Acc. no 5307   l cB (Mor)

Managing Cultural Differences

Effective Strategy and Execution Across Cultures in Global Corporate Alliances

INTERNATIONAL BUSINESS AND MANAGEMENT SERIES

Series Editor: Pervez Ghauri

Published

GHAURI & USUNIER
International Business Negotiations

Forthcoming titles

HENNART & THOMAS
Global Competitive Strategies

SHAFIK
International Privatization

NAUDE AND TURNBULL
Network Dynamics in International Marketing

GEMÜNDEN, RITTER & WALTER
Relationships and Networks in International Markets

Other titles of interest

SANCHEZ, HEENE & THOMAS
Dynamics of Competence-Based Competition

KOSTECKI & FEHERVARY
Services in the Transition Economies

Related journals — sample copy available on request

European Management Journal
International Business Review
International Journal of Intercultural Relations
Long Range Planning
Scandinavian Journal of Management

Managing
Cultural Differences

Effective Strategy and Execution Across Cultures in
Global Corporate Alliances

PIERO MOROSINI

PERGAMON

UK Elsevier Science Ltd, The Boulevard, Langford Lane, Kidlington, Oxford OX5 1GB, UK

USA Elsevier Science Inc., 655 Avenue of the Americas, New York, NY 10010, USA

JAPAN Elsevier Science Japan, Higashi Azabu 1-chome Building 4F, 1-9-15, Higashi Azabu, Minato-ku, Tokyo 106, Japan

First edition 1998

Library of Congress Cataloging in Publication Data

A catalogue record for this book is available from the Library of Congress.

British Library Cataloguing in Publication Data

A catalogue record for this book is available from the British Library.

ISBN 0 08 042762 6

•

Printed and bound in Great Britain by
Biddles Ltd, Guildford and King's Lynn

In memory of Maurizio Marelli and Kohei Takubo.

Contents

Contents

Series Editor's Preface

International business has proved in recent years to be the most dynamic area of business studies. The world economy is becoming globalized, as new blocs and relationships emerge to create a radically different business environment. We have seen the increasing importance of the European Union, the opening up of most of the former centrally planned economies, and a phenomenal growth in emerging markets. All these changes present new challenges and opportunities for academics and practising managers, and highlight the need for more research and publication. This will enhance our understanding of the realities of competition within an increasingly interdependent, yet culturally diverse, business world.

Most universities and business schools now offer international business programmes, at least at graduate level: an MSc in International Business or a Master's degree in International Management. All MBA programmes claim to offer an "international" MBA. Academics and business leaders have both come to appreciate the importance of preparing future managers for the complexities of the new world order.

Consequently, the volume of academic research in international business has increased significantly. Like most business and management literature, it tends to be dominated by a North American perspective, while actual practice varies dramatically and continually adapts to new circumstances. However, as medieval traders, nineteenth-century entrepreneurs and twentieth-century corporations each adopted very different approaches according to the nature of their eras and their own individual perceptions, so the approaches adopted in contemporary international business must reflect the realities of the world in which we live.

The aim of this series is to apply a truly international perspective to the study of international business, with a special emphasis on management and marketing issues. While existing series cover other areas such as finance and economics, there are very few publications covering these issues systematically, apart from the two journals *International Business Review* and *Journal of International Business Studies*. The International Business and Management Series deals with such topics as globalization, international business, negotiations, cross-cultural communication, entry strategies, doing business in different regions, and future trends. Work on competition, the development of international business theory, methodological issues, the results of empirical studies and the findings of practitioners, also fall within its brief.

Throughout, the intention is to provide up-to-date guidance to students and practitioners of international business, and to advance the frontiers of knowledge in this fast-developing field.

University of Groningen,　　　　　　　　　　　　　　　　PERVEZ N. GHAURI
The Netherlands

Preface

Experience

He is truly wise
who's travelled far
and knows the ways of the
world

He who has travelled
can tell what spirit
governs the men he meets

Eddaic Poems — Hávamál, *ca.* 700-900 AD

The initial idea to develop this book occurred to me around 1989, when I was attending doctoral studies in the USA. Mergers and acquisitions (M&As), joint ventures (JVs) and alliances were at the time undergoing unprecedented levels of activity in the USA and elsewhere. Parallel to these developments, highly innovative take-over instruments were making previously inconceivable deals feasible to determined entrepreneurs with financial savvy. Nevertheless, during these years, not many of the academicians or practitioners I knew seemed to regard the cultural or related implementation aspects of M&As, JVs and alliances as particularly critical *vis-à-vis* "strategic" or "financial" factors.

However, by the mid 1990s, this situation had changed remarkably. Based on a growing number of empirical studies published during the first half of that decade, M&A, JV and alliance activity was presenting rather mixed performance results relative to the strategic and financial expectations which had often motivated these agreements. On a more practical note, cultural and organizational complexities were increasingly cited by executives, management consultants and practitioners alike, as critical factors behind many failed M&As, JVs or alliances. Although these types of difficulties were seen as relevant to the performance of both domestic and cross-border deals, the latter usually carried additional complications, ranging from language differences to a myriad of national cultural contrasts which were seemingly pervasive but not always well-defined during the implementation phase of these agreements. Thus, contrary to the prevailing attitude of the previous years, during the mid 1990s many academicians, executives and practitioners were showing a growing interest in the subject of managing across national cultural differences. In fact, while a series of technological, socio-economic and political developments were increasingly fueling the globalization of firms during this post-cold war era — in the process driving international M&A, JV and alliance activity to new record levels — many companies had found themselves struggling to address the practical complexities involved in managing across diverse national cultural environments. Thus, a higher managerial complexity stemming from the globalization of business strategies (often entailing cross-border M&As, JVs and alliances) was not always accompanied by a corresponding increase in a company's practical ability to co-ordinate resources effectively across the different local cultural contexts in which it operated.

Against this background, the topic of national culture has been the subject of contrasting views. On the one hand, national cultural issues are often regarded as an overstated myth from some business and even academic quarters. On the other, national cultural differences are described as nearly insurmountable barriers or amongst the risk factors associated with cross-border M&As, JVs or alliances. Both perspectives have their peculiar drawbacks, though. Many of those highlighting the inflated importance of national cultural issues in international M&As, JVs or alliances as a result end up underestimating the cultural complexities involved in these agreements — only to discover them the hard way. Similarly, executives or practitioners championing national cultural differences as detrimental barriers to global M&A, JV or alliance activity too often regard as cultural what could be better described as a company's internal implementation shortcomings. In spite of this ambiguity, there has been surprisingly little empirical research to support any of the previously mentioned views on culture. Notwithstanding this, strategic, normative or process-based writings attempting to address national cultural issues in international M&As, JVs and alliances have not been particularly missing in the management literature.

This kind of context explains why in this book we approach the issue of managing M&As, JVs and alliances across national cultures from a primarily empirical perspective. As the topic has been the subject of recurrent myths or even prejudice, in Part I we describe the results of a statistical study carried out to test the link between national cultural distance and cross-border acquisition performance. At the same time, we revise the available empirical data complementing our findings from the perspective of international JVs and alliances. Overall, the empirical results described in Part I suggest that national cultural differences are not necessarily detrimental to cross-border M&As, JVs and alliances as has been often assumed in the past. Rather, if managed effectively, national cultural distance can actually enhance performance. However, national cultural issues arising during the implementation of cross-border M&As, JVs and alliances are quite often extremely difficult to manage in practice. Deep-rooted resistance, ceaseless interpersonal conflicts and chronic communication problems can all be motivated or exacerbated by national cultural differences, easily undermining the benefits that are expected from these kinds of agreements — although they might have been soundly conceived *ex ante* from a strategic or a financial perspective. Thus, in Part I we also illustrate how a company's practical co-ordination mechanisms, involving people from diverse national cultural backgrounds, are crucial to co-operatively combine critical resources following overseas M&As, JVs or alliances. Nevertheless, national cultural differences invariably make the development of these global co-ordination mechanisms a time-consuming affair, requiring considerable doses of managerial patience and determination. Paradoxically, this makes such mechanisms rather valuable for a company and extremely difficult to replicate by competitors.

Our empirical findings raise the attention to a company's *social* dimensions and execution skills across national cultures, as strategic sources of competitive advantage in global M&A, JV and alliance activity. The senior executives we approached during our field research, unanimously stressed these pragmatic aspects of management as fundamental to make or break an M&A, JV or alliance in the "real world". In Part II we indeed show how "execution orientation" — a particular combination of strategic vision, leadership, communication and overall execution — is at the very heart of the consistently successful track record in managing global M&As, JVs and alliances, demonstrated by a handful of multinational companies. However, quite surprisingly, the topic of execution has so far received very little attention in the management literature. As already hinted, most of the extensively available writings concerning strategic or implementation aspects of M&As, JVs and alliances take a process or a normative view, seldom addressing the practical business issues and multifaceted managerial context of execution in its own right. These traditional approaches have often single-handedly favored a valuable set of reductionist problem-solving and analytical techniques to address the theoretical and practical issues involved in global M&As, JVs and alliances. However, execution is an inherently holistic and messy phenomenon in the real world, requiring a correspondingly broad-based stream of knowledge that combines both the theoretical and the pragmatic cognitive dimensions. Unlike theoretical knowledge, pragmatic or experience-based cognition (which we also refer to as "gnosis") is to a large extent tacit, and as a result remarkably difficult to either formalize or transfer outside an organization. In particular, gnosis of diverse cultural values and related complexities has recurrently been cited in our research as fundamental to properly execute complex co-ordination functions across borders. In the context of global M&As, JVs and alliances, execution orientation thus highlights the performance effectiveness of more holistic approaches to management theory and practice, combining both formal strategic thinking as well as the tacit knowledge embedded in superior execution..

A large part of the empirical research concerning national culture and management phenomena (including our own statistical analyses in Part I) has been based on numerical models of national culture. Nevertheless, overly relying upon quantitative methodological approaches could lead to under-estimating the significant complexity of national cultural symbols. Indeed, many of the available numerical models of national culture that are utilized in this book have recurrently emphasized its more pervasive and resilient characteristics. However, psychological studies suggest that national cultural symbols are also multiform and unpredictable to a large extent, providing multiple possibilities of variation around central meanings. As a result, although they might be perceived as insurmountable barriers by some, skillful international managers can continuously take advantage of the multiform characteristics of national culture to flexibly adapt and tailor effective managerial principles to the local environment. In this sense, the issue of whether national cultural aspects could be beneficial or detrimental to the performance of managerial phenomena such as cross-border M&As, JVs and alliances might be wrongly stated in the first place. National cultural symbols are highly paradoxical and difficult to manage, but can be practically handled based on correspondingly flexible and holistic execution mechanisms, combining both formal knowledge and experience-based gnosis. Thus, in Part III we describe a variety of such execution mechanisms utilized by leading multi-nationals with extensive M&A, JV and alliance experience, based on a series of in-depth interviews to these companies' CEOs, board members and other highly ranked executives. The particular ways in which these mechanisms fit in with a company's specific context and past experiences provide an insight into how execution orientation can turn national cultural differences into concrete business advantages in relation to cross-border M&As, JVs and alliances.

If national cultural differences are not to be regarded as seemingly exogenous deterrents to global M&As, JVs and alliances, but as complex managerial factors which can be transformed into practical advantages for a company, this could indeed have profound business implications. Some of these are discussed in the concluding chapter of this book, highlighting the potential impact of our findings on various strategic, organizational and government policy areas.

Pellizzano, October 1997   PIERO MOROSINI

Acknowledgments

Many individuals have generously provided their views, support and assistance to the completion of this book. I acknowledge these contributions at the risk of inadvertently omitting some of them. In any event, the numerous errors that might be found in this work are of course the author's sole responsibility.

First of all, I express my gratitude to the friends who initially encouraged me to take on this challenge. Professor Paul Kleindorfer, co-Director of the Risk Management and Decision Processes Center at the Wharton School in Philadelphia, who during the past decade has continuously supported my research endeavors that culminated in this volume. Management Professors Harbir Singh and Ian MacMillan at the Wharton School, as well as Scott Shane at the Sloan School of Management, who provided inspiration and many original ideas to this research. Paul Stonham, editor of the *European Management Journal*, both motivated and guided me in my initial efforts to conceive this publication. Kohei Takubo, who until his untimely death was a Director of the Wharton Regional Representation Office for East Asia in Tokyo, and Ji-Suk Choo, President of Hyosung-BASF in Seoul, both of whom went well out of their way to ensure that I successfully carried out my field work research in the Far East. Brigadier Harry Langstaff, whose example and lessons have positively shaped my early cross-cultural managerial experiences. Nils Linander, whose sympathy has been important throughout my research efforts. My editors Anthony Seward and Sammye Haigh, whose patience and enthusiasm made it possible for me to conclude this work in its present form.

Thanks also to the senior executives who agreed to share their experience and wisdom in the context of this research. In particular, I would like to mention (in alphabetical order): Percy Barnevik, Chairman of Investor and of ABB ASEA Brown Boveri; Jan Ekberg, Board Member of Pharmacia & Upjohn; Atsushi Fukushima, Vice President of Corporate Planning at NEC Logistics; Byung-Ho Kang, President and CEO of Daewoo Corporation; Yotaro Kobayashi, Chairman and CEO of Fuji-Xerox; Lars Lindegren, Senior Vice-President at Pharmacia & Upjohn; Sir Colin Marshall,

Chairman of British Airways; Curt Nicolin, former Chairman and CEO of ASEA; Elserino Piol, former Executive Vice President at Olivetti; Gianmario Rossignolo, President of Electrolux-Zanussi; Iwane Takahara, Counselor Member of the Board at NEC Logistics; and highly ranked executives at Deutsche Bank AG in Frankfurt, as well as Sony Corporation in Tokyo, who preferred to remain anonymous.

A word of gratitude goes to Professor Jean-Pierre Lehmann, Director of the Swiss-Asia Foundation at the IMD in Lausanne, and Tony Cocklin, executive at British Airways in London, for providing their valuable views and support throughout my research work. I also thank Masaru Yoshitomi, Vice Chairman of the Long-Term Credit Bank of Japan Research Institute in Tokyo, and Yukiko Fukagawa, Senior Economist at the same institution, whose advice and comments were particularly useful when carrying out my research work in Japan and the Far East. Thanks also to Örjan Sölvell, Director of the Institute of International Business at the Stockholm School of Economics, and Lena Zander, Research Associate at the same Institute, for their helpful suggestions to my field study.

A very special thanks to Karin, my wife, for her great patience, valuable ideas and enormous help throughout my field work research, case studies, interview transcriptions and reviews of the text. Her love and strength have been with me during the long weekends that it took to conclude this volume.

About the author

Piero Morosini is a Research Fellow at the Risk Management and Decision Processes Center at The Wharton School, University of Pennsylvania, Philadelphia. He has obtained a PhD, an MA and an MBA at The Wharton School, and has graduated in Economics at the Universidad del Pacífico, Lima. Dr Morosini is the author of various scholarly articles on global corporate alliances, execution and cross-cultural management; and has formerly worked in institutions such as McKinsey & Company, JP Morgan, Robert Fleming and the Andean Pact, in several locations across Europe, the US and Latin America. He currently lives and works in Milan, Italy.

Part I
National Cultural Differences and the Performance of Global Corporate Alliances

The Dismal Track Record of Mergers and Acquisitions, Joint Ventures and Alliances

> But when a conqueror acquires states in a province which is different from his own in language, customs and institutions, great difficulties arise, and the excellent fortune and great skill are needed to retain them.
>
> Niccolò Machiavelli — *De Principatibus*

Cross-border M&As, JVs and alliances seem to share at least two characteristics with the marriage trends of the post World War II "Baby Boomers" generation: They have grown explosively during the 1980s and through the 1990s but — less fortunately — they fail about half the time. In particular, the explosive growth of cross-border M&As is a phenomenon which can been traced back to as early as the 1970s, and according to some even to the 1960s, parallel to an increased domestic acquisition activity in the USA and Europe — the world's major economies at the time. From these years, successive worldwide waves of M&As have increasingly resulted in them becoming a major strategic tool of multinational corporations, and *the* preferred mode of internationalization during the last two decades of the 20th century.[1]

Researchers in this field recognize distinctive features characterizing these waves of M&As throughout the post-World War II period. During the 1960s and 1970s, the acquisition activity of major multinational companies tended to follow the logic of *conglomerate* deals, pursuing advantages supposedly embedded in the diversification of financial and operating risks. This type of acquisition activity gave rise to multidivisional and highly diversified organizations such as ITT Corporation and Litton Industries in the USA. However, during the late 1970s and early 1980s, significant market, consumer and technology changes increasingly posed serious demands to these multidivisional types of organizations, based on their limited organizational flexibility and ability to control a broad, and often unrelated range of business interests. Thus, poor managerial control was quoted as a primary reason for the sell-off of around one-third of the business units purchased during the 1960s and 1970s in the USA, while company diversification levels were widely seen as higher than optimal, leading to misallocation of corporate resources through managerial risk aversion.[2] This general situation, coupled with the development of innovative financial techniques such as leveraged buyouts (LBOs) and management buyouts (MBOs), gave rise to the era of debt-laden leveraged acquisitions and *corporate restructuring*, which largely characterized the second wave of acquisitions during the 1980s, conspicuously targeting large and diversified conglomerates.

Corporate restructuring involved major changes in both the composition of a firm's assets and its business strategy in order to improve performance. A post-LBO restructuring program typically led not only to divestiture of a single business unit, but also involved multiple sell-offs across several markets, or even industries, accompanied by massive lay-offs.[3] On the one hand, such corporate restructuring initiatives were triggered by the threat of capital market intervention, a widely used euphemism to describe corporate takeovers during the 1980s. On the other, extensive restructuring followed acquisition by another firm, the company's own management, or even an individual corporate raider, taking place in either a friendly or a hostile fashion. This second wave of acquisitions came to an end by the late 1980s, partly due to the indiscriminate use of debt behind certain corporate restructuring deals, in many cases aggravated by ill-conceived performance expectations and poor post-acquisition results.

The 1990s have seen the blossoming of a slightly different wave of corporate acquisitions world-wide. In a process already started during the previous decade, multinational and internationally oriented companies made increasing use of cross-border M&As to expand operations on a *global* scale. Compared to the era of corporate restructuring, this global wave of M&A activity seemed to broadly favor strategic deals, characterized by relatively debt-free and friendly agreements, and focused on combining the joining companies' complementary resources across borders. Thus conceived, the explosive M&A activity levels arising during the 1980s and the first half of the 1990s have easily dwarfed all previous historical cycles.

Throughout the 1980s the number of cross-border acquisitions increased continuously, making it a significant amount of total acquisition activity by the early 1990s — 95 percent in the case of Japanese companies and 50 percent for EC companies. Within the European Union, for example, cross-border mergers and acquisitions increased sharply since 1986, to reach a peak of nearly 2,000 transactions in 1990, and a record volume of ECU 57 billion in 1995. After a brief slow down in growth during the recessionary years of 1991-1993, worldwide M&A activity resumed again to record highs during the mid 1990s, reaching a total of US$ 1124 billion in 1996. Parallel to this explosive growth, domestic M&As also reached unprecedented levels across major industrialized economies, led by the USA, where M&A activity rose to a record US$ 649 billion in 1996. This represented a substantial increase over the US$ 519 billion mark reached during the previous year, which was itself a record. Nevertheless, either figure comfortably surpassed the 1988 US$ 246.9 billion level, which was the all-time record year for US-based acquisition activity until 1995. However, all previous records for world-wide and US based M&A activity had already been broken within the first ten months of 1997, when it was announced a total of US$ 1305 billion of takeovers globally, with US$ 749 billion worth of M&A transactions in the US alone.[4]

In the case of international (majority and minority) JVs and strategic alliances, these have also experienced substantial growth during the late 1980s and the 1990s, to the point of being perceived as the dominant organizational form of global businesses on the eve of the 21st century. Although by the end of the 1980s these types of co-operation agreements were still rare in certain countries, minority JVs were already becoming a particularly favored internationalization mechanism by companies based in the USA and other developed economies. Thus, during the same years, out of approximately 25,000 foreign affiliates of US-based companies worldwide, minority equity affiliates had already outnumbered both majority and fully owned affiliates put together.[5]

However, although the pace of cross-border M&A, JV and alliance activity has continued to increase at a torrid pace during the last three decades of the 20th century, extensive evidence suggests that their performance has been far from successful. Indeed, since the early 1970s, a growing number of empirical studies carried out by academicians, management consultants and practitioners have consistently reported high failure rates for M&As, JVs and alliances. Remarkably, these studies cover a broad array of performance measures and methodological approaches, including diverse industry sectors, time periods and country samples, and embracing both domestic and cross-border types of deals. Moreover, the gloomy performance record of M&As, JVs and alliances has been researched along the main strategic and financial hypotheses which have been put forward in the management literature to explain why these transactions occur. Not less importantly, a significant part of these findings has drawn attention to the implementation phase of these agreements, highlighting cultural and organizational complexities as critical factors behind their rather mixed economic results.[6]

Severe Implementation Difficulties Following "Strategic" M&A Deals

Despite the fact that the main motives behind a merger or acquisition are usually related to the creation of value, implementation difficulties in integrating resources across the joining companies (typically arising after the conclusion of the deal) have been shown to be particularly severe and detrimental to performance. These integration problems are particularly relevant in the case of related M&A agreements, where greater operating and functional similarities between the companies can be found, underscoring the strategic need to combine their specialized resources in order to create value.[7]

However, many authors have noted that empirical studies in the area of post-M&A performance have generally focused on strategic and financial factors, whereas other aspects, such as cultural and organizational issues, have received considerably less attention. On the one hand, this may be related to the escalating commitment and the peculiar pressure and stress generated during the negotiation phase, generally leading to over-emphasizing analytical approaches at the expense of addressing pragmatic post-integration issues. On the other, the attention of CEOs and senior executives — even those with previous acquisition experience — seems to largely favor strategic and functional areas when considering a merger or acquisition, but dramatically shift to "other" organizational, cultural and personnel-related factors soon after the conclusion of the deal.[8]

Not surprisingly, as a result of the above, "cultural" issues are seldom given serious consideration or play a significant role *vis-à-vis* strategic and financial issues *before* a merger or acquisition agreement takes place. By contrast, from a formal perspective, M&A activity has been typically based on a widely known body of strategic and financial arguments and analytical tools.

The Strategic and Financial Perspectives for M&A Activity

From a theoretical perspective, the numerous arguments explaining M&A activity have been predominantly based on its strategic nature and the financial effects on the bidding firms. These include hypotheses such as: Synergy, relatedness, strategic momentum or organizational inertia. Although these types of arguments have largely prevailed in explaining why acquisitions occur, many other factors have been quoted in the relevant literature, ranging from corporate learning and experimentation, to emotional and psychological elements such as the level of pride and ego characterizing the acquiring company's CEO and top management.[9]

A broad, though useful, characterization of the main hypotheses that have been put forward to explain why acquisitions occur, states that:

> (...) These hypotheses can be broadly categorized as being of two types: value-maximizing and non-value-maximizing theories. The former postulate that acquisitions are motivated by maximizing the value of the firm to stockholders, whereas the latter propose that managers of bidding firms embark on acquisitions to maximize their own utility at the expense of stockholders (perhaps because their compensation is tied to the size of the firm in terms of sales or

assets). The value-maximizing hypotheses of acquisition predict that the wealth of shareholders of both bidding and target firms increases as a result of acquisition, and that positive synergy, or value creation, is evidenced. However, the competing hypotheses predict that the wealth of shareholders of bidding firms falls, that of the target firms' shareholders rises, and no value is necessarily created upon acquisition.[10]

Both categories of hypotheses have been empirically tested from the point of view of the modern financial theory and the strategic management theory. The former has examined the effects of diversification strategies and capital market risk, stating that, although diversification will reduce unsystematic risk, it is not likely to create value for stockholders because systematic risk is not diversifiable. However, managers are not concerned with managing unsystematic and total risk because the stock market will not reward such behavior. The strategic management theory stresses that the process of value creation in merger and acquisitions is based on the strategic fit between the companies involved in such activities. Strategic fit can be loosely characterized as the creation of value based on the combination of the joining firms' specialized resources, given the environmental opportunities and constraints. To explain how this combination can create value, a number of arguments have been put forward. These are mostly centered around the concept of synergy, the sources of which can be generally related to market power, economies of scale and economies of scope.[11]

Strategic Frameworks to Classify M&As

M&As have been classified according to their strategic potential for value creation and the existing relationship between the joining firms. Two such classification frameworks have been widely utilized in the specialized literature.

The first framework, based on the US Federal Trade Commission (FTC) categories, emphasizes on the nature of the business and markets in which a company competes, as well as the supplier-client-competitor or legal relationship between the joining companies. Based on this criteria, acquisitions can be horizontal (emphasizing "same market" or competitor relationship), vertical (emphasizing supplier or client relationship), or conglomerate (emphasizing the relative independence and legal relationship between companies).[12]

The second framework broadly classifies M&As into related and unrelated transactions, emphasizing the strategic potential for transferring functional skills between businesses as a key factor for success across the joining firms. In turn, these functional skills can be further subdivided — e.g. into research and development, production, marketing or distribution areas. In addition, related M&As can be classified into related-complementary and related-supplementary transactions, based on the joining companies' degree of functional, operating or market-based overlap *vis-à-vis* their potential to combine separate but complementary resources.[13]

In a financial context, refinements to the notion of relatedness have proposed it as a strategic source of abnormal returns for the shareholders of bidding firms. From this perspective, a bidding firm will generate abnormal returns *only* when:

- It holds private and uniquely valuable synergistic cash flows with the target
- It can obtain inimitable and uniquely valuable synergistic cash flows with the target
- It holds unexpected synergistic cash flows with the target.[14]

Strategic Frameworks to Classify JVs and Alliances

No precise definition for joint ventures or alliances exists in the international management, business law or accounting literature. Nevertheless, most management authors characterize international joint ventures (IJVs) as separate organizational and legal entities, made up from parts of the parent firms' assets, and headquartered in countries which are foreign from the perspective of at least one of the parent company's operations. The distribution of equity among the parent companies can take different forms, ranging from 50/50 IJVs between two companies, to reduced minority or dominant majority stakes. On the other hand, global alliances encompass a broader range of co-operative agreements, both from the point of view of the participating firms' strategic assets which can be committed to the partnership (from intangible assets such as brand names, to virtually all of a company's assets engaged in the alliance), as well as the legal and organizational forms that can be found (i.e. with or without equity participation, and not necessarily involving separate organizational entities based on overseas locations from one of the partners' operational perspectives).[15]

Thus conceived, the need to combine strategic resource contributions and foster functional co-operation and co-ordination between the partners to create mutual advantages is at the very heart of both IJVs and global alliances. On the one hand, empirical research suggests that both the degree of stability and the partners' ability to obtain advantages from an international joint venture is to an extent dependent upon the categories of strategic contributions that are sought after. In this area, some authors have proposed fifteen categories of JVs, based on the nature of the partners' strategic contributions (e.g. technological know-how, skills learning or entry to new markets). IJVs have been further classified according to the way in which controlling powers are divided amongst the parents and the joint venture itself—leading to "double-parenting" or "multiple parenting" management and operational control structures. These have been shown to affect the IJV's degree of flexibility to adapt to environmental turbulence.[16]

On the other hand, the collaborative purpose of alliances usually involves transaction specific investments between the partners, which are non-redeployable and non-salvageable. The strategic aims of alliances have been categorized within the superordinate levels of management of the multi-national, multicompany team. Thus, multiple networks of "strategic alli-ances" across borders, along with international development projects, are seen as comprising the total global constellation of critical resources available to a multinational company. Managing such global networks constitutes a major challenge across a company's control and structural dimensions, stem-ming from the need to co-ordinate integrated organizational webs, as opposed to bilateral or fragmented systems of subsidiaries, or independent national units. In this context, a number of organizational categories have been proposed to characterize such structural networks of resources, ranging from "heterarchical" forms, to "transnational corporations", "multifocal" or "horizontal" multinationals.[17]

The Mixed Track Record of M&As

As already mentioned, the performance of M&As, JVs and alliances has been extensively examined in a number of empirical studies, most of which sub-scribe to one of the theories, hypotheses or classifications that have been briefly described in the previous paragraphs. Regarding M&As, the evidence that has been produced to support strategic fit theories overwhelmingly sug-gests that these transactions have failed to generate "superior" value or sig-nificantly improve the performance of the joining companies. These findings are entirely consistent with the empirical results provided by management consultancies and M&A practitioners, as well as with anecdotal and specia-lized media evidence. The existing empirical studies examining the perfor-mance of JVs and alliances also report significant failure rates over time.

Although overwhelming, this type of evidence has not been unanimously derived amongst researchers. US-based academicians Singh and Montgomery, carried out one of the few empirical studies showing somewhat positive results for acquisition performance.[18] This study was also based on a US sample from the 1970s, and tested the relatedness hypothesis of acquisi-tions, arguing that a positive relationship existed between performance gains and the degree to which the acquiring and acquired firms shared similar technologies or participated in similar product markets. Their results con-firmed the relatedness hypothesis on the basis of total dollar gains as a per-formance measure. Additional support for this hypothesis was provided shortly afterwards by Shelton, whose empirical findings suggested that acqui-sitions which permitted bidders access to new but related markets created more value for shareholders. A number of other studies also appear to provide some support for the relatedness hypothesis in acquisition activity.[19]

Even if the above-mentioned studies have highlighted relatedness as a key factor for superior acquisition performance, it has been observed that they have generally left unexplained a large variance in the performance variables among acquiring firms, and that their results are inconsistent with each other due to the different paradigms and methodologies utilized.[20] In particular, some of these findings are based on stock returns estimated over a limited time period around the announcement date of an acquisition, making them rather susceptible to the dynamics of a competitive bidding process. Performance measurements estimated on this basis could in fact be pointing out a simple transfer of wealth from the bidding firm's shareholders to the target's shareholders. This exemplifies the practical limitations of such methodological approaches, sometimes readily indicated by their own authors:

> On a pragmatic level this research underscores the need to combine what may be called the theoretical with the practical. In the case of acquisitions, pragmatic issues like implicit and explicit competition for a target firm alter the theoretical expectations of gains from an acquisition transaction.[21]

In sharp contrast with the studies described above, a wide body of empirical literature strongly suggests that acquisition activity has failed to produce superior performance even amongst related firms or, at best, is an inconclusive strategy to induce superior economic performance and value creation. At one end of the spectrum, a study by Chatterjee actually found that targets in unrelated acquisitions perform better than those in related ones.[22] At the other, an empirical research by the same Chatterjee, together with Lubatkin, explored the relationship between systematic risk and relatedness in acquisition activity, based on a sample of 120 large acquisitions in the USA during the 1962-1979 period. It found that, although bidding firms sharing core technologies with targets in non-competing products were able to reduce the systematic risk of their securities, unrelated acquisitions were just as effective in reducing these systematic or environmental risks.[23] During the late 1980s, a study by Lubatkin had already observed that pre-merger abnormal returns for all merger types are positive and significant, but post-merger revaluation is small and insignificant. In addition, he empirically found that related mergers do not create more value than unrelated mergers.[24] In the case of takeovers, Chatterjee added that these types of findings were due to the fact that many of them are motivated primarily by restructuring, not relatedness. The main source of value in these types of operations should therefore reside in the target firm only, rather than the combination of both bidding and target firms. Chatterjee's study provided some empirical support for these hypotheses, particularly in the cases where there was an industry-wide need for restructuring.[25]

A study published in 1992 analyzed the empirical literature on the various factors that influence shareholder wealth creation in acquisitions using a multivariate framework. It reported overall results indicating that shareholders of target firms gain significantly from acquisitions, but those of the bidding firm do not. In addition, the use of stock financing was found to significantly influence shareholders' wealth in both the target and the bidding firms.[26] These types of findings can also be widely recognized in the anecdotal and management consulting evidence.

Moreover, the nature of the markets and businesses in which the acquirer and the target compete, or the existing legal and functional relationship between them, do not appear to significantly influence acquisition performance. Supporting this, an empirical study utilizing the FTC categories of conglomerates and non-conglomerate (horizontal and vertical) acquisitions, examined its overall results over time but reported no significant performance differences across types.[27]

An already mentioned, research work published in 1990 found evidence that financial diversification effects do not play a role in either related or unrelated acquisitions.[28] This study reviewed an abundant empirical literature concerning acquisition performance by the following acquisition types: market power, economies of scale, economies of scope, co-insurance in conglomerate acquisitions and diversification of risk. As a result, the study concluded that the specialized literature provides no evidence that acquisitions have significantly improved economic or financial performance. In the few cases where the empirical evidence appeared to suggest the contrary, unclear and equivocal results were reported.[29]

In a much quoted empirical research work, Porter found a high failure rate in acquisitions, based on the activity of 33 large companies in the USA, during the 1950-1986 period. It was observed that 55 percent of acquisitions in new industries were later divested, with a 74 percent divestment rate in the case of unrelated industries. Similar studies have provided additional empirical support to the high failure rate of acquisitions, as well as the decline in profitability amongst target firms following an acquisition. Overall, some researchers have maintained that, at best, only about half of all M&As have lived up to their initial financial expectations, with failure rates typically falling within the 50-60 percent range.[30]

Some of the earliest pieces of systematic evidence on acquisition performance already highlighted the poor track record of the post-integration and implementation phases. Amongst these, Kitching studied 407 acquisitions in Europe that took place during the 1965-1970 period.[31] Based on subjective assessments provided by the top management of the acquiring companies included in the sample, he concluded that the failure rate had been as high as 50 percent. Insufficient planning and organizational problems during the post-acquisition integration period were major reasons for such a high failure rate. Another study which examined a large sample of US acquisitions during the 1960-1970 period, found that one-third of the business units purchased had already been sold off during the following decade — a pronounced divestment rate primarily attributed to poor managerial control.[32] Additional empirical studies highlighting a generally poor post-acquisition financial performance have attributed these results to a wide array of issues, ranging from implementation drawbacks induced by the acquirer, to executive compensation, personnel and structural changes implanted in the non-acquiring firms.[33]

Anecdotal Evidence Confirms High Failure Rate of Acquisitions

The findings described above are consistent with the empirical literature and anecdotal evidence from both management consulting firms and M&A practitioners, as well as the specialized media.

Regarding the former, McKinsey & Co. found that, based on the cost of capital criteria, 61 percent of the acquisition programs from a sample of 116 US-, Canada- and UK-based companies failed, 23 percent were successful and 16 percent unknown; 86 percent of large acquisitions in unrelated fields failed and 55 percent of the acquisitions of small companies in related fields later failed. Another study by the same management consultancy showed that an unusually high 80 percent of takeovers had at least earned back the cost of capital originally invested; however, these results were based on a restricted sample of largely unrelated LBOs which took place during the 1986-1996 period. The William M. Mercer Group pointed out that, based on share values, divestment rates, or return on investment criteria, most acquisition programs fail. In particular, they noted that: "Acquiring firm's shareholders usually lose as a result of the deal. Acquired firm's shareholders usually benefit, often as a result of the auction process." As mentioned, these types of suggestions have also been highlighted in the academic literature concerning M&A performance. A. T. Kearney notes that acquisitions have largely failed to increase profitability, improve efficiency and expand sales, and do not seem to yield sufficient benefit to any of the parties involved in these transactions. Booz Allen & Hamilton reported a failure rate of about 55 percent, based on the management assessment at 200 diversification programs which took place in Europe between 1970 and 1984.[34]

The specialized media and acquisition practitioners have also highlighted these findings. Amongst the latter, William W. Bain Jr. has stated that:

> A dollar invested in an acquisition has only about a 30 percent chance of creating real economic value — and some who have looked at the record say the success rate is even less. A crap game offers better odds.[35]

An article in *Mergers and Acquisitions* published in 1986 examined the returns on investment of a large company sample relative to the pre-merger or acquisition forecasts. It concluded that 80 percent of M&As were downright disappointments and did not meet the expectations of forecasted returns.[36] *Business Week*'s cover story of 21 March 1988 was, on the other hand, sufficiently explicit in its message: "Most Mergers Don't Work". A special report of the same publication, on 30 October 1995, appeared to be an adequate saga as it was entitled: "The Case Against Mergers. Even in the 90s, most still fail to deliver". This special report described the results of a study examining the stock returns of 150 deals worth more than US$ 500 million during January 1990 through July 1995. The period under observation covered three months before the announcement of the acquisition deal up to three years after. This study pointed out that 30 percent of the deals examined "substantially eroded shareholder returns", 20 percent "eroded some returns", 33 percent "created only marginal returns", and only 17 percent created substantial returns for the shareholders. Similar high failure rates were attributed to cross-border acquisitions, observing that value of cross-border deals was harder to measure relative to domestic ones. These results also highlighted that companies which made no acquisitions during the January 1990-July 1995 period outperformed companies which did, based on returns superior to industry indexes. An article published in the first 1997 issue of *The Economist* similarly reported that most mergers had failed to create shareholder value, mostly due to company managers systematically overlooking the major cultural and organizational complexities involved in integrating the merging firms' operations and informal networks.[37]

JVs and Alliances Are Not Performing Better than Acquisitions

Compared to mergers or acquisitions, the empirical performance of JVs and alliances has been explored less extensively from a statistical perspective. However, the available evidence is delineating strikingly similar performance results *vis-à-vis* acquisitions. Management consultants Bleeke and Ernst examined 49 cross-border alliances during the 1981-1987 period, offering interesting insights into their overall success rate.[38] In their study, success was based on financial and strategic criteria, applied to both the alliance partners separately, as well as measured across both partners' combined operations. The results of this research showed that 53 percent of the cross-border alliances considered were successful for both partners; 33 percent were classified as a failure for both partners, while the remaining 17 percent offered mixed results. The success rate for cross-border alliances was slightly higher amongst those taking place in core or related business areas, and significantly higher in those that were complementary from a geographic stand-point, where these alliances tended to fill functional gaps or share operating costs. Moreover, success rates tended to be higher in cross-border alliances where one partner was a strong performer in its industry and the other a relatively average one. From this perspective, 74 percent of cross-border alliances where both partners were strong in their respective industries were considered successful; while success rate was only 33 percent in alliances with one strong and one weak partner, and 0 percent for alliance agreements between weak partners.

Other studies have also provided evidence of the high failure rates and performance disappointments resulting from IJVs. Those taking place between North American partners on the one hand, and Caribbean, South American, North and East African or Indonesian companies on the other, have been shown to frequently fail in the operational and implementation phases. A generally poor implementation performance has also been found across French-German, US-Russian and US-Chinese joint ventures.[39]

Why Do So Many M&As, JVs and Alliances Fail?

The studies so far reviewed strongly suggest that, based on the available performance record, the strategic and financial value creation hypotheses for M&A activity have generally found rather scant empirical support. Moreover, financial and qualitative performance data accumulated since the early 1970s show that the relatively low success rate of M&As has not risen over time. In spite of this clear evidence, many authors have noted that much attention is focused on strategic and "financial" areas during the planning and negotiation stages of these agreements. As already mentioned, this kind of emphasis might not be exclusive to researchers but appears also to characterize the behavior of many CEOs and senior company executives. Thus, a number of factors, such as insufficient pre-merger planning, inadequate due diligence by the acquirer or merger partner, flawed estimates of possible synergies prior to the deal, or simply paying too much for the target's or merging partner's assets at the outset, are commonly cited as major reasons behind the high failure rates of M&As. By contrast, implementation aspects such as post-integration organizational or cultural issues are comparatively neglected during the evaluation and negotiation phases, but become key to performance after a deal has been concluded. Although these issues are generically applicable to M&A activity, it is apparent that cultural issues will be particularly exacerbated in the case of cross-border situations. In these cases, differences in deep-rooted national values, languages and customs are more likely to exist compared with domestic situations. In turn, these deep cultural differences have been found to significantly affect the organizational characteristics of firms and organizations, for which the implications on the performance of M&As are clearly relevant.[40]

In the case of international JVs and alliances, the situation is remarkably similar. The strategic benefits for company partners to enter new markets, learn skills, gain technology, expand the existing product base, or share fixed costs and investments, have been stressed by researchers and management consultants alike. However, empirical evidence suggests that technical issues are less likely to lead to conflicting situations compared to interrelationship problems during the implementation of international JVs and alliances. Throughout this phase, too much emphasis is usually placed on setting strategic objectives at the cost of ignoring personal interaction aspects involving people from different national cultures. This has been cited as the most critical factor leading to unresolved conflicts and outright failure of an international JV or alliance. To remedy these drawbacks, general attitudes and skills favoring "inter-cultural" effectiveness and international adaptation of company executives have been widely studied and proposed, but often outside their practical context and the relevant business issues.[41]

In spite of this mounting evidence, it has been noted that very few companies look at cultural compatibility and the like as a key part of the attractiveness analysis of M&As, JVs or alliances. This has been partly related to the analytical emphasis of executives and consultants, who generally favor widely known strategic and financial tools that tend to overlook cultural or post-integration issues. In the case of M&As, this tendency to over-emphasize analytical or strategic aspects has also been linked to the particular pressures and stress to conclude a deal that are often created during the negotiation phases. Nevertheless, it has been noted that, even when cultural fit or similar issues are recognized as key aspects in relation to M&A, JV and alliance activity, it is often unclear how to handle them either before or during the implementation phases.[42] One primary reason for this is simply related to the fact that, as observed by many researchers, the problems in this area start with the very definition of what is meant by culture. Although many definitions have proliferated in the literature, the issue remains that values, symbols and beliefs, which are often regarded as central constitutive elements of culture, are notoriously difficult to describe and categorize, and thus defy rigorous formalization. Whilst a comprehensive review of the numerous conceptual approaches developed in this area is beyond the main purpose of this book, a brief introduction to key models of culture is required to properly describe our empirical findings regarding the effects of national cultural differences on cross-border acquisition performance. In these, as well as other management and economic areas, most empirical studies have subscribed more or less explicitly to "ideational" notions of culture. In other words, culture is not strictly viewed as an individual characteristic, but rather as a set of common theories or mental programs that are shared by a group of individuals and pervasively influence their behavior.[43]

Empirically Derived Models of "Culture"

During the late 1970s, the Dutch academician Geert Hofstede developed an empirical model of national culture which has since become widely quoted and utilized by management researchers and practitioners. This model, based on a large statistical survey of the employees of one multinational organization across forty countries, showed that national cultural values vary significantly across four dimensions, which he labeled: power distance, uncertainty avoidance, individualism, and masculinity. These were broadly defined as:

- Power distance: "...the extent to which a society accepts the fact that power in institutions and organizations is distributed unequally".
- Uncertainty avoidance: "...the extent to which a society feels threatened by uncertain and ambiguous situations by providing career stability, establishing more formal rules, not tolerating deviant ideas and behaviors, and believing in absolute truths and the attainment of expertise".
- Individualism: "...implies a loosely knit social framework in which people are supposed to take care of themselves and their immediate families only, while collectivism is characterized by a tight social framework in which people distinguish between in-groups and out-groups; they expect their in-group (relatives, clan, organizations) to look after them, and in exchange for that they feel they owe absolute loyalty to it".
- Masculinity: "...expresses the extent to which the dominant values in society are 'masculine', i.e. assertiveness, the acquisition of money and things, and not caring for others, the quality of life, or people."[44]

Following some authors, we prefer to allude to the latter dimension as "materialism".[45] One of the distinctive characteristics of Hofstede's model of national culture, is that it statistically derived numerical scales to characterize each of the forty countries in the initial sample across all four dimensions.

Contemporary with the publication of Hofstede's work, Schein proposed a broad model of culture, presenting it as a series of three successive and inter-related levels. These were: basic assumption and premises, values and ideology, and artifacts and creations. The first level included "preconscious" notions of the relationship between man and nature, time and space orientations and relationships amongst men. The second level of culture contained deep-rooted values and beliefs influencing ideals, goals and paths of purposeful human action. The third level of culture included such things as language, technology and social organization.[46]

An important idea in the work of Schein is that each successive level of culture is, to an extent, a manifestation of the previous ones, making all three of them highly inter-related (see Figure 1.1). One clear implication of this model is that the culture of a society, a concept akin to national

FIGURE 1.1

The "pervasiveness" of culture

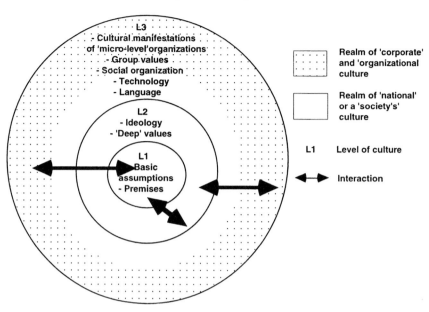

culture, constitutes a most complex and deep-rooted phenomenon that is not easily modified. Another fundamental implication of Schein's model relates to the pervasive effects of culture across virtually all aspects of human action and social interaction. This crucial characteristic of culture has been recurrently highlighted by many researchers, who have found empirical support for the notion that a society's culture is particularly pervasive across sub-cultures.[47] In this sense, Hofstede's national cultural scores can be interpreted as empirical estimates of cultural differences among countries, that are manifested *in spite of* the socialization effect of an international company's sub-culture. Other empirical studies have also reported significant national cultural differences among company employees. For example, in the case of Japanese and American employees of Japanese-owned companies in the USA, these differences persisted even among Americans of Japanese ancestry, or Japanese with extensive living and working experience in the USA.[48]

Further evidence of the pervasiveness of national cultural values across sub-cultures was provided by Hofstede. Based on a model of cultural manifestations from shallow to deep, which can be loosely correlated to Schein's three levels of culture, Hofstede tested the degree to which measurable differences in organizational cultural characteristics could be attributed to a company's unique features (i.e. its corporate history or past leadership), its control and

17

structural systems, or to pre-determined factors such as nationality or industry. This model was then tested empirically on twenty units from ten different organizations in Denmark and the Netherlands, based on *ad hoc* surveys and questionnaires. Analyses of the responses suggested that differences in organizational cultures were largely associated with the diversity across the companies' visible practices. However, differences in cultural values found within these organizations were largely attributed to the nationality and demographic characteristics of their employees. Since both the sample size and the number of countries included in the survey were limited, Hofstede's empirical study on organizational cultures can hardly be interpreted as general or universally applicable. It nevertheless provided interesting insights into several aspects of organizational culture, including an empirical definition of the boundaries between national culture and organizational culture, as well as the theoretical validity of postulating national cultural values as pre-determined factors. Based on the findings of this research, national cultural manifestations are expected to have a pervasive effect on both the nature and the management of an organization's practices, structure or strategy, which in turn influence performance. As a result, certain cultural values in an organization can also be notoriously difficult to change and adapt.[49]

National Culture Pervasively Affects Macroeconomic and Managerial Phenomena

Coherent with the models of culture described above, extensive empirical research findings suggest that differences in deep-rooted cultural manifestations across countries play a significant role in the way in which economic and management issues are addressed and resolved, significantly explaining differences in performance along a variety of phenomena. Some of the main studies in this area are schematically shown in Figure 1.2.

For example, national cultural values, measured from Western and Eastern perspectives, were found to explain more than half the cross-national variance in economic growth over time for samples of eighteen and twenty nations. Cultural differences between countries were also considered to be a major factor influencing the degree of success in the international transfer of critical technologies or managerial techniques between organizations.

Moreover, societies characterized by individualistic and non-hierarchical cultural orientations have been found to be considerably more inventive than others.[50]

Beside these macro-level factors, numerous empirical studies have also explored the effects of national, corporate or organizational versions of culture on a variety of microeconomic and management phenomena. These include recurrent themes in organizational behavior, ranging from the assessment of people and organizational culture fit to the interaction of individual

FIGURE 1.2

The effects of culture on a variety of economic/management phenomena have been studied both theoretically and empirically by many authors (see Notes section at end of chapter for reference details)

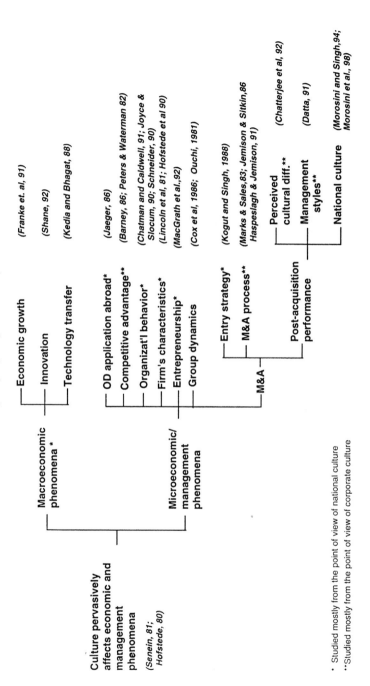

* Studied mostly from the point of view of national culture
**Studied mostly from the point of view of corporate culture

and group values with incentive systems and norms, as well as work adjustment, organizational climate and employee retention. An interesting line of research has examined the effects of cultural differences in ethnic groups and cultural diversity on working behavior and performance within organizations. For example, some empirical studies conducted in the USA suggest that ethnically diverse groups composed of "Asians", "Blacks", "Hispanics", and "Anglos" acted more co-operatively than "all-Anglo" groups. Moreover, these behavioral differences tended to increase when the situational cues favored co-operation. Such differing behavior was found to significantly affect the diversity in performance observed across these multi-ethnic group tasks.[51]

The Role of Culture in M&As, JVs and Alliances

Partly as a result of the increasing empirical evidence highlighting the pervasive influence of culture on the performance of economic and managerial phenomena, and particularly due to the consistently poor track record of M&A, JVs and alliance activity, management researchers have devoted increasing attention to the role played by cultural aspects *vis-à-vis* the performance of these transactions. The evidence so far accumulated suggests that, although both top executives and consultants often regard it as a soft issue, the notion that cultural issues can make or break an M&A, JV or alliance appears to be a hard fact. The empirical data that have been analyzed in this area cover the whole spectrum of culture as characterized above, from "national" aspects to "organizational" and "corporate" aspects. Moreover, the available literature includes studies exploring the influence of cultural aspects on the choice of specific entry modes, the merger or acquisition process *per se*, and post-M&A performance. However, until recently, some important empirical gaps remained in this literature, particularly concerning the influence of national cultural differences on the performance of cross-border acquisitions.

The effect of national culture on acquisition entry strategy

Studies looking at the effects of national culture on the choice of acquisitions as an entry mode generally employ a rational choice perspective, emphasizing the role of the entrepreneur as a rational decision-maker in a relatively transparent market for asset control. The available space for rational decisions broadly includes JVs, acquisitions and greenfield investments. Here, the decision of entry mode appears to be significantly affected by both the country of origin and the "national culture" of a firm. A number of studies have found that European firms are more likely to engage in overseas joint venture activity than American firms. Other authors have reported significantly different patterns of acquisitions among American, British and Japanese corporations. In addition, the relationship between a firm's "national culture" and its preferred mode of entry has been highlighted in the context of ownership policies concerning overseas subsidiaries.[52]

An empirical study by US-based academicians Kogut and Singh provided a systematic statistical test of the effects of national culture on the choice of entry modes.[53] Utilizing Hofstede's national cultural scores, these authors examined the hypothesis that the preference for acquisitions over either JVs or wholly owned greenfields was inversely correlated with the national cultural distance between the investing firm's country of origin and the country of entry. It was further hypothesized that JVs or wholly owned greenfields would be the preferred entry choice when the culture of the investing firm was characterized by a greater uncertainty avoidance. Based on a large-scale sample, Kogut and Singh's research found empirical support for these hypothesis.

Studies concerning the effects of culture on the M&A "process"

A number of authors have focused on the role of the acquisition process itself as a key determinant of M&A outcomes. These studies highlight the complexity and intensity of the activities, tasks and functions taking place prior to the conclusion of an M&A agreement, as major factors influencing performance following the deal. Thus, the level of participation of operating managers and key staff, the degree of involvement of external experts or consultants, and the management approach taken to assess a potential merger or acquisition are among the process factors which greatly affect overall performance, in addition to purely strategic and organizational issues. In particular, it has been suggested that the greater the number and influence which outside advisors have in the process of technical analysis of an acquisition the less attention is likely to be devoted to organizational issues. The level of agreement between top management teams, as well as differences between actual and perceived agreement, has also been recognized as a complex factor affecting both the results of the post-acquisition process as well as the level of interaction between the acquirer and the target during the integration phase.[54]

Studies concerning the effect of culture on post-acquisition performance

Although it had been virtually ignored as a research topic during most of the previous decade, the effects of culture on post-M&A performance have been tested in an increasing number of empirical studies published since the early 1990s. However, these studies have *not* been carried out from a national culture perspective, but rather from the viewpoint of differences in management styles or the perceived cultural differences between the top management teams of the merging companies.

The concept of management styles has been studied from both the organizational fit and organizational culture perspectives. The former relies on a notion of management style which includes a number of elements such as the management group's attitude towards risk, their decision-making approach, and their preferred control and communication patterns. From an organizational culture viewpoint, management style has been prominently described in terms of the managerial or the subjective culture of an organization, influencing its organizational practices and working manifestations.[55]

One empirical piece of research studied the level of compatibility between the buyer's and the target's top management styles (here viewed as a key element of organizational fit) in relation to acquisition performance. Based on a sample of 173 US-based cases in the manufacturing industry, this study found that differences in top management styles had a negative impact on performance across transactions characterized by both high and low levels of post-acquisition integration. In the same study, no relationship was found between reward and evaluation systems and post-acquisition performance.[56]

Another study explored the relationship between the cultural fit of the buyer and the target, and the stock market gains to the acquirer. In this research, the notion of cultural fit was based on the perceived cultural differences between the combined top management teams and the degree of cultural tolerance of the buyer's top management team. The authors of this research found an inverse relationship between perceived cultural differences and shareholder gains. Their analyses provided support for the hypothesis that shareholder gains are significantly dependent upon the degree of "cultural fit" between the merging firm's top management, linking differences in "organizational cultural" aspects to the acquirer's equity value.[57]

Moreover, numerous people-related problems arising as a result of M&As have been widely recognized as being determinant to performance. In particular, the level of cultural fit and job security following these types of deals seem to be key to understanding and anticipating these people-related problems. Typical examples of the latter include: a significant increase in career and financial uncertainty, the lack of transitional support, feelings of alienation and reduced co-worker trust, particularly among an acquired firm's employees. As a result, dissatisfaction, low productivity and morale have been observed following the announcement of a merger or acquisition.[58]

Studies concerning the effects of culture on the performance of cross-border strategic alliances and JVs

Numerous empirical studies have demonstrated that national cultural aspects significantly influence the performance of IJVs and cross-border alliances. The available data cover the assessment, negotiation and particularly the implementation phases of these agreements. Overall, the unobtrusive influence of highly diverse, deep-rooted cultural values on behavior and management systems can lead to unresolved conflict and the lack of compatibility between the partners. These issues, coupled with poor communication and mutual distrust due to misunderstood national cultural differences, have been cited as the most important factors behind the high failure rate of global JVs and alliances. For example, decisions to form an IJV based on sound rational strategies can nevertheless deteriorate in practice as Western executives are faced with day-to-day complications resulting from working in difficult and unfamiliar national cultural environments. Lack of sufficient local knowledge of a foreign country's peculiar cultural and political context, or a short-term attitude *vis-à-vis* developing such knowledge, have also been identified as critical factors leading to flawed partner selection criteria and the early termination of IJVs and cross-border alliances. During the on-going implementation of these agreements, absence of relationship skills and day-to-day unresolved conflicts resulting from differences in deep-rooted values and cultural backgrounds between the partners are often more determinant to performance than market issues *per se.*[59]

Towards a new, "holistic" model of culture's consequences in global corporate alliances?

On the one hand, the available empirical studies we have so far reviewed consistently show a dismal track record for international M&A, JV and alliance activity. On the other, cultural differences are increasingly regarded as factors which pervasively influence a wide array of economic and management phenomena — seemingly including the performance of global M&As, JVs and alliances. What are some of the key implications of these findings which could help us improve both our current managerial understanding and the performance of these international transactions?

The attentive reader has certainly noticed that many sets of hypotheses have been proposed in the past to support a company's M&A, JV and alliance activities. Regarding M&As, for example, it has been hypothesized that "value creation" is not a crucial issue, because these transactions supposedly involve a simple transfer of benefits from the buyer's to the target company's shareholders. However, value creation theorists argue that M&As, JVs and alliances can be significantly motivated by a number of strategic benefits, based on relatedness, learning, market power, or potential economies of scale and scope. Another set of hypotheses seemingly takes a process view, drawing attention to the pre-acquisition planning or deal negotiation phases, as well as the degree of cultural compatibility between the merging or partner firms, as determinant factors in a company's M&A, JV and alliance activity. Additional hypotheses such as these have been proposed in the past, and new ones will undoubtedly be advanced in the future to explain why these transactions occur, and what are the actual benefits they bring to a firm.

Nevertheless, the considerable empirical evidence which has so far been produced to evaluate the performance of M&As, JVs and alliances is both remarkable and challenging in that it has consistently reported high failure rates across nearly *all* of the above-stated sets of hypotheses. Is this to be taken as increasing evidence that the strategic importance of these transactions has been significantly over-estimated in the so-called global economy? Is there a critical set of variables that might have been consistently overlooked and which could explain why most M&As, JVs and alliances fail? Have our concepts of performance been too narrowly conceived in the past? Are the expectations underlying most global M&As, JVs and alliances too high or unrealistic prior to the deal? Particularly when confronted with the stubbornly high failure rates of these transactions both globally and over time, a researcher or company executive alike could easily conclude that our current strategic and organizational approaches might contain only a partial set of all the relevant explanatory variables of M&A, JV and alliance performance. In the absence of more complete models to satisfactorily explain both the nature and the dismal performance of global corporate alliances, new and more holistic approaches certainly deserve serious consideration.

These types of reflections have induced us to conceptualize a specific organizational model to guide our research on national cultural differences and the performance of global M&As, JVs and alliances. In this model, we recognize that most of the hypotheses that have been previously put forward to explain M&A, JV and alliance activity (i.e. predominantly based on strategic or financial arguments) can be regarded as valid to a significant extent. However, the organizational views that underlie these hypotheses stress a fundamental dichotomy between a firm's *internal* structural factors and an *external* marketplace. As a result, the performance of an M&A, JV or alliance is largely seen as a function of elements that are either *internal* to the acquiring, target or partner companies (such as their financial, strategic or marketing assets), or mostly belonging to the *external* realm of a firm's marketplace (i.e. market power or related "synergies" which can be attained through an acquisition or a strategic alliance). Following these organizational views, management researchers often address national cultural differences as merely exogenous factors to a company, representing potential risks for a cross-border acquirer or partner. The latter must endeavor to measure such cultural risks and include these assessments when deciding about and implementing overseas M&As, JVs or alliances.

However, these organizational approaches tend to only partially address the complexity of cultural symbols in relation to management phenomena. Indeed, in the "real world", deep-rooted national cultural values can be thought of as pervasively underlying the particular ways in which a company behaves and relates to the social community to which it belongs. From this perspective, apart from strictly *internal* or *external* factors, an organization needs to be described in terms of its *social* components in order to fully understand how it achieves results in the marketplace, and what is the role that cultural values play in this process. Indeed some authors have suggested that this type of holistic view of the firm may increasingly supersede our current organizational approaches:

> After World War I and Alfred Sloan's reorganization of General Motors Corporation (and culminating in the 1950s with the decentralization of the American General Electric Company), we superimposed on [Henri] Fayol's model a structure called the "business unit". It tries to balance the *internal* concern for getting the work done with the *external* concern of serving the market. It is still the most widely accepted approach and underlies all of the present discussion of balancing "core competencies" and "market focus" as well as the present concern with re-engineering.
>
> But now a totally different approach is emerging, not replacing the older approaches but being superimposed on them: it says that the purpose of organizations is to get results *outside*, that is, to achieve performance in the market. The organization is, however, more than a machine, as it is in Fayol's structure. It is more than economic, defined by results in the marketplace. The organization is, above all, *social*. It is people. Its purpose must therefore be to make the strengths of people effective and their weaknesses irrelevant. In fact, that is the one thing only the organization can do — the one reason why we have it and need to have it.[60]

A firm's *social* components are concerned with how it acts and obtains results as part of a living community, thus including such aspects as:

- How a company executes complex co-ordination functions involving both *internal* and *external* resources.
- How it develops critical networks and learns within its community.
- How its people communicate and collectively foster a social sense of identity.

In the context of global M&As, JVs and alliances, we maintain that national cultural differences are closely linked to a company's multiple *social* dimensions, some of which are both extremely complex to handle practically and determinant to performance. In particular, a company possessing the pragmatic skills to continuously co-ordinate resources from M&As, JVs and alliances across diverse national cultural contexts can build concrete advantages in a way that is difficult to replicate by competitors. We argue that this is the case because the co-ordination mechanisms that work effectively across diverse national cultures are holistically based on both knowledge and on the surrounding sea of cultural symbols, metaphors and norms which we capture with the ancient Greek notion of *gnosis*. This concept is central to the topic of this book and will be developed in more detail in the following chapters.

Gnosis is a cognitive dimension subjectively grounded on experience-based (or *tacit*) understanding of complex phenomena such as national cultural symbols, group metaphors and social norms. A firm's *gnostic* dimensions deeply pervade its organizational and cultural milieu, uniquely characterizing the way it acts, communicates and obtains results in the marketplace. Thus conceived, *gnosis* is time-consuming to attain and difficult to codify, but correspondingly hard to imitate by competitors. Underpinning these views, proponents of the firm as a *social* community have found empirical support to the notion that it specializes in the creation of tacit knowledge and "idiosyncratic technologies" which are slower to transfer outside the firm and extremely difficult to formalize, but which can be recombined at lower cost in wholly owned subsidiaries relative to third parties.[61]

Following this approach, a firm can be conceived in terms of its specific set of *internal, external* and *social* conditioning factors. These are not to be thought of as independent from one another, but as mutually interacting in a highly complex way. In particular, the peculiar *gnostic* characteristics of each firm will uniquely and comprehensively shape its cultural behavior, social norms, group metaphors and tacit communication. Thus, in the context of an M&A, JV or alliance, a firm's *social* conditioning factors are important not only in an abstract sense but also in relation to how any two merging or partner companies will interact to blend and enrich each others' *internal* and *external* factors, and *how* they will execute critical co-ordination mechanisms that are determinant to performance. This interacting model is schematically represented in Figure 1.3.

In this model, the interaction of two firms' conditioning factors is a function of the targeted changes which the merging or partner companies decide to undertake. During an initial phase, a firm's *internal, external* and *social* factors are pre-positioned to match both the nature and amount of structural change required. This will take into account not only "financial", "strategic" or other functional dimensions but also a firm's national cultural characteristics, its reflective knowledge, its knowledge about another firm's conditioning factors, its *gnostic* and leadership qualities, its pragmatic skills, etc. In some cases, for example, an international acquirer could decide to implement minimum or no significant changes on a target's operations. In others, significant changes could be sought in an overseas M&A, JV or alliance, inducing major demands on a company's resources—i.e. to pre-position key managers lacking the required co-ordination skills across borders, or a sufficient *gnosis* of diverse national cultural contexts.

FIGURE 1.3

Conditioning factors in an M&A, JV or alliance

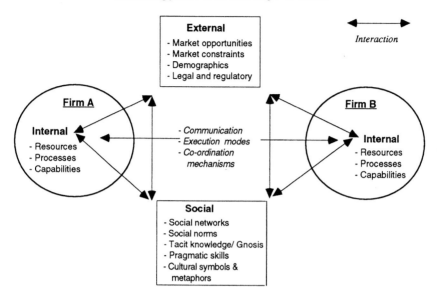

The second stage in this model, is characterized by increasing demands on a company to timely achieve the targeted changes following a cross-border acquisition, or within a newly formed JV or alliance abroad. At this stage, specific execution modes and mechanisms will lead to the expected results not only based on their intrinsic functional or technical value, but also on the degree to which they are adapted to their relevant national cultural contexts. Here, a company's *gnosis* of the confounding factors arising from another firm's cultural symbols, tacit norms and group metaphors will become crucial to effectively carry out critical co-ordination and communication mechanisms across borders.

Thus, in this model, achieving performance results in M&As, JVs and alliances across national cultures is not only dependent on a company's *internal* or *external* conditioning factors, but also represents a holistic *social* endeavor deeply embedded in the fabric of *gnosis*. However, this is also why no one-sided recipe or codified strategic approach might be available to describe a company's consistently successful M&A, JV and alliance activity across national cultures. In this area, holistic research and managerial approaches — encompassing both theoretical and pragmatic cognition — seem to be required in order to improve our understanding and the performance results of these transactions.

Our proposed model also highlights subjective experience and the pragmatic aspects of management as critical to the performance of M&As, JVs and alliances across national cultural differences. This might appear surprising to some, in view of the abundant management literature that is available concerning M&A, JV and alliance "implementation" aspects. However, our particular focus favors the concrete execution modes and mechanisms utilized by international acquirers, joint venturers or company partners to manage effectively across specific national cultural contexts, rather than the archetypal or process-oriented approaches which have largely characterized the literature concerning the implementation aspects of these transactions.

In the remaining chapters of Part I we will empirically test some of the crucial assumptions underlying our proposed model, based on a sample of cross-border acquisitions. First, we will examine the link between national cultural distance and cross-border acquisition performance. Although systematic empirical evidence has been conspicuously missing in this area, it is somewhat surprising that a number of researchers have forcefully referred to a cultural myth supposedly involved in over-estimating the role of national cultural issues in the context of cross-border acquisitions.[62] However, equally compelling myths are typically proposed as counter-arguments to these notions, based on the presumed detrimental effects of national cultural distance on cross-border acquisition performance. Until recently, both types of arguments have been widely circulated in business and even academic quarters without systematic evidence to support either position.

Following these analyses, we will examine the link between national cultural differences, post-acquisition execution modes and performance. If a company's pragmatic modes of execution are relevant to the performance of M&As across national cultures, this would suggest that some of the *social* aspects of a firm are at least as important as its *internal* and *external* components. More holistic strategic and organizational approaches to global M&As — and, to an extent, also JVs and alliances — could thus be justified, encompassing a company's tacit cognition, pragmatic skills, social community and its subjective experience of diverse national cultural contexts. Such is the subject that we will develop in the next chapters of this book.

Notes and References

[1] Cartwright, S. and C. L. Cooper. "The role of cultural compatibility in successful organizational marriage", *Academy of Management Executive*, 7, 1993, pp. 57-70; Melin, L. "Internationalization as a strategy process", *Strategic Management Journal*, 13, Special Issues, 1992, pp. 99-118; Root, F. *Entry Strategies for International Markets*, Lexington Books, Lexington, MA, 1990.

[2] Williamson, O. E. *Marchets and Hierarchies: Analysis and Antitrust Implications*, Free Press, New York, 1975; Ravenscraft, D. and F. Scherer. "The profitability of mergers", *International Journal of Industrial Organization*, 7, 1989, pp. 101-116; Hoskisson, R. E., M. A. Hitt and C. W. Hill. "Managerial risk taking in diversified firms. An evolutionary perspective", *Organization Science*, 1991, pp. 296-313; Markides, C. C.

"Consequences of corporate restructuring: ex ante evidence", *Academy of Management Journal*, 35, 1992, pp. 398-412.

[3] Hoskisson, R. E. and T. A. Turk. "Corporate restructuring: governance and control limits to the internal capital market", *Academy of Management Review*, 15(3), 1990, pp. 459-477.

[4] European Commission Directorate General for Economic and Financial Affairs. *European Economy*, Supplement A, *Economic Trends*, No. 7, ISSN 0379-2056, July 1996; *The Economist*, 9 November 1996, p. 38; *The Economist*, 4 January 1997, p. 21; *Business Week*, 30 October 1995, p. 56; *Financial Times*, Friday, 31 October 1997, p.9.

[5] Perlmutter, H. V. and D. A. Hennan. "Cooperate to compete globally", *Harvard Business Review*, March-April, 1986, pp. 136-152; Lichtenberger, B. and G. Naulleau. "French-German joint ventures: cultural conflicts and synergies", *International Business Review*, 2 (3), 1993, pp. 297-307; Franko, L. G. "Use of minority and 50-50 joint ventures by United States multinationals during the 1970s: the interaction of host country policies and corporate strategies", *Journal of International Business Studies*, XX (1), Spring, 1989; Contractor, F. and P. Lorange. *Cooperative Strategies in International Business*, D. C. Heath, Lexington, MA, 1987.

[6] Seth, A. "Sources of value creation in acquisitions: an empirical investigation", *Strategic Management Journal*, 11, 1990, pp. 431-446; Chatterjee, S., M. Lubatkin, D. Schweiger and Y. Weber. "Cultural differences and shareholder value in related mergers: linking equity and human capital", *Strategic Management Journal*, 13, 1992, pp. 319-334; Datta, D. K. "Organizational fit and acquisition performance: effects of post-acquisition integration", *Strategic Management Journal*, 12, 1991, pp. 281-297.

[7] Salter, M. S. and W. A. Weinhold. *Diversification through Acquisitions: Strategies for Creating Economic Value*, Free Press, New York, 1979.

[8] Morosini, P. "Effects of national culture differences on post-cross-border acquisition performance in Italy", Doctoral Dissertation, Management Department, The Wharton School, University of Pennsylvania, 1994; Marks, M. "Merging human resources", *Mergers and Acquisitions*, 17(2), 1982, pp. 38-42.

[9] Porter, M. E. *Competitive Strategy*, Free Press, New York, 1980; Salter, M. S. and W. A. Weinhold. *Op. cit.* 1979; Amburgey, T. and A. Miner. "Strategic momentum: the effects of repetitive, positional, and contextual momentum on merger activity", *Strategic Management Journal*, 13, 1992, pp. 335-348; Håkanson, L. "Learning through acquisitions", *International Studies of Management and Organization*, 25 (1-2), 1995, pp. 121-157. A study at the Columbia University business school suggested that CEOs with "bigger egos" — i.e. measured by relative compensation and media exposure — tend to pay higher acquisition premiums (quoted in *Business Week*, "The case against mergers. Even in the '90s most still fail to deliver", 30 October, p. 59).

[10] Seth, A. "Value creation in acquisitions: a re-examination of performance issues", *Strategic Management Journal*, 11, 1990, p. 100.

[11] There is a vast specialized literature concerning the concept of "synergy" and related issues in merger and acquisition activity. The following references can provide a suitable introduction for the interested reader: Lubatkin, M. and H. O'Neill. "Merger strategies and capital market risk", *Academy of Management Journal*, 30 (4), 1987, pp. 665-684; Chatterjee, S. "Type of synergy and economic value: the impact of acquisitions on merging and rival firms", *Strategic Management Journal*, 7, 1986, pp. 119-139; Salter, M. S. and W. A. Weinhold. *Op. cit.*, 1979; Singh, H. and C. Montgomery. "Corporate acquisition strategies and economic performance", *Strategic Management Journal*, 8, 1987, pp. 377-386; Eckbo, B. "Horizontal mergers, collusion and stockholder wealth", *Journal of Financial Economics*, 11, April 1983, pp. 241-273; Stillman, R. "Examining antitrust policy towards horizontal mergers", *Journal of Financial Economics*, 11(1-4), April 1983, pp. 225-240; Porter, M. E. *Op.*,

cit., 1980; Scherer, F. *Industrial Market Structure and Economic Performance*, Rand McNally, Chicago, IL, 1980; Wiggins, S. "A theoretical analysis of conglomerate mergers", in R. Blair and R. Lanzilotti (eds), *The Conglomerate Corporation*, Oelgeschlager, Gunn & Hain, Cambridge, MA, 1981, pp. 53-70; Baumol, W., J. Panzar and R. Willig. *Contestable Markets and the Theory of Industry Structure*, Harcourt Brace Jovanovich, San Diego, CA, 1982; Teece, D. "Economies of scope and the scope of the enterprise", *Journal of Economic Behavior and Organization*, 1(3), September 1980, pp. 223-247; Willig, R. "Multiproduct technology and market structure", *American Economic Review*, 69(2), May 1979, pp. 346-351; Williamson, O. E. "The modern corporation: origins, evolution and attributes", *Journal of Economic Literature*, 19, December 1981, pp. 1537-1568; Stigler, G. "A theory of oligopoly". In G. Stigler (ed.), *The Organization of Industry*, Irwin, Homewood, IL, 1968, pp. 39-63.

[12] Seth, A. "Sources of value creation in acquisitions: an empirical investigation", *Strategic Management Journal*, 11, 1990, pp. 431-446; Seth, A. "Value creation in acquisitions: a re-examination of performance issues", *Strategic Management Journal*, 11, 1990, pp. 99-115.

[13] Salter, M. S. and W. A. Weinhold. *Op. cit.*, 1979; Singh, H. and C. Montgomery. *Op. cit.*, 1987.

[14] Barney, J. "Returns to bidding firms in mergers and acquisitions: reconsidering the relatedness hypothesis", *Strategic Management Journal*, 9, 1988, pp. 71-78.

[15] Lichtenberger B. and G. Naulleau. *Op. cit.*, 1993; Shenkar, O. and Y. Zeira. "Human resource management in international joint ventures: directions for research", *Academy of Management Review*, 12 (3), 1987, pp. 546-557; Contractor, F. and P. Lorange. *Op. cit.*, 1987; Young, R.G. and Bradford, S. Jr. *Joint Ventures Planning and Action*, Arthur D. Little, New York, 1977.

[16] Blodgett, L. "Partner contributions as predictors of equity share in international joint ventures", *Journal of International Business Studies*, 22 (1), 1991, pp. 63-78; Geringer, J. M. "Strategic determinants of partner selection criteria in international joint ventures", *Journal of International Business Studies*, 22 (1), 1991, pp. 41-62; Evan, W. M. (ed.) *Inter-organizational Relations*, University of Pennsylvania Press, Philadelphia, 1978.

[17] See: Hedlund, G. and J. Ridderstråle. "International development projects", *International Studies of Management and Organization*, 25 (1-2), 1995, pp. 158-184; Contractor, F. and P. Lorange. *Op. cit.*, 1987; Hedlund, G. "The hypermodern MNC—a heterarchy? *Human Resource Management*, 25 (1), Spring 1986, pp. 9-25; Bartlett, C. A. and S. Ghoshal. *Managing Across Borders: The Transnational Solution*, Harvard Business School Press, Cambridge, MA, 1989; Doz, Y. L. *Strategic Management in Multinational Companies*, Pergamon Press, Oxford, 1986; White, R. E. and T. A. Poynter. "Organizing for a world-wide advantage", in C. A. Bartlett, Y. Doz and G. Hedlund (eds), *Managing the Global Firm*, Routledge, London, 1990, pp. 95-116; Rindfleisch, A. and J.B. Heide. "Transaction cost analysis: Past, present and future applications", *Journal of Marketing*, 61 (4), 1997, pp. 30–54.

[18] Singh, H. and C. Montgomery. *Op. cit.*, 1987.

[19] Shelton, L. "Strategic business fits and corporate acquisition: empirical evidence", *Strategic Management Journal*, May-June 1988, pp. 279-288; Elgers, P. and J. Clark. "Merger types and stockholder returns: additional evidence", *Financial Management*, 1980, pp. 66-72; Lubatkin, M. "Merger strategies and stockholder value", *Strategic Management Journal*, 8(1), 1987, pp. 39-53; Kitching, J. "Why do mergers miscarry?", *Harvard Business Review*, 45(6), 1967, pp. 84-101.

[20] Chatterjee, S. *et al. Op. cit.*, 1992; Lubatkin, M. *Op. cit.*, 1987.

[21] Singh, H. and C. Montgomery. *Op. cit.*, 1987, p. 385.

[22] Chatterjee, S. *Op. cit.*, 1986.

[23] Chatterjee, S. and M. Lubatkin. "Corporate mergers, stockholder diversification, and changes in systematic risk", *Strategic Management Journal*, 11, 1990, pp. 255-268.

[24] Lubatkin, M. *Op. cit.*, 1987.

[25] Chatterjee, S. "Sources of value in take-overs: synergy or restructuring — implications for target and bidder firms", *Strategic Management Journal*, 13, 1992, pp. 267-286.

[26] Datta, D. K., G. E. Pinches and V. K. Narayanan. "Factors influencing wealth creation from mergers and acquisitions: a meta-analysis", *Strategic Management Journal*, 13, 1992, pp. 67-84.

[27] Wansley, J., W. Lane and H. Yang. "Abnormal returns to acquired firms by type of acquisition and method of payment", *Financial Management*, 12(3), Fall 1983, pp. 16-22.

[28] Seth, A. "Sources of value creation in acquisitions: an empirical investigation", *Strategic Management Journal*, 11, 1990, pp. 431-446.

[29] The studies revised by A. Seth included: Eckbo, B. *Op. cit.*, 1983; Stillman, R. *Op. cit.*, 1983; US Federal Trade Commission. *Economic Report on Conglomerate Merger Performance*, Washington, DC, November 1972; Kim, E. and J. McConnell. "Corporate mergers and the coinsurance of corporate debt", *Journal of Finance*, 32(2), May 1977, pp. 349-365; Asquith, P. and E. Kim. "The impact of merger bids on the participating firms' security holders", *Journal of Finance*, December 1982, pp. 1209-1228; Choi, D. and G. Philippatos. "An examination of merger synergism", *Journal of Financial Research*, 6(3), 1983, pp. 239-256; Shrieves, R. and M. Pashley. "Evidence on the association between mergers and capital structure", *Financial Management*, Autumn 1984, pp. 39-48; Langetieg, T., R. Haugen and W. Wichern. "Merger and stockholder risk", *Journal of Financial and Quantitative Analysis*, 15(3), September 1980, pp. 689-717; Firth, M. "Synergism in merger: some British results", *Journal of Finance*, 33(2), May 1978, pp. 670-672.

[30] Porter, M. E. "From competitive advantage to competitive strategy", *Harvard Business Review*, 65(3), 1987, pp. 43-59; Ravenscraft D. and F. Scherer. *Op. cit.*, 1989; Cartwright S. and C. L. Cooper. *Op. cit.*, 1993; Young, J. "A conclusive investigation into the causative elements of failure in acquisitions and mergers", in S. J. Lee and R. D. Colman (eds), *Handbook of Mergers, Acquisitions and Buyouts*, Prentice Hall, Englewood Cliffs, NJ, 1981, pp. 605-628.

[31] Kitching, J. *Acquisitions in Europe*, Business International, 1973.

[32] Ravenscraft D. and F. Scherer. *Op. cit.*, 1989.

[33] Schmidt, D. and K. Fowler. "Post-acquisition financial performance and executive compensation", *Strategic Management Journal*, 11, 1990, pp. 559-569; Sutton, R. "Managing organizational death", *Human Resource Management*, 22, 1983, pp. 391-412; Haspeslagh, P. C. and D. B. Jemison. *Managing Acquisitions: Creating Value through Corporate Renewal*, Free Press, New York, 1991.

[34] McKinsey & Co., Financial Post Conference, 8 November 1988; Booz Allen & Hamilton Inc. *Strategy & Business*, Quarterly Review; William M. Mercer's Strategy and Organization Group. *Making Mergers Work*, 1988, Toronto, Canada; A.T. Kearney. *Corporate Marriages: 'Til Death Do Us Part?*, 1989; *The Economist*, 4 January 1997, p. 61.

[35] Bain, W. Jr. "Shopping for companies", *Across the Board*, July-August 1986, p. 44.

[36] Anderson, R., M. Feldman and M. L. Marks. "Life after the deal", *Mergers and Acquisitions*, November-December, 1986, p. 62.

[37] *The Economist*, 4 January 1997, pp. 61-62; "The Case Against Mergers" (cover story), *Business Week*, 30 October 1995; "Most Mergers Don't Work" (cover story).

[38] Bleeke, J. and D. Ernst. "The way to win in cross-border alliances", *Harvard Business Review*, November, 1991, pp. 127-135; Ernst, D. and J. Bleeke. *Collaborating to Compete*, John Wiley, New York, 1994.

[39] Radway, R. J. "Joint ventures with foreign partners: capital, control and culture problems", *The Currency Forecasters Digest*, November-December, 1986, pp. 24-30; Lane, H. W. and P. W. Beamish. "Cross-cultural cooperative behavior in joint ventures in LDCs", *Management International Review*, Special Issue, 1990, pp. 87-102; Lichtenberger, B. and G. Naulleau. *Op. cit.*, 1993; Beamish, P. W. *Multinational Joint Ventures in Developing Countries*, Routledge, London, 1988; Beamish, P. W. and H. Y. Wang. "Investing in China via joint ventures", *Management International Review*, 29(1), 1989, pp. 57-54; Gunther, R. "Cross-cultural conflicts in China and Russia", *Wharton Alumni Magazine*, Fall 1996, p. 25.

[40] Weber, Y., O. Shenkar and A. Raveh. "National and corporate cultural fit in mergers/acquisitions: an exploratory study", *Management Science*, 42(8), August 1996, pp. 1215-1227; Lincoln, J., M. Hanada and J. Olson, "Cultural orientations and individual reactions to organizations: a study of employees of Japanese-owned firms", *Administrative Science Quarterly*, 26, 1981, pp. 93-114.

[41] Lane, H. W. and P. W. Beamish. *Op. cit.*, 1990; Moran, R. "Cross-cultural dimensions of doing business in Latin America", in D. R. Shea, F. W. Swacker, R. J. Radway and S. T. Stairs (eds), *Reference Manual on Doing Business in Latin America*, University of Wisconsin, Milwaukee, 1980.

[42] Morosini, P. *Op. cit.*, 1994; Jemison, D. B. and S. B. Sitkin. "Corporate acquisitions: a process perspective", *Academy of Management Review*, 11(1), 1986, pp. 145-163; Marks, M. *Op. cit.*, 1982.

[43] See: Wiener, Y. "Forms of value systems: a focus on organizational effectiveness and cultural change and maintenance", *Academy of Management Review*, 1988, 13(4), pp. 534-545; Barney, J. "Organizational culture: can it be a source of sustained competitive advantage?", *Academy of Management Review*, 11(3), 1986, pp. 656-665; Barley, S. "Semiotics and the study of occupational and organizational cultures", *Administrative Science Quarterly*, 28, 1983, pp. 393-413; Gregory, K. L. "Native-view paradigms: multiple cultures and culture conflicts in organizations", *Administrative Science Quarterly*, 28, 1983, pp. 359-376; "Ideational" notions of culture are also well illustrated in Keesing, F. *Cultural Change: An Analysis and Bibliography of Anthropological Sources to 1952*, Stanford University Press, Stanford, CA, 1953.

[44] Hofstede, G. *Culture's Consequences: International Differences in Work-Related Values*, Sage Publications, Beverly Hills, 1980, pp. 45-46.

[45] McGrath R., I. MacMillan, E. Ai-Yuan Yang and W. Tsai. "Does culture endure or is it malleable? issues for entrepreneurial economic development", *Journal of Business Venturing*, 7, 1992, pp. 441-458.

[46] Schein, E. "SMR Forum: does Japanese management style have a message for American managers?", *Sloan Management Review*, 23(1), 1981, pp. 55-68; also see: Schein, E. *Organizational Culture and Leadership: A Dynamic View*, Jossey-Bass, San Francisco, 1985.

[47] Barney, J. *Op. cit.*, 1986; Deal, T. and A. Kennedy. *Corporate Cultures*, Addison-Wesley, Reading, MA, 1982; Jaeger, A. "Organization development and national culture: where's the fit?", *Academy of Management Review*, 11(1), 1986, pp. 178-190.

[48] Lincoln, J. *et al. Op. cit.*, 1981.

[49] Hofstede, G., B. Neuijen, D. Daval Ohayv and G. Sanders. "Measuring organizational cultures: a qualitative and quantitative study across twenty cases", *Administrative Science Quarterly*, 35, 1990, pp. 286-316.

[50] Franke, R., G. Hofstede and M. Bond. "Cultural roots of economic performance: a research note", *Strategic Management Journal*, 12, 1991, pp. 165-173; Kedia, B. and R. Bhagat. "Cultural constraints on transfer of technology across nations: implications for research in international and comparative management", *Academy of Management*

Review, 13(4), 1988, pp. 559-571; Shane, S. "Why do some societies invent more than others?", *Journal of Business Venturing*, 7, 1992, pp. 29-46; Jaeger, A. *Op. cit.*, 1986.

[51] Studies on the impact of culture on organizational behavioral aspects include: O'Reilly, C. A. III, J. Chatman and D. Caldwell. "People and organizational culture: a profile comparison approach to assessing person-organization fit", *Academy of Management Journal*, 3, 1991, pp. 487-516; Schein, E. *Op. cit.*, 1985; Chatman, J. "Improving interactional organizational research: a model of person-organization fit", *Academy of Management Review*, 14, 1989, pp. 333-349; Schneider, B. "The people make the place", *Personnel Psychology*, 40, 1987, pp. 437-453; Joyce, W. and J. Slocum. "Strategic context and organizational climate", in B. Schneider (ed.), *Organizational Climate and Culture*, Jossey-Bass, San Francisco, 1990, pp. 130-150; Sheridan, J. "Organizational culture and employee retention", *Academy of Management Journal*, 35(5), 1992, pp. 1036-1056. "Multiethnic-group" performance has been studied by a variety of authors. A good introduction to the subject can be found in Cox, T., S. Lobel and P. L. McLeod. "Effects of ethnic group cultural differences on co-operative and competitive behavior on a group task", *Academy of Management Journal*, 34(4), 1991, pp. 827-847.

[52] See: Wilson, B. "The propensity of multinational companies to expand through acquisitions", *Journal of International Business Studies*, 12 (Spring/Summer), 1980, pp. 59-65; Rappaport, A. "Strategic analysis for more profitable acquisitions", *Harvard Business Review*, 57, 1979, pp. 99-110; Salter, M. S. and W. A. Weinhold. *Op. cit.*, 1979; Puxty, A. "Some evidence concerning cultural differentials in ownership policies of overseas subsidiaries", *Management International Review*, 19, 1979, pp. 39-50; Stopford, J. and K. Haberich. "Ownership and control of foreign operations", in M. Ghertman and J. Leontiades (eds), *European Research in International Business*, North-Holland, Amsterdam, 1978, pp. 141-167; Robinson, R. "Management attitudes toward joint and mixed ventures abroad", *Western Business Review*, 1961.

[53] Kogut, B. and H. Singh. "The effect of national culture on the choice of entry mode", *Journal of International Business Studies*, Fall 1988, pp. 411-432.

[54] Druker, P. "The five rules of successful acquisition", *Wall Street Journal*, 15 October 1981; Searby, F. "Control postmerger change", *Harvard Business Review*, 47(5), 1969; Jemison, D. B. and S. B. Sitkin. *Op. cit.*, 1986.

[55] "Organizational fit" studies on management styles, include: Covin, J. and D. Slevin. "The influence of organizational structure on the utility of an entrepreneurial top management style", *Journal of Management Studies*, 25(3), 1988, pp. 217-234; Khandwalla, P. *The Design of Organizations*, Harcourt Brace Jovanovich, New York, 1977; Miller, D. "Strategy, making and structure: analysis and implications for performance", *Academy of Management Journal*, 30(1), 1987, pp. 7-32. Management style research from the perspective of "organizational culture" is exemplified by: Roberts, K. "On looking at an elephant: an evaluation of cross-cultural research related to organizations", *Psychological Bulletin*, 74, 1970, pp. 327-350; Bhagat, R. and S. McQuaid. "Role of subjective culture in organizations: a review and directions for future research", *Journal of Applied Psychology*, 67(5), 1982, pp. 653-685; Sathe, V. *Culture and Related Corporate Realities*, Irwin, Homewood, IL, 1985.

[56] Datta, D. K. *Op. cit.*, 1991.

[57] Chatterjee, S. *et al. Op. cit.*, 1992. In this study, the dimension of "cultural tolerance" utilized was based on an "acculturation" model for acquisitions developed during the late 1980s (see: Nahavandi, A. and A. Malekzadeh. "Acculturation in mergers and acquisition", *Academy of Management Review*, 13(1), 1988, pp. 79-90).

[58] Marks, M. and P. Mirvis. "The stiff challenge in integrating cross-border mergers", *Mergers and Acquisitions*, January-February, 1993, pp. 37-41; Mirvis, P., M. Marks and A. Sales. "A conceptual history of the impact of a corporate acquisition", in E. E.

Lawler (Chair), *Acquisition. Symposium at the American Psychological Association Meeting*, Los Angeles, 1983; Hirsch, P. and J. A. Andrews. "Ambushes, shootouts, and knights of the round table: the language of corporate take-overs", in L. Pondy, P. Frost, G. Morgan and T. Dandridge (eds), *Monograph in Organizational Behavior and Industrial Relations*. Vol. 1: *Organizational Symbolism*, JAI Press, Greenwich, CT, 1983, pp. 145-155; Levinson, H. "The psychological roots of merger failure", in H. Levinson (ed.), *The Great Jackass Fallacy*, Harvard Graduate School of Business Administration, Division of Research, 1973.

[59] The "unobtrusive" influence of national culture in IJVs and alliances has been discussed in various studies, including: Hofstede, G. *Op. cit.*, 1980; Perlmutter, H. V. and D. A. Heenan. *Op. cit.*, 1986; Lane, H. W. and P. W. Beamish. *Op. cit.*, 1990; Lane, H. W. and J. J. Di Stefano. *International Management Behavior: From Policy to Practice*, Nelson Canada, Scarborough, Ontario, 1988; Beamish, P. W. *Op. cit.*, 1985; Geringer, J. M. *Op. cit.*, 1988; Lichtenberger, B. and G. Nalleau. *Op. cit.*, 1993; Shenkar, O. and Y. Zeira. *Op. cit.*, 1987; Beamish, P. W. and H. Y. Wang. *Op. cit.*, 1989.

[60] See an introduction by Peter F. Drucker in *The Organization of the Future*, Hesselbein, F., M. Goldsmith and R. Beckhard (eds), San Francisco, Jossey-Bass, 1997, pp. 4-5.

[61] Kogut, B. and U. Zander. "Knowledge of the firm and the evolutionary theory of the multinational corporation", *Journal of International Business Studies*, 26, 1993, p. 636.

[62] Kanter, R. M. "Change in the global economy". Rosabeth Moss Kanter interview by Paul Stonham, Editor, *European Management Journal*, 12(1), March 1994.

CHAPTER 2

Myths and Evidence Concerning the Role of National Cultural Differences in Merger and Acquisition Performance

It must be considered that there is nothing more difficult, more dangerous or more apt to miscarry than an endeavour to introduce new institutions. For he that introduces them will make enemies of all those who do well out of the old institutions, and will receive only cool support from those who would do well out of the new ones.

Niccolò Machiavelli — *De Principatibus*

Despite successive and increasing waves of M&A, JV and alliance activity since the 1970s, substantial empirical evidence shows that these fail about half of the time. Most surprisingly, although extensive studies on the critical success factors of M&As, JVs and alliances have been carried out and widely circulated during the past decades, the available evidence reviewed in the previous chapter suggests that their failure rate has remained unchanged well into the 1990s. Partly due to this dismal track record, cultural issues, from being initially neglected relative to strategic and financial factors, have attracted growing attention as critical aspects *vis-à-vis* performance. As a result, increasing empirical research shows that, despite having been largely dismissed as a myth by some, cultural issues significantly influence the performance of M&As, JVs and alliances throughout the assessment, negotiation and implementation phases. Particularly in the case of cross-border acquisitions, national cultural differences have been shown to pervasively influence a myriad of behavioral and pragmatic aspects which are relevant to organizational performance. However, until recently, a remaining gap in the empirical literature covering these aspects concerned the link between national cultural distance and cross-border post-acquisition performance.

"Myth" of National Cultural Differences as Insurmountable Barriers to Cross-Border M&A

Notwithstanding the lack of systematic evidence, a number of researchers, management consultants and company executives have recurrently emphasized the supposedly detrimental influence of national cultural distance in cross-border M&A activity.[1] Such a tendency — or myth? — to put national cultural distance in a consistently negative light might be partly the result of empirical evidence stemming from closely related fields. On the one hand, the specialized literature concerning IJVs and alliances has overwhelmingly associated national cultural differences with chronic inter-relationship problems and unresolved conflicts between the partners, often leading to severe communication gaps and outright failure. On the other, many of the concerns about cultural distance that have been put forward in the literature concerning post-acquisition performance are based on corporate cultural differences. From this perspective, higher levels of cultural distance between firms have been associated with a greater degree of conflict and process losses during the day-to-day post-acquisition implementation period.[2]

Thus, direct extrapolation of empirical evidence from related areas might be one factor supporting the myth of national cultural distance as inherently detrimental to cross-border acquisition performance. However, a potentially more insightful explanation concerns the somewhat indiscriminate reference to national cultural aspects and manifestations as largely *external* factors from a managerial perspective — presumably as a result of the pervasive and resilient characteristics of deep-rooted cultural symbols. These views explicitly or implicitly underlie most research studies that have looked at national culture as a risk factor, or as a rigid pre-condition *vis-à-vis* cross-border acquisitions and similar situations.[1]

However, whereas national cultural symbols have been shown to be notoriously difficult to formalize and modify, from a company's viewpoint they need not be consequently regarded as insurmountable barriers, intractable aspects, or largely exogenous variables which are to be appraised and measured similar to systematic risk factors. Indeed, the same empirical literature that has examined national cultural distance in the context of IJVs and alliances, as well as studies looking at corporate cultural differences in relation to post-acquisition performance, have often regarded these issues as essentially endogenous to management. Seemingly less noticed by the proponents of national culture as a risk factor, this empirical evidence suggests that the source of such risks might not be unilaterally ascribed to cultural aspects, but could just as well be conceived as a function of a company's practical ability to handle national cultural aspects in an international acquisition. In these areas, most of the studies concerning national cultural differences have explored their influence on the performance of IJVs. On the one hand, managers' particular attitudes towards national cultural differences, and not cultural diversity *per se*, have been recognized as the real determinants of positive or negative performance outcomes in these types of partnerships.[3] On the other, further evidence is clearly pointing out the crucial importance of cross-cultural skills and managers' ability to handle day-to-day inter-relationship aspects, to effectively build enduring and co-operative IJVs. Thus, even in culturally distant or unfamiliar countries from a Western perspective, such as "developing" or "emerging" economies, it is not any particular or "given" environmental factor which can make or break such a partnership, but rather the company managers' commitment, patience and ability to work and adapt to difficult conditions and different cultures overseas, as well as to build critical "local" knowledge and networks of relationships in these countries. As a result, the skills to handle national cultural differences in an IJV, have also been linked with a company's consistent ability to recruit, select, compensate and train expatriate managers who can adapt and function effectively in overseas locations. Similarly, studies showing the detrimental effects of cultural distance between firms during the post-acquisition period explicitly assert that these performance outcomes are dependent upon the specific steps taken by the acquirer during the implementation phase.[4]

Most of the contrasting arguments to the notion of national cultural distance as a risk factor in international acquisitions crucially highlight the role of a company's pragmatic ability to manage these aspects. This particular kind of perspective might further explain why national culture appears to have often been regarded as a rather exogenous managerial factor by researchers in this field. Indeed, the resilient and penetrating nature of deep-rooted cultural values has led to logical conceptions of national culture akin to "mental programs", shared by groups of people and based on clearly identifiable and measurable dimensions that are *given* and not modifiable within the boundaries of an organization. From this perspective, national cultural dimensions have been likened to a hardly changeable mental software, distinguishing some categories of people from others, and pervasively affecting group as well as individual behavior. Within an organizational setting, these collective cultural programs are postulated as mechanistically causing specific behavioral orientations, which in turn influence certain economic or managerial outcomes.[5]

In spite of being widely utilized by management researchers, such conceptions of national culture may tend to overlook the complex psychological nature of the deep-rooted symbols underlying national culture. Unlike signs, these symbols have been described as embedded in words or images with dynamic meanings which are beyond conscious interpretation or logical codification. Hence, in addition to resilience and pervasiveness, a fundamental (though somewhat paradoxical) characteristic that has been associated with deep-rooted cultural symbols is constituted by their highly dynamic and unpredictable nature, providing virtually limitless possibilities of slight variations around a "central" meaning.[6] This crucial characteristic is not always well captured by the available empirical models of national culture, which are instead numerically based on factor constructs that inherently represent average features.[5] Although rather useful from a methodological perspective — i.e. to statistically correlate "national cultural" scores with a variety of economic and managerial phenomena — when transferred to more practical business dimensions these kinds of models face basic limitations to fully apprehend the wide context, dynamicity and unpredictability of national cultural manifestations. However, from a practical managerial perspective, it is precisely these multiform and dynamic characteristics of deep-rooted cultural symbols which might be particularly valuable to the *skillful* company manager overseas, allowing him/her to continuously devise ways to work inside and around highly diverse national cultural environments. In the case of IJVs between companies based on Western versus developing nations, it has indeed been observed that the latter countries' local cultural scene continuously changes over time.[7] Similarly, in the case of cross-border acquisitions, national cultural manifestations might be crystallized in practice through a myriad of dynamic possibilities, providing a critical space of options for international managers to effectively handle its more resilient and pervasive characteristics.

Complexity of National Cultural Issues Requires Pragmatic Skills

It follows that national cultural distance *per se* need not be conceived as necessarily detrimental to an international acquirer, joint venturer or partner. Rather, it is a company's ability to handle complex national cultural issues in these situations which can be ultimately regarded as determinant to performance. However, researchers in this area have widely recognized that, under certain circumstances, managing national cultural aspects can be very difficult indeed. Particularly in the context of a firm's internationalization, it has been observed that national cultural differences might be increasingly complex to manage the more a target's country of origin is culturally distant or unfamiliar from the acquirer's own national cultural perspectives. Swedish researchers at the University of Uppsala coined the term "psychic distance" between countries in relation to factors influencing a firm's degree of familiarity with a foreign market. These factors included differences between the culture and language of an acquirer's and a target's countries of origin, potentially disturbing the flow of communication between firms following an acquisition. As a result, these researchers argued that a gradual approach was preferable in the context of a firm's internationalization process, initially favoring culturally close locations over more distant ones.[8]

Further evidence of the difficulty in handling national cultural issues during cross-border acquisitions relates to their potential for nurturing deep-rooted resistance and intense conflict between different groups of people. The anthropological research highlights numerous instances of basic antagonism, widespread human alienation and exacerbated "tribal" conflict between members of different ethnic and cultural groups, which can be both non-rational and enduring. As mentioned, the specialized management literature has also reported fundamental people-related conflicts, lack of transitional support and feelings of alienation following the announcement of an acquisition.[9] However, when these transactions take place across culturally distant countries, deep-rooted differences are likely to further *anchor* and reinforce potentially hostile reactions as well as basic dissension between members of the acquiring and the target firms. This could seriously complicate the smooth execution of internal post-acquisition co-ordination and co-operation functions across national borders, thus affecting the potential performance benefits resulting from the combination of the merging firms' critical resources.

Overall, failure to properly manage a cross-border M&A, JV or alliance appears not to be unilaterally related to insurmountable "structural barriers" arising from distant or highly diverse national cultural values. National cultural differences are to be considered amongst the dynamic contextual characteristics of international M&A, JV or alliance activity. However, it is the acquirer's practical ability to manage complications eventually arising from these contextual characteristics which often makes the difference between success or failure, even within the most familiar national cultural environment from a given company's viewpoint. Nevertheless, the notion that a company can derive lasting practical advantages from its ability to consistently manage complex cross-cultural situations, such as the implementation of international M&As, JVs and alliances, may seem to be an excessive suggestion from certain perspectives. As mentioned, the so-called cultural myth or stereotype involved in systematically over-estimating the effects of national cultural differences on cross-border M&As, JVs and alliances has often been recognized in the relevant literature.[10] However, the opposite view — i.e. considering these business situations as essentially "culture-free" — usually follows these observations and could be just as detrimental to their success. Thus, in the following paragraphs we present some practical instances illustrating how national cultural differences can represent significant challenges in relation to the implementation of cross-border M&As and alliances, highlighting the importance of a company's pragmatic skills in effectively handling these challenges, and occasionally turning them into concrete advantages.

The *Culturally Unnatural* Process of Integrating M&As and Alliances Across National Borders

National cultural issues were particularly complex to handle in the large-scale, cross-border merger leading to the formation of ABB, the global electrical engineering group. This was largely due to the presence of several national identities prior to the merger: ASEA's Swedish origins, and Brown Boveri's historically strong and highly autonomous Swiss, French, German and Italian companies. Indeed, many of the initial doubts about the viability of such a combination often stressed the century-old historical infighting between Brown Boveri's autonomous national companies and the expectation that these would be reinforced and fueled over time when confronted with the differences in national cultural values, regulatory and institutional environments of Sweden's ASEA. In addition, these companies were highly representative and most visible industrial symbols in their home countries, being amongst Europe's oldest and more respected industrial concerns in their own right when the merger deal was announced (1987). Therefore, the task of merging both companies was, from the very beginning, indistinguishable from that of handling their national constituencies' deep-rooted, cultural resistances and conservative "instincts".

As mentioned, the profound pervasiveness and resilience of national — or more pointedly, "tribal" — cultural resistances across people's behavior have been widely studied in management, and constitute a classic subject in anthropological research. The former have highlighted the inward orientation and lack of cosmopolitan attitudes which are characteristic in countries showing markedly uncertainty avoidant and non-individualistic national cultural traits.[5] In turn, anthropological studies have stressed the deep-rooted human dichotomy between "we" and "they" categories, the relatively universal phenomenon of dehumanizing one's enemies or antagonists, and the important role that tribal and local cultural differences have in generating human conflicts.[9] As a result, in the case of a major international merger, the overall process of building and co-ordinating critical resources across countries can be rendered extremely difficult and complex to implement in practice by these different national and tribal cultures. This was a particularly relevant factor regarding the particular "multidomestic" organizational structure which ABB decided to implant following the 1987 merger between ASEA and Brown Boveri. This structure relied heavily on the company's practical ability to smoothly execute complex co-ordination functions between its global technology-based organizational units and its multidomestic network of small local profit centers.[11] Here, the crucial role played by the existing deep-rooted cultural differences across ABB's numerous national constituencies was not easy to ignore. Their resilience and penetrating nature required a correspondingly deep understanding, tolerance and patience to be dealt with effectively in practice. Moreover, underlying all these difficulties, the attempt to continuously carry out global co-ordination functions and build a multidomestic structure based on people whose profound cultural "instincts" were often heavily "local" was found to be a deeply disturbing and *unnatural* process. The strong, basic reactions which were often found as a result usually manifested themselves through a country's institutional and corporate framework as clusters which exerted a stubborn influence against specific changes both inside and outside the company boundaries. Percy Barnevik, ABB's Chairman and the company's former CEO, thus observes that, in the context of a radical company transformation such as the merger between ASEA and Brown Boveri, the relevance of these deep-rooted "instincts" and cultural resistances acquired a distinct and concrete dimension:

> From the perspective of a local company's employees, the multidomestic organization presents strong national roots and loyalties, encompassing "their" Government, "their" Union, "their" friends, and "their" town. And in the event of a corporate turnaround or a major company transformation effort, these clusters of people sometimes will address a local company manager as if he or she had to "defend" his or her country. But when people become deeply disappointed, then you have to look at how they behave. The clusters strongly manifest themselves. You can see "tribal" reactions among people, with many of them becoming deeply disappointed and angry during the implementation of a difficult corporate transformation.

As a result, the culturally *unnatural* characteristic of building a global structure across national roots can easily throw into disarray even a carefully thought through organizational design in practice. In the case of ABB, the situation was further complicated by the need to operate as a network of 5,000 small profit centers maintaining strong national cultures and "local" identities, within an overlay of global co-ordination functions. The crucial difficulties of running such a contradictory organization are candidly and explicitly acknowledged in ABB's "Book of Values", a document containing the company's basic guidelines of behavior, which has been widely circulated internally following the 1987 merger between ASEA and Brown Boveri:

> The true merger process does not come automatically or naturally — it is unnatural and takes management determination.

It is possible to find many instances in ABB's past to illustrate the practical experiences which may have led to such internal policy statements. In effect, the company found that efforts to create such an *unnatural* global co-ordination structure faced a staunch internal resistance within certain countries' institutional fabrics (or "clusters"), which were often well organized and historically embedded in their national cultural values. For instance, in Germany's strongly consensual and conservative cultural environment, Brown Boveri had to confront an epic resistance from some of the most powerful unions in the industrialized world following its merger with ASEA. As is well known, the German unions, along with the government's and the industry's representatives, form part of the country's "tripartite" economic system which, since the end of the Second World War, has consensually decided on far-reaching annual agreements regarding such sensitive issues as pay rises, wage contracts and corporate lay-offs. Such a well-defined institutional structure has in the past been associated with the country's specific national cultural characteristics, strongly favoring "uncertainty avoidant" and consensual behavior.[5]

In such a powerfully organized social environment, the decision to restructure Brown Boveri's German operations — involving proposed job losses of 4,000 people — found a determined and often violent internal resistance. Not only the unions, but also other highly visible institutions and personalities across the whole country, were literally mobilized against ABB's proposed restructuring plan. These included the local politicians, management representatives, the common people, and even religious leaders, who protested openly under unprecedented media attention. As a result, there were public demonstrations, explicit threats, physical obstructions and strong pressures on ABB's management to drop its restructuring plan. Eberhard von Koerber, then the company's appointed top executive in Germany, was given uninterrupted police protection during those critical years. More importantly, these events took place during the early stages of the merger, at the very core of Brown Boveri's largest operations, which, as mentioned, had been at the center of one hundred years of infighting amongst their Swiss, German and Italian constituents.

In such a difficult context, the very credibility of the merger between ASEA and Brown Boveri was put at stake from the outset, and the company's determination to carry it through was severely tested after it decided to bluntly target Brown Boveri's most visible subsidiary early on. Nevertheless, after the German unions realized that by not accepting the company's restructuring program it would altogether move a large part of its manufacturing operations outside the country, ABB was able to carry out its plans with some modifications. These included 2,500 job losses instead of the 4,000 which had been initially proposed, contingent on a significant increase in productivity in a number of factories which were not closed.

Was this the specific result of working in an unfamiliar, foreign cultural and institutional environment, or a case uniquely influenced by some significant national cultural distance between, say, German values and ASEA's Swedish culture? In the light of the difficulties faced by ASEA in Sweden — its own historic home turf — during the 1970s, and particularly throughout the early 1980s, the answer is decidedly negative. In effect, during this period ASEA had to confront the Swedish unions' strong opposition to the radical, "American-style" lay-offs which the company had to carry out in order to boost its declining profitability. These were the years when Curt Nicolin, both as one of ASEA's most visible leaders and as the President of the Swedish Industry Association (SAF), achieved an almost legendary clout in the country by his tough, some say ruthless, negotiation style with Sweden's powerful unions which, as in the case of Germany, had historically been a dominant and highly organized economic force in the country. These were also the years when Barnevik, as a newly appointed CEO of ASEA, had to conduct an unprecedented large-scale restructuring of the company's operations. Throughout this process, Barnevik found in Sweden the same type of wide-ranging, determined and often violent resistance which von Koerber had to face in Germany. In particular, the plant closures, including some of ASEA's, and Sweden's, most historically revered industrial symbols, were highly diffi-cult, intensely emotional events which, Barnevik confesses, at times tended to wear down even the most determined corporate leader. In fact, the way ASEA's profound transformation was publicly labeled during those years—ranging from "ASEA's cultural revolution" to "Percy's Reign of Terror"—reflects both the epochal, shocking effect it had on the company's employees and the extreme difficulty of carrying it through in the context of the company's highly patriarchal and conservative culture, the stiff opposi-tion from Sweden's powerful employee unions, and the country's notoriously generous social welfare state—keenly weary of corporate lay-offs.

Thus, it was perhaps in ASEA's own home country that some of ABB's leaders sharpened their hard-won practical skills to handle many of the prac-tical complications and deep-rooted cultural obstacles often associated with major cross-border mergers. Here, the strong initial resistances against a radical company transformation plan were reinforced and *anchored* in a socie-ty's deep-rooted cultural values, often manifesting themselves through the country's specific institutional fabric. In addition, the different corporate values of the merging companies usually contributed to further *anchor* the employees' national and tribal cultural mechanisms of resistance against the *unnatural* changes brought by the need to co-ordinate globally across nationalities. According to Barnevik, this is not only characteristic of ABB's post-merger integration experiences, but it has also been the case of many other companies that have been built through major cross-border, or even domestic M&As. In fact, although it could be argued that in cross-border situations language differences and the like can further complicate corporate cultural resistances, these appear to be no less formidable for the local man-agers themselves:

> You are often faced with a "tribal" mentality when you try to carry out a merger across different national or corporate cultures. In ABB, you have per-haps the most extreme case of a corporate merger across cultures in our size category. And the fact that we have a relatively short history is also a big challenge. We are making steady progress but we must speed it up. We strive to be the best. But some patience is required and one shouldn't underestimate the magnitude of the challenge.

How does one deal with all these formidable, culturally rooted obstacles in practice? This is, quite simply put, the domain where *superior execution skills* can make all the difference. These are the "practicalities" which make it possible for a company to succeed in the enormous task of building a global structure which can actually generate and sustain competitive advantages over time. Although seemingly simple from a conceptual standpoint, these practicalities are often extremely difficult to implement in the context of cross-border M&As and alliances, partly due to the above described deep-rooted resistances and cultural differences. In ABB's *unnatural* quest to build a global, multidomestic structure in practice, the company has to face the day-to-day, strenuous task of working against nature with vision, patience, tolerance and sheer determination. Here, it is only after uninterrupted, enormous efforts to instill global values and behavior in ABB's employees around the world since the 1987 merger that Barnevik can acknowledge some visibly encouraging results:

> But it was only after eight years that people really started to understand and accept the message, that they needed to work together cooperatively as one company. You can't have single stars and still manage to merge a company as large and complex as ABB's.

However, if it is based on such *culturally unnatural* principles, is ABB's global structure poised to last, to survive its current management generation? Or is *nature* going to take its long-term course, with all the various national values and "tribal instincts" of the company's constituencies ultimately encroaching its painfully crafted multidomestic framework of global co-ordination? Barnevik answers:

> You need to be a little humble and acknowledge that when you are sitting in your ivory tower, you may think that you have done "this" and "that". But then you meet people, three, four, or five layers down, and realize that you haven't done that much. This is like democracy: you have to fight for it all the time. It's the same when you try to decentralize a large company. We are decentralized now, but the "organizational gravity" always leans towards centralizing again.

So far, ABB's global crusade seems to have served the company and its shareholders well. Only eight years after the merger, the company's revenues had more than tripled, reaching US$ 34 billion at the end of the fiscal year 1995.[12] In the same year, it achieved a 28 percent return on equity, a level of profitability that the merging companies had never reached in the past, and for the first time surpassing the 25 percent internal goal set shortly after the 1987 merger between ASEA and Brown Boveri. Parallel to these achievements, the company's productivity levels and global network increased significantly after the merger. As a result, ABB's global and multidomestic structure became a widely studied and emulated organizational design, obtaining nearly every prestigious recognition for distinguished management awarded by the international business community.

However, most importantly, during the mid 1990s, some of the industry's largest players were increasingly regarding ABB as their greatest competitor, the rival to beat.[13] These are, in Barnevik's view, the outcomes of the company's key advantages — the other side of the difficult and *culturally unnatural* process of building a global co-ordination structure which works in practice across national borders:

> We talk a lot about the challenge of managing the national cultural complexities with this company, even after almost ten years. However, some of our competitors haven't even started, and when they try to become truly global, and grow their businesses over here in Europe, for example, then they will have to go through all these problems: The local regulations, learning how to work effectively with the unions, becoming an insider in each country. It will be very difficult for them.

The banking industry: are functional skills "effortlessly" transferable across national cultures around the world?

Investment banking has often been referred to as one of the few truly global industries, where it is claimed that certain functional skills and capabilities can be transferred effortlessly across countries with little regard for national cultural differences. Similar views have also been applied to other financial activities commonly regarded as truly global, such as securities sales and research. Robert M. Baylis, a former Vice Chairman of Credit Suisse First Boston Inc., observes:

> Regarding specific processes and incentives which are key to create a learning organization, I believe in most investment banks you will find that functional skills are considered the only key, and are considered transferable around the world in capital markets.

In fact, it could be argued that the merger between Credit Suisse and US-based First Boston was a forerunner of the kind of cross-border banking deals combining commercial and investment banking which took place in Europe since the late 1980s. During the early 1970s, Credit Suisse formed an investment banking joint venture with White Weld, a London-based concern. Then, in 1978, it bought a minority and subsequently a majority in First Boston's London Merchant Bank and merged Credit Suisse White Weld with it. Credit Suisse First Boston (CSFB), the resulting joint company, soon became London's top Eurobond house, remaining a leading force in this market throughout the mid 1990s, albeit keeping its operations separated from both Credit Suisse's and First Boston's. Baylis notes that, as a result, there was no real merger between Credit Suisse and First Boston, nor were any integration efforts carried out beyond the previously mentioned investment banking operations. National cultural differences were not weighed as an issue when integrating First Boston's merchant bank into Credit Suisse White Weld:

> Cultural differences were not really considered other than as they related to language differences. The strains that resulted were between CSFB (the merged London Merchant Bank) and First Boston. Attempts to achieve one corporate culture mission statement, etc., at the merchant banking firm were unsuccessful and not fully supported by senior management. I think one would find in studying investment banks, that the return on human and dollar capital is probably the most important driving force.

Thus, difficulties in creating a common culture "at the merchant banking firm" are largely attributed to the change in First Boston's ownership structure brought in by the merger with Credit Suisse White Weld. This created problems at the top management levels of the acquired investment bank, previously organized as a partnership:

> In most firms the only significant stake holder are the partners or managing directors. In a firm where the majority owner is different from this group there are some obvious strains.

In 1989, Credit Suisse created a holding structure for the whole group, leading to higher organizational flexibility among the group's subsidiaries. Although a subsequent centralization of management along functional lines seems to have been met with cultural resistance internally, at the time it was argued that these were related to the organizational change rather than to the merger *per se*.

However, in April 1996 it was publicly disclosed that CS Holding was taking the first steps to integrate more closely its commercial and investment banking operations. In Germany, Credit Suisse and CSFB agreed to merge their commercial and investment banking businesses, respectively, in a joint venture two-thirds owned by Credit Suisse and one-third by CSFB. This development was viewed by CSFB executives as an experiment which, if successful, could provide a "model" for other parts of the organization, such as the UK-based 4,000-strong CS group. It involved establishing significantly greater co-ordination functions between the bank's investment banking and traditional commercial banking subsidiaries *vis-à-vis* the client base. However, significant difficulties in carrying out such cross-functional co-ordination in practice were apparent after CSFB executives emphasized in the media that independence was key to their creativity as an investment bank and, accordingly, the planned reorganization was not meant to tie the group's commercial and investment banking businesses "too close" together to undermine such independence. As a result of these types of reports, some observers at the time started to openly refer to CSFB's organizational complexities as significantly culture-related, suggesting that: "...its [Credit Suisse's] CS First Boston arm has, to put it mildly, had its ups and downs. The cultures of the US investment bank and the Swiss banking giant have not bedded conspicuously well."[14]

Such events seem to further illustrate the sharp distinction between formalizing an appealing organizational design and actually executing it. Even within the global banking businesses, *execution skills* seem to be crucial to establishing and managing complex co-ordination functions across highly diverse informational contexts, including the national and corporate cultural resistances which may arise. Thus, despite being amongst the first to combine commercial and investment banking operations through its CSFB joint venture in 1978, by 1996 the CS Holding group was being viewed as lagging relative to other institutions such as Swiss Bank Corporation and Deutsche Bank. In fact, although the latter institutions entered investment banking later than Credit Suisse did, they were quicker to integrate commercial and investment banking. In this sense, Credit Suisse's failed merger attempt with UBS during early 1996 was seen by many as an overdue response to its Swiss-based rivals determined inroads into the profitable global investment banking business. In particular, Swiss Bank Corporation's acquisition of S.G. Warburg Group plc in 1995 had catapulted the joint company to the top of the European investment banking leagues, while Credit Suisse's 69 percent stake in CSFB was not turning out to be a particularly good investment according to some analysts, despite CS' equity capital infusions of more than US$ 700 million since 1990.[14] It is possible that, as CS Holding's attempts to integrate its commercial and investment banking operations gain momentum across national borders, cultural issues, beyond mere language differences, may turn out to be increasingly important practical aspects of the bank's global transformation efforts.

Since early 1995, Deutsche Bank appeared to provide vivid illustration of just these types of issues when it started to actively integrate its international network of investment banking, trading and asset management acquisitions. As part of an aggressive internationalization effort started during the early 1980s, Deutsche Bank had acquired Banca d'America e d'Italia (BAI) in 1986, and Banco Comercial Transatlántico S.A. in Spain, followed by the acquisition of Italian Banca Popolare di Lecco SpA in 1993. The following year, Deutsche Bank bought Sharps Pixley Group, a metal trading concern, and in 1995 Finanza e Futuro, Italy's second largest direct sales force brokerage house at that time, with a sizable asset management operation. Moreover, since the early 1990s it had engaged in the most determined and extensive international "head-hunting" operation ever attempted in the banking industry, attracting highly ranked executives, and even entire working divisions, away from its competitors. However, perhaps the bank's most notorious acquisition took place in 1989, when it paid £950 million (around DM 2.7 billion) for London-based Morgan Grenfell, an old and most established English merchant bank. In order to minimize potential cultural conflicts between the German and the Anglo-Saxon constituencies, Deutsche Bank opted for an initial hands-off management style after the acquisition.

Therefore, until 1995 Morgan Grenfell was kept at arm's length from Deutsche Bank's operations, largely as a financial participation. However, during early July 1995, Deutsche Bank publicly announced that it was moving towards integrating its world-wide investment banking business under the name Deutsche Morgan Grenfell (DMG), bringing together its operations with those of the former Morgan Grenfell. A management committee of sixteen people was formed, which included three non-British executives and others recently hired from competing merchant banks, such as Merrill Lynch and S. G. Warburg.[15] This committee markedly differed from Morgan Grenfell's previous top management organization, which had remained unchanged and traditionally dominated by long-standing company executives of British nationality. Here, Deutsche Bank's executives utilized euphemisms to describe the difficulties which this management committee faced as a result of the changes introduced. Thus, including "all these Americans" and "people from other companies" in the top management ranks of DMG was generally viewed as "not easy" to former Morgan Grenfell executives who were used to a management structure with "no outsiders". It was also mentioned that favorable market conditions during 1995 have significantly contributed to "sort out management problems" as a result of the DMG integration.

Both CS First Boston and DMG are examples of commercial banks' strategic attempts to create plausible global investment banking capabilities through cross-border acquisitions or JVs. In these, and other similar operations, it has been observed that the aggressive, deal-oriented and equity culture usually associated with Anglo-Saxon investment and merchant banks, does not easily blend well with the more conservative culture of certain commercial banks. This might be especially the case within highly conservative national cultural environments, such as Germany's and Switzerland's, where extensive branch networks, conventional financial intermediation and traditional deposit-taking remain considerably more characteristic of commercial banking relative to the USA or the UK. Thus, as in the case of ABB, national cultural resistances and deep-rooted reactions can be greatly reinforced and further *anchored* as a result of the differing corporate cultures that may exist at the base of an international M&A.

During early September 1996, unexpected events at DMG's Asset Management division (MGAM) provided a highly visible example of how such mutually reinforcing cultural resistances can be suddenly set-off. A fund manager admitted having overstepped internal supervisory controls, leading to a loss of US$ 279 million and the suspension of three Morgan Grenfell listed funds. As Deutsche Bank stepped in to cover the financial damage that had been inflicted, the affair may have been a notorious reminder of the possible downsides of DMG's Anglo-Saxon and aggressive investment banking culture, just as in the past a significantly increased profitability had provided ample evidence of its benefits.[16] As a result, these events were seen as complicating the sensitive task of weaving together DMG's "Anglo-Saxon" culture with the more conservative one of its German parent. Indeed, during the weeks following the MGAM affair, wide media coverage reported a growing tension between the London-based Anglo-Saxon management of DMG and their Frankfurt-based German colleagues. Uncertainty as to whether Deutsche Bank would attempt to reassert control of its more independent DMG operations appeared to spark reactions somewhat reminiscent of the "tribal" and "deep-rooted" cultural resistance described in relation to ABB's merger. However, things appeared to settle as it was announced that Rolf Breuer, a Deutsche Bank director, would succeed Hillmar Kopper as Chief Executive in May 1997. Although it was perhaps not entirely devoid of significance that such an announcement should be made only a few weeks after the MGAM affair, Deutsche Bank's choice was widely interpreted as reassuring of its long-stated commitment to turn itself into a global investment banking powerhouse, firmly rooted in international financial centers such as London.

National governments can anchor deep-rooted, "tribal" resistances in the international airline business

Sometimes "tribal" and deep-rooted national cultural resistances can be sparked and *anchored* not so much based on the acquiring or target companies' internal situations, but as a result of direct and pervasive government intervention in the business. This appears to be a relevant issue in the international airline business, an industry where people's natural openness to work across borders (independently of nationality) is usually described as an intrinsic requirement to perform normal working routines, particularly customer-related. This can prove to be quite an advantageous characteristic in the context of global co-operation and international alliances. Sir Colin Marshall, Chairman of British Airways, stresses these aspects when describing the development of the company's extensive network of international alliances and cross-border partnerships:

> National cultures are diverse from country to country, and this is a relevant issue to consider when entering an international alliance or an acquisition. However, I would dare to say that, in the case of the airline business, this has to be put into context. And this is mostly, I would say, due to the fact that there is such a thing as an "airline culture" around the world, no matter which nationality a particular carrier bears. Much like there might have been a "sailors culture" across the many Mediterranean maritime states a number of centuries ago. Similarly, we share some common feelings, or outlooks, or what have you, but you can

really tell when you find "airline people". And this might be related to the fact that, being by definition an extremely secular, international and travel-intense business, people in our industry tend to be more open, able and willing to work across diverse national cultures and values, more internationally-minded so to speak. It happens routinely, every day, that a large number of our employees has a face-to-face contact with colleagues and clients from the most diverse ethnic groups and cultural values you can think of. And the same goes for many other airlines. So, we share this sort of "airline culture", and English is widely spoken internationally, which helps a lot.

Therefore, it is maintained that the significant resistances that airline executives have often found when carrying out international M&A and alliances are rather the result of the direct participation of national governments which has historically dominated this industry. Says Marshall:

However, the real barriers to globalization, to cross-border growth by acquisitions and alliances, derive from the way the airline industry has evolved after WWII. As you may recall, this goes back to the Chicago Conference in 1944, when the Allied countries met to discuss the post-war commercial aviation outlook and policies on an international scale. It was already there that the Americans proposed deregulation as a basic market policy. However, the European governments naturally presented resistance to this concept at the time, largely because, unlike the Americans, European airlines had been completely blown out by the war. So, they opted for a sort of protectionist type of framework, with a strong and direct participation of governments in the commercial aviation business. This was chiefly represented by the idea of national sovereignty incorporated to the commercial air transportation area, and by the fact that most commercial air carriers after the war (in Europe and elsewhere outside the US) were in fact public companies, "national airlines", owned and managed by the government, which by the way, was also the case of British Airways before privatization. Strange as it may seem today, this protected environment may have actually served European commercial aviation at the time, as it might have helped it survive and grow from the damage caused by WWII.

British Airways (BA) was the first national air carrier to be privatized in 1985. This undoubtedly gave it a strong impetus towards globalization across national borders and cultures, as well as contributing to a world-wide improvement of their service and operations. In turn, this led to its consistently being ranked amongst the most profitable international air carriers in the world, gaining the top place in May 1996 when it reported record pre-tax profits of £585 million (US$ 889 million). A major factor leading to these remarkable results has been based on BA's customer service focus and an extensive international network developed through acquisitions and alliances. By mid 1996, these included TAT European Airlines and Air Liberté in France, Deutsche British Airways in Germany, and a cross-shareholding alliance with USAir.

Building on this international base, in June 1996 BA dwarfed any previous cross-border alliance ever attempted in the industry, after it successfully concluded a long-awaited agreement with US-based American Airlines (AA). The combined group was poised to take a dominating 60 percent share of the lucrative transatlantic flight routes between the USA and London, enhancing Heathrow's position as the world's leading international air hub. However, shortly after announcing their deal, the BA-AA alliance became a good example of how government intervention could pervasively influence the developments in this industry, sometimes inducing deep-rooted, tribal resistances with rather concrete effects. Just as it had been the case with the alliance between United Airlines of America and Germany's Lufthansa, the signing of an "open skies" treaty between the US and the UK governments was being put forward as a prerequisite to clear the way for BA and AA to effectively combine their transatlantic routes. The issue was further complicated in July 1996, when six major US-based carriers — including some of the most powerful figures in US aviation — jointly signed a letter calling on President Bill Clinton to halt open skies negotiations with the British government, arguing that it was planning to use the BA-AA alliance to restrict competition. Similar claims were made in the UK by Virgin Atlantic, a BA competitor standing to lose much ground as a result of the BA-AA alliance. In what was seen as an additional, unexpected setback to the BA-AA alliance, USAir initiated legal action against its partner BA, linking its opposing claims to those of Virgin Atlantic. A virulent campaign ensued, mixing emotional recriminations with openly chauvinistic remarks against the BA-AA deal, duly accompanied by concrete legal actions, further delays and antitrust investigations. In the midst of these events, it was announced during the second half of 1996 that USAir and BA will terminate their broad alliance partnership, with the latter company selling its 25 percent equity stake in USAir. At the same time, more investigators, involving not only the US and the UK government officials but also "supernational" organizations such as the European Union, stepped in to review the BA-AA deal from their own perspective. Although large-scale international alliances such as these are bound to routinely raise antitrust concerns from government regulators in almost any industry, Marshall observes that governments' traditional involvement in the airline business makes it particularly vulnerable to deep-rooted resistance and jingoism, manipulating the perceived need to protect national interests:

> We live in a different world today. Governments in Europe and elsewhere are less willing and able to sustain certain public expenses and unprofitable participation in industries presumed to be strategic in one sense or another. Protectionist measures may make sense in exceptional historic circumstances, but in the case of commercial air transportation, I believe that the present trend is, and should be, towards widespread deregulation and privatization. From business perspective, it is the lack of deregulation, and the strong national government participation in our industry, that may actually be inhibiting glo-

balization across cultures, and national cultural differences are not to be blamed. The latter in fact, are sometimes turned into an obstacle or utilized as contentious arguments by interested governments or national authorities. And this is not only in our business, but you see and can expect that in any businesses where national governments get substantially involved in one way or another.

As a result, paradoxically, major cross-border M&A or alliances which might be expected in such increasingly global industries are nearly unthinkable in the case of the "international" airline business. National sovereignty can easily turn any such a transaction into an exceedingly complex bilateral affair between governments, with the shadow of deep-rooted resistance permanently hanging over what can be swiftly portrayed as a threat to a country's cherished patrimony. Says Marshall:

> Say we bought Air France tomorrow (and this is purely hypothetical). As a result, we could in fact be involved in direct flights between Paris and New York. But you will have to expect a strong protest from the American government, fueled by their domestic air carriers strong opposition to such a deal, arguing, perhaps, that no "British" carrier could obtain advantages "in France" and "in the US" without the US getting a reciprocal advantage "in Britain". In a deregulated environment, however, this would be seen as a result of completely natural business and competitive dynamics. So, you can see why we need today a strong impetus towards privatization and deregulation: The idea of national sovereignty in the commercial air transportation business should be dropped, and the participation of national governments and authorities ought to be reduced to a level compatible with deregulated markets. This will benefit competition, will benefit the consumer, and will allow our industry to effectively globalize its operations across borders and national cultures.

A concrete illustration of such an hypothetical situation was provided during October 1996, after BA announced its intention to acquire Air Liberté, a loss-making French domestic carrier. With the prospect of a fierce battle for market share between BA and Air France in the background, BA's CEO Robert Ayling publicly offered some employment guarantees, a return to profitability within three years and the commitment to keep the target's French identity, apparently aiming at preventing local concern about Air Liberté falling into foreign hands. In spite of these pledges, BA's bid to buy Air Liberté drew increasing criticism in France, as it was widely portrayed as a direct threat to the state-owned carrier Air France. An outburst of protests involving union labor and left-wing political opposition parties followed in due course, also coinciding with the intended sale of part of the state-owned Thomson group to Korea's Daewoo, as well as negotiations by the UK-based General Electric Company (GEC) to take a share of Framatome, France's nuclear engineering company. The protests escalated to the point that, during late October, reports in the UK business media were openly warning against a nearly xenophobic reaction threatening French sales to foreign investors. As a result, BA, which had formerly asked the European Commission to block the sale of Air Liberté to a French company on the grounds of illegal use of state aid, was now potentially facing even the prospect of a parliamentary inquiry over its bid to buy Air Liberté (which effectively materialized in the case of the proposed GEC-Alsthom and Framatome merger). However, in November 1996 BA effectively won the battle for Air Liberté, when a commercial tribunal in Creteil accepted its plan to invest FFr 440 million (US$ 86 million) in the French carrier, in exchange for a 67 percent stake. At the same time that BA's bid was finally approved, UK and US negotiators were announcing a meeting in Washington to resume talks aimed at negotiating an open skies agreement between the two countries. These were to take place following the UK government approval to the controversial BA-AA alliance in December 1996, contingent upon BA effectively selling 168 take-off and landing slots at London's Heathrow airport.

In spite of their occasionally managing to negotiate through these deep-rooted national resistances, the above instances illustrate how, in the case of international air carriers such as BA, global expansion through M&As and alliances has to routinely face the mixed realities of national sovereignty and the resulting local or national government interventions. The latter can considerably complicate a company's planned expansion as a result of institutional and legal complexities, sometimes escalating to the point of nurturing reactions which display a deep-rooted fear of what may be perceived or portrayed as a threat to a country's national patrimony.

Wide social anchors to deep-rooted opposition against "foreign" acquirers

Sometimes government intervention is not necessarily what determines a deep-rooted reaction against a foreign acquirer. In these cases, a wider base of tribal hostility can be formed across a country's social groups and institutions, which can exert a much stronger influence over an international acquirer's plans. In such situations, a country's general and specialized media, ample sectors of the business community, and even academicians or management consultants might deliberately or inadvertently contribute to create and sustain a general sense of antagonism or self-defense against specific countries or corporate groups seen in a menacing light.

Executives at Sony hint that such a situation was faced by a number of Japanese companies with large operations in the USA during the late 1980s. At that time, lagging accomplishments relative to Japan's industrial productivity growth and general economic performance, as well as an increasing Japanese market dominance in semiconductors, consumer electronics, automobiles and other key industrial sectors in the USA, made the "Japanese threat" an everyday topic of discussion and profound concern in the American psyche. The latter was continuously fueled by ceaseless media reports, academic studies and management debates providing evidence of the growing gaps between the USA's overall economic performance and Japan's. As a result, while some influential researchers, management consultants and executives demonstrated boundless admiration for Japanese organizational achievements, business methods and approaches, others were equally extreme in their criticism of their real or perceived detrimental aspects. This latter tendency had a rather dark side to it, made evident throughout the early 1990s when the somewhat standard practice of Japanese-bashing by US government officials over the issue of an ever-growing and unfavorable trade gap with Japan appeared to reach new heights of intensity. However, what both of these contrasting views on Japan showed in common at that time was a clear emphasis on portraying the radical national cultural differences and "unique" Japanese cultural traits versus those of the USA as crucially underlying the social and economic differences observed between the two countries. Apart from the rather extreme views on the Japanese economic performance which proliferated during these years, there were remarkably few empirical studies carried out to explain the superior performance of some Japanese companies relative to American ones. Nevertheless, these few empirical studies generally tended to emphasize the key role of systematically implementing sound management practices, as opposed to insurmountable advantages supposedly rooted on unique national cultural traits.[17]

Despite having already become an American household name comparable to many of the country's classic consumer icons, Sony executives maintain that the general views of the Japanese during the late 1980s in the USA greatly affected some of the company's operations in that country. In 1989 Sony Corp. acquired Columbia Pictures and TriStar Pictures, some of the USA's most prestigious and well-known Hollywood studios, as part of the company's strategic aim to combine "hardware and software" in the consumer electronics business, and to turn itself into a global electronics and entertainment powerhouse in the 21st century. However, only five years later, in 1994, Sony announced a write-off of US$ 3.2 billion to cover losses associated with their movie business acquisitions, raising its investments in Hollywood to a total of US$ 8 billion according to some estimates made in 1996.[18] During the same year, the head of Sony's film division was dismissed, raising new concerns on the company's growing difficulties to carry out its stated aim to introduce cost controls and generally a more modern management into Hollywood's star-driven operations. Although a large part of this performance can be undoubtedly attributed to strategic or financial miscalculations, as well as corporate cultural differences, executives at Sony's headquarters in Tokyo argue that the strong feelings aroused *vis-à-vis* the Japanese business impact on the USA at the time of their movie studios acquisitions in that country had an unexpectedly significant effect on their ability to swiftly implement their post-acquisition integration plans:

> Sony has always believed in allowing local management to run its own operations. For us, Columbia Pictures was no exception. We acknowledged that its local management had a great experience in the entertainment business, and so we let them manage their operations autonomously. However, although we had expected some strong reactions when we acquired the movie studios in the US, in retrospect I can say that we were a bit surprised at how strong these reactions really were. In a way, Columbia Pictures represents an important part of the American culture, and this was seen by some as falling into foreign hands. In some instances, our acquisition — just as other Japanese companies' acquisitions in the US at the time — were actually described as some kind of threat. And these circumstances made our communication efforts extremely challenging after the acquisition of Columbia Pictures. We had our plans for the company, but it became clear that it would be very challenging to implement them within the prevailing environment. Now [in mid 1996] the whole situation has changed. America has regained its competitiveness and its economy continues to show strength and vitality, and so their perception of the Japanese has also changed. We are not perceived so much of a threat anymore, for we Japanese also have our problems.

A similar wide base of deep-rooted resistances was faced by Korea's Daewoo in France, following their intention to acquire Thomson Multimedia. This purchase would have turned Daewoo into the largest producer of TV sets in the world, with an estimated annual production of 16 million units — surpassing Sony's 12 million. Daewoo and the France-based Lagardére group made a joint bid for control of the state-owned Thomson group, which had been offered for sale in an early privatization effort by the French government in February 1996. After the French government initially announced on 16 October that it had decided to favor Lagardére-Daewoo's bid over Alcatel's (a diversified French industrial conglomerate), Lagardére was to keep Thomson CSF to form Europe's largest professional/defense electronics company. In addition, under the terms agreed in their joint offer, Daewoo was to undertake a symbolic payment of FFr 1 to take control of the heavily under-capitalized and indebted Thomson Multimedia. However, after these terms were made public in France, they provoked such vigorous reactions and protests from the country's labor unions and political opposition parties that the international business media did not hesitate to use strong terms to describe them, ranging from "nationalistic" to "chauvinistic" or even "xenophobic", and raising doubts in the stock markets as to whether the French government would be able to proceed with the sale. It did not help that Daewoo had pledged to create 5,000 jobs in France, committing to make this country the center of its world-wide FFr 13 billion five-year investment plan, or that it was picking up around FFr 5 billion of Thomson Multimedia's sizable debt (after an injection of FFr 11 billion by the French state). French workers had already built stiff resistance against Daewoo's acquisition of Thomson Multimedia prior to the conclusion of the privatization deal, with representatives of France's CGT Union in Thomson's plants rallying around the objective of keeping the company in national hands. However, these events looked set to further escalate a few weeks after the sale of the Thomson electronics group, when the head of Lagardére was put under formal investigation for alleged misuse of the company's assets. At the same time, critics of the privatization within France were reported to claim that the French state was paying too much to reduce the Thomson group's debt, and that the sale of Thomson Multimedia to Daewoo would put the company's technological inventions in foreign hands. At the end of a public debate of mounting intensity along these lines, on 4 December 1996 it was announced that the French government had suspended the privatization of the Thomson group following the rejection of the Lagardére offer by an independent commission (a step which was contemplated in advance in the procedure of the sale). This commission based its decision on concerns that Daewoo's offers to invest in and create additional jobs within Thomson Multimedia were "unenforceable", and that the sale would hinder the French state from obtaining a return on investment on the group's technological developments. However, it was not entirely clear the extent to which these concerns had weighed the fact that Thomson Multimedia's technological expertise had been partly developed by RCA, a US company that it had acquired back in the 1980s, or that Daewoo's past successes in turning around major and financially troubled public companies within Poland or the Czech Republic put it in a seemingly strong position to effectively rescue state-owned Thomson Multimedia. As a result, this decision was widely perceived to be linked with a certain part of the French public's strong antagonism to the sale of national assets to Korea's Daewoo. Thus, the Korean government demanded official explanations from its French counterpart shortly after the suspension of the Thomson privatization, warning of a possible deterioration of relations between the two countries, while the French Finance Minister was forced to make a strong appeal to foreign investors not to affect their business decisions in the country as a result of these events.

Skills to Manage National Cultural Complexities can be Difficult to Copy

Thus, practically handling the nastier and less comfortable aspects associated with diverse national cultural environments requires substantial doses of managerial determination, patience, flexibility and openness, combined with an extensive and direct interaction within the foreign country. As a result, cross-cultural *execution skills* are often developed upon pragmatic knowledge that is in itself significantly embedded in the target country's local culture, as well as in a company managers' subjective experiences over a long time period. The latter allow a company to effectively manage complex post-acquisition integration tasks across highly diverse national cultural environments, in spite of the potential information gaps and discontinuities, or deep-rooted conflicting situations which could be associated with these national cultural differences. However, the existence of difficult and continuously changing local cultural environments, as well as the practical complexity and time-consuming demands required to develop such cross-cultural *execution skills*, are fundamental reasons why these are often hard to replicate by competitors. Therefore, an international acquirer possessing these types of skills could implant critical post-acquisition integration functions across national cultural environments in ways that are not easily copied by other firms. Hence, paradoxically, cross-cultural *execution skills* might represent a potentially valuable competitive advantage for an international acquirer, based on its systematic ability to attract and develop managers capable of handling complex national cultural integration issues.

For example, learning to work effectively within certain developed as well as "emerging" economies, where the local institutional and political scenes are particularly volatile, can easily become a long-term proposition for an expatriate manager. At a minimum, this may require his/her extensive immersion and direct exposure to the local cultural ways of doing things.[7] However, a company with the cross-cultural *execution skills* to manage effectively in these countries could rapidly implant practical co-ordination mechanisms to combine the merging companies' critical resources across borders. More generally, a company which is quicker to act and faster than its competitors in executing complex tasks across culturally distant countries can learn new things and carry out complex co-ordination functions with significant cost advantages compared to less skilled companies. This can lead to quicker integration of M&As internationally, thus continuously enriching a company's global constellation of available resources and strategic options. Moreover, the ability to swiftly integrate M&As across national cultures allows a company to react timely and take advantage of market opportunities across certain industrialized as well as "developing" or "emerging" countries, where market growth and profitability can be high relative to mature economies, but where cultural and other environmental difficulties may act as powerful deterrents to less skilled companies.

National Cultural Differences Bring Valuable Organizational Routines

Regarding the national cultural facets of international M&A activity, not every potential competitive upside results from the ability to manage its less pleasant aspects. Proponents of a resource-based view of the firm have argued that human capital advantages often lie in the administrative routines and repertoires that firms develop to make decisions, to govern the allocation of resources, to formulate strategy, to interact with shareholders, or to make use of assets. Routines and repertoires have been defined as the ways in which a firm typically undertakes aspects of organizing its business activities, including such things as R&D procedures, policies for supervising subordinates, and procedures for scanning the competitive environment. For administrative routines and repertoires to create a sustainable competitive advantage, they must not be easily imitated by other firms. This is the case of organizational routines that are developed in interaction with a firm's history and peculiar institutional environment. Indeed, such interaction leads to the development of a unique and firm-specific set of organizational routines and repertoires. Even though these unique routines and repertoires are often seen by managers of other firms to be valuable, they might be difficult to copy for competitors that followed different historical development paths, or lack a critical access to the same institutional environment as the advantaged firm.[19]

Both the institutional environment and the historical paths leading to a firm's unique routines and repertoires appear to be embedded in the national culture of its founders and the national circumstances of their founding. Some routines, like the process of innovating and inventing, are more common in some national cultures than in others. National culture has also been linked with the decision-making practices used by firms, affecting the choice of certain strategies, as well as the way in which organizations work with stakeholders such as employees, suppliers and customers. Moreover, national cultural values have been linked to a preference for investing in R&D, engaging in large-scale restructuring efforts, utilizing computer-based technologies, training personnel and hiring outside resources. As a result, some of the organizational routines and repertoires potentially leading to a firm's sustainable competitive advantages tend to be national culture constrained, which makes them difficult to be replicated in other environments.[20]

Multinational corporations may need to own a diverse set of routines and repertoires if they are to compete in a diverse and rapidly changing world. In an uncertain environment, it is difficult for managers to know ex-ante what routines and repertoires will lead to sustainable competitive advantage and performance. Given the difficulty of forecasting valuable future routines and repertoires, a firm competing on a global scale may benefit from having access to a relatively large and diverse pool of routines and repertoires, thus increasing the chances that it will possess those that prove to be valuable in the future. Cross-border acquisitions provide a mechanism to access a broad and diverse pool of national culture-embedded routines and repertoires without creating the developmental path that leads to them. Some authors have indeed maintained that acquisitions across national cultures could enhance firm performance by making available to the organization a pool of critical skills and resources not previously accessible to the organization.

Access to routines and repertoires via acquisition of a firm in another national culture could enhance the performance of the combined organization through learning and specialization. Organizations in some national cultures are unable or unwilling to develop certain routines because they lack a history of that "way of doing things" or because certain ways of working are not compatible with their cultural beliefs. National culture leads and contributes to the adoption of country-specific routines for how certain tasks should be accomplished. It is less costly to have people perform tasks in ways appropriate for their national cultural values than to have them carry out tasks in ways that are less culturally acceptable. For example, the acceptability of freedom from organizational control varies across national cultures. Consequently, it has been shown that it is less costly to innovate in the context of some national cultures than in others. Following a cross-border acquisition, the two organizations interact and learn from each other at various operating levels, pooling their organizational routines and adopting ways of working that are specialized to their local contexts. However, critical routines and repertoires embedded in national culture will materialize into concrete performance benefits, to the extent that the bidding firm has the ability to properly handle complex organizational and cross-cultural co-ordination functions during the post-acquisition integration phase.[21]

In the case of the 1984 acquisition of Italian-based Zanussi by Sweden's Electrolux, company President Gianmario Rossignolo points out that leveraging on Zanussi's historical strengths, local cultural routines and repertoires and established institutional network was at the very heart of the acquirer's strategic aims. The practical implications of these objectives pervaded both the organizational structure that was established, as well as Rossignolo's insistence on *keeping* the large majority of Zanussi's employees in place following the Electrolux acquisition. These employees were seen as embedding the company's traditional core skills in the innovative design and development of electrodomestic products such as dish washers, washing machines and dryers. Moreover, all of Zanussi's established brands were also maintained and fully integrated into Electrolux's global product portfolio after the acquisition.

During the 1978-1984 period, Zanussi's management had adopted a diversification strategy in unrelated fields, spending over Lit 127 billion (at 1985 value), mostly by diverting investments away from its core businesses. As a result, the development of new products faltered and the company lost market share to competitors in its traditional areas of competence. In addition, its diversification investments did not yield the expected results, leading to a series of losses until 1984. Nevertheless, when Electrolux came to the financial rescue of Zanussi during that year, it was to leverage on the company's historical strengths, which had remained essentially intact in its core product areas. Thus, in less than two years, Rossignolo was able to turn around the company by divesting from its non-core areas, launching new lines of electrodomestics, and reinvesting in R&D and product development. As a result,

Electrolux-Zanussi returned to profitability by 1986, and subsequently showed growing business trends. However, Rossignolo remarks that being able to absorb Zanussi's Italian creative routines and repertoires in design and product development was dependent upon the organizational skills to implant a decentralized post-acquisition structure highly integrated with Electrolux's other product areas:

> Zanussi was the largest manufacturer of washing machines [in Europe prior to Electrolux acquisition]. This was not by chance, because at Pordenone [a North-Eastern Italian city where the company is headquartered] they have washing machines in the blood. You cannot invent an industry from scratch, destroying what is already there. You need to understand that history has more strength than the stupidity of man. And Hans Werthen [CEO of Electrolux in 1984], who is a man of high intelligence and a good common sense would say: "Why should I locate the headquarters for washing machines in Sweden when the best engineers, production methods, etc. are in Italy?" Of course the head-quarters remained in Sweden, but we introduced business lines. For example, products across the "Wet" business line — that is washing machines, dish washers and dryers — are developed from Italy, and this covers strategy, R&D, marketing etc. However, we have located the "Cold" business line — that is, refrigerators — in Sweden, because the best skills for these products are in that country.

National cultural differences are not necessarily detrimental, but undeniably difficult to handle in the context of cross-border M&As, JVs and alliances. Correspondingly, the cross-cultural *execution skills* to manage national cultural complexities often take time to develop, and are based upon direct interaction with the local environments, as well as on the managers' subjective skills and extensive experiences in culturally distant countries. Paradoxically, it is precisely these characteristics that render such skills potentially valuable for companies, as they might be difficult to copy by competitors lacking these cross-cultural exposure and subjective experiences. Not less importantly, acquisitions in culturally distant countries might give access to critical routines and repertoires that are uniquely embedded in a firm's national cultural environment, and are hard to develop within another firm's country culture.

As a result, national cultural distance could actually have a beneficial performance impact for a company with the cross-cultural *execution skills* to co-ordinate and integrate its global constellation of resources, including those brought in through international M&As, JVs and alliances. These arguments will be empirically examined in the next chapter, based on a sample of cross-border acquisitions.

Notes and References

[1] David, K. and H. Singh. "Sources of acquisition cultural risk", in G. von Krogh, A. Sinatra and H. Singh (eds), *The Management of Corporate Acquisitions*, Macmillan, 1994.

[2] Shenkar, O. and Y. Zeira. "Human resource management in international joint ventures: directions for research", *Academy of Management Review*, 12(3), 1987, pp. 546-557; Lane, H. W. and P. W. Beamish. "Cross-cultural cooperative behavior in joint ventures in LDCs", *Management International Review*, Special Issue, 1990, pp. 87-102; Buono, A., J. Bowditch and J. Lewis, "When cultures collide: the anatomy of a merger", *Human Relations*, 38, 1985, pp. 477-500.

[3] Lichtenberger, B. and G. Naulleau. "French-German joint ventures: cultural conflicts and synergies", *International Business Review*, 2(3), 1993, pp. 297-307.

[4] Cross-cultural studies addressing the key importance of inter-relationship skills in IJVs, include: Lane, H. W. and J. J. Di Stefano. *International Management Behavior: From Policy to Practice*, Nelson Canada, Scarborough, Ontario, 1988; Lane H. W. and P. W. Beamish. *Op. cit.*, 1990. In the case of acquisitions, a number of researchers have pointed out the crucial relevance of the acquirer's implementation capabilities in resolving "cultural" problems during the integration phase, which seemingly are the reason of many M&A failures (see: Haspeslagh, P. C. and D. B. Jemison. *Managing Acquisitions: Creating Value through Corporate Renewal*, Free Press, New York, 1991).

[5] Hofstede, G. *Cultures and Organizations: Software of the Mind*, McGraw-Hill, London, 1991. See also: Hofstede, G. *Culture's Consequences: International Differences in Work-Related Values*, Sage Publications, Beverly Hills, 1980.

[6] See: *Man and His Symbols*, edited by C. G. Jung, Dell Publishing, 1968. A rather partial view of deep-rooted symbols might not be the only limitation of empirical models of "national culture" describing it as a "mental software". Taking such analogy too literally could indeed result in a tendency to over-simplify the flexibility, creativity and unpredictability of the human mind's intelligent functions. Researchers in the field of artificial intelligence, attempting to build a "software" complex enough to replicate human conscious and intelligent structures, have often referred to the "holistic" and self-referential characteristics of the human mind as paradoxical logical deterrents, so far systematically preventing the successful realization of this scientific ambition (see a description of the paradoxical characteristic of human intelligent functions in Chapter 4).

[7] Lane, H. W. and Beamish P. W. *Op. cit.*, 1990.

[8] Johanson, J. and J. Vahlne. "The internationalization process of the firm: a model of knowledge development and increasing foreign market commitments", *Journal of International Business Studies*, 8 (Spring-Summer), 1977, pp. 23-32; Hornell, E., J. Vahlne and F. Wiedersheim-Paul. *Export och Utlandsetableringar*, Almqvist & Wiksell, Uppsala, 1973.

[9] For an insightful anthropological discussion on deep-rooted human conflict based on ethnic group factors and the like, see: *To See Ourselves as Others See Us: Christians, Jews, "Others" in Late Antiquity*, J. Neusner and E. S. Frerichs (eds), Scholars Press, Chico, CA, 1985. Also see: Barber, B. *Jihad versus McWorld*, Random House, 1995; Keesing, F. *Cultural Change: An Analysis and Bibliography of Anthropological Sources to 1952*, Stanford University Press, Stanford, CA, 1953.

[10] Kanter, R. M. "Change in the global economy". Rosabeth Moss Kanter interview by Dr. Paul Stonham, Editor, *European Management Journal*, 12(1), March 1994.

[11] See a more detailed description of ABB's organizational structure in Chapters 4 and 8.

[12] See: ABB's 1995 Annual Report.

[13] A senior executive of General Electric has been quoted as saying: "The lights are going all over Europe, and the buccaneers have been turned loose. Among them is Percy Barnevik — this Swede with a beard who swings from country to country like the actor Errol Flynn, cutting deals and forming alliances… A convalescing GE power systems may find him the most formidable adversary it has ever faced." (See: Simons, R. and C. Barlett. "ASEA Brown Boveri", *Case Study Harvard Business School*, 9-192-139, 1992, p. 4.) Also, the Managing Director at Mitsubishi's power plant division stated in 1994: "Our greatest rival is no longer the US firm General Electric. The one we have to be most on guard against is ABB." (See: *Nikkei Business*, 1994, No. 1. pp. 19-22.)

[14] See: *Financial Times*, editorial page of 31 October 1996 as well as the 15 April 1996 issue. Also, see: *Business Week*, 22 April, p. 44.

[15] In March 1997, DMG's management committee consisted of thirteen members with the following nationalities: Eight British, four Americans and only one German.

[16] Although public figures were not available, during 1996 it was widely believed that DMG represented the lion's share of Deutsche Bank's increasing profits. Our own research, based on informal interviews, suggests that, during that time, as much as one-third of the profits may indeed be attributable to DMG's global investment banking and asset management operations. In addition, DMG seems to have contributed to a major transformation in Deutsche Bank's earnings structure, which in 1996 included as much benefits from fee-based income and other non-lending activities as from profits on traditional commercial banking (see an interview with Hilmar Kopper, Chairman of Deutsche Bank, in the *Financial Times*, 13 May 1997, p. 19).

[17] See, for example: Gavin, D. A. "Quality on the line", in *Managerial Excellence. McKinsey Award Winners from the Harvard Business Review (1980-1994)*, Harvard Business School Press, Boston, 1996.

[18] *The Economist*, 21 September 1996, pp. 75-76.

[19] This section is based on: Morosini, P., S. Shane and H. Singh. "National cultural distance and cross-border acquisition performance", *Journal of International Business Studies*, (forthcoming publication), March 1998. See also: Barney, J. "Firm resources and sustained competitive advantage", *Journal of Management*, 17(1), 1991, pp. 99-120; Barney, J. "Organizational cutlure: Can it be a source of sustained competitive advantage?" *Academy of Management Review*, 11(3), 1986, pp. 656-665; Fiol, M. "Managing culture as a competitive resource: An identity-based view of sustainable competitive advantage", *Journal of Management*, 17(1), 1991, pp. 191-211; Collis, D. "A resource-based analysis of global competition: The case of the bearings industry", *Strategic Management Journal*, 12 (Summer), 1991, pp. 49-68.

[20] Schneider, S. and A. DeMeyer. "Interpreting and responding to strategic issues: The impact of national culture", *Strategic Management Journal*, 12, 1991, pp. 307-320; Kreacic, V. and P. Marsh. "Organisation development and national culture in four countries", *Public Enterprise*, 6, 1986, pp. 121-134; Shane, S. "Why do some societies invent more than others?", *Journal of Business Venturing*, 7, 1992, pp. 29-46; Pettigrew, A. "On studying organizational cultures", *Administrative Science Quarterly*, 24, 1979, pp. 570-581.

[21] Morosini *et al., Op. cit.*, 1998. Also see: Haspeslagh, P. C. and D. B. Jemison. *Op. cit.*, 1991; Ghoshal, S. "Global strategy: An organizing framework", *Strategic Management Journal*, 8, 1987, pp. 425-440; Jemison, D. B. and S. B. Sitkin. "Corporate acquisitions: A process perspective", *Academy of Management Review*, 11(1), 1986, pp. 145-163.

CHAPTER 3

Strategic Link Between National Culture, *Execution* and Acquisition Performance[1]

The more alike people become, the more sensitively they react to differences.

Alexis de Tocqueville

In the previous chapter, it was suggested that, either from the perspective of national cultural distance or from the viewpoint of national culture-embedded routines and repertoires, a company's cross-border acquisition outcomes seem to be significantly dependent on *execution*. This managerial dimension can be understood from a transformational perspective as a continuous flux of practical mechanisms that are carried out mobilizing a critical array of organizational resources — *internal, external* and *social* — leading to distinct outcomes of increasing complexity.[2] Here, an examination of the national cultural aspects related to cross-border acquisitions has drawn the attention to a series of cross-cultural *execution* mechanisms as potentially significant to performance. On the one hand, some mechanisms can be useful to smoothly handle co-ordination functions across borders following the acquisition, in spite of serious informational discontinuities and potential conflicts associated with national cultural distance between the bidding and the target companies. On the other, a number of *execution* mechanisms — perhaps closely related to the former — can allow an overseas acquirer to integrate diverse routines and repertoires that are uniquely embedded in the merging organization's specific national cultural environments.

In either case, proper implementation of these mechanisms during the post-acquisition integration phase usually requires a long-term and subjective familiarity of key company managers' with the target company's national cultural context. These characteristics make cross-cultural *execution* mechanisms both difficult and time-consuming to develop, particularly by companies lacking long-term and direct exposure to different national cultures. From the perspective of an international acquirer, this makes competitive advantages grounded on cross-cultural *execution* mechanisms, potentially valuable and sustainable over time.

From a complementary viewpoint, it has been suggested that access to a diverse pool of routines and repertoires uniquely embedded in different national cultures, can have a beneficial performance impact for a firm competing on a global scale. Cross-border acquisitions in culturally distant countries provide access to significantly diverse routines and repertoires which can be utilized to enhance the combined firm's competitive advantage and performance over time. Indeed, in the context of a cross-border acquisition, national cultural distance has been defined as representing distance in the norms, routines and repertoires for organizational design, new product development, and other aspects of management which are found in the acquirer's and the target's countries of origin. Extensive empirical research has shown that specific routines and repertoires are both critical to post-acquisition performance *and* vary significantly across countries, in direct association with the national cultural distance between them. For example, innovation, inventiveness, and entrepreneurship have been found to vary significantly according to the degree of cultural "individualism" across countries. It has also been shown that organizations in countries that are significantly distant along the "uncertainty-avoidance" and "power-distance" national culture dimensions, present specific differences in terms of their decision-making practices and their power and control structures. National cultural distance between countries has also been associated with significant differences in their legal systems, incentive routines, administrative practices and working styles.

If, as we argued before, the ability to develop certain routines and repertoires is partly dependent on the national cultural environment in which firms operate, multinational firms will find that cross-border acquisitions in culturally distant locations tend to be more valuable, because a greater national cultural distance makes it more likely that the target will provide a set of routines and repertoires that are significantly diverse from the bidding firm's own set, and which are difficult to replicate in the acquirer's country of origin — or vice versa. Since these different routines and repertoires can be utilized to significantly transform a firm's business strategy, structure and operations in order to improve performance, a cross-border acquisition might be interpreted as a mechanism for the bidding (or the target) firm to access different routines and repertoires that are missing in its own national culture and have the potential to enhance the combined firm's competitive advantage and performance over time. However, a company's ability to absorb these potentially beneficial routines and repertoires is ultimately dependent upon the concrete steps taking during the post-acquisition phase, where the acquirers' execution skills can vary greatly from case to case.[3]

National cultural distance could enhance cross-border post-acquisition performance

As a result, not only could it be argued that national cultural distance is not necessarily detrimental to cross-border acquisitions, as has been usually maintained. Rather, if handled effectively from an *execution* perspective, national cultural distance could actually enhance post-acquisition performance. Moreover, these performance benefits seem to be difficult to replicate by competitors lacking the practical knowledge inherent in cross-cultural *execution* mechanisms, or without a proper access to critical routines and repertoires embedded in culturally distant countries.

A *Holistic* Methodological Approach to Capture National Cultural Complexity

In order to test the above supposition, we carried out the first empirical examination of the link between national cultural distance and cross-border acquisition performance. Due to the limited ability of the available empirical models of national culture to capture its more complex, multiform and dynamic attributes, we utilized a blend of complementary methodologies to adequately examine the role played by national cultural distance on cross-border acquisition performance. On the one hand, we carried out a questionnaire-based survey across a sample of cross-border acquisitions, and utilized Hofstede's national culture scores to design a quantitative model that rigorously tested the link between national cultural distance and post-acquisition performance. A separate model, based on the same sample data, explicitly measured the significance of *execution* aspects *vis-à-vis* the observed empirical results. On the other hand, we carried out a series of qualitative interviews with thirty-one senior executives in thirteen multinational corporations with extensive cross-border M&A, JV and alliance experience. The latter included a number of companies that were part of the quantitative model sample, being backed up with an in-depth clinical and case study research concerning these firms' international M&A, JV and alliance activities. Such a combination of a strictly quantitative as well as qualitative empirical methodological approaches was expected to capture both the systematic link between national cultural distance and cross-border acquisition performance, as well as the multiform context and dynamicity of the specific *execution* mechanisms underlying this link. Moreover, the use of both questionnaire-based surveys and direct senior executive interviewing approaches avoided the potential drawbacks associated with the exclusive use of either methodology.[4]

Previous cross-cultural management studies in the areas of corporate acquisitions, JVs and alliances have favored a mixture of methodologies and multi-disciplinary research approaches. These tend to provide more realistic insights, not only into the cultural factors that are more susceptible to numerical representation, but also *vis-à-vis* the wider context, breadth and depth of motivations, issues and decisions that are relevant to the highly complex phenomena of national culture. Moreover, it has been observed that research approaches combining both quantitative and qualitative methodologies, allow for a deeper understanding and sharper delineation of concept domains. The latter tends to avoid a "large database mentality" or "multi-variate number crunching" tendencies which can be particularly detrimental in cross-cultural management studies. In addition, explicitly introducing practicing managers and senior executives to develop mutual knowledge on the subject under study is an approach akin to "action research", potentially increasing and complementing the validity of both statistical analyses and case studies. Action research and participant-oriented methodological approaches have been variously described as more relevant to managerial practice, *vis-à-vis* the traditional positivistic (anti-positivistic), case study, and grounded theory-building research processes. Participatory action research allows for a broader and more holistic conception of knowledge — i.e. not constrained by scientific cognitive approaches, but including the subjective, observer and practical cognitive perspectives. Not less importantly, a critical mixture of methodological approaches appears to be well suited to reflect an author's or a team of researchers' diverse academic, managerial and cross-cultural backgrounds.[5]

A Quantitative Model of National Cultural Distance

A detailed questionnaire was designed, and around 400 companies which had engaged in cross-border acquisitions in Italy were invited to participate in the survey. These companies represented a large part of the cross-border acquisition activity taking place in Italy between 1987 and 1993. Out of the 400 companies invited, 73 responded positively to the research project's invitation, and a total of 64 responded to the questionnaire. To ensure data reliability, only information from companies for which performance data could be independently verified from archival sources was utilized. The responses of 52 companies could be verfiied in this way, and therefore the quantitative empirical analysis was based on the responses of these 52 companies.[6] The questionnaires covered cross-border transactions in which one of the partners — either the acquirer or the target company — was always Italian. The non-Italian partners were of Western European or US nationality. The higher country frequency — besides Italy — belonged to US, UK and France, whereas other nationalities present in the sample included: Switzerland, Belgium, Germany, Austria, Netherlands, Finland and Sweden. Appropriate tests were conducted which demonstrated that the sample was not statistically biased.

The questionnaire distributed to the sample of companies included a request for a series of operating financial data during the year when the acquisition took place, two years before and two years after. The choice of a two-year series of performance data in the survey was based on a wide body of relevant literature suggesting that the first two years after an acquisition are critical to its overall performance. After the first year — and particularly by the end of the second year following the acquisition — the process of joining the organizations usually has been completed and the results of the underlying integration effort can be measured effectively.[7]

Based on these data, we designed a bivariate linear regression model to empirically test our hypothesis on the link between national cultural distance and cross-border acquisition performance. Regarding the model's dependent variable — acquisition performance — we found that market-based measures, although often suggested in the relevant literature as superior alternatives, had a limited applicability in the particular context of our sample.[8] One of the main reasons for this is that a large part of it was made up of family- or privately-owned companies not listed in the stock market. Moreover, the Italian stock market is considerably small relative to other developed economies, both in terms of the number of companies quoted and as a proportion of the total size of the economy. As a consequence, the acquisition activity taking place through the Italian stock market is not always representative of the total level of M&A activity. In addition, during the time period covered by the survey, a number of the stock markets of countries well represented in the sample (i.e. Italy, France, Germany) followed substantially diverse regulatory frameworks relative to the US or the UK stock market regulations, offering a rather heterogeneous degree of market efficiency.[9]

However, operating and productivity-based measures have been widely used in the strategic management literature as dependent variables measuring performance. This type of approach was entirely feasible in the context of the present research, as the questionnaires distributed to the sample provided with a five-year series on the acquired companies' net sales, net income and number of employees (for the year of the acquisition, two years before and two years after). Based on this data, we decided to utilize sales, profitability and productivity growth as our performance variables for two main reasons. First, these measures appeared to be appropriate to characterize the performance of a process-based operating phenomenon such as the implementation of cross-border acquisitions, within a one- to two-year period. Secondly, sales, profitability and productivity growth are performance measures which have been often used in the strategic, management-consulting and specialized media literature. Growth in sales, for example, has been used extensively as a measure of performance in strategic management research, including studies on post-acquisition performance. Industry profits have been studied in relation to competitive performance and the underlying industry and market structure. Regarding productivity variables, diverse measurements based on operating variables and the number of employees (i.e. sales per employee) have been previously utilized in the management literature as a performance variable linked to a business, an industry or indeed a country's performance or competitive advantage.[10]

We estimated gains in productivity and profitability growth, as the growth differential "after" versus "before" the acquisition took place. This is a quite stringent measure of performance, as gains in growth will turn out positive only when there was positive growth after the acquisition *and* the post-acquisition growth was greater than the pre-acquisition growth over the same time period. In addition, we also estimated these performance measures based on percentage growth following the acquisition. All the performance measures designed were estimated over a one-year as well as a two-year period, because we wanted to examine whether our hypothesized link depended significantly on the time-frame.

Regarding independent variables, we utilized Hofstede's national culture scores to measure national cultural distance. These scores have been criticized on the basis of the representativeness of the sample, the validity and universality of the dimensions studied, as well as the methods utilized to construct the scales. Nevertheless, Hofstede's national cultural measurements retain a number of unique and appealing characteristics for the researcher. On the one hand, as previously mentioned, his model was based on a large-scale empirical survey across countries and provides quantitative estimates for national cultural traits. On the other, the overall validity and reliability of Hofstede's national cultural scores appears to hold both over time and across related dimensions. Quantitative estimates of national cultural scores carried out more than a decade after the publication of Hofstede' model, nevertheless led to highly correlated indices. In addition, direct correlation has been found between Hofstede's and other researchers' indices measuring culture-related factors across countries, such as: Leadership and initiative, personal and interpersonal values, and country-level medical factors measuring stress and extroversion.[11]

Thus, national cultural distance was measured utilizing a multidimensional index that estimated the difference between Italy and the other countries of origin, along Hofstede's national culture scores for: Power distance, uncertainty avoidance, materialism/nurturing and individualism/collectivism.[12] There are significant methodological advantages to using Hofstede's scores as a measure of national cultural distance rather than administering a questionnaire on national culture to managers in the companies in a given sample. First, this could in fact avoid the problem of common method variance, in which the same individuals answer questions about both firm performance and national culture.[13] As a result, respondents show a tendency to address queries on both national cultural aspects *and* research hypothesized effects, in essentially the same way. By employing a national culture scores from an external source, we avoided the problem of common method variance. Second, the use of Hofstede's national culture scores circumvents the problem of retrospective evaluation of national culture. Since people tend to be ethnocentric and prefer similarity, if surveyed after the acquisition, members of acquiring firms might "remember" the national culture of a target firm as being more similar than it really was. The design of our study avoids this problem by using national culture scores from an external source that is not dependent on the memory of the respondents within the company sample. The national cultural distance estimates utilized in our study are illustratively shown in Figure 3.1.

In addition, we introduced relatedness and company size as control variables in the bivariate regression model. The notion of relatedness is commonly found in the literature of strategic fit and M&A performance. As mentioned, it has been postulated that related acquisitions — as opposed to unrelated ones — lead to a superior performance because the former have the strategic potential of transferring functional skills between businesses, which are important for the success of both the acquired and the acquiring firms. On the other hand, size is normally used as a control variable in the empirical literature of M&A performance from both the strategic and financial points of view, as well as from the perspective of organizational and cultural differences. The relative sizes of the merging companies has also been studied in relation to the choice of post-

FIGURE 3.1

Countries in our sample ranked according to their national culture distance to Italy

Countries	National Culture Distance to Italy
Sweden	82.02
Netherlands	61.48
Finland	51.48
Austria	45.48
United Kingdom	44.83
Spain	39.74
USA	35.07
France	34.63
Belgium	29.03
Switzerland	24.68
Germany	20.54

acquisition management approach, timing and type of leadership, as well as top management turnover following the acquisition.[14]

Uncertainty avoidance on the part of the acquirer has also been highlighted as influencing post-acquisition performance and was therefore controlled for in our study. Uncertainty avoidance has been associated with a preference for organizational rules and procedures favoring monitoring, planning and control, which in turn have been found to affect post-acquisition performance. It has also been observed that uncertainty avoidant countries favor short-term feedback, leading to top-down types of post-merger management approaches which are generally fast to implement and lead to quick sales growth.[15] Due to this, we argue that uncertainty avoidance will have a beneficial impact on post-acquisition performance. In order to control for this variable in our study, we used Hofstede's national culture scores for the uncertainty avoidance of the acquiring firm's country of origin.

Controlling for the year of the acquisition was also necessary because national and international economic and financial conditions vary over time and have a clear impact on the performance of all acquisitions. Moreover, important political, economic and financial changes took place in Italy during the period under consideration in this research, particularly during 1991, as a result of which a large-scale devaluation took place in the next year, forcing the Italian government to withdraw the Lira from the European Monetary System (EMS) of minimal exchange rate fluctuations between the main European currencies. These events affected the performance of the acquisitions under study, as many of the Italian companies acquired were export-oriented (e.g. textiles and clothing industry). We controlled for the year of acquisition using "dummy" variables in our model.

In addition, research has documented industry differences in the preference of acquisitions as an entry mode. Moreover, strong patterns are present in the preference for acquisitions across services and manufacturing industries. These industry differences in the preference for acquisition as an entry mode suggest that industry might have an effect on post-acquisition performance. Therefore, through the use of "dummy" variables, we controlled for acquisitions in four key industrial sectors in which there was significant acquisition activity during the period under study: Banking, textiles and clothing, waste management, and pharmaceuticals.[16]

Execution modes

In our empirical model, we also controlled the post-acquisition *execution* aspects carried out across the transactions included in our sample. As previously discussed, a fundamental part of our hypothesis concerning a positive link between national cultural distance and cross-border acquisition performance is based on the notion that the acquirer's *execution* dimensions play a key role underlying this link. Regarding this, the specialized literature has found that post-acquisition "integration modes" are critical for the strategic and financial success of M&As. The existing approaches include prescriptive frameworks for preparatory measures, to studies on the role of "acculturation" processes, organizational culture and management turnover in the post-M&A integration process.[17]

However, formally capturing the dynamicity of an acquirer's execution dimensions in relation to a phenomena as complex and multiform as national culture can be rather difficult. This was particularly the case for our study, where the limited sample size made it necessary to numerically represent these execution dimensions within a narrow interval in order to conduct regressions at adequate levels of statistical significance.[18] Thus, we broadly differentiated the post-acquisition *execution modes* carried out by the acquirer, based on the degree of post-integration which was sought after with the target company, as well as the predominant source of value in the acquisition (i.e. synergies between the acquirer and the target, or benefits based on the target firm only). As a result, three post-acquisition *execution modes* were defined: "integration", "restructuring" and "independence". Their characteristics are given in Figure 3.2.

In order to determine the post-acquisition *execution mode* in each of the transactions in the sample, these "modes" were described in detail within the survey, explicitly asking the respondents which definition best suited the approach actually implemented by the acquirer following the conclusion of the deal. Control questions were also included in the questionnaire to ensure that respondents consistently identified a specific *execution mode*.[19]

Our characterization of post-acquisition *execution modes* offers some key differences with previous conceptions put forward in the literature concerning cultural issues and post-acquisition "integration strategies" or "integration modes". Indeed, a large part of this literature has developed "acculturation modes" or "cultural fit" integration approaches that employ theoretical constructs and conceptual categories to describe cultural phenomena. Hence, although they are presented as addressing "the different ways through which the culture, organizational practices, and systems of two companies can be combined,"[20] acculturation modes have been described as ill-defined and lacking a clear connection with the concrete and functional aspects of post-acquisition management.[21] Similar observations have been made on the literature concerning cultural fit between an acquirer and the target. This literature maintains that cultural analyses ought to be carried out both prior and during the post-acquisition integration process, in order to minimize culture-related complications.[22] However, the cultural fit approaches that are suggested as a result, are prevalently based on theoretical constructs that are difficult to both formalize and operationalize from a functional business perspective. As a result, the practical value of cultural fit, acculturation and integration types of models has been described as inherently limited in the context of a post-acquisition integration phase:

FIGURE 3.2

Basic characterization of post-acquisition execution modes

	Integration	Restructuring	Independence
Managerial approach	Bottom up	Top Down	Limited change
Main focus of intervention	Across both acquirer and target	Focus mostly on the target firm	Limited or no intervention
Main decision-makers	Empowered teams or managers	CEO or transition leader	Pre-existing management
Benefits best captured	Skill transfer and revenue enhancement	Cost savings	Continuity
Number of people involved	Many	Many	Few (typically only top management)
Time frame to achieve targets	Medium/ long term	Short term	Continuity
Working style	• Many teams and processes • Horizontal • Decentralized decision making	• Common process across teams • Hierarchical • Centralized decision making	Limited change
Degree of structural change achieved by acquirer	High	High/ Medium	Low
Advantages/ disadvantages	Participatory, creative and high morale, but not always enough focus on savings	Can achieve big savings fast, but risking low morale and exaggerated focus on process	Minimal disruption after acquisition, but little opportunity to build "new" company

In sum, there is a large upsurge of literature on the benefits of conducting a "cultural fit" analysis to predict the type of problems that can occur during the integration process. Many of these articles often end with recommendations such as "incentives should be offered to ensure that appropriate acquisitions are made" or "that meetings should be held to ensure a smooth integration process without any emerging problems". Sadly, such "prescriptive" type of articles are in abundance and they suffer from a lack of both theoretical and practical applicability.[23]

By contrast, although still limited to fully capture the dynamicity of cross-cultural *execution* dimensions, our definition of post-acquisition *execution modes* concretely emphasizes some of the key functional categories underlying an implemented course of action. These broadly include: The managerial approach carried out to integrate the two companies (i.e. "top-down" or "bottom-up"), the main focus of intervention by the acquirer, the main decision-makers during the post-acquisition period, the degree of structural change carried out by the acquirer, the working style and the time-frame for achieving post-acquisition targets. As a result, by defining post-acquisition *execution modes* in terms of functional business dimensions rather than mostly conceptual cultural categories, we could control for the impact of these aspects *vis-à-vis* national cultural distance in our empirical model.

Our Results Confirm that National Cultural Distance is Positively Linked to Cross-border Acquisition Performance[24]

The statistical results of the regression model supported our hypothesis, indicating that national cultural distance was positively correlated with post-acquisition performance, and that this correlation was statistically significant. In other words, after controlling for year, industry, size, relatedness, post-acquisition *execution modes* and the acquirers' uncertainty avoidance, the greater the national cultural distance between the acquirer and the target, the greater the productivity gains and sales growth rate over the one-year and the two-year periods following the acquisition. There were no significant differences in these results when considering Italian companies in the role of acquirers or targets.

Looking specifically at the control variables, our results suggest that the effect of uncertainty avoidance national cultural index was rather small. Our findings also indicated that the degree of relatedness between the acquirer and the target did not influence performance during the one-year and two-year post-acquisition period. The effects associated with the size variable were negative and significant when utilizing percentage growth in sales as the performance measure, but the magnitude of this effect was also very small. Also in relation to percentage growth in sales, the variable controlling for the year of the acquisition "1991", was positive and approached statistical significance. As mentioned, 1991 was characterized by momentous political, fiscal and monetary policy events with few precedents in Italian post-war history, which may have affected both the level of activity and the relative performance of cross-border acquisitions in Italy during the years around 1991. In relation to this, the variable controlling for the textiles and clothing industry had a significant and positive effect on post-acquisition percentage growth in sales, possibly reflecting the export-oriented nature of this industry within Italy, which makes it particularly sensitive to currency devaluation.

The statistical results concerning the variable controlling for post-acquisition *execution modes* indicated that it had an effect on performance, but at relatively low significance levels. However, an important part of our arguments postulated that the acquirer's *execution modes* might underlie any potentially beneficial performance effects linked to national cultural distance. It is possible that accounting for such "modes" as individual variables is not adequately representing the fit between the acquirer's execution dimensions and the target's national cultural traits. As mentioned, previous research has suggested that it is a company's approach towards national cultural differences, and not diversity *per se,* which determines the actual positive or negative outcomes in an IJV.[25] Similarly, in the context of cross-border acquisitions, it could be argued that the acquirer's implementation of specific *execution modes* that are compatible with the target company's national cultural traits, could have a significant impact on performance. To operationalize these additional notions in our model, it was necessary to design a variable measuring the *interaction* between the acquirer's *execution modes* and the target's national cultural traits, and subsequently test the effects of this *interaction* variable on cross-border post-acquisition performance.

Significance of "National Culture Compatible" *Execution Modes* on Acquisition Performance[24]

Most of the empirical literature on the effects of culture on acquisition activity and performance has surprisingly focused on the effects of cultural traits *alone.*[26] In particular, this literature seldom refers to cultural issues in relation to the myriad of practical and functional dimensions which are critical to the performance of a post-acquisition process across borders. However, it could be argued that the bidding firm's implementation of alternative post-acquisition *execution modes* will find different degrees of compatibility or acceptability, depending upon the target's specific national cultural characteristics. In turn, such a degree of cultural compatibility will significantly influence a target company's organizational responses during the post-acquisition integration phase.[27] Thus, we hypothesize that there is an *interaction*, between, on the one hand, the target company's national cultural traits, and, on the other, the post-acquisition *execution mode* chosen by the acquirer and implemented after the deal. The effects of this *interaction* will positively or negatively influence performance depending on the degree to which the post-acquisition *execution mode* implemented by the acquirer is compatible with the target company's national cultural characteristics.

One of the main reasons for studying this interaction concerns its performance implications on both the buyer's decision to make a cross-border acquisition, and on the practical managerial approach chosen and carried out after the deal. In effect, although an international buyer could readily recognize the influence of environmental factors on post-acquisition performance, many authors have maintained that national culture is a deep-rooted phenomenon which is notoriously difficult to change in the context of a specific management situation. Therefore, from the buyer's perspective, the target company's national culture is a *given*, not subject to change — at least within the short to medium term.

However, national cultural manifestations are also multiform and dynamic, providing a space of critical implementation options which an international acquirer can leverage on during the integration phase, by adapting and tailoring its *execution* approach to the target's particular cultural and environmental *context*. In other words, the acquirer can select and carry out a post-acquisition *execution mode* which is compatible with the target company's specific national cultural context. Such a "national culture compatible" *execution mode* can lead to positive performance outcomes relative to alternative approaches that are less acceptable in relation to the target's national cultural characteristics. To develop our specific working hypotheses in this area, we focused on Hofstede's uncertainty avoidance and individualism/collectivism dimensions, which were found to be a key source of national cultural distance between the acquirers and the targets that were part of the empirical sample.[28]

Interaction between execution modes *and the target's uncertainty avoidance*

In the country sample utilized, Hofstede's uncertainty-avoidance and power-distance dimensions were found to be rather highly correlated, and therefore nearly interchangeable scales at a technical level. However, apart from purely technical factors, uncertainty avoidance has been described as significantly influencing the choice, direction, implementation and outcome of an acquisition. The importance of uncertainty-avoidant behavior in relation to the post-acquisition *execution mode*, essentially reflects the difficulty of integrating foreign management and staff after the deal. Furthermore, organizations in countries that present relatively high uncertainty-avoidant characteristics, also show a greater resistance to change, a lower acceptance of conflict, a reduced labor mobility and an emphasis on ritualistic and formal processes.[29]

Thus, we postulate that target companies in highly uncertainty-avoidant countries will be more affected when the acquirer's post-acquisition *execution modes* require some form of combination of both companies' human resources after the acquisition. Whereas the latter will be most difficult in the case of an *integration* mode, in the case of a *restructuring* mode, its emphasis on highly structured processes and approaches will contribute to minimize the negative effects of uncertainty. Conversely, we postulated that, when the buyer leaves the target company relatively *independent*, this will lead to higher cross-border acquisition performance the more the target's national culture is uncertainty-avoidant.

Interaction between execution modes and the target's individualism

On the other hand, in Hofstede's work, individualism/collectivism and materialism/nurturing were the national cultural dimensions that accounted for the greatest variance in work-goal priorities. However, extensive research suggests that the individualism/collectivism polarity is particularly relevant to creativity, innovativeness, entrepreneurship, and to the performance of multi-ethnic teams and group tasks. Therefore, individualism appears to be a fundamental cultural dimension influencing the performance effectiveness of the numerous team-based and technical engagements which form the core of any post-acquisition implementation phase.

Organizations in highly individualistic countries tend to stress innovation, initiative, empowerment of employees, freedom and financial and social rewards for achievement. Individualism has also been found to be associated with a society's cosmopolitan orientation. These traits can be particularly suited to facilitate the integration of foreign management after a cross-border acquisition, as well as the implementation of bottom-up types of post-acquisition approaches favoring skill transfer and revenue enhancement.[30]

Based on the above, we hypothesize that target companies in highly individualistic countries will best realize the potentially beneficial effects when the acquirer's post-acquisition *execution mode* favors *independence*. Conversely, the implementation of a *restructuring* post-acquisition mode will be more difficult the more the target's national culture is characterized by individualism, due to the highly structured and relatively centralized characteristics embedded in this type of approach. However, negative effects could be reduced when the buyer implements an *integration* post-acquisition mode, emphasizing bottom-up managerial approaches, team-based, horizontal working styles, empowerment of teams and managers, and skill transfer.

Link Between "National Culture Compatible" *Execution Modes* and Cross-border Acquisition Performance

We designed a coefficient to quantitatively measure the *interaction* between, on the one hand, the acquirer's post-acquisition *execution mode* and, on the other, the target's national cultural traits.[31] Similar to our previous model, we utilized gains in profitability and productivity growth as performance measures, controlling for the degree of relatedness and size of the acquisition.

Based on this bivariate regression model, we found that our *interaction* coefficient was statistically significant on a one-year basis. In other words, controlling for relatedness and the target company size, the *interaction* between the acquirer's post-acquisition *execution mode* and the target company's specific national cultural characteristics, was found to significantly affect cross-border acquisition performance one year after the acquisition.

However, different national cultural traits affected diverse performance measures. The uncertainty avoidance/post-acquisition mode *interaction* showed a strong relationship with gains in profitability growth, whereas the individualism/post-acquisition mode *interaction* significantly affected gains in productivity growth. Our intermediate results confirmed the stability of these findings, suggesting that the coefficient measuring the *interaction* between the acquirer's post-acquisition *execution modes* and the target's national culture, had a greater influence on performance compared with variables measuring the target's national cultural traits *alone*.[32]

The particular direction of this interaction supported our hypotheses. Based on the results of our model, the more the target company's national culture was characterized by a higher uncertainty avoidance index (i.e. Italy, France), the more an *independence* mode led to positive gains in profitability growth one year after the acquisition. Both *integration* and *restructuring* post-acquisition *execution modes* were associated with negative gains in profitability growth one year after the acquisition, although, in the case of *restructuring*, this was rather minimal compared to *integration*. Conversely, in countries with lower uncertainty-avoidance levels (i.e. UK, USA, Sweden), *integration* led to highly positive results, whereas both *restructuring* and *independence* were associated with negative gains in profitability growth one year after the acquisition. *Independence*, however, appeared to be much more detrimental to performance compared with a *restructuring* post-acquisition mode in lower uncertainty-avoidant societies.

In the case of the individualism/post-acquisition mode *interaction*, our results also presented some stability when including both the control variables and the target's cultural indices for individualism. Although the full model did not show an appropriate significance level, the *interaction* coefficient was statistically significant. This provides some support to the notion that the individualism/post-acquisition mode *interaction* does have an influence in gains in productivity growth one year after acquisition. However, these results support our hypothesized effects only partially. As expected, in highly individualistic societies (i.e. Italy, USA, UK) an *independence* post-acquisition *execution mode* does appear to lead to higher gains in productivity growth one year after the acquisition, compared to either *restructuring* or *integration*. However, *restructuring* seems to be associated with higher gains in productivity growth relative to an *integration* post-acquisition mode. These results do not support our hypothesis, which favored *integration* over *restructuring*, based on the argument that the former post-acquisition mode, commonly associated with bottom-up approaches and the empowerment of employees, would be best suited to individualistic societies. Indeed, rules have been associated with bureaucracy and as a result are often referred to with negative connotations in relation to the emphasis on freedom and initiative which characterizes highly individualistic societies. Nevertheless, our results suggest that this need not be the case, as good rules — though not likely to be as noticeable as bad ones — can have a beneficial impact on an organization. The effects of a restructuring *execution mode* on post-acquisition performance are therefore mixed. On the one hand, they can stress form over content in certain activities which are critical to post-acquisition performance, such as monitoring, planning and control. On the other, good rules are not necessarily constraining; they can actually lead to more structured environments, encouraging innovation amongst executives and higher intellectual flexibility. In turn, these could lead to higher productivity in a post-acquisition context.[33]

We integrated in a single model all of our results in this area, which are schematically shown in Figure 3.3. Based on our findings, *integration* post-acquisition modes lead to higher gains in profitability growth, followed by *restructuring* and *independence*, in target companies based in "Anglo-Saxon" countries such as the USA (i.e. lower uncertainty avoidance and power distance, *and* higher individualism). Conversely, in countries with higher uncertainty avoidance and power distance but lower individualism (such as France), the *execution mode* which suited the target company best in terms of gains in profitability growth was *independence*, followed by *restructuring* and *integration*. Similar results correspond to gains in productivity growth, if we consider, on the one hand, "Central European" national characteristics (e.g. Germany: Relatively lower uncertainty avoidance, power distance *and* individualism) and, on the other, Southern European national characteristics (e.g. Italy: Relatively higher uncertainty avoidance, power distance *and* individualism). Although these results are not to be taken as prescriptive due to the rather limited country sample utilized, they do point out the significant empirical link found between the acquirer's *execution modes*, the target's national cultural characteristics, and cross-border acquisition performance.

FIGURE 3.3

"National culture compatible" post-acquisition execution modes and performance

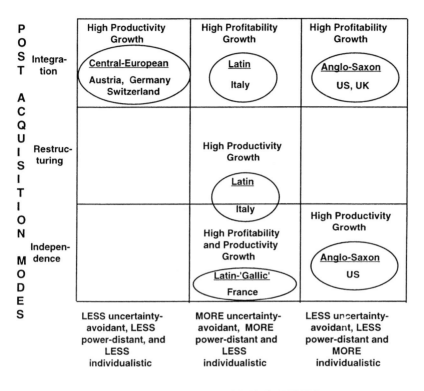

Key Implications and Main Limitations of our Quantitative Findings

Our findings suggest that acquisitions in culturally distant countries are not necessarily detrimental to performance, as it has been often assumed in the past, largely based on theoretical arguments or rather anecdotal evidence. On the contrary, our empirical model showed a positive association between national cultural distance and cross-border acquisition performance. Moreover, crucially underlying any positive performance effects, our results highlight the degree of "national cultural compatibility" found between an international acquirer's post-acquisition *execution modes*, and the target company's country culture. Although national culture has been shown to be notoriously resilient, especially in the short term, our results suggest that even one year after a cross-border acquisition the fit between the buyer's *execution modes* and the target's national cultural traits seems to significantly influence performance. Thus, conveniently handled from an *execution* perspective, cross-border acquisitions allow a company to take advantage of attractive market opportunities overseas, in spite of the potential difficulties involved in managing within culturally distant environments. In addition, cross-border acquisitions might provide a mechanism for companies to access diverse routines and repertoires uniquely embedded in culturally distant countries, which can be utilized to enhance the combined firms' performance.

These results suggest that international acquirers should take a broad look at the factors potentially influencing performance, not only addressing strategic aspects such as relatedness or synergy, but also national cultural factors and pragmatic *execution* dimensions.[34] In this sense, national cultural issues, as well as an acquirer's *execution* capabilities to handle them, should be explicitly addressed during the planning, negotiation and implementation of cross-border acquisitions, with a degree of managerial attention and resources that is comparable to the levels usually associated with strategic and financial aspects. Failure to do this in the past might be partly responsible for the relatively poor performance record of international acquisition activity.

Our findings provide evidence that seems to contrast with the gradual pattern of internationalization proposed by some theorists, suggesting that companies start by entering countries that are culturally close to their own in order to learn and perform well when expanding into culturally distant locations.[35] However, our results suggest that if companies do enter culturally distant countries, they can perform well relative to acquisitions in culturally closer countries. A certain tendency to favor acquisitions in culturally closer locations can be explained in two ways. First, managers may be inclined to follow strategies that are to their own benefit, whether they enhance firm performance or not. Substantial evidence exists for managers adopting strategies that are in their own interests rather than in the interests of shareholders, and expansion into culturally similar countries may be yet another example of this agency problem.[36] Second, it has been suggested that managers use satisficing search strategies when they look for acquisition targets.[37] When pursuing acquisition targets abroad, managers are more familiar with national cultures similar to their own than with distant ones, and the associated cost of gathering information about the former is generally lower than the cost of obtaining data about the latter. As a result, managers may be satisficing on acquisitions in similar national cultures, even if acquiring targets in more distant national cultures could be potentially more beneficial to the bidding company. Both of these tendencies might be underestimating the potential advantages for a firm to develop the practical *execution* capabilities to manage acquisitions effectively across culturally distant locations. Since developing these capabilities has been described as a significantly complex and time-consuming managerial effort, *execution*-based advantages across culturally distant countries could indeed be difficult to copy by competitors.

Our empirical analyses presented a number of limitations which suggest topics of further research. The empirical sample was made up of cross-border acquisitions in which one of the acquisition partners was always Italian, and the other either of European (non-Italian) or US "nationality". In addition, the performance measures we utilized could be regarded as partial *vis-à-vis* other operational and market-based indicators which could provide more general results. Moreover, the impact of other variables such as corporate culture and firm strategy, which could be influencing cross-border acquisition performance, were not explicitly considered in the empirical models designed. Not less importantly, although our empirical sample focused on cross-border acquisitions, it could be argued that some aspects of the link we found between national culture, *execution modes* and performance, may also apply to overseas JVs and alliances.

Moreover, a paramount limitation of the empirical results so far presented concerns a number of key questions left unanswered by the quantitative methodological approach. On the one hand, although our use of post-acquisition *execution mode* variables highlighted the relevance of practical functional business dimensions to handle the target's national cultural characteristics, these dimensions were operationalized at a rather high level. Thus, these *execution modes* are not describing in detail the concrete mechanisms utilized by managers of multinational corporations to decide about and handle acquisitions in culturally distant countries. In particular, the specific *execution* mechanisms through which cultural factors might influence performance — i.e. based on learning and specialization — were not spelled out as independent variables in the model. This limits the extent to which such a quantitative model can explain exactly *how* acquirers in culturally distant locations manage to carry out complex co-ordination functions across borders despite deep-rooted cultural resistance, or can access diverse routines and repertoires which are potentially beneficial to performance.

The above limitations may also highlight more general methodological shortcomings of quantitative models of national culture. These types of approaches are certainly a required step to rigorously test hypothesized empirical links involving national cultural aspects and managerial phenomena. However, once these links have been analytically validated, quantitative models could be rather cumbersome to characterize the complexity of both national culture and the *execution* dimensions to manage it in the "real world". Indeed, as previously mentioned, these models' numerical reliance on average national cultural dimensions across countries tends to make them inherently limited to represent the multiform and dynamic characteristics of deep-rooted cultural symbols. Similarly, the variability and richness of detail underlying the *execution* mechanisms associated with such multiform phenomena are not well captured by broad post-acquisition *execution mode* variables. In either case, properly characterizing these aspects within a quantitative model might require a massive amount of empirical data in order to derive statistically significant and stable results from it. However, even if such a large data sample was available to the researcher, it is questionable whether predominantly quantitative exercises could offer more significant insights into the contextual and practical aspects of cross-cultural *execution mechanisms*. Indeed, some authors have highlighted that in the real world standard statistical procedures cannot be applied without massive violation of assumptions which, particularly in the case of cultural symbols, concern irrational and fickle human behavior, uncontrolled and multiple interaction amongst variables, unwieldy decision-making and perpetually changing contextual conditions.[38]

Placing our Quantitative Findings Into a Wider Business *Context*

Thus, in order to complement and further enrich our quantitative findings, we carried out a series of senior executive interviews in multinational companies with extensive cross-border M&A, JV and alliance experience, some of which had been part of the survey sample. The interviewees were mostly board members, CEOs or highly ranked executives with direct decision-making and long-term involvement in their company's M&A, JV and alliance activities, throughout the assessment, negotiation and implementation phases. Both the managerial level and specific experiences sought in the interviewees intended to increase the external validity of the responses obtained, to an extent avoiding potential problems of hindsight rationalization or partial knowledge of the business situations examined.[39] A detailed case study research of these companies, particularly focusing on their M&A, JV and alliance activities, preceded every interview. In addition, follow-up questions were carried out in most cases, either with the main interviewees, or with other company executives and managers. Altogether, the main interviewing sessions and follow-up meetings were carried out during 1995 through to 1996.

The companies were chosen along specific representativeness criteria, from a geographic, industry sector, internationalization stage, and level of M&A, JV or alliance activity across culturally distant locations. Thus, we combined some companies well into globalization, such as ABB or British Airways, with others which had started their global expansion more recently, such as Deutsche Bank or Pharmacia & Upjohn. In addition, we ensured that a number of senior executives from Swedish-Italian acquisitions such as Pharmacia-Farmitalia Carlo Erba, and Electrolux-Zanussi were included amongst the interviewees, given that the national cultural distance between Sweden and Italy was found to be the highest within the empirical sample utilized in the first part of our research (see Figure 3.1). Moreover, senior executives from Japanese and Korean companies, such as NEC, Fuji-Xerox, Sony and Daewoo,were also interviewed in this part of our research, in order to complement the overly Western company sample initially utilized. The interviews were carried out in a structured way, to examine in detail the companies' experience in relation to the practical and strategic aspects of managing M&As, JVs and alliances across culturally distant or unfamiliar environments. An important part of these interviews was devoted to the nature and role played by *execution* mechanisms *vis-à-vis* the performance outcomes obtained. The main results of these interviewing sessions are described in Part III.

However, prior to that, in Part II, we will discuss in more detail the notions of *execution* in relation to national cultural differences in cross-border M&As, JVs and alliances. Indeed, an important part of the arguments and quantitative analyses so far presented has centered around the key role played by *execution* dimensions in potentially turning national cultural complexities into lasting practical advantages in the context of international M&As, JVs and alliances. Nevertheless, when trying to find conceptual support and explanations to these notions within the available management literature, a primary difficulty has been the lack of publications directly dealing with these issues. Although there is an abundant literature concerning implementation aspects of cross-border M&As, JVs and alliances, this is mostly made up of normative or process-oriented studies, rarely addressing the practical business issues, concrete outcomes and specific context within which *execution* takes place. Hence, in Part II we will discuss some initial arguments concerning the nature and relevance of the managerial dimensions of *execution* in relation to cross-cultural M&As, JVs and alliances. In particular, we will examine whether and how these dimensions could underpin lasting practical advantages for global acquirers, joint venturers or company partners.

Notes and References

[1] The empirical results discussed in this chapter are largely based on a research project carried out by the author at The Wharton School, University of Pennsylvania, Philadelphia. The detailed research findings have been published in: Morosini, P., S. Shane and H. Singh. "National cultural distance and cross-border acquisition performance", *Journal of International Business Studies*, in press; Morosini, P. and H. Singh. "Post-cross-border acquisitions: Implementing 'national culture compatible' strategies to improve performance", *European Management Journal*, 12(4), December 1994; Morosini, P. "Effects of national culture differences on post-cross-border acquisition performance in Italy", Doctoral Dissertation, Management Department, The Wharton School, University of Pennsylvania, 1994.

[2] *Execution*, as such, is a topic that has so far received surprisingly little attention within the management field. See Part II for a more detailed discussion on key aspects, concepts and implications related to managerial *execution* dimensions.

[3] See: Jemison, D. B. and S. B. Sitkin. "Corporate acquisitions: a process perspective", *Academy of Management Review*, 11(1), 1986, pp. 145-163; Bartlett, C. A. and S.

Ghoshal. *Managing Across Borders: The Transnational Solution*, Harvard Business School Press, Cambridge, MA, 1989; Hofstede, G. *Culture's Consequences: International Differences in Work-Related Values*, Sage Publications, Beverly Hills, CA, 1980.
[4] Langlet, P. and B. Wärneryd, *Att Fråga- Om Fråga Konstruktion vid Intervju och Enkät Undersökning*, Statistiska Centralbyrån, 1980; Lundahl, U. and P. H. Skärvad, "Utredningsmetodik för Samhällsvetare", Studentlitteratur, 1982.
[5] Von Krogh, G., J. Roos and K. Slocum. "An essay on corporate epistemology", *Strategic Management Journal*, 15, 1994, pp. 53-71; Parkhe, A. " 'Messy' research, methodological predispositions, and theory development in international joint ventures", *Academy of Management Review*, 18(2), 1993, pp. 227-268; Chakravarthy, B. S. and Y. Doz. "Strategy process research: focusing on corporate self-renewal", *Strategic Management Journal*, 13, 1992, pp. 5-14; Glaser, B. G. and A. L. Strauss. *The Discovery of Grounded Theory*, Aldine, Chicago, IL, 1967; Eisenhardt, K. M. "Building theories from case study research", *Academy of Management Review*, 14(4), 1989, pp. 532-550; Yin, R. K. *Case Study Research*, Sage, Beverly Hills, CA, 1984; Lane, H. W. and P. Beamish. "Cross-cultural cooperative behavior in joint ventures in LDCs", *Management International Review*, Special Issue, 1990, pp. 87-102.
[6] In our regression model, sample size oscillated between 50 and 52, comfortably exceeding the sample size of 35 which has been shown to be adequate to conduct statistical tests at 5 percent level of significance (see: Mazen, A., M. Hemmasi and M. Lewis. "Assessment of statistical power in contemporary strategic research", *Strategic Management Journal*, 8(4), 1987, pp. 403–410).
[7] Jemison, D. B. and S. B. Sitkin. *Op. cit.*, 1986; Marks, M. "Merging human resources", *Mergers and Acquisitions*, 17(2), 1982, pp. 38-42; Balloun, J. and R. Gridley. "Post-merger management — Understanding the challenges", *The McKinsey Quarterly*, 4, 1990.
[8] See: Woo, C., G. Willard and U. Daellenbach. "Spin-off performance: a case of overstated expectations?", *Strategic Management Journal*, 13, 1992, pp. 433-447.
[9] Marelli, M. "Struttura di correlazione dei rendimenti e applicazioni della moderna teoria del portafoglio", *Finanza, Imprese e Mercati*, 3rd quarter, 1994; Attanasio, O. and L. Rigotti. "Efficenza del mercato borsistico: Un analisi di 30 titoli e 6 settori". In: A. Penatti (ed.), *Il Rischio Azionario e la Borsa*, pp. 201-236. Egea, Milan, 1991.
[10] See, for example: Stiles, C. H. "The influence of secondary production on industry definition in the extended vertical market model", *Strategic Management Journal*, 13, 1992, pp. 171-187; Brooks, 1973; Lustgarten, S. H. "The impact of buyer concentration in manufacturing industries", *Review of Economics and Statistics*, May 1975, pp. 125-132; MacDonald, J. M. "Market exchange or vertical integration: An empirical analysis", *Review of Economics and Statistics*, May 1985, pp. 327-331; Powell, T. "Organizational alignment as competitive advantage", *Strategic Management Journal*, 13, 1992, pp. 119-134; Caves, R. E. and R. M. Bradburd. "The empirical determinants of vertical integration", *Journal of Economic Behavior and Organization*, 9, 1988, pp. 265-279; Caves, R. E. and P. Ghemawat. "Identifying mobility barriers", *Strategic Management Journal*, 13, 1992, pp. 1-12; Istvan, R. L. "A new productivity paradigm for competitive advantage", *Strategic Management Journal*, 13, 1992, pp. 525-537; Stalk, G. Jr. "Time: the next source of competitive advantage", *Harvard Business Review*, July/August 1988, pp. 41-51.
[11] Jaeger, A. "Organization development and national culture: Where's the fit?", *Academy of Management Review*, 11(1), 1986, pp. 178-190; Kogut, B. and H. Singh. "The effect of national culture on the choice of entry mode", *Journal of International Business Studies*, Fall 1988, pp. 411-432; Shane, S. "Cultural differences in innovation championing strategies", Doctoral Dissertation, Management Department, The Wharton School, University of Pennsylvania; 1992; Haire, M., E. Ghiselli and L.

Porter. *Managerial Thinking: An International Study*, John Wiley, New York, 1966; Gordon, L. V. *Survey of Interpersonal Values — Revised Manual*, Science Research Associates, Chicago, 1976; Lynn, R. and S. L. Hampson. "Fluctuations in national levels of neuroticism and extroversion, 1935-1970", *British Journal of Social and Clinical Psychology*, 16, 1977, pp. 131-137.

[12] This measure was based on Kogut, B. and H. Singh's index (*Op. cit.*, 1988). We defined it as:

$$CD_j = \sqrt{\sum_{i=1}^{4}(I_{ij} - I_{iI})^2}$$

where:
CD_j: is the cultural difference for the jth country
I_{ij}: Hofstede's index: ith cultural dimension and jth country
I: indicates Italy.

[13] For a discussion of the problem, see: Shane, S. 1995. "Uncertainty avoidance and the preference for innovation championing roles", *Journal of International Business Studies*, 26(1): 47-68.

[14] Salter, M. S. and W. A. Weinhold. *Op. cit.*, 1979; Shrivastava, P. "Post-merger integration", *Journal of Business Strategy*, 7, 1986, pp. 65-76; Singh, H. and C. Montgomery. "Corporate acquisition strategies and economic performance", *Strategic Management Journal*, 8, 1987, pp. 377-386.

[15] Hofstede, G. *Culture's Consequences: International Differences in Work-Related Values*, Sage Publications, Beverly Hills, 1980; Achtmeyer, W. and M. Daniell. "How advanced planning widens acquisition rewards", *Mergers and Acquisitions*, 23(1), 1988, pp. 37-42; Morosini, P. and H. Singh. "Post-cross-border acquisitions: Implementing 'national culture compatible' strategies to improve performance", *European Management Journal*, 12(4), December 1994, pp. 390-400.

[16] Caves, R. "Multinational enterprise and economic analysis", 1982, Cambridge, UK; Cambridge University Press; Kogut, B. and H. Singh. *Op. cit.*, 1988.

[17] Previous publications by the author have denominated "Post-acquisition strategies (PAS)" what we rather call post-acquisition *execution modes* in this volume. While in these publications PAS were already defined as the integration modes *actually implemented or carried out* by a cross-border acquirer, this denomination could nevertheless mislead the reader into identifying them with ex-ante integration strategies, pre-acquisition "acculturation" modes or similar concepts which have sometimes utilized analogous terminology (See, for example: Shrallow, D. A. "Managing the integration of acquired operations", *Journal of Business Strategy*, 6(1), 1985, pp. 30-36; Nahavandi, A. and A. Malekzadeh. "Acculturation in mergers and acquisition", *Academy of Management Review*, 13(1), 1988, pp. 79-90; Drucker, P. "The five rules of successful acquisition", *Wall Street Journal*, 15 October 1981; Balloun, J. and R. Gridley. *Op. cit.*, 1990). By contrast, the denomination *execution modes* emphasizes post-acquisition management approaches that were actually *carried out* by the cross-border buyer, and retrospectively specified in a survey two years *after* the acquisition took place. As described in more detail in the remainder of this section, these are among the main characteristics that differentiate our post-acquisition *execution modes* from similar notions that have been put forward in the management literature (See: Morosini, P. and H. Singh. *Op. cit.*, 1994).

[18] Although our sample comfortably exceeded the size of 35 which has been shown to be adequate to conduct statistical tests at the 5 percent level of significance (see specific

reference in note 6 in this chapter), the independent variables already specified in our model limited the number of additional variables which could be included while retaining statistical significance. For more details, see appendix and: Morosini, P. *Op. cit.*, 1994, chapters 9 and 11; Morosini, P. *et al.*, *Op. cit.*, 1998).

[19] For more details, see: Morosini, P. *Op. cit.*, 1994.

[20] Nahavandi, A. and A. Malekzadeh. *Op. cit.*, 1988, p. 83.

[21] For a concise review of the management literature concerning post-acquisition integration "modes", see: Janson, L. "Towards a dynamic model of post-acquisition cultural integration". In: A. Sjögren and L. Janson (eds), *Culture and Management in a Changing Europe*, Multicultural Centre, Botkyrka, and Institute of International Business, Stockholm, 1994, pp. 127-152. Also see: Weber, Y., O. Shenkar and A. Raveh. "National and corporate cultural fit in mergers/acquisitions: An exploratory study", *Management Science*, 42(8), August 1996, pp. 1215-1227. A number of these approaches utilize the concept of acculturation, a notion studied since the end of the 19th century by both anthropologists and cross-cultural psychologists. It is normally defined as a process of "changes induced in (two cultural) systems as a result of the diffusion of cultural elements in both directions" (Berry, J. W. "Acculturation as varieties of adaptation". In: *Acculturation*, ed. A. M. Padilla. Boulder, Colo. Westview Press, 1980, p. 215), in this case in relation to the acquirer's and the target's "cultures" during the post-acquisition period.

[22] Buono, A., J. Bowditch and J. Lewis. "When cultures collide: The anatomy of a merger", *Human Relations*, 38, 1985, pp. 477-500; Cartwright, S. and C. L. Cooper, "The role of cultural compatibility in successful organizational marriage", *Academy of Management Executive*, 7, 1993, pp. 57-70.

[23] See: Janson, L. *Op. cit.*, 1994, p. 131. "Acculturation modes" and "cultural fit" integration approaches have undoubtedly contributed to define the possible options broadly available to a corporate buyer in order to keep a newly acquired company. From a wide perspective, however, this is not at all uncharted territory. On the contrary, Machiavelli's writings during the early years of the XVI century — at the height of the Italian Renaissance, curiously contained most of the essential elements that are present in the current literature of "acculturation modes" or "integration approaches" (although within an obviously different context):

> When states that are newly acquired have been accustomed to liberty and to living under their own laws, there are three ways of maintaining them. The first is to ruin them; the second is to reside there in person; and the third is to allow them to live under their old laws, while exacting tribute from them and setting up an oligarchy which will keep them loyal to you.
>
> (*The Prince*, Nicolò Machiavelli. In particular, see chapter III: "Of Mixed Principalities")

Thus, in Machiavelli's writings, the first way for a Prince to keep newly acquired states is to destroy them, a way comparable to the "absorption" or the "assimilation" approaches in the post-acquisition literature. The second is for the Prince to integrate his newly acquired state by taking residence in these new dominions, something akin to the "symbiosis" or "integration" post-acquisition modes. Finally, the third way is to let the newly acquired state keep its old laws, and limit all intervention to the exaction of tribute and the creation of an oligarchy faithful to the Prince in the new state, a way similar to the "preservation" or the "separation" post-acquisition approaches (see: Haspeslagh, P. C. and D. B. Jemison. *Managing Acquisitions: Creating Value through Corporate Renewal*, Free Press, New York, 1991). It certainly did not escape the acute intellect of the Florentine, that a conceptually possible fourth way to maintain a newly acquired state which does not involve an effective intervention by the Prince (something akin to the "holding" or "deculturation" processes proposed by modern post-acquisition researchers), cannot be considered an integration approach. This has also been recognized in the current literature concerning post-acquisition integration (Janson, L. *Op. cit.*, 1994). Another crucial difference between Machiavelli's writings and the authors who have looked at post-acquisition "acculturation modes" and "integration approaches" in modern times, is that the former, while recognizing the significant importance of culture-related factors when facing the problem of maintaining a newly acquired state, goes on to explain and characterize the different options available to the Prince in a rather practical way, replete with what today would be called case stories. In effect, Machiavelli's poignant work is keenly aware of the audience to which it is ultimately destined to: Princes, political and military leaders, all of whom he advises in pragmatic, concrete terms. Here, cultural and other key factors are duly taken into account in relation to the specific decisions and choices that need to be carried out in order to maintain a newly acquired state in the most advantageous way to the acquirer. Although his specific advice has not always been encouraged or praised throughout the centuries, it is hardly surprising that Machiavelli's writings and influence have outlived him to the present day (See: Machiavelli, Niccolò. *The Prince*, Everyman's library, J. M. Dent & Sons, London; Charles E. Tuttle Co., Rutland, Vermont; translated by Bruce Penman, 1992).

[24] See some results of the statistical tests carried out in the appendix. For more details, see: Morosini, P. *et al.*, *Op. cit.*, 1998; Morosini and Singh, 1994; Morosini, P. *Op. cit.*, 1994.

[25] Lichtenberger, B. and G. Naulleau. "French-German joint ventures: Cultural conflicts and synergies", *International Business Review*, 2(3), 1993, pp. 297-307.

[26] Chatterjee, S., M. Lubatkin, D. Schweiger and Y. Weber. "Cultural differences and shareholder value in related mergers: Linking equity and human capital", *Strategic Management Journal*, 13, 1992, pp. 319-334; Shanley, M. T. and M. E. Correa. "Agreement between top management teams and expectations for post-acquisition performance", *Strategic Management Journal*, 13, 1992, pp. 245-266; Datta, D. K. "Organizational fit and acquisition performance: effects of post-acquisition integration", *Strategic Management Journal*, 12, 1991, pp. 281-297.

[27] Weber *et al.*, *Op. cit.*, 1996; Lincoln *et al.*, *Op. cit.*, 1981.

[28] For an analysis of the national cultural traits significantly underlying the national cultural distance measure in our sample, see: Morosini, P. *Op. cit.*, 1994, p. 64.

[29] See: Morosini, P. *Op. cit.*, 1994. Also see: Kogut, B. and H. Singh, *Op. cit.*, 1988; Haspeslagh, P. C. and D. B. Jemison, *Op. cit.*, 1991; David, K. and H. Singh, *Op. cit.*, 1994; Marks, M. "Organizational adjustment to uncertainty", *Journal of Management Studies*, 14, 1977, pp. 1-7.

[30] Hofstede, G. *Op. cit.*, 1980; Balloun, J. and R. Gridley, *Op. cit.*, 1990; Pursche, W., *Op. cit.*, 1990; Haspeslagh, P. C. and D. B. Jemison, *Op. cit.*, 1991; Cox, T., S. Lobel and P. L. McLeod. "Effects of ethnic group cultural differences on co-operative and competitive behavior on a group task", *Academy of Management Journal*, 34(4), 1991, pp. 827-847; Triandis, H. "Cross-cultural studies of individualism-collectivism", in J. J. Berman (eds.), *Nebraska Symposium on Motivation: Cross-Cultural Perspectives*, Vol. 37, University of Nebraska Press, Lincoln, 1989, pp. 41-133.

[31] The interaction coefficient was defined as:

$$I_j = \lambda \times \delta_j$$

I: interaction between the target's national culture traits and the post-acquisition strategy implemented by the acquirer

λ: acquirer's post-acquisition *execution mode* (-1 = independence, 0 = restructuring,

1 = integration)

δ: the target's centralized national culture index

$_j$: the target country's specific national culture trait index: (i.e. uncertainty avoidance, or individualism/collectivism, as defined by: Hofstede, 1980).

The use of centralized indices reduces the possibility of finding spurious correlations in a bivariate regression model such as the one we utilized to test our hypotheses. This is particularly relevant when including cultural indices of countries which rank relatively "high" (or "low") in Hofstede's (1980) scales. In addition, the (-1, 0, 1) categorical variable for "independence", "restructuring" and "integration" post-acquisition strategies, respectively, is ordinarily specified to indicate the relative degree of change expected by the acquirer after the cross-border acquisition (for more details, see: Morosini, P. and H. Singh, *Op. cit.*, 1994).

[32] See some of the statistical results in the Appendix. For more details, see: Morosini, P. and H. Singh, *Op. cit.*, 1994.

[33] Perrow, C. *Complex Organizations: A Critical Essay*, Scott, Foresman, Glenview, IL, 1972; Hofstede, G., *Op. cit.*, 1980; Haspeslagh, P. C. and D. B. Jemison, *Op. cit.*, 1991; Baker, C. R. "An investigation of differences in values: accounting majors versus non accounting majors", *Accounting Review*, 51, 1976, pp. 886-893; Inkson, J. H., J. P. Schwitter, D. C. Pheysey and D. J. Hickson. "A comparison of organization structure and managerial roles: Ohio, USA and the Midlands, England", *Journal of Management Studies*, 7, 1970, pp. 347-363; Kohn, M. L. "Bureaucratic man: a portrait and an interpretation", *American Sociological Review*, 36, 1971, pp. 461-474.

[34] Datta, D. K. *Op. cit.*, 1991; Chatterjee, S. *et al. Op. cit.*, 1992.

[35] Johanson, J. and J. Vahlne. "The internationalization process of the firm: A model of knowledge development and increasing foreign market commitments", Journal of International Business Studies, 8 (Spring-Summer), 1977, pp. 23-32.

[36] Jensen, M. and W. Meckling. "Theory of the firm: managerial behavior, agency costs, and ownership structure," *Journal of Financial Economics*, 3, 1976, 305-360; Amihud, Y. and B. Lev. "Risk reduction as a managerial motive for conglomerate mergers", *Bell Journal of Economics*, March, 1981, 605-617.

[37] Cyert, R. and J. March. *A Behavioral Theory of the Firm*. Englewood Cliffs, NJ: Prentice Hall, 1963.

[38] Parkhe, A. " 'Messy' research, methodological predispositions, and theory development in international joint ventures", *Academy of Management Review*, 18(2), 1993, pp. 227-268.

[39] Regnér, P., "Swedish mergers and acquisitions in the US — Acquisition performance and strategic acquisition factors". Institute of International Business, Stockholm School of Economics, 1996.

Part II
Execution Advantages in Global Corporate Alliances

Why Can *Superior Execution* Lead to Practical Advantages in Global Mergers and Acquisitions, Joint Ventures and Alliances?

> The desire to acquire territory is a very common and natural thing; and when a man who is capable of doing it makes the attempt, he will generally be praised, or at least not blamed; error and blame arise when a man lacks the necessary ability and still wants to make the attempt at all costs.
>
> Niccolò Machiavelli — *De Principatibus*

The empirical study described in the previous chapters provided evidence that national cultural differences between an acquirer and a target are not necessarily detrimental to the performance of cross-border acquisitions. Rather, if handled effectively, they can actually enhance performance. Supporting this, our findings indicated a positive association between national cultural distance and cross-border acquisition performance. Moreover, this positive association was significantly explained by the bidding firm's implementation of specific *execution modes* that were compatible with the target's national cultural characteristics. Our findings thus highlighted the acquirer's particular set of *execution skills* as a key factor explaining the performance of cross-border acquisition activity, along with the strategic and financial considerations which have often been proposed in the past. More generally, our findings raise the question: To what extent does a company's superior *execution skills* in handling national cultural differences become critical to building lasting practical advantages via cross-border M&As, JVs and alliances?

Addressing such a question could have profound implications from a number of perspectives. If superior *execution skills* can indeed underpin lasting competitive advantages in the marketplace, then the pragmatic knowledge embedded in a company's *execution* mechanisms must be given extreme importance. However, if this pragmatic knowledge could be technically formalized in all, or at least in most, relevant managerial circumstances, this would make it effectively transferable across company boundaries, and therefore few or no lasting advantages could be derived from *execution* over time. In addition, if most of the managerial aspects which are relevant to the generation of sustainable competitive advantages were ultimately related to formal, technological, or methodological knowledge (i.e. as in "strategic thinking" in a restricted sense), then it is apparent that the role of *execution* could be best stated in terms of a company's structured application of rather explicit and declarative know-how. From such a perspective, a firm's unique advantages in the marketplace are less associated with pragmatic knowledge or *superior execution*, but largely become a function of its ability to continuously devise superior strategies to outcompete its rivals, through the formal application of scientific and technological knowledge, as well as highly routinized implementation processes.

These assertions have been heavily criticized in the past by both management researchers and consultants. On the one hand, technological know-how, declarative knowledge, analytical frameworks and the like, have been found to be increasingly codifiable and transferable across company borders. By contrast, *execution skills* are embedded in procedural knowledge, practical methods, cultural behavior, social networks, and organizational routines and repertoires that often resist comprehensive formalization, and are difficult to develop or copy by competitors.[1] Overly analytical, formal and academic approaches to management have been identified as unsuitable to capture the richness of detail, increasing turbulence and complexity of the "real world", thus leading to mediocre business practices and a declining overall economic performance. Even more poignantly, some authors have maintained that management practitioners and consultants suffer from a fundamental loss of credibility dating back to the 1970s, as a result of their acting as if the world was infinitely more certain and simple than it is in reality, or as if it was susceptible to proper understanding based on a body of analytical knowledge and tools.[2]

On the other hand, the limitations of analytical approaches have been linked to their inherent tendency to systematically break down the totality of a complex managerial situation into separated and independent entities, or *problems*. Thus, the resulting problem-solving approach very effectively unwinds complex managerial situations into simpler components and discrete units, but often at the cost of losing sight of the fundamental relationship that exists between them. Richard Ackoff aptly characterized this dilemma in a 1979 article provocatively entitled "The Future of Operational Research is Past":

> Managers are not confronted with problems that are independent of each other,
> but with dynamic situations that consist of complex systems of changing pro-

blems that interact with each other. I call these situations messes. Problems are abstractions extracted from messes by analysis; they are to messes as atoms are to tables and charts... Managers do not solve problems: they manage messes.[3]

Supporting the above, some authors have maintained that the limitations of strategic planning approaches are tightly related to its paramount reliance on analytical methods, whereas true strategic thinking is supposedly based on synthesis, involving "messy processes of informal learning", creativity and intuition. Compared to the decidedly analytical approaches that have been previously described, these types of views appear to attach greater value to the pragmatic aspects of management, although mostly as key inputs to strategic thinking. Thus, they still stop short of the notion that lasting practical advantages in the marketplace could be traced back to a company's superior *execution skills* in their own right. In particular, some authors have noted that the international business literature has overwhelmingly focused on the strategic aspects involved in cross-border M&As, JVs or alliances, whereas practical issues related to the effective implementation of these agreements have not been adequately or sufficiently addressed. Strategy formulation is perceived by these authors as an analytical cognitive process, while the effective implementation of international M&As, JVs and alliances also requires different skills — i.e. to properly handle intense interaction between people from different countries and highly diverse cultural backgrounds. However, the dismal track record of international M&A, JV and alliance activity, can be significantly attributed to difficulties in managing these kinds of implementation issues.[4]

The above observations are intended to highlight the difficulties implicit in one-sided attempts to understand a company's critical advantages when approached from a practical perspective, rather than a wholesale criticism of strategic thinking, or the associated analytical, formal and problem-solving aspects of management. In this sense, our research on cross-border M&As, JVs and alliances has provided illustration of how the *execution* of any particular strategic design or corporate vision in a complex reality requires a stream of both theoretical and practical knowledge — i.e. employing logical, synthetic and analytical approaches but not being bounded by them. The issue of how a company holistically combines both types of knowledge to generate *superior execution* is therefore critical to understanding whether it can consistently lead to lasting practical advantages in the marketplace.

The general distinction between two types of knowledge and the inherent duality of approaches to attain it has often been highlighted in the management literature. On the one hand, logic, objective, formal and quantifiable knowledge can usually be documented in a complete way through explicit processes, routines, procedures and codes. On the other, the qualitative, subjective, experience-based and intuitive knowledge is exceedingly difficult to document in a complete way. It thus remains tacit within groups or individuals to a significant level.[5] We argue that this basic distinction is funda-mental to the notion of *superior execution*, to the extent that it relies on parti-cular combinations of formal as well as experiential knowledge which might be both difficult to attain and to copy. As previously mentioned, routines and repertoires significantly embedded in tacit or experiential knowledge have been found to be slower to transfer outside a firm's boundaries, and corre-spondingly more difficult to imitate by competitors over time.[1] Thus, from this perspective, the critical issues underlying *superior execution* seem to be less related to the possession of knowledge *per se*, but to *knowability*; i.e.:

- How groups and individuals acquire and use objective-formal, as well as subjective-experiential, types of knowledge, to fundamentally grasp, understand and act upon complex phenomena.
- How an organization devises practical ways to combine, interact and complement objective-formal and subjective-experiential knowledge in order to attain *superior execution* in a managerial context.

Besides management, *knowability* has been a central subject of study in a number of fields, including philosophy, psychology, neurology, genetics, linguistics, mathematics, cybernetics and artificial intelligence. Although the importance of logical approaches *vis-à-vis knowability* has been tradition-ally stressed in these disciplines, in later years there has also been a con-comitant emphasis on the essential role played by intuitive and experiential mechanisms.

However, in a wider sense, the fundamental philosophical quest inherent in *knowability* is far older and deeper to mankind. In fact, recognition of the fundamental importance of both the theoretical and the experience-based aspects of knowledge to reach an intimate understanding of "things" follows rather ancient philosophical, scientific and religious traditions of thought in both Eastern and Western civilizations. Both traditions have at various times attempted to gain an understanding of this relationship in order to attain "true" knowledge. Although a detailed study of these approaches is beyond the central argument of this book, a discussion of selected aspects is required to further characterize the relevance of *knowability* versus the managerial concept of *execution*. In particular, we will examine how the one-sided attempt to derive a company's advantages based on analytical and formal methods seems to curiously mirror historical efforts to logically formalize the issue of *knowability* within philosophy, mathematics, psychology and other sciences, during the past two centuries or even before. As these efforts notoriously led to unresolved logical conundrums and paradoxes in most of these disciplines, it is interesting to explore whether the responses that evolved could in turn shed light on the issue of *knowability* in managerial *execution*.

Gnosis and the Ancient Recognition of a Dual Approach to *"Knowability"*

The ancient Greeks distinguished between scientific or theoretical knowledge and knowledge through direct observation and experience. The Greek word for knowledge is *gnosis*, which is broadly equivalent to the Latin *cognoscere*, and the Sanscrit *jnana*. However, during the first and second centuries AD, the word *gnosis* was widely utilized in Greek philosophical circles to denote a deep understanding of phenomena based on intuition and insight gained through direct experience, in sharp contrast to the sort of scientific knowledge that had been pursued by thinkers such as Socrates, Plato or Aristotle during the classical period of Greek philosophy (around the 6th and 5th centuries BC). Indeed, the "Gnostic" or "Gnosticist" philosophical and religious movements that arose in Greece during the first centuries of the Christian era were partly a response to a perceived intellectual failure of the established scientific and religious systems to provide satisfactory answers to *knowability* and other fundamental human issues. Curiously, similar affirmations have also been made to characterize the rise of modern Gnosticism.[6]

Although it tacitly or explicitly underlies a wide number of ancient as well as modern writings or authors commonly referred to as "Gnostic" or "Gnosticist", *gnosis* as a concept is neither identical nor exclusively bounded to this literature. Thus, the use of the word *gnosis* in the context of this book, is not grounded on any specific secular or religious doctrinaire interpretation of the term in either the ancient or the modern intellectual streams of Gnosticism.[7] Rather, by *gnosis* is denoted the intuitive process of gaining a deep insight of oneself and nature, attained through an intimate and personal *relationship* between self and object, and implying a direct acquaintance, acceptance and equality between both. This is akin to the ancient philosophical interpretation of *gnosis* as "understanding intuition", or the modern psychological one as "perception by way of the unconscious".[8] By contrast, the scientific and logic-based knowledge of an object requires *separation* of the object and the subject, the latter placed on a higher epistemological position to master the former. In the continuation of this book, we will retain the distinction between the predominantly conceptual, objective, and logic "knowledge" and the mostly experience-based, subjective and intuitive *gnosis*.

During the 6th century BC, Pythagoras (582-500 BC) maintained that scientific knowledge was both indispensable and sufficient to gain a deep understanding of the nature of things. However, Plato (427-347 BC) observed that scientific knowledge only constituted a pre-education (*propaideia*), and that *knowability* of a subject was to be achieved through the dialectic method, a process defined as *noêsis*, or the act of gaining insight through the interaction of scientific knowledge (*episteme*) and articulated intuition (*dianoia*). Aristotle (384-322 BC) espoused a dualistic view of the world: On the one hand, the common world was available to all men, and was a world of ideas (a notion first advanced by Plato); on the other, each individual's experience nurtured its own reality, without which the former world of ideas would not exist (*causa efficiens et causa finalis*). Two centuries before Aristotle, Mahavira (599 BC) a "great teacher" in the Jain tradition in India, had recognized a distinction between theoretical knowledge and "acquaintance" (or experience-based insight) in the realm of the spirit. However, true *knowability* was to be based on formal contemplation, as good or bad actions, personal activities and individual experiences (*karma*) were seen as binding a person to a cyclical round of rebirth. In China, K'ung-fu-tzù (born around 551 BC and latinized in the West as Confucius) developed "the way" (*Tao*), a mode of life based on formal, strictly codified behavior reflecting virtue and harmony. Meng K'o (born in 372 BC and also known as Mencius), perhaps the greatest of Kung's successors, enlarged the logical and ritualized dimension of Confucian tradition by adding the idea that moral, ethical and other insights could be gained by direct, inner experience rather than through formal processes of study, reflection and self-control. Such notion is also present in Ch'an Buddhism, introduced in Canton around 520 AD by Bodhidharma, a legendary Indian monk. The Ch'an meditation school, maintained that "it is not by examining the things around us or by gathering information that true insight is won; rather it is found in spontaneous experience".[9] These views were in contrast with the idealist Mahayama Buddhism, which saw all phenomena as mental products, and the distinction between an outside world and the world of experiences as the result of a false projection of ideas.

Also since antiquity, an inherent preference for either formal (logical, objective) or gnostic (experiential, subjective) approaches to *knowability* have been associated with differences based on gender, or underlying a fundamental duality in the arts. In China, Lao Tzu, who is supposed to have been an earlier contemporary of K'ung, developed an idea of Tao which was broader than the one present in Confucianism. It described Tao as the principle which underlies and controls the universe (much like the Greek philosophical notion of *Logos*). The *Tao tê Ching*, a book commonly attributed to Lao Tzu, makes a distinction between a male, or active, principle of knowledge and creation, and a female, or passive, principle. A similar distinction is present in Chuang Tzu's influential Taoist writings, which identifies a polarity between the *yin* (feminine) and *yang* (masculine) energy underlying all cosmic phenomena. The Confucianists positive pursuit of good is *yang*, whereas relativity about ethical judgments beyond good and evil are *yin*. However, a key notion in classical Taoism is that the female principle has a deeper significance, and it is through achieving *wu-wei* (an effortless state of mind sometimes interpreted as inaction) that a deep insight into Tao can be attained.

Writing on the eve of the 20th century, Friedrich Nietzsche (1844-1900) observed that the antithetical Apollonian-Dionysiac duality inherent in the ancient Greeks' creative tendencies, was fundamental to a proper understanding of their aesthetic artistic doctrines and mystical traditions.[10] Attic plastic arts, above all architecture, were Apollonian in spirit and embodied in visual creations expressing the mode of existence of the theoretical man (*principium individuationis*). Socrates was the archetype of such a man, a "theoretical optimist" whose confidence in science and logic to guide life and pursue intimate *knowability* of things found its supreme aesthetic expression within the serene, formal and balanced limits of doric architecture. By contrast, the Dionysiac spirit arose from the limitations inherent in this theoretical man: "When the inquirer, having pushed to the circumference, realizes how logic in that place curls about itself and bites its own tail, ... "[11] Thus, the turbulent Attic music was a Dionysiac art *par excellence*, not based on the visual, formal and logic aesthetic principles of plastic arts, but inciting the soul to experience a deep understanding of the "thing-in-itself" of every phenomenon in a symbolic and intuitive way.

The Modern Conundrum Involved in One-Sided Approaches to *Knowability*

Well into the 20th century, empirical psychological research examining the issue of *knowability* has arrived at findings paralleling in certain aspects the ancient dichotomies prompted by the philosophical and religious speculation. Women have been found to privilege intuitive and subjective ways of knowing, relying much more than men on direct experience, relationships and "real talk". By contrast, men prefer to attain knowledge through objective approaches, emphasizing individualism, rational and abstract thinking, and public speaking.[12] From the point of view of self-knowledge, Swiss psychologist Carl G. Jung (1875-1961) observed that the *anima* was one crucial component of the individual psyche, corresponding to the maternal Eros, and embodying all the outstanding characteristics of a female. Its complement, the *animus*, was the mind or spirit, corresponding to the paternal, masculine Logos. According to Jung, men's psyche is generally dominated by the *animus*, with the *anima* as its projection-making factor; whereas in women the opposite situation can be observed.

Thus, not surprisingly, the ancient epistemological duality transcending most philosophical, religious and psychological approaches to the problem of *knowability* has also found its way into modern Western philosophy and science — albeit in a much less poetic way. One of the first manifestations of this ancient dichotomy in modern times was embodied by the contrasting views of philosophical empiricism and idealism. John Locke (1632-1704) was a chief exponent of the former school, maintaining that all ideas come from experience — simple ones directly, and complex ones from the mind operating on simple ideas. Thus, perceptions were critical to attain knowledge of material objects, primary perceptions being akin to simple ideas, whereas second-

ary perceptions were associated with complex ideas. In developing his philosophical empiricism, Locke was greatly influenced by the ground-breaking
discoveries of some of his contemporaries, particularly in the field of mathematics, which encouraged the view that the entire universe could be
described and analyzed on the basis of formal and mathematical representations (a view that continues to seduce many of today's scientists). Amongst
these was René Descartes (1596-1650), whose publication of *Géométrie* in 1637
brought together classic geometry and algebraic functions. Also around this
time, Sir Isaac Newton (1642-1727) in England and Baron Gottfried Wilhelm
von Leibniz (1646-1716) in Germany, simultaneously, but independently,
developed a method for calculating areas contained within mathematical
functions (hence "calculus"). The latter method proved to be astonishingly
versatile to analyze physical and astronomic phenomena, and thus became
the cornerstone of both the Newton and Leibniz scientific systems, generally
aimed at devising:

> ...a general method in which all truths of reason would be reduced to a kind of
> calculation. At the same time this would be a sort of universal language or
> scripts, but infinitely different from those projected hitherto; for the symbols
> and even the words in it would direct the reason; and errors, except for those of
> fact, would be mere mistakes in calculation.[13]

Seldom in history has an ambitious scientific aspiration been so powerfully
stated. There is little doubt that Newton's and Leibniz's contributions, more
than those of anyone before or immediately after, made possible the development of modern Western science as we know it, particularly in the fields of
physics, astronomy and mathematics. As mentioned, their views profoundly
influenced philosophers such as Locke, who entertained the notion that all of
nature could be apprehended through direct observation and the proper
application of compelling analytical tools such as calculus. However, in
spite of Locke's reliance on experience as the source of human knowledge,
David Hume (1711-1776) demonstrated the inherent contradictions of
empiricism when taken to its ultimate consequences. He argued that, regardless of its plausibility, any causality assumptions could be made about an
event or phenomena which would be necessarily true as long as no logical
contradiction could be proved. As a consequence, Hume effectively denied
causality, maintaining that the sole criterion of necessary truth is whether or
not a proposition can be denied without contradiction. If Hume pointed out
the logical limitations of pure empiricism, Bishop George Berkeley (1685-
1753) did exactly the same, but from the opposite pole of philosophical
idealism. Berkeley's writings emphasized that knowledge is inseparable
from the notion of perception of space, which in turn is the result of visual
and muscle sensations and memory. He agreed with Locke's assumption that
all knowledge comes from perception, but took it much further, denying that

there existed primary or secondary perceptions. Instead, perceptions were concrete and not independent from reality. However, the logical consequence of this view was the so-called nominalism, based on denial of the reality of the physical world, and the belief that all we can know and experience were our ideas.

Holistic Responses to the Conundrum: The Limits of Logics

Berkeley and Hume illustrate the philosophical conundrum underlying most one-sided approaches to *knowability* when carried out to their ultimate logical consequence. In effect, starting from a similar source — i.e. Locke's fundamental reliance on knowledge-through-experience — these thinkers arrived at entirely opposite conclusions, but equally reaching a logical deadlock: on the one hand, denial of causality; on the other, denial of the physical world.[14] As a result, Arthur Schopenhauer (1788-1860), and particularly Immanuel Kant (1724-1804), proposed attempts to reconcile the rather bizarre conclusions of one-sided philosophical empiricism and idealism. In his *Critique of Pure Reason*, first published in 1781, Kant asserted that inherent structures in the mind in fact mediated all analytical, and especially synthetic, judgments. Although physiological and psychic functions impose sensorial limitations on people, so that we are not able to ultimately apprehend the "thing-in-itself" (*das ding an sich*), the mind was organized in true categories through which man's perception of the outer world took place. As a consequence, all of man's perception ultimately is psychological. Kant's recognition of the crucial role played by the inherent structures of the human mind and psyche is often seen as initiating present-day philosophical approaches to the issue of *knowability*, as well as inaugurating modern psychology. Moreover, his approach to *knowability* can be described as holistic, as opposed to one-sided. This is aptly summarized in Kant's famous assertion that:

> ...thoughts without content are empty, and intuitions without concepts are blind.[15]

In other words, *knowability* holistically encompasses both logic and intuition, a priori theoretical judgments and experience, as well as both the physical and psychological aspects of human perception. Although not historically new or unprecedented,[16] the concepts developed by Kant and Schopenhauer deeply pervaded successive philosophical and psychological views on the issue of *knowability*. Amongst the former, Nietzsche was amongst the first to recognize that these philosophers' paramount achievement had consisted of showing the inherent and real limits of logic to understanding the intimate nature of things. In effect, Nietzsche identified this limitation as the major flaw underlying modern Western civilization (or Alexandrian culture, as he called it). Thus, universal reliance on scientific thought to unveil the mysteries of nature was a truly modern tragedy of Alexandrian culture. As a result, in his book *The Birth of Tragedy*, originally published in 1872, Nietzsche anticipated a new system of morals based on a reinterpretation of the ancient Greek tragedy. The latter was understood as a holistic union of the classic duality: The logic-concrete and structured spirit of Apollo, and the mythical-symbolic and intuitive Dyonisiac spirit of primordial reality. This was intended to subdue the limits of Western scientific cultural values:

> The extraordinary courage and wisdom of Kant and Schopenhauer have won the most difficult victory, that over the optimistic foundations of logic, which form the underpinnings of our culture. Whereas the current optimism had treated the universe as knowable, in the presumption that eternal truths, and space, time, and causality as absolute and universally valid laws, Kant showed how these supposed laws serve only to raise appearance — the work of Maya — to the status of true reality, thereby rendering impossible a genuine understanding of that reality: in the words of Schopenhauer, binding the dreamer even faster in sleep. This perception has initiated a culture that I dare describe as tragic. Its most important characteristic is that wisdom is put in place of science as the highest goal.[17]

In psychology, the work of Jung also recognized the profound limits of logic from the viewpoint of self-knowledge and the world of human psyche. As is well known, the concept of symbol is central to Jungian psychology, along with the exploration of dreams and the unconscious, and the notion of archetypes. According to Jung, the conscious side of man, his personality and self-realization, were outward manifestations of the unconscious, which preceded all conscious understanding. (This notion has found some support in the empirical research of the neurology of the human brain, identifying its inner cortexes with a primitive or prehistoric brain, and the outer cortexes with the developed brain and its main conscious thinking functions.[18]) In this, Jung's views departed quite radically from Sigmund Freud's (1856-1939), who is generally credited with bringing the unconscious side of the psyche into the modern world's attention, though largely as a depository of (sexually-related) conscious repression. In contrast to this perception, Jung's holistic psychological approach saw the conscious and the unconscious as interactive component parts of the human psyche. *Knowability*, and the intimate understanding of things, were thus deeply influenced by this immanent psychic duality:

> Logical analysis is the prerogative of consciousness; we select with reason and knowledge. The unconscious, however, seems to be guided chiefly by instinctive trends, represented by corresponding thought forms — that is, by the archetypes.[19]

To conclude this discussion, we observe that the holistic responses to the issue of *knowability* developed in philosophy and in psychology since the 17th century, can be closely linked with the increasing realization of the limits of logical methods of cognition, as well as the rediscovery of unconscious and intuitive phenomenon in the human psyche. However, well into the 20th century, the study of self-referential paradoxes in the field of logic itself, as well as within mathematics, led to surprisingly similar holistic developments in these disciplines, provoking profound effects across many other related natural and social sciences.

The 20th Century Conundrum: Logical Evidence of the Limits of Logic

It is quite ironic that the most powerful evidence yet of the limits of logic *vis-à-vis* the issue of *knowability* was to be derived within the quintessential "logical" science of mathematics. This started with a conundrum involving logical attempts to formalize the mathematical notion of infinite, an issue which can be traced back to the modern discovery of calculus. In effect, although Newton's and Leibniz's calculus depended heavily on infinite processes to estimate the area contained under a mathematical function, a formal approach to treat the notion of infinite was largely missing in their writings. This was already noticed and criticized by their contemporaries, amongst them Berkeley. One generation later, Karl Weierstrass' (1815-1907) development of "limits" provided an elegant way to express the concept of infinite utilizing finite mathematical constructs.[20] However, during Weierstrass' lifetime, George Cantor (1845-1918) re-proposed the dilemma of infinity from a different (and still unresolved) perspective, within the theory of sets.[21] In addition, an Italian mathematician and contemporary of Cantor, Giuseppe Peano (1858-1932), developed a small set of properties through which the core of number theory could be derived using mathematical induction (thus referred to as *Peano arithmetic*). Partly as a result of the paradoxical results of Cantor's transfinite set theory, and the stunning possibilities of Peano's mathematical formalism, a number of mathematicians took two basic approaches to develop unique and complete mathematical systems in which all such issues could be logically resolved. These were the "logician" and the "formalist" approaches, which in some respects mirrored the empiricist and idealistic responses sparked by Locke's one-sided philosophical approach to *knowability* a century earlier.

In their voluminous *Principia Mathematica*, Bertrand Russell (1872-1970) and Alfred North Whitehead (1861-1947) developed a major effort to devise a "complete" logical mathematical system of number theory.[22] Since mathematics, physics, astronomy and a very large category of scientific fields in Western civilization are crucially based on natural numbers, a complete system of number theory could in principle have been applied to describe the mechanics of the whole universe, placing *knowability* within the grasp of logics, and thus fulfilling Leibniz's and Newton's intellectual aspirations, which had preceded Russell's by more than two centuries. Russell's belief that such a complete logical system could be mathematically derived was greatly influenced by both Peano's formal arithmetic and by the work of logician George Boole (1815-1864), who had developed laws of thought or propositional syllogisms to represent deductive reasoning.[23] However, during the development of his numerical system, Russell discovered that Cantor's paradoxical mathematical notion of the "set of all sets" potentially applied to all logical systems.[24] As a result, he has been credited as re-discovering the role of paradoxes in modern logics. Even simple statements such as: "This sentence is false", evidence logical paradoxes according to Russell. In other words, a logical paradox is a statement that:

> ...if assumed to be true, leads to the conclusion that the statement is false. If assumed to be false, it implies that it is true. Hence, "an assertion whose truth or falsity is undecidable".[25]

Although undecidable logical paradoxes had been already recognized in antiquity, both within Greek philosophy and Zen Buddhism doctrines,[26] Russell reformulated this notion and placed it at the very heart of the modern mathematical and logical systems. His findings had deeply disturbing effects to the work of Gottlob Frege (1848-1925), whose aspiration of combining formal logic with number and set theory found an unassailable barrier in these logical paradoxes. However, it should be noted that Russell himself was unable to offer satisfactory solution to the paradoxes he had unveiled. In *Principia Mathematica*, Russell and Whitehead simply developed constructs which "by definition" avoided Cantor's paradoxical results—but without resolving them.[27] This approach was criticized by formalist mathematician David Hilbert (1862-1895), and by Kurt Gödel (1906-1978). Hilbert failed to provide a rigorous proof that Russell and Whitehead's *Principia Mathematica* was both a consistent (i.e. free of contradiction) and complete system, but as a result concluded that many formal axiomatic systems for mathematical logic were conceivable, his own program being in some ways an attempt to devise a formal system alternative to Russell's. Gödel, on the other hand, doubted that any complete and consistent system of number theory could be developed at all, following exclusively logical and formal approaches, such as Leibniz, Newton, Russell, Hilbert, Frege and Peano had variously attempted. This to contemporaries may have seemed to be a rather radical stance, but what made Gödel's observations rather difficult to ignore is that he was able to present them with all the rigor and logic of a mathematical proof.

Gödel's proof of his "Incompleteness Theorem" has been referred to as a modern landmark in logical thought, its influence and significance comparable with Kant's or Einstein's chief achievements.[28] In proving his central theorem, he followed two steps. First, by mapping the entire elementary arithmetic onto a finite sequence of whole numbers (so-called "Gödel numbers"), he devised an extraordinarily rigorous way to make comprehensive statements about both real numbers and statements involving real numbers (such as numerical formulae, propositions and theorems), based on a relatively contained and finite numerical sequence. In order to conceive the powerful significance of Gödel's mathematical code, consider a finite set of English words which could be mapped onto the totality of the English language plus every single text, sentence and phrase that has ever been written in English! Gödel's mathematical code has been referred to as "self-referential" in that it utilizes numerical signs to make comprehensive statements about numerical signs and relationships. However, as a result, the Gödel numbers could provide an exhaustive representation of the whole universe of number theory, including the mathematical equivalents of the logic paradoxes unveiled by Russell, which are also self-referential in nature. In other words, statements referring to the statements themselves, as in: "This sentence is false".

The second step was proving the "Incompleteness Theorem" itself, of which an English language paraphrase has been offered by Hofstadter:

> All consistent axiomatic formulations of number theory include undecidable propositions.[29]

Using his numerical code, Gödel was not only able to prove that Russell's and Whitehead's logical system of *Principia Mathematica* was incomplete, but that this applied to any related logical-axiomatic system of number theory. In other words, in a number of finite steps, Gödel found rigorous and logic proof that all axiomatic systems of number theory included statements for which no proof of truth or falsity could be possibly derived based on logical methods. As a result, both the formalists and logicians historic attempts to create complete and consistent axiomatic systems of number theory were shown to be inherently fruitless, as were any previous or future attempts based on formal or logic methods.[30]

Thus, based on the extraordinarily high standards of rigor embedded in the Gödel numbers, the "Incompleteness Theorem" offered logical proof that mathematics transcends logic. In other words, logic was shown to be a subset of mathematics, and not the other way round. However, if this is the case, what is there in mathematics that goes beyond logic? After Gödel's work, one modern answer to this question has been to rekindle the ancient notions of mathematical intuition and the archetypal nature of numbers, no longer in a metaphorical but in a strictly literal way. Hence, some mathematicians such as Mostowski have expressed the need to build "intuitive mathematics" in the hope of arriving at complete numerical systems. Others have bluntly argued that mathematicians should have the courage to recognize the reality of numerical forms, which "indeed have an existence that is independent of the mind considering them".[31] Roger Penrose has highlighted the "profound and timeless reality" of mathematical concepts such as the system of complex numbers, describing them as objects with a life of their own, the pre-existent properties of which are only discovered by mathematicians. Such holistic ideas have been echoed by physicists such as Paul Davies. Similarly, psychologists such as Jung have described numbers as possessing independent archetypal reality, a notion that goes back to Pythagoras and Plato.[32]

However, the implications of Gödel's "Incompleteness Theorem" appear to transcend even mathematics, and it is just relatively recently that we have started to understand their pervasive influence in other fields where logical methods are involved. Not only has it been shown that any such formal system rich or complex enough to produce self-referential statements necessarily contains logically undecidable paradoxes. In reality, complex natural systems seem also to possess self-referential properties which can be termed paradoxical, in a way which closely parallels Gödel's mathematical notions.

Beyond the Realm of Logics: Complexity, Paradoxes and Self-Reference in the Natural World and the Social Sciences

Since Gödel's original publication of his "Incompleteness Theorem" in 1931, self-referential paradoxes have been explored in relation to a variety of phenomena across diverse fields, including the natural and the social sciences. A key notion involving Gödelian paradoxes — both in the natural world and in the case of mathematical and logical systems — is that they seem to be absent in relatively simple systems and phenomena, but emerge whenever these are complex enough to include self-referential statements, behavior or processes. Amongst the processes closely linked with self-reference in nature are the so called "strange loops". These phenomena take place when, starting from any given point, upwards or downwards patterns in a hierarchical system lead back to the starting point, in a seemingly infinite fashion. Such strange loops — inherently involving a paradox between finite and infinite motions — have been given ample artistic representation, with astonishing esthetic effects of illusion and double meaning.[33] More importantly for our topic, strange loops and paradoxical, self-referential behavior have been found to be central to the functioning processes of many complex natural systems — in particular those associated with conscious and intelligent structures.

Strange loops have been identified at the core of the mental rules governing intelligent behavior. Scientists and researchers in the field of artificial intelligence (AI) have likened the flexibility, creativity, ambiguity, and unpredictability associated with intelligence, to a tightly codified set of strange-loop programs. Thus, paradoxically, heavily formal and rigid rules with self-referential and strange-loop properties, could lead to flexible AI programs.[34] Moreover, the analogy between self-referential paradoxes and intelligence has been very clearly stated by some researchers. Under these views, the complexity involved in "Gödelian questions" of self-referential awareness is what differentiates an intelligent brain from a machine. If the complexity of our machines could reach the level in which (without external additions) it could engage in self-referential processes — i.e. reflect upon its own performance in a critical way — then it could be possible to speak of intelligent machines analogously to intelligent brains. This notion is intrinsically holistic: Unlike a machine, the performance of a conscious brain is more than the sum of its parts — and that "more" is given by the ability to ask self-referential Gödelian questions. As a result, a conscious being intrinsically is a holistic unity. Thus, any references to the parts of a conscious mind are not to be taken literally, but only figuratively.[35]

In Jungian psychology, all of the deeply paradoxical phenomena associated with the human psyche stem from the inherently self-referential nature of consciousness: A conscious psyche is aware of itself, yet it is also embedded in transcendental, unconscious, and collective archetypal realities. This was essentially termed the "paradox of the Self", from which all other paradoxes of the psyche originate. According to Jung, the Self is a timeless, immanent reality, the contextual entity in which an individual's body, soul, mind and spirit can be integrated in a balanced whole.[36]

In anthropology, Gregory Bateson described all living creatures as open systems in relation to their surrounding environment, possessing a highly complex feedback loop structure.[37] This is an inherently self-referential structure, in the sense that the living system provides information about itself, and that information is used to produce changes which are in turn fed back again into the system, in a seemingly infinite loop. However, at every feedback loop, the living organism acquires information of higher complexity, in order to produce a better performance or an improved adaptation to its environment. Thus, self-referential properties in relation to the contextual environment are at the very heart of the living organism's complex evolutionary capabilities.

Within the social sciences, management and organization theories have advanced a number of metaphors describing organizations as living systems in Bateson's sense.[38] Curiously, these metaphors have often been proposed as a response to the inadequacy of mechanistic conceptions of organizations (i.e. the so-called "classical" or "scientific" management theory[39]) to deal with the complexity and fluidity of today's world. Thus, on the one hand, concepts such as "bounded rationality" have questioned the human brain's ability to handle the complexity of issues related to management and organizations, purely based on rational grounds:

> *The capacity of the human mind for formulating and solving complex problems is very small compared with the size of the problems whose solution is required for objectively rational behavior in the real world.*[40]

On the other hand, a number of authors have identified relatively recent technological, economic and social trends as having led to a sharp increase in environmental fluidity during the last quarter of the 20th century. Far from reaching a more stable state, such trends are expected to reinforce each other, fueling ever increasing levels of environmental fluidity well into the 21st century.[41]

As a result, conventional management theories based on Cartesian or reductionist paradigms have been sharply criticized. The latter are based on the scientific reduction of management phenomena to tractable analytical units, and utilize model representations grounded on structural or dynamic steady-state equilibrium, which have proved very limited in handling environmental fluidity. As an alternative, some authors have explored self-organizational frameworks, viewing corporations as organisms in perpetual adaptation and change for survival in a turbulent environment.[42] From these perspectives, even the mechanisms that govern evolution are subject to evolution themselves. Therefore there exist not only adaptive or morphostatic changes in an organization (also called autopoietic, or changes that fundamentally preserve the pre-existing structure), but also self-renewal morphogenetic changes that radically transform the existing organizational structure and replace it with a new one characterized by a higher degree of complexity. Self-organizational metaphors have influenced evolutionary theories of the firm, which highlight the role of knowledge and human cognition in relation to the development of organizational capabilities.[43]

From a similar perspective, H. A. Simon's concept of bounded rationality underlies his brain metaphor for organizations.[44] He postulated that organizations, like people, make decisions based on incomplete information and bounded rationality. Therefore, the limitations of the human brain to retain and process information are of fundamental importance for decision-making. Within this metaphor, the term "satisficing" was coined to describe behavior geared to achieving a set of pre-established goals — as opposed to classical "maximizing". Simon's metaphor is one of the key organizational notions underlying the theory of institutional economics, proposing a view of human nature and the relationship between markets and firms which is described as realistic compared to the standard neoclassical economic analysis. Bounded rationality, satisficing and other related notions can also be found underpinning large areas of modern decision theory.[45]

Connectedness Amongst the Mathematical, the Natural and the Organizational Systems

The connections between the physical, mathematical, biological and organizational systems which have been proposed so far have taken the form of metaphors. The utility of such interpretative mechanism in science, particularly when applied to living organizations, has been recognized by some authors, highlighting that:

> (...) our theories and explanations of organizational life are based on metaphors that lead us to see and understand organizations in distinctive yet partial ways. Metaphor is often just regarded as a device for embellishing discourse, but its significance is much greater than this. For the use of metaphor implies a way of seeing that pervade how we understand our world generally. For example, research in a wide variety of fields has demonstrated that metaphor exerts a formative influence on science, on our language and on how we think, as well as on how we express ourselves on a day-to-day basis.[46]

In fact, when linking Gödel's mathematical findings on the incompleteness of axiomatic systems to parallel phenomena in the natural world, Hofstadter presents a strictly metaphorical approach.[47] The discussions that are thus derived are conceptually born, rather than strictly a matter of mathematical cognition. Although this remains an insightful approach, a number of scientists have argued for an even more literal interpretation of the fundamental linkage between the mathematical, biological and psychological "worlds", a notion which has rather ancient philosophical and religious precedents.[16] Nobel prize winner and physicist Wolfgang Pauli and psychologist Carl Jung, worked together to develop the idea that an area of interrelation existed among microphysics, the unconscious psyche, and the biological processes. Curiously, structural complexity and the associated self-referential paradoxical concepts were already seen by Pauli and Jung at the heart of the singular parallelisms underlying a potential "one-ness" of archetypal, biological and physical phenomena. These views have also deeply influenced the development of relatively new sciences such as cybernetics, artificial intelligence and systems theory.[48]

This discussion thus highlighted that, whether they can be seen as real or "just" metaphorical, the linkages between self-referential paradoxical phenomena in the logical, psychological and biological systems are far from trivial. Rather, we have described how these linkages have already in the past been metaphorically extended to certain areas of economics and management, such as institutional economics, organizational theory, and the evolutionary theories of the firm. In all these disciplines, the concept of self-referential complexity, closely associated with the issue of *knowability*, has been shown to characterize important phenomenon which seem to defy purely logical methods of inquiry, thus stressing the need for fundamentally more holistic responses.

Holistic *Execution* and the Paradoxes of Management

As in the mathematical, biological and psychological fields, many critical aspects of the managerial activity have to come to terms with self-referential paradoxes and complex phenomena. Within highly stable company environments, it could be argued that *knowability* can be neatly attained based on explicit rules, formal knowledge and codifiable procedures. Likewise, many simple, logically conceived mathematical systems (i.e. lacking self-referential axiomatic statements) can be both complete and consistent. However, highly fluid environments appear to set-off paradoxical feedback loops within a company, oscillating between different — and often contradictory — informational contexts. Thus, the need to co-ordinate and control along multiple contextual dimensions and within rapidly changing environments, leads to highly complex internal company structures, where routine *execution* mechanisms can no longer be carried out solely based on formalized knowledge or codified procedures.

For example, a company's or an industry's expansion during the globalization stages often brings the need to effectively co-ordinate resources across highly diverse global and local informational contexts, involving people possessing vastly different deep-rooted national cultural backgrounds. As a result, from a cognitive perspective, it could be argued that *execution* mechanisms within these stages will have to constantly evolve and adjust through complex organizational routines, leading not only to a formal adaptation but also to an experience-based, intuitive transformation. This will require that both the individuals and entire areas of the organization continuously attain *gnosis* of the deep-rooted cultural symbols and manifestations characterizing their diverse and hardly predictable local informational contexts, as a crucial complement to purely formal and technical knowledge.

Some empirical studies have indeed provided support to the notion that firms specialize in the creation and transfer of knowledge with a significantly tacit content, "that is difficult to understand and codify."[49] Continuous transfer and recombination of this kind of knowledge leads to the creation of idiosyncratic technologies within firms, which some are able to transfer at a lower cost to wholly owned subsidiaries relative to third parties. Based on these types of findings, evolutionary theories of the firm have proposed to understand multinational corporations not as organizations arising from failures in the knowledge markets, but rather as social communities specializing in the rapid and efficient creation and transfer of knowledge, the latter term encompassing not only declarative know-how but especially procedural and tacit knowledge. A firm's boundaries thus denote qualitative changes in the reservoir of social and contextual knowledge available to people inside the organization, requiring a complex set of explicit and tacit rules of co-ordination and a structured identity to continuously influence the direction and search of learning in a way that lowers the costs of communication.[50] Hence, in relation to what firms *do* in practice, it can be argued that these four tightly interrelated aspects — self-referential complexity, informational context, environmental fluidity, and cognitive holism — constitute key dimensions to characterize *execution* from the perspective of it being a potential source of lasting practical advantages to the firm (see Figure 4.1).

This definition of *execution* closely parallels the genetic process known as epigenesis. Through this process, a *genotype* (i.e. a set of basic chemical elements and genetic information contained in DNA molecules) is transformed into a distinct and specific physical organism, called *phenotype*. However, the process of epigenesis itself consists of a series of ill-understood and exceedingly complex chemical reactions and feedback loop cycles.[51] Analogously, in the context of a firm, *execution* consists of a continuous transformational flux, where, starting from a given set of (internal and external) strategic, financial, technological, human and intangible inputs, small tasks interact with multiform feedback cycles to generate distinct outcomes or states of higher complexity. True, a number of tasks are discrete, routine and strictly internal to the firm, yet they need to be executed. However, from a transformational perspective, these are to be considered part of, rather than strictly equal to, *execution*.

Our analogy, however, doesn't stop there. Some geneticists have observed that the popular belief that DNA molecules contain all the chemical compo-

FIGURE 4.1

The key dimensions of execution

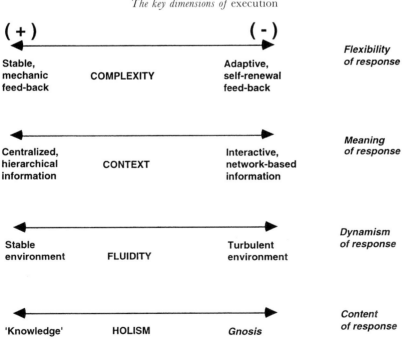

nents and instructions necessary to produce a phenotype is profoundly flawed. In effect, so far, an isomorphic correspondence between genotype and phenotype has only vaguely and rather figuratively been established.[52] In reality, the unique and distinct meaning inherent in any given DNA molecule can only be extracted within its chemical context. This includes information outside the DNA, which is combined with the chemical content inside the genotype in order to transform it into a concrete physical organism. Parallel phenomena have been studied within the theory of solid state physics. Physicist Werner Heisenberg (1901-1976) found that at the sub-atomic level the relationship between "subject" and "object" that takes place under direct observation originate changes which make such a distinction irrelevant — both observer and the observed object become a single system. The interaction between particles (such as electrons and photons) follows strange-loop type of patterns, where particles cannot be defined outside their dynamic context but only in relation to other particles.[53] Also, both in psychology and within action theories of communication, it has been argued that, although individual symbols can be singled out from each other, their inherent meaning is awakened in the context of a constellation of other symbols. This connectedness of symbols often occurs through complex functions resembling recursive, strange loop networks.[54]

Similarly, a firm's practical advantages can never be completely derived *a priori* in direct correspondence to a firm's given internal inputs (i.e. strategic, financial, technological, human or intangible). These inputs are akin to the firm's organizational DNA, which can only attain specific meaning and full realization within the informational context of *execution*. In turn, the latter is fundamentally affected by highly complex psychological and environmental phenomena, such as cultural symbols or technological innovations, which are extremely difficult to rigorously formalize or categorize.[55] As a result, a firm's peculiar *execution* context (as well as the associated *execution skills* and specific outcomes) may constitute to a significant extent a rather uncodifiable and unpredictable dimension. Contrary to this viewpoint, strategic planning theorists have argued that most, if not all, of a firm's actual advantages can be internally derived from strategic approaches based on forecasting models and factual information, carried out through formal processes largely detached from the practical aspects of *execution*. Such views, implicitly reducing *execution* to a sort of formal appendix of strategic thinking (i.e. within the operational, tactical or implementative dimensions of the firm), have been described by some authors as dangerously fallacious.[56] In sharp contrast with such strategic planning approaches or with earlier theories of the firm emphasizing the advantages of its internal knowledge and capabilities, evolutionary authors have stressed the importance of the informational context to the firm. As mentioned, such evolutionary views recognize networks of interacting firms, procedural coordination and learning, tacit and social knowledge, location and identity, as well as evolutionary mechanisms in relation to the market environment, amongst the key factors underlying what firms do and why certain firms show superior performance.[57]

If informational context characterizes the meaning of a firm's particular *execution* response, the required degree of *execution* flexibility is given by the level of complexity within the underlying organizational feedback structure of the firm. The existence of feedback mechanisms in an organization makes it a self-referential entity in a Gödelian sense. In the case of firms, this is an almost tautological consequence of a critical reliance on contextual knowledge for survival, and the fact that they are partly made up of human beings whose brains are the self-referential structures *par excellence* in the natural world. Therefore, from a knowledge-based perspective, firms are to be considered self-referential entities in all but the most stable competitive environment.[58] The complexity of a firm's feedback structure is thus crucially linked to the fluidity of the environment in which it operates. In logical, physical and biological systems, a self-referential structure leads to paradoxical behavior once a critical level of complexity is reached. Analogously, a relatively stable firm environment can be dealt with based on linear, one-dimensional feedback structures and simple performance measures.[39] However, a highly fluid, or turbulent environment can be associated with a firm's highly complex feedback cycles along multiple organizational dimensions. In this area, management authors have characterized a dramatic increase in environmental fluidity, significantly affecting the ways in which firms operate. Thus, the years between the mid 1960s and the early 1970s are described as a period during which systematic turbulence suddenly and unexpectedly arose across all dimensions of industrialized societies. Turbulence has ever since manifested itself through the interaction of on-going powerful trends which continuously reshape the existing social structures in various, irreversible and unpredictable ways. Among these trends we may mention market globalization, the ever-increasing rate of technological change, the explosive growth of information and the means to process it, the radical transformations in labor and capital markets, etc.[59] Continuous reinforcement of these developments will necessarily pose increasingly complex, paradoxical barriers (or opportunities) to *execution*, with all the related implications in terms of the *execution skills*, infrastructural and strategic capabilities required. Hence, from the viewpoint of a firm's *execution* dimensions, turbulent environments demand more dynamic responses, in the same way that highly complex feedback structures in the firm should result in more flexible *execution* responses.

Overall, the firm's cognitive understanding of its informational context, its level of self-referential complexity and the fluidity of its environment, are what inherently determines the content of any particular *execution* response. As mentioned, under certain circumstances these factors can result in paradoxical phenomena with regards to *execution*, thus requiring procedural, intuitive and experience-based cognitive structures. This is what makes the *execution* content a fundamentally holistic dimension, including both logic-based, objective knowledge, as well as experience-based, subjective *gnosis*. For instance, it has been stressed that market phenomena such as globalization are generally associated with a significant increase in environmental fluidity. Within such a competitive setting, a firm's expansion modes often routinely include cross-border M&As, JVs and alliances. National cultural differences have been found to significantly affect the performance of these types of expansion modes, due to the pervasive influence of deep-rooted cultural symbols, values and archetypes.[60] Here, the fundamental limits of logical methods and objective knowledge to grasp such symbolic and archetypal entities have been initially pointed out in psychology.

Jung defined the archetypes as *primordial images* of the collective unconscious, stemming from a common atavic (and probably pre-conscious) past. They are also sometimes associated with a sort of ancient race memory from pre-historic stages of mankind. According to Jung, an unsuspected amount of human creativity — i.e. the artistic, as well as most of the mythical, religious and philosophical developments that have come to characterize the deep-rooted cultural and epochal aspects of nations, are archetypal in nature. However, when he sought after the archetypes during his clinical experiences, *Jung encountered personal and cultural symbols in his patients' dreams but no firm traces of the archetypes themselves*. Thus, he concluded that, although the archetypes constitute the underlying unconscious psychic realities, they remain empty until the individual's experiences fill it with symbolic content.

In turn, symbols were words or images with meanings beyond conscious, rational or logic interpretation. Whereas the inherent meaning of a sign can be completely mapped onto a codified system, symbols are not isomorphic — i.e. they cannot be completely described in terms of another logic structure. Thus, symbols provide vast possibilities of variation around a central meaning, inherently defying any exhaustive formal or logic categorization. Culture was one of the key dimensions along which variations of symbolic constructs took place, according to Jung. Thus, referring to linguistic symbols, he observed:

> Each word means something slightly different to each person, even among those who share the same cultural background. The reason for this variation is that a general notion is received into an individual context and is therefore understood and applied in a slightly individual way. And the difference of meaning is naturally greatest when people have widely different social, political, religious, or psychological experiences.[61]

Jung's description of symbols has greatly influenced our modern views of human culture. In the management literature, symbols and archetypal constructs are virtually unanimously considered as central constitutive elements of culture.[62] In related social sciences such as linguistics, communications, and political sciences, symbolic concepts of cultural tradition, knowledge and cognition are paramount to modern theories of communicative action.[63] The resulting notion of culture is thus highly paradoxical: Although seen as a major pervasive influence across a wide range of human and social fields of activity, it is notoriously difficult to formalize, and therefore defies rigorous logical definition.

In order to reach a non-trivial cognitive understanding of cultural — and other human psychic symbols in practice — Jung's response was inherently holistic. Almost paraphrasing Kant's earlier philosophical reflections, Jung argued that intuitive understanding and a personal relationship with the symbolic phenomena were essential to experience their intimate meaning, but that this insight needed to be complemented by conscious and logical cognition. Thus, referring to the symbolic interpretation of dreams, Jung observed that:

> Intuition is almost indispensable in the interpretation of symbols, and it can often ensure that they are immediately understood by the dreamer. But while such a lucky hunch may be subjectively convincing, it can also be rather dangerous. It can so easily lead to a false feeling of security. The safe basis of real intellectual knowledge and moral understanding gets lost if one is content with the vague satisfaction of having understood by "hunch". One can explain and know only if one has reduced intuitions to an exact knowledge of facts and their logical connections.[64]

From his holistic perspective, Jung warns of an over-reliance on intuitive mechanisms to attain a cognitive understanding of symbols. Conversely, when discussing cognitive approaches in relation to scientific phenomena, he guards against exclusively logical methods:

> Here they [imagination and intuition] play an increasingly important role, which supplements that of the "rational" intellect and its application to a specific problem. Even physics, the strictest of all applied sciences, depends to an astonishing degree upon intuition, which works by way of the unconscious (although it is possible to demonstrate afterward the logical procedures that could have led one to the same result as intuition).[64]

Here, as mentioned, Jung's notion of "perception by way of the unconscious" is akin to our use of the term *gnosis*. Similarly, the holistic dimension of *execution* along "knowledge" and *gnosis*, echoes Jung's own complementary view of psychological perception — crucially stressing the importance of direct experience and relationship with the subject to attain an intimate level of cognitive understanding.

Holistic Execution Responses can be Difficult to Copy

Whereas logical methods and objective knowledge have been invariably identified as a key cognitive dimension in management, the notion of *gnosis* as its indispensable complementary pair has received much less attention — even from the viewpoint of implementation or similar *execution*-like perspectives. However, the pervasive relevance of deep-rooted cultural symbols, and the existence of similarly complex or paradoxical managerial phenomena, suggests that *gnosis* can be considered the key complement of objective knowledge within the holistic dimension of *execution*:

- It largely relies on experienced-based mechanisms, being guided — but not bounded — by theoretical, logical and formal thought.
- Through understanding intuition, it conveys to the dimensions of *execution*, critical information which is exceedingly difficult — if not impracticable — to codify, formalize or made predictable within explicit systems, i.e. in relation to direct experience of deep-rooted cultural symbols, creativity, procedural behavior and other similar complex and paradoxical phenomena.
- It attains intimate cognitive familiarity based on a direct relationship with the subject, unconstrained by epistemological hierarchies.

Holistic *execution* responses can be difficult to imitate by competitors based on some of the characteristics inherent in their *gnosis* content. As mentioned, whereas the explicit nature of formal procedures and codified routines makes these mechanisms increasingly transferable outside the firm, a more tacit knowledge content is considerably slower to transfer beyond a firm's boundaries.[50]

This makes execution-driven advantages potentially strategic for a firm competing in the global economy. In the next chapter, we will examine how these holistic advantages can be generated over time, particularly within the context of global corporate alliances. Specifically, we will illustrate the way in which some sophisticated post-merger structural designs — as in the case of the multidomestic company — continuously foster global advantages based on their "execution orientation".

Notes and References

[1] Kogut, B. and U. Zander. "What firms do? Coordination, identity and learning", *Organization Science*, in press. Also see: Morosini, P., S. Shane and H. Singh. "National cultural distance and cross-border acquisition performance", *Journal of International Business Studies*, in press.

[2] Bartlett, D. L. and James B. Steele. *What Went Wrong*, Andrews and McMeel, Kansas City, 1992; Hayes and Abermath, quoted in *"Managerial Excellence"*. Also, see: Schon, D. *Reflective Practitioner*, Basic Books, New York, 1983.

[3] This passage was quoted in a foreword by R. Gupta to: *Managerial Excellence.* McKinsey Award winners from the *Harvard Business Review* (1980-1994), Boston, Harvard Business School Press, 1996. The original article can be found as: Ackoff, R. "The future of operational research is past", *Journal of Operational Research Society,* 30(2), 1979, pp. 93-104.

[4] Mintzberg, H. "The fall and rise of strategic planning", *Harvard Business Review,* January-February 1994, pp. 107-114; Porter, M. E. "The state of strategic thinking", *The Economist,* 23 May, 1987, p. 21; Lane, H. W. and P. Beamish. "Cross-cultural cooperative behavior in joint ventures in LDCs", *Management International Review,* Special Issue, 1990, pp. 87-102; Barkema, H. G., J. Bell and J. M. Pennings. "Foreign entry, cultural barriers and learning", working paper, Management Department, The Wharton School, University of Pennsylvania, Philadelphia, December 1993.

[5] Nonaka, I. "A dynamic theory of organizational knowledge creation", *Organization Science,* 1, 1994, pp. 14-37.

[6] For a detailed study of ancient Gnosticism see: Harnack, *History of Dogma,* translated by Neil Buchanan *et al.,* Vol. 1, Boston, Little Brown, 1899, Chapter 4; Nock, A. D. "Gnosticism", *Harvard Theological Review,* 57, October 1964, pp. 255-279; "Proposal for a terminological and conceptual agreement with regard to the theme of the colloquium", in U. Bianchi (ed.), *Le Origini dello Gnosticismo,* supplements to *Numen,* Vol. 12, Brill, Leiden, 1967, pp. xxvi-xxvii; Bultmann, R. *Theology of the New Testament,* translated by K. Grobel, Vol. 1, Scribner, New York, 1951; Rudolph, K. *Gnosis,* translated by R. McLachlan Wilson *et al.,* Harper and Row, San Francisco, 1983; *The Nag Hammadi Library in English,* 3rd edn, J. M. Robinson (ed.), Harper and Row, San Francisco, 1988. Eric Voegelin and Hans Jonas are often quoted as the "pre-eminent" authorities of modern Gnosticism. See: Voegelin, E. *Science, Politics and Gnosticism,* Regnery Gateway Editions, Chicago, 1968; Jonas, H. *The Gnostic Religion,* 2nd edn, Beacon Press, Boston, 1963.

[7] Perhaps the only common element characterizing the utilization of the term *gnosis* in the context of religious and intellectual movements is that, both in ancient and modern times, it has been loosely adopted to underlie a wide plurality of tendencies — sometimes even contradictory ones. For example, the word *gnosis* was broadly utilized in ancient Greece and Rome, in relation to both philosophical or religious doctrines based on subjective experience and individual thought, as opposed to those emphasizing formal, ideological or dogmatic approaches. Thus, Gnostic and mystery religions, such as the secretive Orphic, Eleusian and Dyonisian rites, emphasized their devotees' highly personalized and direct religious experience to attain *gnosis* of God and one-self (understood as "true knowledge", or "individual insight"), as opposed to the strictly magical, formalized or revealed interpretations of God present in many ancient Semitic and Middle Eastern religions. Under a Gnostic view, ritual was intended io fundamentally change a man's life through a personal transcendental experience in which knowledge of oneself and a direct encounter with the divine took place (Graves, R. *Greek Myths*: I, revised edn, Penguin Books, 1960; Smart, N. *The Religious Experience of Mankind,* Fount Paperbacks, January 1977). Similarly, the so-called Gnostic Christianity was embedded in a plurality of interpretations of Jesus's teachings and Christian tradition, largely based on a free, direct and transcendental personal experience — sharply contrasting the dogmatic, revealed and highly formalized interpretation favored by the early Christian Churches' hierarchies of Rome and Constantinople. As a result, during the first two centuries AD, the Mediterranean world witnessed continuous, and often violent, conflicts between Gnostic Christians and the Christian devotees of the emerging institutionalized Churches. This eventually resulted in a comprehensive obliteration of Gnostic Christianity as "heresy", to the

extent that much of our present knowledge of their thought and traditions has come through the surviving condemnatory writings of the early Church fathers (Pagels, E. *The Gnostic Gospels*, New York, Vintage Books, September 1989; Angus, S. *The Mystery-Religions and Christianity*, Carol Publishing Group, 1966). However, even within the 20th century, the writings of Victor White (a Catholic priest) can give an idea of how liberal and sectarian the utilization of the terms *gnosis* or Gnostic has been in the past. He observed that even St. Paul and Church fathers such as Clement of Alexandria "accounted *gnosis* among one of the most precious of the gifts of the Spirit to the Christian Church" (Segal, R. *The Gnostic Jung*, Princeton University Press, 1992, p. 203). Thus, the Church's ancient antagonism was not directed against Christian Gnostics, but towards Christian "Gnosticists" (which apparently included, according to White, all those whose "Gnosticist" views were not in agreement with the Catholic Church).

Thus, during the 20th century, the situation has remained somewhat similar from the viewpoint of the broad utilization of the word *gnosis* and the like — except that antagonism against specific Gnostic movements has not always reached the violent overtones of the early Christian period. Segal (*op. cit.*, 1992) observes that the term "Gnostic" or "Gnosticism" has been liberally applied to a broad number of movements and authors (a disparate list including Goethe, Byron, Simone Weil, More, Calvin, Marx and Hitler), many of whom had no knowledge of ancient Gnostic writings, held openly contradictory positions, or could be more accurately classified under "existentialist", "millenarian", or "nihilist" denominations. Nevertheless, beyond the confusing use of the term, there is little doubt that a revival of philosophical Gnosticism can be detected during the early 20th century, in many ways paralleling the ancient Gnostic's disillusion with scientific systems of knowledge and ethical or dogmatic religious principles. Thus, a list of truly modern Gnostics (whom — among other characteristics — knew and found inspiration in ancient philosophical Gnosticism) could include Nietzsche and Jung. On the one hand, in works such as *The Birth of Tragedy* and *The Genealogy of Morals* Nietzsche attempted to create a new system of (non-Christian) morals based on a reconciliation between scientific (or Apollonian) knowledge and insightful, deep (or Dyonisiac) understanding of the world. On the other, Jung (based on a study of 10th century Christian manuscripts of the Gnostic Gospel of Thomas, found in Egypt near the town of Naj 'Hammadi in 1945), asserted that Christian Gnostics were less concerned with the relationship between man and God, and more interested in the psychological problem of the human Self. In this, Jung recognized Gnostic Christians as truly ancient forerunners of his own psychology and theories of the Self. Thus, Jung saw a modern flowering of Gnostic thought and tendencies in the 20th century man's fascination with understanding the unconscious, and saw alchemy as the medieval connection between ancient and modern Gnosticism (see: Bousset, W. *Hauptprobleme der Gnosis*, Vandenhoeck & Ruprecht, Göttingen, 1954. Also see: Robert A. Segal's introduction to *The Gnostic Jung*, 1992, pp. 3-52. This latter text includes a wide bibliography of Jung's "alchemical" and "Gnostic" writings).

[8] See: Jung, C. G. *The Collected Works of C. G. Jung*, Vol. 10: *Civilization in Transition*, Bollingen Series XX, G. Adler and R. F. Hull, (eds), Princeton University Press, Princeton, 1964.

[9] Smart, N. *The Religious Experience of Mankind*, Fount Paperbacks, 1977, p. 234.

[10] See: Nietzsche, F. *The Birth of Tragedy and the Genealogy of Morals*, Doubleday, New York, 1956. For an excellent modern review of Dyonisiac myths and rituals, see: Kerényi, K. *Dioniso*, Adelphi, 1992.

[11] Nietzsche, F. *Op. cit.*, p. 95.

[12] Gilligan, C. "In a different voice: women's conceptions of self and of morality", *Harvard Educational Review*, 47, 1977, pp. 481-517; Gilligan, C. *In a Different Voice: Psychological Theory and Women's Development*, Harvard University Press, Cambridge, MA, 1982; Piercy, M. "Unlearning to not speak", in M. Piercy, *To Be of Use*, Doubleday, New York, 1973, p. 38; Belenky, M. F., B. McVicker Clinchy, N. R. Goldberger and J. M. Tarule. *Women's Ways of Knowing. Development of Self, Voice and Mind*, Basic Books, 1986.

[13] From Leibniz' *De Arte Combinatoria*, first published in 1666. Quotation in: Robertson, R. *Jungian Archetypes*, Nicolas-Hays Inc., York Beach, ME, 1995, p. 30.

[14] However grotesque they may seem at first, such conclusions were neither isolated developments nor dependent on the underlying epistemological approach adopted by these philosophers. Rather, as described in the remaining parts of the chapter, similar conundrums occurred during the 20th century — this time as a result of a fundamental and rather one-sided reliance on *knowability*-through-logic.

[15] Quotation in: Robertson, R. *Op. cit.*, p. 34.

[16] Examples of holistic or organic philosophical and religious doctrines can also be found in antiquity. For example, the philosophical school of Stoicism, founded by Zeno of Citium (335-263 BC) maintained the organic unity of the universe as a single whole. Thus, a "wise man" was not to be detached from worldly affairs or solely contemplative, but was rather courageous, tolerant and self-controlled in the practical fulfillment of his duties. Lucius Annaesus Seneca (4 BC–65 AD) championed Stoic morals and codes of behavior that were widely adopted by the nobility in Roman times. A century later, Marco Aurelio (Roman Emperor between 161 and 180 AD) was seen by his contemporaries as the ideal personification of the Stoic Man, who exerted wide religious and political tolerance. In pre-Confucian China, Lao Tzu's notion of Tao was also an organic one, underlying all natural processes and causes — much like the Mother Goddess of ancient Mediterranean religions.

[17] Nietzsche, F. *Op. cit.*, p. 111. Nietzsche's moral system antagonized Christian ethics which — according to the philosopher — had exorcised man's Dyonisiac spirit as "evil", but only at the cost of inhibiting the deep-rooted human creative and living instincts. In this, Nietzsche anticipated 20th century psychological and neurological research on the key role of the unconscious on human outward creative, artistic and cultural impulses. This notion is at the roots of Nietzsche's often misunderstood assertions on Christian religion, and his interpretation of the Anti-Christ. (See: Nietzsche, F. *Thus Spoke Zarathustra*.)

[18] The literature on Jungian psychology is vast. For the unaware, however, perhaps the best introduction is a book co-authored by Carl Jung himself (Jung, C. G. *Man and His Symbols*, Dell Publishing, 1968). An interesting introduction to modern aspects of the neurology of the brain can be found in Bodmer, W. and R. McKie. *The Book of Man. The Quest to Discover Our Genetic Heritage*, Abacus, London, 1994.

[19] Jung, C. G. *Man and his Symbols*, Dell Publishing, 1968, p. 67.

[20] See: Boyer, C. B. *A History of Mathematics*, Princeton University Press, Princeton, 1968; Struik, D. J. A. *A Concise History of Mathematics*, 4th revised edn, Dover, New York, 1987.

[21] This was embedded in Cantor's unresolved "continuum hypothesis". For a more formal examination of the problem of infinity in Cantor's theory of sets, see: Cohen, P. *Set Theory and the Continuum Hypothesis*, W.A. Benjamin, Menlo Park, CA, 1966; Boyer, C. B. *Op. cit.*, 1968; Bell, E. T. *Development of Mathematics*, McGraw-Hill, New York, 1940.

[22] The mathematical notion of completeness is a complex one. However, in the context of mathematical systems such a Russell's *Principia Mathematica*, a complete system could be simplistically described as one in which formal and logical proof of truth

or falsity can be derived for any of the system's internal statements. In other words, completeness of the mathematical system is given by the fact that we can logically demonstrate the truth or falsity of any of its inherent statements (in Russell's case, the mathematical system was the full arithmetic of the natural numbers or integers — upon which much of mathematics has been developed). Conversely, when it can be shown that there exists a category of mathematical statements for which no proof of truth or falsity can be derived (so called undecidable statements or propositions), the underlying system is called "incomplete". See: Benacerraf, P. and H. Putnam (eds), *Philosophy of Mathematics: Selected Readings*, Cambridge University Press, Cambridge, 1983.

[23] "Boolean" propositions are much used in computer science, artificial intelligence and other related fields. During the 19th century, deductive reasoning patterns were also developed by another English logician, Augustus De Morgan.

[24] See: Boyer, C. B. *Op. cit.*, 1968; Bell, E. T. *Op. cit.*, 1940.

[25] Robertson, R. *Op. cit.*, 1995, p. 127.

[26] Even if the modern philosophical fascination with logical paradoxes is relatively recent, these have profoundly captivated human intellect since antiquity. During the 6th century BC, Epimenides, a Greek poet born in the island of Crete, proposed a famous ancient paradox when he stated that "all Cretans are liars". A century later, a Greek philosopher, Zeno of Elea, was called "inventor of paradoxes". In 5th century BC China, a central branch of the Ch'an school (or Meditation School — a blending of Buddhist and Taoist ideas first advanced by Bodhidharma, an Indian monk) developed a notion of *knowability* as intrinsically paradoxical. This branch of thought spread greatly in Japan, and is referred to as Zen Buddhism after some of the meditation techniques involved. One of these was based on "question and answers" (WEN-TA in Chinese, or MONDO in Japanese). Another technique that came to characterize Zen Buddhism was based on the so called "Zen riddles" or "public documents", as the verbal riddles between Masters and disciples were recorded and collected. Thus, to an extent, Zen Buddhism doctrines were contained in these public documents, named KUNG-AN in Chinese, or KOAN in Japanese. They are an odd sort of writings emphasizing the profound mystery and paradoxical undecidability involved in attempting to reach a true understanding of the universe.

[27] For example, as in Russell's theory of descriptions, or his theory of types. Russell defined "classes" which did not include themselves — hence avoiding by definition Cantor's paradoxical "continuum hypothesis" of the "set of all sets", which has remained unresolved. See: Russell, B. *Introduction to Mathematical Philosophy*, Dover Publications, New York, 1933.

[28] For a detailed discussion of Gödels "proof", see: Shanker, S. G. *Gödel's Theorem in Focus*, Routledge, London, 1988. Also see: Davis, M. *The Undecidable*, Raven Press, Hewlett, NY, 1965. Rather accessible descriptions of both the theorem and its profound significance to modern thought, can also be found in: Robertson, R. *Op. cit.*, 1995; and Hofstadter, D. R. *Gödel, Escher, Bach: An Eternal Golden Braid*, Vintage Books, New York, 1989.

[29] See: Hofstadter, D. R. *Op. cit.*, 1989, p. 17. The reader may be forgiven for not attempting to go over Gödel's original mathematical proof of the "Incompleteness Theorem" (originally published in German in 1931). Nevertheless, the mathematically minded readers can find an English translation in Gödel, K. *On Formally Undecidable*, Basic Books, New York, 1962.

[30] Again, Gödel's proof refers to all axiomatic number systems complex enough to include self-referential paradoxical statements, such as Russell's and Whitehead's. Axiomatic number systems which do not include these types of paradoxes can be

completely and consistently defined, but these are exceedingly basic and simple mathematical systems.

[31] See: Davis, P. J. and R. Hersh. *The Mathematical Experience*, Houghton Mifflin, Boston, 1981, p. 319.

[32] See: Mostowski, A. *Sentences Undecidable in Formalized Arithmetic: An Exposition of the Theory of Kurt Gödel*, North-Holland Publishing Company, Amsterdam, 1952; Davies, P. *The Mind of God*, Penguin Books, 1992; Jung, C. G. *Man and his Symbols*, Dell Publishing, 1968.

[33] Nobel Prize winner Gabriel Garcia Márquez has created a massive "strange loop" structure in *Cien Años de Soledad*, a landmark of 20th century literature. The novel ends with the main dynastic character, Aureliano Buendía, nearly reading about his own death in a century-old *pergamine* in Macondo, but dying before arriving at the final — and fatal — sentences. In music, a number of Johann Sebastian Bach's towering compositions, such as his Musical Offering, have been shown to possess an underlying strange loop structure in the form of canons and fugues; in the visual arts, M. C. Escher's drawings, lithographs and woodcuts abound with representations of strange loops that offer astounding illusory and unexpected effects, which are also present in the works of surrealist painters René Magritte and Salvador Dalí (Hofstadter, D. R. *Op. cit.*, 1989). However, perhaps the greatest visual representation of a strange loop structure is Diego Velázquez' most famous masterpiece: "Las Meninas", a painting completed in 1656, and currently hanging at the El Prado museum in Madrid. It represents the Spanish Royal Infanta as a child in a wide room inside a Royal Palace (sometimes identified as the Madrid's Alcázar). She is surrounded by her court of young female servants and a pet. In the background, a nun and an old figure converse calmly, while Velázquez has represented himself besides the Infanta, staring appraisingly towards the spectator from behind a large canvas he is painting. However, the spectator soon realizes that the royal couple must be posing beside him/her, as their image is reflected in a mirror situated several steps behind Velázquez' self-portrait and besides an open door through which a man is exiting the room. The extraordinary atmosphere of the composition, and Velázquez' supreme mastery of color and technique prompted critic Téophile Gautier's exclamation: "But, where is the painting?"

[34] Similar self-referential computer programs underlie the so-called "Artificial Life" (AL) models. See: Jackson, P. C. *Introduction to Artificial Intelligence*, Petrocelli Charter, New York, 1975; Davies, P. *The Mind of God*, Penguin Books, 1992.

[35] See: Lucas, J. R. "Minds, machines and Gödel", *Philosophy*, 36, 1961, p. 112. Also, see: Turing, A. M. "Computing machinery and intelligence", *Mind*, LIX (236), 1950.

[36] Jung, C. G. *Aion. Researches into the Phenomenology of the Self*, Princeton University Press, 1978.

[37] See: Bateson, G. *Steps to an Ecology of Mind*, Ballantine Books, New York, 1972.

[38] Ulrich, H. and G. J. B. Probst (eds) *Self-Organization and Management of Social Systems*, Springer-Verlag, 1984; Maturana, H. R. and F. Varela. "Autopoietic systems", Report BCL 9.4, Biological Computer Laboratory, University of Illinois, Urbana, IL, 1975; Checkland, P. *Systems Thinking, Systems Practice*, John Wiley, 1981; von Bertalanffy, L. *General Systems Theory: Foundations, Development, Applications*, Braziller, New York, 1968.

[39] See: Taylor, F. W. *What is Scientific Management?*, *Management Classics*, 2nd edn, Goodyear, Santa Monica, CA.

[40] Simon, H. A. *Models of Man*, John Wiley, New York, 1957, p. 198.

[41] Emery, F. and E. Trist. "The causal texture of organizational environments", *Human Relations*, 18, 1965, pp. 21-32; Jantsch, E. *The Self-Organizing Universe*, Oxford, Pergamon Press, 1980.

[42] Ulrich H. and G. J. B. Probst. *Op. cit.*, 1984; Maturana, H. R. and F. Varela. *Op. cit.*, 1975; Baumol, W. and J. Benhabib 1989. "Chaos: Significance, mechanism and economic applications", *Journal of Economic Perspectives*, 3(1); Winter, S. "Survival, selection and inheritance in evolutionary theories of organizations", in J. V. Singh (ed.), *Organizational Evolution: New Directions*, Sage, Newbury Park, CA, 1990; Yovits, J. and Goldstein (eds), *Self-Organizing Systems*, Spartan Books, 1962.

[43] Winter, S. "Four Rs for profitability: Rents, resources, routines and replication", in C. A. Montgomery (ed.), *Resource-based and Evolutionary Theories of the Firm: Towards a Synthesis*, Norwell, MA, 1995, pp. 147-178; Winter, S. "Knowledge and competence as strategic assets", in D. J. Teece (ed.), *The Competitive Challenge: Strategies for Industrial Innovation and Renewal*, Ballinger, Cambridge, MA, 1987, pp. 159-184.

[44] Simon, H. A. "Theories of bounded rationality", in C. McGuire and R. Radner (eds), *Decision and Organization*, North-Holland Publishing Company, Amsterdam, 1972, pp. 161-176; Simon, H. A. *Design of a Brain*, Macmillan, New York, 1965.

[45] Gans, J. S., "On the impossibility of rational choice under incomplete information", *Journal of Economic Behavior and Organization*, 29(2), 1996, pp. 287-309. Bui, T. X., "Evaluating negotiation support systems: a conceptualization", Proceedings of the twenty-seventh annual Hawaii international conference on System Sciences, Wailea, HI, USA, 4-7 January 1994. Langley, A. "Formal analysis and strategic decision making", *Omega*, 19(2-3), 1991, pp. 79-99.

[46] Morgan, G. *Images of Organization*, California, Sage Publication, 1986. Also see: Black, M. *Models and Metaphors*, Ithaca, NY, Cornell University Press, 1962. In psychology, "instruction by metaphor" has been recognized as central to Self-knowledge. Knowing metaphorically is not restricted to rational, logical, or empirical thinking based on objective data, but in addition it provides intuitive insights into the symbolic and ambiguous meanings of complex situations (see: Kopp, S. *If You Meet the Buddha on the Road Kill Him*, BY, Bantam Books, 1985).

[47] Hofstadter, D. R. *Op. cit.*, 1989.

[48] See: Jung, C. G. and W. Pauli. *The Interpretation of Nature and the Psyche*, Pantheon Books, New York, 1955. Also see: Boden, M. *Artificial Intelligence and Natural Man*, Basic Books, New York, 1977; von Bertalanffy, L. *Op. cit.*, 1968; Anderson, A. R. (ed.), *Minds and Machines*, Prentice-Hall, Englewood Cliffs, NJ, 1964. Prior to Jung and Pauli, parallelisms underlying the "one-ness" of Man and the Universe were highlighted towards the turn of the 20th century by another Nobel prize winner, Spanish physician Santiago Ramón y Cajal, who stated that: "As long as our brain is a mystery, the universe — the reflection of the brain's structure — will also be a mystery".

[49] Kogut, B. and U. Zander. "Knowledge of the firm and the evolutionary theory of the multinational corporation", *Journal of International Business Studies*, 26, 1993, p. 636.

[50] See chapter 9 for an illustration of the concepts developed in this section, in the context of Fuji-Xerox international expansion efforts. See also: Kogut, B. and U. Zander. "What firms do? Coordination, identity and learning", *Organization Science*, in press.

[51] See: Lehninger, A. *Biochemistry*, Cambridge University Press, New York, 1976.

[52] Within mathematics, isomorphisms occur when one mathematical construct can be completely and exhaustively mapped onto another (which mirrors such characteristics — the former). The concept of isomorphism is also widely utilized in other disciplines such as logic, linguistics and communications.

[53] See: Heisenberg, W. *The Physical Principles of the Quantum Theory*, Dover Publications, New York, 1949.

[54] Habermas, J. *The Theory of Communicative Action*. Vol. 1: *Reason and the Rationalization of Society*, Beacon Press, Boston, MA, 1984; Hofstadter, D. R. *Op. cit.*, 1989; Jung, C. G.

The Collected Works of C. G. Jung, Vol. 5: *Symbols of Transformation*, 2nd edn of 1952, Bollingen Series XX, G. Adler and R. F. Hull (eds), Princeton University Press, Princeton, 1967.

[55] Kogut, B. and U. Zander. "What firms do? Coordination, identity and learning", *Organization Science*, in press; Mintzberg, H. "The fall and rise of strategic planning", *Harvard Business Review*, January-February 1994, pp. 107-114; Kogut, B. and U. Zander. "Knowledge of the firm, combinative capabilities and the replication of technology", *Organization Science*, 3, 1992, pp. 383-397; Schein, E. "SMR Forum: Does Japanese management style have a message for American managers?", *Sloan Management Review*, 23(1), 1981, pp. 55-68.

[56] Mintzberg, H. *Op. cit.*, 1994.

[57] Kogut and Zander. *Op. cit.*, 1992; Kogut and Zander. *Op. cit.*, 1993; Szulanski, G. Appropriating Rents from Existing Knowledge: Intra-Firm Transfer of Best Practice, Doctoral Dissertation, INSEAD, 1995, UMI Number 9600790; Winter. *Op. cit.*, 1987.

[58] Simon, H. A. *Op. cit.*, 1957; March, J. G. and H. A. Simon, *Organizations*, John Wiley, New York, 1958; Winter. *Op. cit.*, 1987; Ulrich, H. and G. J. B. Probst. *Op. cit.*, 1984.

[59] Emery, F. and E. Trist *Op. cit.*, 1965; Jantsch, E. *Op. cit.*, 1980.

[60] Morosini, P. "The effect of national culture differences on post-cross-border acquisition performance in Italy", Doctoral Dissertation, Management Department, The Wharton School, University of Pennsylvania, 1994; Kogut, B. and H. Singh. "The effect of national culture on the choice of entry mode", *Journal of International Business Studies*, Fall 1988, pp. 411-432.

[61] Jung, C. G. *Man and his Symbols*, Dell Publishing, 1968, p. 28.

[62] Barley, S. "Semiotics and the study of occupational and organizational cultures", *Administrative Science Quarterly*, 28, 1983, pp. 393-413; Gregory, K. L. "Native-view paradigms: multiple cultures and culture conflicts in organizations", *Administrative Science Quarterly*, 28, 1983, pp. 359-376; Schein. *Op. cit.*, 1981.

[63] Habermas, J. *Op. cit.*, 1984.

[64] Jung, C. G., *Man and his Symbols*, Dell Publishing, 1968, p. 82.

CHAPTER 5

Generating *Execution-Driven* Advantages

> A good general, a well-organized system, good instruction, and severe discipline, aided by effective establishments, will always make good troops, independently of the cause for which they fight.
>
> Napoleon Bonaparte

The dimensions of *execution* described in Chapter 4 have been represented along a continuum, thus suggesting that a holistic property fundamentally applies to all four. But even without this geometric suggestion, our previous discussion has stressed the tight interrelation between complexity, informational context, environmental fluidity and the cognitive content of *execution*. As in the case of the human mind, it could be argued that referring to the "parts" or "dimensions" of *execution* is to only be understood in figurative terms, as in reality it is invariably crystallized as an indivisible unit (see Figure 5.1).[1]

Still, thinking of the "dimensions" of *execution* can be useful, especially when trying to understand how it can generate advantages over time. Take the cognitive dimension of *execution*. It could be argued that, as the key levers of *execution* change over time, so its content will include different combinations of "knowledge" and *gnosis*. For example, from a firm's perspective, key *execution* levers may include:

- technology
- degree of connectedness with the local markets
- internal co-ordination across multiple informational contexts.

At every stage the cognitive content of the *execution* responses will be holistically based on both "knowledge" and *gnosis*. However, just as the characteristics of these *execution* levers may vary over time as a function of both market and internal factors, also the *execution*-driven advantages will be

FIGURE 5.1

Execution *as an organic whole*

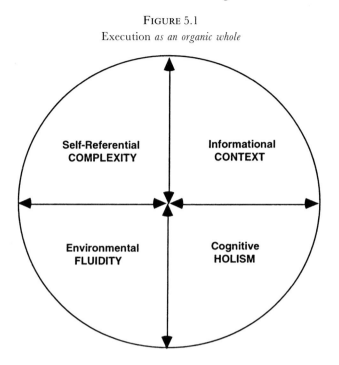

based on alternating dominant contents of either formal knowledge or experience-based *gnosis*.

A Dynamic View of *Execution-Driven* Advantages

These concepts are graphically shown in Figure 5.2. The dynamic process of market evolution has been schematically represented in three fundamental stages to illustrate how, from a company's perspective, the evolution of key scientific and market-based levers duly affect the organic dimensions of *execution* over time. An initial stage is characterized by the presence of emerging and ill-defined technologies, and the corresponding uncertainty as to their real viability. This is a stage akin to the primordial mist of evolutionary processes. In a second stage, an array of technological possibilities has been narrowed down to a few viable options, and technical standards insinuate themselves with increasing clarity. During the subsequent and last stage, technological developments have achieved full maturity, and well-known formal methods and techniques, as well as incremental innovations, flow with increasing speed across the marketplace, hardly constrained by country-based or international restrictions.

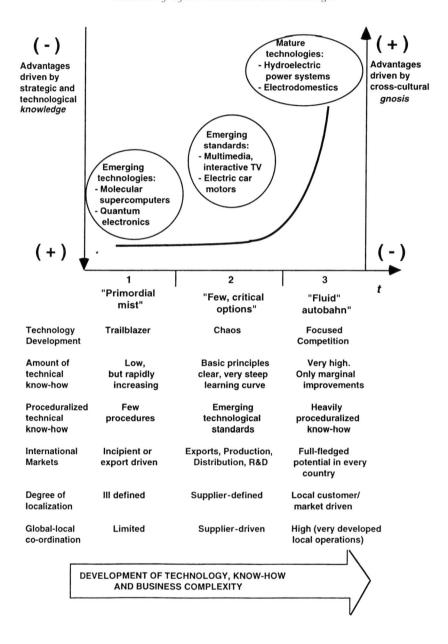

FIGURE 5.2

Evolution of a firm's execution-*driven advantages*

DEVELOPMENT OF TECHNOLOGY, KNOW-HOW
AND BUSINESS COMPLEXITY

At first, technological development is largely a pioneering undertaking, where a very low initial amount of technical know-how needs to be rapidly increased by continuous innovation. In such an environment, a very high degree of technological experimentation is required, not restrained within heavily proceduralized frameworks. International markets are seldom a key lever during this initial stage, largely due to the lack of reliable technological standards. As a result, operations tend to largely lie within the restricted geographic boundaries of the original technological developments. It could be argued that within the primordial mist stage of technological evolution, scientific and technologically based knowledge content will constitute the dominant aspect of *execution*-driven advantages. Although it has been shown that, even within scientific areas, the ability to experiment and innovate is significantly dependent on intuition, actual technologically driven business advantages at this stage stem from the way in which these scientific creative intuitions are formalized in due course, so that the market viability of products based on the new technologies becomes less and less unclear.[2]

During the second stage, scientific experimentation converges towards a few technological standards, around which much learning and technical know-how are rapidly accumulated. The full potential and the practical applications of these emerging technological standards are made clear within this stage, and as a result, business growth accelerates. However, a fundamental lack of experience with regards to modes of competition, commercial approaches, investment models and internationalization modes, eventually leads to highly unstable, or even openly chaotic rivalry patterns amongst competitors within the emergent businesses or industries. Moreover, international markets, degree of localization and global co-ordination at this stage are mostly supplier-defined, around a well-established core of products, services and functions. Although the technical knowledge content of *execution* is still critical at this stage, *gnosis* of foreign cultural, regulatory, social and infrastructural aspects become increasingly important to it, as the internationalization of the firm's operations proceeds.

During the third stage, specific rivalry patterns between competitors emerge which are clearly recognizable, but the competitive environment becomes highly fluid, driven by an increasingly mature technological base. Thus, on the one hand, competition becomes highly focused, as advantages based on either technical know-how or strategic modes are rapidly matched or copied by competitors. On the other, as maturing technologies lead to highly formalized and proceduralized know-how, relatively marginal improvements take place at great speed and hit the marketplace with ever-decreasing lead times. However, as the associated technological knowledge moves within increasingly fluid environments, even small-sized or agile local competitors become increasingly able to replicate some of the firm's core portfolio of products and services. Hence, the required degree of localization becomes significantly greater, as the firm will seek to exploit the full potential of international markets based on an expanded set of high value added products and services around established technologies. It is also at this stage that the firm increasingly seeks to expand its geographic reach, including markets which are culturally distant or unfamiliar. While local operations move from being predominantly supplier-driven to increasingly customer and market-driven, also the internal co-ordination mechanisms of the firm become significantly more complex, in order to both cope with an expanded informational context and to timely generate business advantages from it. Thus, contradictory demands between global and local organizational dimensions may lead to paradoxical phenomena, both from an internal control perspective, as well as from the viewpoint of the diversity of the national cultural and local informational contexts that need to be simultaneously co-ordinated. As a result, *execution* advantages are increasingly driven by the ability to co-ordinate the company's global reservoir of technological know-how and business knowledge across the highly diverse local cultural and informational contexts. However, the different local contexts in which the firm operates usually are difficult to formalize in a comprehensive way or to become fully routinized, and therefore *gnosis* becomes increasingly crucial to manage the global and local co-ordination functions required.

The notion that the content of *execution* greatly varies over time can also be illustrated from the viewpoint of individual business processes. For example, the key *execution* levers of an M&A, JV or alliance may vary over time, as these move from the planning through to the negotiation and implementation phases. Whereas proper application of analytical and formal approaches is particularly critical during the planning phase of M&As, JVs and alliances, direct experience, intuitive understanding and cultural familiarity might become more and more determinant during the subsequent negotiation, and particularly throughout the implementation phases.[3] Accordingly, in the latter phases business advantages related to *execution* will be increasingly reliant on *gnosis*. Hence, the application of a simple principle remains in this example, that wherever critical managerial activities and co-ordination functions become significantly more complex—i.e. due to expanded informational contexts involving highly diverse cultural, organizational and institutional dimensions, the more the reservoir of experience-based, subjective *gnosis* becomes crucial to a firm's cognitive *execution* dimensions (see Figure 5.3).

This highly schematic representation around a limited number of key *execution* levers and dimensions, nevertheless illustrates how evolution of the technological and competitive environments may dramatically affect the way in which the content of *execution* varies over time, influencing the business advantages that a firm can derive at different stages. So far it has been argued that, as a competitive environment becomes more fluid and global around relatively mature technologies, a firm's internal co-ordination functions will become correspondingly more complex, and so *gnosis* of the highly diverse

FIGURE 5.3

"Execution-*driven*" *advantages throughout the temporal phases of an M&A, JV or alliance*

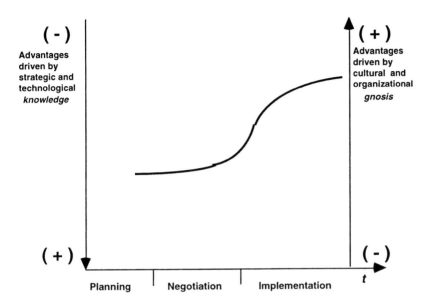

local cultural and informational contexts in which a firm operates will become increasingly relevant to the routine *execution* of these co-ordination mechanisms. Whereas technological and functional knowledge tends to become more proceduralized and transferable within increasingly fluid environments, a firm's *gnosis* is considerably more difficult to transfer outside its boundaries, as it is embedded in intuitive, experience-based and tacit cognitive mechanisms.[4] Thus, at this stage, the *gnosis* content of *execution* may become increasingly crucial to the generation of practical business advantages.

However, the actual ways in which *execution*-driven advantages might be generated will vary greatly from industry to industry, and from case to case. In some industries such as electrodomestics and industrial design, and also within certain service-oriented businesses, significant technology, product or market-based innovations may arise as a result of the firm's *gnosis* of local cultural values, customs or idiosyncrasies which are then adopted on a global scale. In other industries such as pharmaceuticals, it could be argued that customary international patent protections of a firm's product, technology and process-based innovations, makes formal knowledge a very crucial component of *execution*-driven advantages, well into the maturity stages of any particular technology, product or process innovation. However, in this indus-

127

try the local *gnosis* is also fundamental for the marketing of the products developed.

The "multidomestic" company provides a good illustration of how *execution*-driven advantages can be actually articulated within a global market context and around relatively mature technologies, generating organizational responses which need to be flexible and dynamic, yet complex; deeply embedded in multiple informational contexts, yet tightly co-ordinated across highly diverse cultural, social and institutional environments. ASEA Brown Boveri (ABB), the leading electrical engineering group, has been widely studied in the past as an archetypal example of this type of multidomestic organization, a term coined by the company's Chairman and former CEO Percy Barnevik. Although ABB's competitive edge has in the past been largely associated with its formal structural design *per se*, examining the way it works from a practical perspective reveals that many of the company's advantages can be actually traced back to its *execution skills* and ability to co-ordinate paradoxical organizational dimensions within highly fluid environments. Similar to ABB, we also found that a number of other companies, showing such diverse organizational structures as British Airways, Electrolux or Daewoo, nevertheless consistently stress their organizations' *execution* dimensions and skills as key factors leading to practical business advantages in the global marketplace.

ABB: An *Execution*-Oriented Multidomestic Organization

During the mid 1990s, the so-called multidomestic company was being increasingly referred to as a new type of organization, heralded as ideally suited for the post-industrial age. Percy Barnevik is generally credited as a model designer and a pioneer of this type of organization, formed after the 1987 merger between Sweden's Allmänna Svenska Elektriska Aktiebolag (ASEA) and Switzerland's Brown Boveri. During the eight-year period of Barnevik's tenure as the company's CEO, ABB grew from a US$ 18 billion combined turnover in 1988 to US$ 34 billion in 1995, with dramatic increases in profitability, efficiency and international coverage. Indeed, the fact that this company was initially created, and subsequently expanded through major cross-border M&As, JVs and alliances (numbering a total of 160 acquisitions by the end of 1995), has undoubtedly given it some of its initial multidomestic imprints. Says Barnevik:

> What we try to do is to create a new type of company. We put together a company with a chunk of Scandinavia, Central Europe, America, Italy and the rest of Southern Europe, and created a new company. We have 17 different nationalities in this small building [ABB's headquarters in Oerlikon, Switzerland], mixed teams everywhere. We also have deep roots going back many years in many countries. For example, in Italy we go back to 1898 with

Tecnomasio. We have roots in America from the 1920s, and through the Westinghouse [acquisition] from 1880. We even have companies in the Czech Republic from Napoleonic times. So all these country organizations have long local traditions. They're Finnish or Norwegian or Italian. You can't say that they've become Swiss or Swedish just because you put the headquarters somewhere.

ABB's multidomestic organization aims to reap global benefits of scale and scope while deliberately maintaining strong local and national cultural identities within the countries it operates in. This might appear to be an exceedingly, and perhaps unnecessary complex pursuit, according to pundits who argue that increasing globalization will rapidly erase national differences and significantly homogenize consumer tastes around the world — not just within the more industrialized areas.[5] However, on the opposite side, a number of scholars maintain that there is no evidence that such a global homogenization process is taking place in practice, and that local differences will continue to reaffirm themselves in an increasingly interdependent world economy.[6] In reality, both tendencies might be at work simultaneously. On the one hand, growing government deregulation, increasingly fluid technological environments, and the ever decreasing costs of information and transportation imply that global economies of scale and scope will continue to represent a distinct advantage over national or even regionally oriented companies. On the other, strong cultural, historical and environmental differences among countries will continue to exist during the foreseeable future (paradoxically reinforced in certain cases, as a response to some of these global socio-economic trends), making it necessary for a company to establish deep local roots in the domestic markets. Such seemingly contradictory scenarios appear to underpin ABB's organizational design, as it intends to simultaneously take into account both the differing national contexts in which it does business, and the increasing opportunities for realizing global business advantages. Thus, running such an organization implies putting in place a highly complex structure where local units and national cultural values efficiently co-exist within a global framework. Observes Barnevik:

> So the question was: Can you really run a global multidomestic group and have strong national organizations with national people running it, and still have global overlay, with a global umbrella culture above the Swedish, Italian or American culture in those companies? Can you get the full benefits from being three times as big as anybody else in certain areas, such as transformers, where we have the advantage of 30 companies around the world, billing US$ 1.2 billion? Can you still run them as family companies but have common structure in standardization, global supply, access to the world market, rotation of people and best practice internally? Can you reap this economy of scale, economy of scope, while you have these nationalities?

Thus, paradoxes — in the Gödelian sense — lie at the very heart of the multidomestic company.[7] Opposite forces in the competitive environment constitute the essential mold of such managerial paradoxes: To be simultaneously global and local, not just metaphorically but also in real competitive terms. To combine the agility and local identity of small-sized, domestic competitors in every country it operates in, while at the same time consistently achieve global economies of scale and scope across a number of functional areas. This initial paradox poses a second one at the organizational level, embedded in the need to simultaneously operate within two clearly distinguishable informational contexts. On the one hand, the local context, ABB's multidomestic organizational dimension, is made up of 1,000 separate companies, which are in turn divided into 5,000 profit centers across the different countries it operates in. On the other, the global context, represented by ABB's four business segments — power generation, power transmission and distribution, industrial and building systems and financial services — constitutes the company's world-wide pool of technologically and financially based resources available to the local profit centers. Thus, responding to the contradictory demands of its competitive environment, the need to execute a functioning organizational fabric deeply rooted in both global and local contextual dimensions lies at the heart of ABB's internal paradoxes. Says Barnevik:

> That's where you talk about the contradictions, to be domestic, local, national, yet at the same time to be global. To be small with 5,000 profit centers, each with its own balance sheet, and to be big with respect to finance, research and other resources. You need to retain national identity. You don't want to make Germans out of the Italians, you don't want to make the Germans less formal. Can you still have a global umbrella policy where people pool together, and share group values while deep down they have other values?

Beyond the possible appeal of a multidomestic design, self-referential paradoxes may inevitably arise from an *execution* perspective in a company which intends to be both global and local. Co-ordination flaws, lack of alignment or even open infighting between the different multidomestic organizational dimensions can in practice take the form of downward feedback and control cycles from a global organizational perspective (or upwards from a local one) — closely resembling the "strange loops" found in certain biological systems. In effect, if the global organizational dimension of the company becomes excessively involved in *execution* routines across every local informational context, it will then have to be comprehensively endowed with both "knowledge" and *gnosis* of all its relevant functional, technological, customer base, human resources, national cultural and institutional aspects, and even day-to-day management aspects. As a result, such an organization would become irremediably centralized over time — thus inhibiting *execution* dynamism at the local levels. Conversely, if the *execution* dimensions of every local company or profit center were to comprehensively cover areas such as technology, R&D, product and production allocation, purchasing, and business know-how, then the company as a whole will lose its potential advantages of size, scale economies, standardization and the like. Over time, such a company will resemble a vast collection of independent but highly overlapping businesses, with little global co-ordination and rather simplistic feed-back structures underlying *execution* at the local levels.

Within biological and information systems, paradoxical strange loops arising from seemingly infinite upwards or downwards cycles, are avoided through recursion mechanisms. A recursive pattern closely resembles self-referential paradoxes, except that it continuously re-defines a strange loop in simpler versions of itself.[8] Similarly, at the organizational level, ABB's multidomestic structure is based on a fundamentally recursive response to avoid strange loops in its control and feedback mechanisms, harmonizing *execution* routines from both the local and the global perspectives. The main characteristic of such a response has been the reduction of complex co-ordination functions within a limited number of business areas (BAs) and their corresponding "global managers". In this way, ABB has clearly focused the local and global organizational roles within their respective informational contexts, while at the same time thrusting most of the paradoxical complexity of global co-ordination functions upon a relatively few managers. On the one hand, this ensures that ABB's local companies and profit centers retain structural simplicity and flexibility, developing a high level of *gnosis* of the national contexts they operate in, comparable to any other domestic competitor. Barnevik explains:

> You have to be simple. The person running our standard motors business in Germany doesn't need to be a global giant. He needs to be a good German manager. He doesn't need to know the power plant business. He doesn't need to know South America. But he needs to know the export countries he sends motors to. He needs to know the German market and his German employees, and he needs to know motor technology. But that's what all motor managers have to do, even a family company in Germany has to have that knowledge.

On the other hand, as mentioned, organizational simplicity at the local level implies that the sheer complexity of globally co-ordinating all these highly focused country-based organizations dramatically falls upon the global managers. From an *execution* perspective, this implies that the business areas and global managers have to effectively make practical sense of ABB's global pool of resources, providing every BA with a world-wide strategic sense of direction, timely achieving financial results and profitability targets, monitoring risk management, proposing acquisition, divestment and investment decisions, as well as co-ordinating global R&D, product development, internal and external market allocations and sourcing, internal and between-countries pricing policies, know-how and technology transfer, purchasing, quality and product and manufacturing allocations... This is quite a demanding charter according to any corporate standards. Explains Barnevik:

> At the top it may be complicated. I and my people at the top have to understand the power plant business which involves billion dollar projects running over five years. We have to understand emerging markets build up and industrialized markets. We have to understand the different national cultures that we operate in. But the thousands of managers in Italy, and Mid West America and China, or wherever, they need to know their countries. They're all part of a network, they reap the benefits out of that.

As a result, it is not difficult to see why the ability to identify, recruit, develop and nurture people with the unusual skills and broad cultural understanding required from an ABB global manager becomes one of the paramount challenges to execute in practice the potential benefits underlying the company's global co-ordination structure. These global managers are the key to make such an organization work effectively within a functioning matrix structure, by continuously co-ordinating the multidomestic local organizations with a critical pool of global knowledge and resources. In fact, most of ABB's *execution*-driven advantages could be traced back to the way in which about 500 global managers co-ordinate effectively across over 40 local organizations and 5,000 profit centers with 200,000 employees, across more than 140 countries and counting on only 200-strong staff support in headquarters (see Figure 5.4).[9]

An internal company document, referred to as ABB's "Policy Bible", or ABB's "Book of Values", provides some practical insights into the type of profile and abilities required from the company's global managers. ABB's Book of Values is a widely circulated and exacted text within the company, containing highly pragmatic, down-to-earth guidelines of behavior for its managers across the globe. Regarded as a sort of internal constitution of the company's values, its presence dates back to the very outset of ABB's original merger, when the company's top management — seemingly pervaded by a sense of missionary feeling — introduced it during a large information meeting held in January 1988 in Cannes for 250 ABB key managers. In this and subsequent versions of this document, the characteristics of ABB's global managers are indeed described not only in terms of the wide array of technical knowledge and functional competence required for the job, but also based on what we have referred to as *gnosis*. In effect, although the company has established English as its official language world-wide, and has also instituted common reporting standards and procedures, only a fraction of the company's global managers and employees are likely to have a fluent command of English at any given time — or to feel at ease with all of its standard procedures. In spite of this, ABB's global managers are nevertheless required to co-ordinate global resources across national

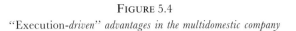

FIGURE 5.4

"Execution-driven" advantages in the multidomestic company

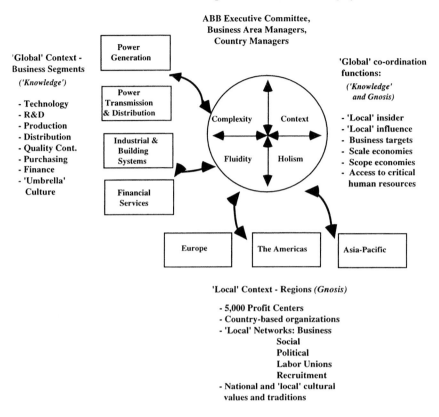

borders, continuously and from day one. Such a complex task visibly demands at every stage of *execution*, a holistic combination of both technical knowledge and *gnosis* of the differing local cultures and environments. Selected excerpts of ABB's Book of Values suggest that this is indeed the case:

- We must eliminate any "us versus them" attitude. There are different ways of achieving results. *What works well in one local and cultural context may not work equally well in another.*

(...)

- We must be aware of the risks of miscommunication and misunderstanding. *English is a foreign language* to a majority of our employees. We therefore need to spend time on communication, repeating key messages and checking that they are understood as intended.

(...)

- With its broad multicultural scope and its complex organization, the Group requires upper-level managers with skills that go *beyond technical competence and managerial efficiency. ABB managers must have an exceptional grasp of differing traditions, cultures, and environments.* They must be effective team players who can bridge contradictions, build mutual support, and achieve consensus.[10]

In addition, as *gnosis* fundamentally relies on experience-based, intuitive mechanisms, ABB's Book of Values correspondingly accords to foster a proactive attitude amongst its global managers, and to continuously stimulate direct international experiences through personnel rotations:

- General Principles of Management Behavior
  1. To take action (and stick out one's neck) and do the right things is obviously the best.
  2. To take action and do the wrong thing is second best (within reason and a limited number of times).
  3. Not to take action (and lose opportunities) is the only non-acceptable behavior.

(...)

- We must speed up the flow of managers across organizational and geographical borderlines. At higher levels horizontal moves should be used to create challenges and opportunities. Only in exceptional cases should transfers be stopped because that person is badly needed where he/she is.[10]

To be endowed with both the technical knowledge and *gnosis* required to work co-operatively across borders, local cultures and country-specific environments, an ABB global manager requires quite exceptional reserves of talent, energy, commitment and determination. These are highly proactive individuals who spend most of their working time on the road, establishing and developing direct relationships with all the relevant local and global company employees at various levels, and unwieldy complex co-ordination functions within close contact with "their" markets anywhere in the world.

Thus, it is — again — the ability to continuously identify and develop a critical number of professionals with such a unique set of *execution skills* and multicultural outlook which largely determines the practical advantages of ABB's functioning multidomestic structure:

> If I needed 5,000 global managers I would give up because there aren't that many around. There are a relatively few people who have the right mix of character, experience, etc. So, if you have an organization which requires too many global managers, it won't work. You can say it's a beautiful concept, but it won't work.

As a result, ABB's functioning global co-ordination structure, based on the unusual *execution skills* of 500 global managers within thirty-seven BAs ensures that the local profit centers and local organizations co-operate and share critical resources across borders, thus generating access to global economies of scale, scope and business knowledge. In addition, the company's small headquarters — radically reduced from 4,000 to 200 in one of Barnevik's first initiatives after becoming ABB's CEO in 1987 — has effectively pushed decentralization over to the 5,000 profit centers which were created after the merger. Each of these centers was in general designed as a relatively small unit, which seldom exceeded 250 employees, following one of Barnevik's "simple" management principles dating back to his early experiences as Executive Vice President at Sandvik AB, a Swedish specialty steel and tools manufacturer. This fabric of small profit centers made it possible to extensively promote a dynamic and responsive working orientation across ABB's local businesses, discouraging bureaucracy and fostering entrepreneurship and customer-oriented attitudes throughout the organization. As a result of these developments, many of the associated benefits of centralized control under a single or a few dominant nationality base, as often found in multinational organizations, have been lost. In effect, when comparing ABB's postmerger organizational characteristics to those of his competitors, Barnevik openly recognizes this feature:

> Now, they [General Electric] have of course advantages by being all Americans, in the top and on the board. They speak the same language, they understand each other, it's easier to avoid misunderstandings, and so on. Siemens in Germany, of course, has the same big advantage. Having the same nationality management all close by in one country, helps.

On the one hand, Barnevik decisively points out that, although more centrally controlled multinational organizations manage to avoid getting by ABB-type of "internal contradictions", they are also lacking in flexibility, dynamism and *gnosis* of the "local" informational contexts of *execution*:

> If you have a centralized organization, the downside is limited to a certain point. You can control the whole business from your head office. But the upside is also limited. A centralized organization creates a big bureaucracy, it's slow, and far from the customers, and they don't understand the national cultures where you have to operate now, such as Asia for example, or Eastern Europe.

On the other hand, effectively generating the benefits associated with a multidomestic structure, requires a constantly functioning and smooth co-ordination between ABB's global and local informational contexts. Therefore, such potential gains need to be put into the perspective of the significant risks, difficulties and complexity of the global managers co-ordination tasks. These significantly depend on their *execution skills* to effectively manage across ABB's multiple organizational dimensions, while keeping an exceedingly thin headquarters base, avoiding duplications across national markets and businesses, and eliminating potential internal competition in overlapping areas. Says Barnevik:

> If this [ABB's] organization is not managed well, then it can be a problem. It can be fragmented. It can be torn by internal rivalry. There can be duplications. It can be difficult to pull together from different countries for a plant, when Siemens has it all in Germany, within the same town. So, if you do this poorly, the company can perform quite poorly. On the other hand, it has an enormous upside.

Undoubtedly, the formal principles underlying a multidomestic structural design carry strategic significance. However, it is apparent that over time, ABB's organizational principles can be applied, adopted, imitated and pursued by watching competitors everywhere. Indeed, whereas the company's structural design has been widely studied by corporations, academicians, management consultants and practitioners around the world, most of its imprints have also been anticipated, or outright implemented, by a handful of internationally oriented companies prior to ABB. However, from a practical perspective a multidomestic structural design is inherently paradoxical, relying on seemingly contradictory aims which can hardly be reconciled based on a purely formal approach. Here, Barnevik hints that the holistic *execution skills* of ABB's global managers to work co-operatively across borders and local cultures, harmonizing complex upwards and downwards organizational loops, are critical to generating the company's practical business advantages. Such skills are notoriously difficult to develop, as they are deeply embedded in both technical competence and first-hand *gnosis* of the company's co-ordination functions across its local informational contexts. However, they are correspondingly hard to formalize, imitate or transfer outside the company's boundaries. Barnevik observes:

> Why did a company like AEG, after 25 years, decline and disappear? That's 160,000 people, a company that was once a pioneer. Dead. Another company, Emerson Electric in America, [by the end of 1995] had grown 48 quarters in a row. Of course, the difference is in *execution*! Often people ask me: "Mr. Barnevik, what is the secret? How could you make the [ABB] merger? How can you create a [global] culture across borders? How do you do that?" And they think there's a hidden strategy that is very intellectually advanced, and sophisticated and impressive, hidden from the outside world. But when you go through it, there's no big secret. There are some basic principles: Trust people. Develop people. Rotate people. That type of thing. There is nothing impressive about that. Nothing to write about. And that is why most management books are worthless. They go to a successful company, interview the successful CEO and write down what he does. But you can't write that down. It's how you behave, how you act, your style, how you communicate, how you reach down to

the grass roots, how you mobilize 25,000 managers. How you do that is difficult to write in a book.

Difficult as it might be to represent in a book, it is nevertheless insightful to portray the way in which internationally oriented companies approach *execution*, and how the continuous implementation of a number of apparently "simple" mechanisms can create lasting practical advantages in the marketplace.

Execution orientation: disentangling a modern management conundrum?

The key dimensions of *execution*: complexity, context, fluidity and holism have been represented so far as a continuum along a pair of complementary opposites, tightly related within an indivisible totality. This stresses the intrinsically holistic nature of *execution*, and herein lies the essence of what could be termed a modern conundrum of management. Whereas it has been shown that — since the late 18th century — successive developments in philosophy, mathematics, psychology, and other related disciplines, have increasingly resulted in holistic solutions to overcome the paradoxical limits of one-sided approaches to *knowability*,[11] the same cannot be confidently said from the perspective of management. Indeed, apart from a few specific areas, an overwhelming one-sided reliance on analytical approaches, technical methods and explicit processes continues to characterize much of management science, to the extent that, within certain academic and management consulting circles these appear to be nearly tantamount to strategic thinking, strategic planning, and even to larger areas of implementation and organization theory. Thus, although evolutionary approaches to the firm, knowledge-based managerial theories and a few areas in organizational behavior have increasingly highlighted the importance of subjective, intuitive, experience-based mechanisms and procedural knowledge in relation to the practical aspects of a firm's performance, such emphasis has been relatively recent. By contrast, vast areas of management science appear to have almost exclusively relied on logical methods and approaches, seemingly embodying an epistemological illusion first ascribed to 19th century science:

> ... the illusion that thought, guided by the thread of causation, might plumb the farthest abysses of being and even *correct* it. This grand metaphysical illusion has become integral to the scientific endeavor and again and again leads science to those far limits of its inquiry where it becomes art — *which, in this mechanism, is what is really intended.*[12]

Although they continue to bizarrely pursue one-sided methods of inquiry, it has been mentioned that the inherent limitations of formal management approaches have not remained unnoticed. Far from it, overly analytical tools, two-dimensional thinking and control-oriented mindsets have been variously described as simplistic, fallacious and even detrimental to manage in the real world.[13] Indeed, such formal approaches implicitly rely on a dualistic rupture of organizational structures into "thinking" and "doer" categories, or between strategic and implementation functions, which has curiously survived the early classical management theorists well into the modern strategic planning approaches. In effect, even those who have criticized analytical, formal and objective approaches as inherently impractical to manage in the real world, have mostly done so from the perspective of reforming the thinking function of the organization.[14] As a result, complex and paradoxical managerial realities are seldom addressed outright from a holistic perspective, but are rather continuously defined away based on different epistemological categories. Not surprisingly, these approaches often fall short of spelling out the *execution* dimensions of management — although recognizing some of its basic imprints from a distinctly one-sided perspective:

> The essential problem in organizations today is a failure to distinguish *planning* from strategizing. Planning is about programming, not discovering. Planning is for technocrats, not dreamers.[15]

> Strategic planning, as it has been practiced, has really been *strategic programming*, the articulation and elaboration of strategies, or visions, that already exist.
>
> (…)
>
> …strategy making is a process interwoven with all that it takes to manage an organization.
>
> (…)
>
> Real strategists get their hands dirty digging for ideas, and real strategies are built from the occasional nuggets they uncover.
>
> (…)
>
> But where in the planning literature is there a shred of evidence that anyone has ever bothered to find out how it is that managers really do make strategies?[16]

If the effectiveness of overly formal management approaches is indeed limited to deal with paradoxical issues in the real world, then this last question points out a potential way out of the conundrum. Although it has in the past been answered from a rather one-sided strategic perspective, in the context of our research we found that considerably more holistic responses seem to be at play within highly successful organizations. Thus, in the face of national cultural-related or similar paradoxical complexities arising in cross-border M&As, JVs and alliances, the question may become even more insightful when directed to identify where a company's practical advantages really lie: Are they a rather isomorphic result of strategy-making, strategizing and the like, or are the dimensions of *execution* significantly more important than previously thought? Indeed, in the cases we examined, a clear *execution orientation* was found underlying a company's transformational responses, intrinsically encompassing a holistic content of both "knowledge" and *gnosis*, of strategic steering and experience based intuition, at every stage.

True, it can be argued that intuition, creativity and synthesis have also in the past been advocated as significant constitutive elements of strategic planning and the like. However, hardly codifiable and formalizable phenomena, as well as the associated paradoxical managerial realities, suggest that it is from the perspective of direct experience and *execution orientation* that a critical totality of strategic and other formal organizational inputs can be holistically embraced — rather than the other way round. In effect, in our research we examined how, in the context of cross-border M&As, JVs and alliances, such a fundamental holistic integration seems to take place through the *execution orientation* of senior executives as well as key operational and line managerial levels within an organization.

Notes and References

[1] See: Lucas, J. R., "Minds, machines and Gödel", *Philosophy*, 36, 1961, p. 112. Also, see: Turing, A. M., "Computing machinery and intelligence", *Mind* LIX (236), 1950.

[2] This topic has been extensively studied in the management literature. It has been suggested that companies behaving as "early movers" — and not the original innovators — are often the ones which thrive from a new significant innovation or technological breakthrough. Thus, if the ability to innovate is what makes any further technical developments possible, what ultimately carries the financial premium usually associated with such innovations, is the ability to rapidly create commercially viable products based on reliable production and distribution systems around a new technology or business concept. Amongst the classic examples of early movers taking full advantage of other company's initial innovations, one could include: Microsoft's dominance of the PC operating systems market (and perhaps also the Internet navigator market), as well as an array of consumer electronics and other similar products successfully developed and marketed by Japanese companies around technological breakthroughs initially created elsewhere. See: Nonaka, I. "A dynamic theory of organizational knowledge creation", *Organization Science*, 1, pp. 14-37; Reich, R. B. and E. D. Mankin. "Joint ventures with Japan give away our future", *Harvard Business Review*, March-April, 1986, pp. 78-86.

[3] Morosini, P. and H. Singh. "Post-cross-border acquisitions: implementing 'national culture compatible' strategies to improve performance", *European Management Journal*, 12(4), December 1994, pp. 390-400; Datta, D. K. "Organizational fit and acquisition performance: effects of post-acquisition integration", *Strategic Management Journal*, 12, 1991, pp. 281-297; Achtmeyer, W. and M. Daniell. "How advanced planning widens acquisition rewards", *Mergers and Acquisitions*, 23(1), 1988, pp. 37-42; Rappaport, A. "Strategic analysis for more profitable acquisitions", *Harvard Business Review*, 57, 1979, pp. 99-110.

[4] Kogut, B. and U. Zander. "What firms do? Coordination, identity and learning", *Organization Science*, in press.

[5] See, for example: Levitt, T. "The globalization of markets", in *International Business Classics*, Lexington, Toronto, 1988; Ohmae, K. "The global logic of strategic alliances", *Harvard Business Review*, March-April, 1989, pp. 143-155.

[6] See: G. S. Kindra (ed.), *Marketing in Developing Countries* (foreword by P. Kotler), Croom Helm, London, 1984; Wind, Y. in V. Mahajan and Y. Wind (eds), *Innovation Diffusion Models of New Product Acceptance*, Cambridge, MA, Ballinger, 1986; Kotler, P., D. H. Haider and I. Rein. *Marketing Places: Attracting Investment Industry and Tourism to Cities, States and Nations*, The Free Press, New York, 1993.

[7] The paradoxical characteristics of the multidomestic company have been highlighted before. See: Handy, C. "Balancing corporate power: a new federalist paper", in *Managerial Excellence. McKinsey Award winners from the Harvard Business Review (1980-1994)*, Boston, Harvard Business School Press, 1996; Also see: Ghoshal, S. and C. A. Bartlett. "Changing the role of top management: beyond structure to processes", *Harvard Business Review*, January-February, 1995, p. 86.

[8] Hofstadter, D. R. *Op. cit.*, 1989, p. 127.

[9] 1995 figures from ABB's internal sources.

[10] Morcos, R. "Percy Barnevik and ABB", case study 05/94-4308, INSEAD, Fontainebleau, 1994. Italics have been included by the author.

[11] As previously indicated, this essential quest presents much older antecedents. In effect, it is hard not to see the ancient philosophical parallels to the modern holistic approaches to *knowability*. In ancient Greece and Rome, the Stoic school of philosophy maintained the organic quality of the universe, based on the "life-giving tension" of complementary pairs of opposites (*tonos*). Similar notions were developed within Taoism, in the 5th century BC, where the common principle underlying all natural processes was based on the interaction between the opposite *yin* (feminine) and *yang* (masculine) energy. Also, the ancient Greek tragedy was seen by Nietzsche as a reconciliatory ritual between man's "rational" Apollonian spirit and Dyonisiac "instincts".

[12] Nietzsche, F. *The Birth of Tragedy and The Genealogy of Morals*, Anchor Books, New York, 1956, p. 93.

[13] Mintzberg, H. "The fall and rise of strategic planning", *Harvard Business Review*, January-February 1994, pp. 107-114; Porter, M. E. "The state of strategic thinking", *The Economist*, 23 May, 1987, p. 21; Lane, H. W. and P. Beamish. "Cross-cultural cooperative behavior in joint ventures in LDCs", *Management International Review*, Special Issue, 1990, pp. 87-102; Barkema, H. G., J. Bell and J. M. Pennings. "Foreign entry, cultural barriers and learning", working paper, Management Department, The Wharton School, University of Pennsylvania, Philadelphia, December 1993.

[14] Schon, D. *Reflective Practitioner*, Basic Books, New York, 1983; Mintzberg, H. *Op. cit.*, 1994.

[15] Hamel, G. "Strategy as revolution", *Harvard Business Review*, July-August, 1996, p. 71.

[16] Mintzberg, H. *Op. cit.*, 1994, pp. 107, 114, 111 and 110, respectively.

CHAPTER 6

Execution Orientation to Handle National Cultural Differences in Global M&As, JVs and Alliances

> Generals-in-chief must be guided by their own experience or their genius. Tactics, evolutions, the duties and knowledge of an engineer or an artillery officer may be learned in treatises, but the science of strategy is only to be acquired by experience, and by studying the campaigns of all the great captains.
>
> Napoleon Bonaparte

A number of authors have in the past sought to classify internationally oriented companies based on various attributes such as their organizational characteristics, operational structure and strategic design. The resulting categories, ranging from "transnational" to "multifocal" and the like, often emphasize underlying structural factors, such as configuration of assets, relative international presence, the nominal role of the overseas operations, formal mechanisms of knowledge creation and diffusion inside the organization, and even the number of different nationalities to be found in a company's key managerial ranks.[1]

Although insightful, these categorizations are largely based on organizational design and formal attributes. As a result, they often fall short of identifying the specific factors leading to an organization's practical advantages internationally, how these factors can be developed and nurtured, and how they evolve over time *vis-à-vis* the competitive environment. After all, internationally oriented companies competing in the same industries, sharing fundamental strategic aims and presenting highly similar organizational characteristics and archetypal structural designs can consistently show vastly different performances in the management of their cross-border operations. In this context, it is difficult to point out an area where such contrasting experiences present themselves more dramatically than in the way internationally oriented companies conduct their cross-border M&A, JV and alliance activities. Although managing major domestic M&As, JVs and alliances is often an extremely hard test for any organization, whenever these activities involve dealing with foreign and significantly different deep-rooted cultural values and environments, a company's overall practical abilities or shortcomings in mobilizing and co-ordinating key resources across borders are invariably exposed. Thus, abundant anecdotal evidence illustrating failed cross-border M&A, JV and alliance efforts has often emphasized the national cultural risks and culture-related barriers involved in such international transactions, particularly within highly different or distant national cultural environments.

However, it could be argued that a critical test of a truly globally managed company might reside in its ability to generate specific and lasting competitive advantages across the local marketplaces and differing national cultures, through the effective and *practical co-ordination* of a world-wide pool of critical resources. In particular, when a company's international growth and expansion modes include cross-border M&As, JVs and alliances, as seems to be increasingly the case, national cultural issues are likely to be further complicated by the diverse corporate cultures and strong sensitivities which usually arise during the integration phase. The consistent ability to manage and co-ordinate resources effectively in these demanding situations is often more revealing of an internationally oriented company's practical competitive advantages than any organizational archetypes it may have chosen to present to the external world. Thus, generating sustainable advantages based on the *practical ability* to establish and run a functioning world-wide co-ordination appears to set apart an organization that truly manages resources globally from one that largely acts as a collection of international companies or subsidiaries, operating under a certain business logic within a single legal entity or ownership structure. Describing the particular organization which was built after the 1987 cross-border merger between ASEA and Brown Boveri, in the electrical engineering industry, Barnevik remarks:

> You can say companies like Nestlé are very domestic, although the largest part of their revenues takes place outside Switzerland. They have an Italian ice cream company for Italy, and local brand names in different countries. So that's one type of multinational business with a relatively limited global structure. Now ABB builds power plants in Asia with ABB companies participating from Europe and America working cross-borders. We have almost half of our invoices going between companies in the group. So this is a global network. You can't compare it to Nestlé or some of these other multinationals.

ABB is indeed a case in point to illustrate the conspicuous difference that exists between a company's rational choice of an external organizational archetype and its actual ability to generate competitive advantages based on continuous co-ordination of a global constellation of resources, including M&As, JVs and alliances. In fact, following what at the time was regarded as the largest cross-border merger that the business world had seen, ABB's multidomestic matrix structure was identified as a distinct source of competitive advantage. However, the supposedly unique multidomestic and federation type of organizational principles championed by ABB had been pioneered many decades ago by companies such as Royal Dutch Shell and Cable & Wireless. Such structural designs were often pursued with the aim of creating highly de-centralized, flexible and relatively autonomous national subsidiaries, in contrast with the rigidity associated with more globally centralized organizations. Companies such as IBM, General Electric, Johnson & Johnson and Coca Cola in the USA, Grand Met, Ciba Geigy and British Petroleum in Europe, as well as Sony and Honda in Japan, have at different times attempted to approach a federation type of structure with increasing interest.[2] Recognizing this, Barnevik observes that the basic organizational principles underlying a multidomestic design have been extensively studied and pursued by a number of industrialists, including some of ABB's closest competitors:

> If you read his [Jack Welch, CEO of General Electric] annual report you can see that we have the same ideas. We want to build around the world. We want to be borderless. We want to encourage initiative. Break down the barriers, make the business more entrepreneurial. A number of companies are moving in this direction. It's not something that is patented in any way.

Thus, it is maintained that a multidomestic organizational design, based on such well-understood and sought after conceptual principles, may not be what actually makes a practical difference in global performance over time. Instead, some of the unique advantages of a truly globally managed company seem to be grounded in its *practical ability* to make such an organization work across national borders and different cultures, overcoming its internal contradictions, organizational risks and operational complexities. Barnevik remarks:

> Now of course many people say it is impossible. Can you have so many profit centers? Can you control all these national organizations? Don't you fight internally? Don't you get lots of duplications with all these companies, trying to do the same thing, running into each other? How can you achieve economies of scale with so many units? The art is not in the concept because if you could write down how to do all that in three pages, then anyone could do it. *The thing lies in **execution**.* Implementation. Actually doing it. Not getting stuck.

The international experience of companies such as ABB also evidence how the vague and negative references often associated with cultural risks or national cultural distance in most cases ought to be balanced with the degree to which a company demonstrates specific *execution skills*, managerial willingness and determination when handling such issues in practice. National culture and other related complexities usually are found in varying degrees when companies operate abroad in the context of major M&As, JVs and alliances. Nevertheless, too often in the past the lack of *execution skills* to handle such complications, or plainly lousy management, have been indiscriminately mixed with arguments which emphasized supposedly insurmountable cultural complications and national cultural barriers. Such a tendency has been noted not only in the USA and Europe, but also in Japan and other countries which have witnessed a significant increase in the level of cross-border M&A, JV and alliance activity. Supporting this, Masaru Yoshitomi, Vice-Chairman at The Long-Term Credit Bank of Japan, and one of the country's leading experts in foreign direct investment, has observed that:

> ...the most popular explanation (or excuse) for the bitter experience [of Japanese multinationals] in the United States or Europe, is that, after all, national cultural distance is too large and too costly to compensate [based on] the growth of the acquired firms.

Moreover, in this area it has been suggested that managers consistently favoring expansion into locations that are culturally close to their own may often be inclined to follow strategies that are to their own benefit rather than in the interest of shareholders, independently of whether they enhance company performance or not.[3] These might be particularly relevant observations on the eve of the 21st century, when increasing globalization trends create unprecedented business opportunities for internationally oriented companies, often in so-called emerging economies which are seldom familiar to industrialized countries from a cultural standpoint. Here, it is the *execution skills* required to co-ordinate globally across local borders and national cultures which are ultimately seen as creating lasting practical advantages. Explaining ABB's pioneering entry into Eastern Europe following the fall of the Berlin Wall, Barnevik remarks:

> Cultural distance is not relevant for us. We have factories in more than 100 countries. It is not a matter of: Is the culture right for us in Romania? Any culture is right for us! But that's not saying that you underestimate difficulties with the national cultures. Is this an issue of evaluating a foreign culture in our case? No. This is a question of: How do you turn around that company in Ukraine? How do you make an ABB company in five years, with our values, a full member of the family, with the accounting, quality and all the ideas we have regarding success in business? People who from the start don't speak much English, don't understand pricing, a market economy, or how to motivate others.

Thus, it is maintained that specific *execution skills* such as these are, in practice, at the very heart of ABB's competitive edge. These enable the company to turn the seemingly insurmountable contradictions of a multidomestic organization into practical advantages stemming from global co-ordination functions across borders and national cultures. These co-ordination capabilities are considerably difficult for competitors to copy, because they are embedded in common behavior, organizational routines and repertoires, and deep *gnosis* of the local informational contexts. Says Barnevik:

> The big advantage is, of course, a powerful, cost-competitive Group, with economies of scale, combined with local people in each country who know their customers. If you can create that type of organization, then you are a winner and nobody can catch up with you. You have an organizational edge, an advantage that is very, very difficult to copy. It takes decades. Technology flows around faster and faster and is easy to copy. Methods, processes are more difficult because they take longer time to copy. If the Japanese can make a car in nine hours it is difficult to copy. Likewise, organization, structure, values are all extremely difficult things to copy.

Because they continue to be increasingly used by internationally oriented companies as key mechanisms to compete on a global scale, the *execution skills* required to integrate and co-ordinate cross-border M&As, JVs and alliances into an organization's world-wide constellation of resources are seen as critical advantages in major industries. In the case of ABB, the company was built through a cross-border merger leading to one of the world's largest electrical engineering groups. Shortly after this merger, the company's *execution skills* to turn around acquisitions allowed it to swiftly expand its multidomestic organization at a rate which exceeded one acquisition per month. These included both large acquisitions in industrialized markets, such as US-based Combustion Engineering, as well as a myriad of small-sized, pioneering transactions across the Eastern European countries and other transitional economies. The speed at which these companies have been integrated within ABB's co-ordination structure, as multidomestic units in their own right, uniquely characterizes the company's practical global advantages. Barnevik observes:

> We acquired Combustion Engineering in America [in 1988], the biggest boiler company in the world. We also acquired part of Westinghouse and a number of other American companies. Then we moved into Eastern Europe and Russia, where we now [at the end of 1995] have 60 companies. And then we bought a lot out in Asia. Overall, we have bought 160 companies, including the smaller ones. No company or very, very few companies in our size category, has anything resembling this type of background.

In the pharmaceuticals industry, where the global nature of the demand and the increasing scale of R&D investments required to produce new drugs have been driving an unprecedented surge in major cross-border M&A, JV and alliance activity since the late 1980s, an annual report published by the Swedish-Italian Pharmacia group in 1994 candidly stated that " . . . there are three key areas that are important to managing in a changing environment: expertise, new products and an *ability* to restructure."[4] And shortly after Pharmacia merged with US-based Upjohn in November 1995, creating the world's fifth largest pharmaceutical company at that time, the next annual report restated the key importance of swiftly integrating acquisitions and alliances into the company's global resources: " ... [our] strategy relies on the following points: leveraging our already strong position in key therapeutic areas and building and focusing our R&D efforts around them; taking full advantage of developed and developing markets all over the world; and *making acquisitions or entering strategic partnerships to complement internal growth.*"[4] Jan Ekberg, Board Member of Pharmacia & Upjohn stresses that the *practical ability* and *execution skills* which are critical to successfully integrating these cross-border acquisitions and alliances constitute an important competitive advantage *vis-à-vis* a company's stated strategic aims:

> You say that about 50 percent of acquisitions fail. But I think that in the case of cross-border acquisitions the percentage of failure is higher: In our experience, maybe as much as two thirds of them fail. Do you know what is the main reason behind these failures? I wouldn't say that it's something to do with the [pre-acquisition] analyses or the [strategic] fit, or anything of that sort. It's how to handle the merger or acquisition, How to implement it: That is where most of these transactions fail. Take Ciba Geigy. They are still Ciba and Geigy, and that is a problem of managerial skill: How to make the merger, how to run the processes, how to make people come together after the merger.

The acquisitive Korea-based Daewoo group provides another example supporting the notion that *execution skills* are in practice what ultimately makes or breaks a merger, acquisition or alliance, particularly those taking place in different or relatively unfamiliar national cultural environments. Daewoo's highly successful turnaround of major acquisitions in Eastern Europe started right after the fall of the Berlin Wall in 1989, as well as the group's pioneering establishment of joint ventures in Vietnam, North Korea and other "emerging" economies in the Far East during approximately the same time period. President and CEO Byung-Ho Kang observes:

> Companies from Europe or the United States often find that implementing cross-border mergers or acquisitions is very difficult, especially within the so called emerging economies. But in our experience, it is possible to turn around acquisitions in emerging markets in a short period of time. However, most companies find this quite hard to do, and failure rates across these cross-border acquisitions are therefore very high, for example in Eastern Europe or across the socialist countries of the Far East. But of course, it is not only Korean companies that can turn around these acquisitions, although some of them can do much better than others. What plays an important role in the end is the ability to carry out the practical things, such as rotating people or implementing the working methods and procedures. How you do all this is crucial to performance.

To say that most M&As, particularly across borders, fail in the execution stages of implementation, often due to cultural and organizational barriers, is not a new observation. On the contrary, this has often been highlighted in the specialized literature.[5] However, it is surprising that although the importance of the practical aspects of managing M&As has been widely recognized in the past, relatively little attention has been given to the *execution skills* which appear to be so critical to make these transactions work in practice. Our research findings suggest that, even if some of the basic principles underlying the successful implementation of cross-border M&As might be far from new or unfamiliar to managers of internationally oriented companies at large, these nevertheless appear to be extremely difficult to apply in practice, partly as a result of the day-to-day difficulties of managing diverse people within different national cultural environments. It has been indeed argued that this is one of the chief reasons why superior *execution skills* can become a source of lasting practical advantages over competitors. A strikingly similar observation can be made of cross-border JVs and alliances, where the failure rates appear to be even higher than those commonly associated with acquisitions.[6]

In the cases utilized to illustrate these notions within the context of our research, it is not always easy to draw a clear line showing where tribal resistance grounded on national cultural differences end, and where the sheer individual- or group-based interests start. Similarly, although they have been shown to be markedly different,[7] it is sometimes difficult to point out a sharp divider between national or corporate cultural aspects in the face of the mutually reinforcing deep-rooted resistance against radical company transformations that may arise in the context of cross-border M&As, JVs or alliances. Based on the experiences of companies such as ABB, British Airways, Credit Suisse, Daewoo, Deutsche Bank or Sony, national and corporate cultural resistances to international M&A or alliances are in certain cases found to closely strengthen each other through *anchoring* mechanisms, involving a complex and not always foreseeable web of personal, group and institution-based manifestations, both inside and outside company boundaries. These may range from labor organizations, to political parties, regional authorities, official regulatory bodies and internal company employees.

However, in spite of these types of difficulties, a number of companies have expanded globally through M&As, JVs and alliances carried out within a remarkably short time period and across highly diverse national cultural environments. In certain cases, companies like ABB or Daewoo have extensively acquired in locations where national cultural diversity was mixed with a little previous exposure to basic capitalist practices or Western ways of working, such as the former European communist regimes or the ex-Soviet Republics. Across these situations, specific *execution skills* have been important factors for these companies to manage such deep-rooted resistances, in certain cases turning national cultural difficulties into concrete business advantages.

Identifying *execution skills* as a key factor to effectively handle national cultural issues and resistances that often arise in a cross-border M&A, JV or alliance, inevitably raises the attention to the experience, character and personal abilities of a company's leaders and key managerial levels, as well as its corporate history and cumulative experiences over time. Moreover, a country's history and industrial development may also contribute to shape the cultural openness and cosmopolitan orientation of its people, which has been cited as an important element to effectively carry out business activities across highly diverse national cultural environments. Although these factors have been researched in the past, the emphasis has often been on exploring how they influence a company's corporate culture, management style or strategic vision, rather than in relation to how these may influence the development of a company's *execution skills*, or people's openness to work co-operatively across national cultural differences.

Executives Focused on *Execution*

The concept that corporate leaders often shape a company's culture, management style, strategy, and overall historic developments, has been widely studied in management theory.[8] The notion that a company can distinguish itself from its competitors based on its *practical ability* and *execution skills* to consistently managing complex situations effectively across national cultures, arguably stems from the very top of an organization, firmly embedded in the personal character, subjective experiences and overall abilities of its leaders over time.

Some authors have in the past highlighted a "bias for action" underlying the excellence of certain companies, arguably demonstrated by their degree of "organizational fluidity" when carrying out task-force and project- team work, and their willingness to experience first as opposed to emphasizing bureaucratic and over-analytical processes.[9] Although this remains an insightful approach, a certain tendency to favor managerial action *per se* can be detected in this literature. By contrast, in our study we have continuously corroborated the sharp *execution orientation* of corporate leaders in many multinational companies. Contrary to the largely detached and strategically focused image which is sometimes associated with senior managers and corporate leaders,[10] the executives we approached in our research often exemplified a critical mix of sound strategic thinking *and* a nearly obsessive and direct involvement in the implementation of major corporate efforts such as global M&As, JVs and alliances. Throughout our study we thus found innumerable instances illustrating these corporate leaders' *execution orientation* and hands-on dedication to bring key people together across borders and national cultures, from the top management through to the grass-roots of the organization, in order to implant critical global co-ordination functions through strenuous direct involvement, highly effective communications and personal example.

Is this a case of systematically overlooking or underestimating the visionary, strategic or analytical aspects of management? On the contrary, the executives we interviewed as part of our research in many cases preside over outstanding companies, with performance and managerial qualities that have been recognized and even proposed as models by strategy researchers, management thinkers and the specialized media alike. Rather, *execution orientation* highlights a particular combination of strategic vision, leadership, communication and overall execution which — albeit fairly diverse elements in strategy, style, corporate values and competitive environments — we have found as a common thread throughout our study. In the context of a major cross-border merger such as ABB, Barnevik has summarized the inherent challenges that this holistic combination presents:

> A key concern for me is, how do you reach deep down with communication and establish two-way communication? *I used to say that five or ten percent of management is strategic thinking, ninety to ninety-five percent is execution*. A large part of execution is communication, motivating people and making them "buy in", be committed. In our case we must communicate with 25,000 managers, who in turn must communicate with everybody else in the organization. That is a gigantic task. In doing so, we always cheat ourselves at the top. We think that we have made a revolution, certain memos have gone out, a re-organization has taken place. But we have only touched the surface of this gigantic organization. Lots of people haven't even heard about our plan of action; they don't care about it; they don't understand it. So the magnitude of reaching down, communicating, converting, influencing people is enormous. One has to be humble when confronted with that task.[11]

These leaders' distinct, hands-on *execution orientation*, and the keen emphasis put on fast, continuous and effective communication from the top management through to the bottom of the organization, is ceaselessly remarked in the context of major cross-border M&As and alliances. British Airways leaders' *execution orientation* extends to both building living corporate values through continuous communication, as well as the daily management of operations — including the practical integration of the company's major network of international alliances and commercial partnerships. Sir Colin Marshall, a former Chief Executive and subsequently the company's Chairman, is described by his close associates as a leader sharply centered upon execution — on "getting the job done" — with a working approach characterized by a nearly obsessive focus on customer service and a tremendous grasp of detail. Whereas a number of analysts have in the past pompously described Sir Colin Marshall's decisive tenure as CEO (from 1985 to 1995), as British Airways' "era of global expansion", he unassumingly refers to it as "the era of the customer, the period when the company rediscovered customer service". Such a direct, open, no-nonsense and down-to-earth management style has come to characterize British Airways' leadership. Says Marshall:

> Regarding leading and communicating with people, we have a commonly accepted mission and goals, which we continuously share with every one of our employees, including some of our operations with our international partners. In order to ensure this happens, Bob Ayling [British Airways' CEO] involves himself personally through all these aspects of communications. (...) Then, there is our global co-ordination of resources and operations, which takes place within our Executive Committee. All our Regional Directors periodically present their business cases in order to request aircraft, crew levels and other resources inside this Committee, which allocates them based on the business merits of each proposal. Bob Ayling is himself routinely involved in these decisions and leads the Committee, which shows better than anything the hands-on management style of this company, and the practical importance we place on international co-ordination of operations.

In the case of Daewoo's acquisitive spree in Eastern Europe right after the fall of the Berlin Wall in 1989, Kim Woo-Choong, the group's founder and Chairman, took a decidedly hands-on, executive role to personally lead the restructuring and integration of such acquisitions, ranging from automotive factories in Romania, Poland and the Czech Republic, to shipbuilding wharves in Romania and bearing production plants in Hungary. During the early 1990s, he decided to move permanently to Eastern Europe to personally oversee and get involved in the massive efforts which were required to revamp entire industrial sectors in these previously communist regimes that had frightened off most Western investors at the time. Thus, based on the results it has obtained so far, it is difficult to ignore that a significant element leading to Daewoo's swift and large-scale turnaround of its Eastern European acquisitions has been their leaders' *execution orientation* and hands-on direct involvement. By 1996, these managerial skills had helped to transform the group into a sizable producer of cars, automotive parts, electronic home appliances, ball bearings and ships, in a region adjacent to the European Union markets. Following in Kim's footsteps, a sharp *execution orientation* can also be found in the leaders of all the other major parts of Daewoo's industrial conglomerate. Kang remarks:

> Our company founder and Chairman, Mr. Kim, at present [during mid 1996] spends most of his time in Poland and other Central European countries, where he is directly involved in the restructuring of our acquisitions. Mr. Kim is reorganizing entire industries in some of these countries, for example the automotive industry, or Romania's shipbuilding industry, where he is carrying out a major restructuring job similar to the one he implemented here in our [Korea's] ship-building industry several years ago. In all these cases, Mr. Kim is directly involved, for example in managing the outsourcing activities, or re-educating and training our Central and Eastern European employees. He understands their industries very well, and believe it or not, he is almost twenty four hours working, although we can reach him almost any time. Likewise, as CEO of Daewoo's Trading Division I like to personally visit all of our offices, at least once a year. It's very demanding, but if I meet my local managers personally it makes it much easier for us to communicate in the future.

Gnosis and Direct Experience Underlying the *Execution Orientation* of Company Leaders

In our research, we found further illustration of how these leaders' clear *execution orientation* goes together with a detailed, down-to-earth knowledge of their industries, a first-hand exposure to different national cultures and environments, and an ability to pragmatically adapt common managerial principles to their company's specific circumstances. Hence, these leaders' *execution skills* are deeply grounded in a series of direct experiences, in many cases leading to a nearly obsessive focus on key business principles dating back to their very early professional activities. The intimate degree of cognitive familiarity which is achieved through such a continuous *execution orientation* and subjective experiences is thus akin to the previously described notion of *gnosis*. In the remainder of this section, we provide some illustration of how the interplay between a leader's raw personal qualities and formative corporate experiences can lead to their peculiar *execution-oriented* leadership imprints.

In the case of Percy Barnevik, there has been so much written about his leadership traits in the business media and specialized literature, that by the mid 1990s this corporate leader had become something akin to a business icon, some sort of management superstar. Nevertheless, for all the myth built around his personality, Barnevik comes across as an austere, no-nonsense, and down-to-earth individual, not inclined to hyperbole, but sharply focused on carrying out what he sees as his corporate mission. An articulated, passionate and effective speaker, given to relentlessly persuade, motivate and intimidate others, Barnevik is described by his ABB colleagues as an intellectually bright, impatient and restless person. During the 1975-1979 period, as President of Sandvik in the USA, Barnevik started to apply a number of basic management principles with a skill that would make him a legendary business leader a few years later. Through steady dedication, sound strategic thinking and a passion for *execution*, for carrying out and acting upon decisions, he managed to rationalize Sandvik's US business, and to triple sales to US$ 250 million, against seasoned competitors such as General Electric and US Steel. He thus became a good illustration of a basic management principle inserted in ABB's Book of Values, establishing that: "Taking action and do a reasonable amount of mistakes it's good enough—but not to take action is the only non-acceptable behavior". Barnevik considers these experiences, as well as those stemming from his subsequent dramatic turnaround of ASEA, as consolidating his *execution orientation* and forming the particular organizational *execution skills* which would allow him to face the challenges involved in building ABB in 1987:

> I did the same thing in Sandvik twenty-five years ago, I did the same thing in ASEA when I came there. I did the same thing in Finland, and with

Combustion Engineering when we got them in. I did the same thing with Brown Boveri when they joined. So I've done it many times, you know, in a bigger and bigger scale. So it's not that I'm experimenting. I see that it works. But of course, it becomes more complex and bigger and bigger every time. I've been twenty-five years in the business of implementing this type of global, decentralized matrix structure around the world. And in the end it comes down to communication, dedication, having the right people.

Barnevik likes to point out that his obsession with execution and decentralization can be traced back to his family printing business in Simrishamn (Southern Sweden), where he had a first-hand experience of the benefits of the entrepreneurship, responsiveness and concreteness associated with well-run small companies. Many years later, he would describe his own corporate career as a continuous effort to implant these kind of family business, decentralized and entrepreneurial spirit, inside large corporations. At ABB, Barnevik has managed to turn around a sizable industrial group through large-scale rationalization, global co-ordination, productivity increases, technology enhancements and cross-border M&As, JVs and alliances. As a result, only seven years after the cross-border merger that created it, ABB revenues more than tripled to reach US$ 33.7 billion in 1995, with the company's stock capitalization multiplying in excess of twenty times. Through this highly successful corporate transformation, ABB's leaders have crafted a multidomestic organizational fabric, combining strong local identities and national cultures with the ability to perform critical global co-ordination functions in practice. Thus, ABB's organizational design has become a widely studied model, its structural principles being pursued by many internationally oriented companies. Paradoxically, although management writers, researchers and consultants often highlight the strategic and conceptual merits of such an organization, Barnevik himself has consistently stressed the importance of *execution orientation* and *execution skills* to build the practical advantages associated with a multidomestic design. Accordingly, his working style has been consistently characterized by his colleagues, clients and close competitors, as extremely hands-on, with an astonishing capability to endure exceedingly long working hours and punishing schedules. This demanding working style was indeed cited as a factor, when in October 1996 it was announced that Barnevik was to step down as ABB's CEO, to become the company's Group Chairman. However, more importantly, this event highlighted a key characteristic of an *execution-oriented* company, that it can live after its leaders — even one as influential as Barnevik — have concluded their executive roles.

In the commercial air transportation business, Sir Colin Marshall's international outlook and career-long obsession with customer service started with his very first working experience during the early 1950s, in war-torn Britain. As a cadet purser on the former Orient Line, then a primary shipping transport for British immigrants to Australia, he still recalls that the voyage from

Tilbury docks took about six weeks, with "much potential for friction and general dissatisfaction between passengers and crew". After he and other perceptive crew members implanted a few, very basic service improvements, the passengers were generally satisfied and led relatively peaceful and "mostly hassle-free shipboard lives". However, it was a few years later, as a junior management trainee with Hertz (the car rental corporation) in Chicago, that these rudimentary customer service ideas were firmly shaped into the corner-stone of Marshall's future business strategy and execution:

> It is now no big deal for those of us who travel frequently to the USA, but I was mightily impressed by the fact that [even in a relatively humble restaurant] the coffee came, unsolicited, like magic, the instant I sat down — and my cup was replenished automatically, thereafter. For somebody used to poor old-war Britain, this was rocket science, in terms of customer service. So, too, were incredible things like valet parking, supermarket bag packing and "flub stubs" which guaranteed no-quibble refunds if the product or service was argu-ably not up to scratch. These acts of seeming kindness did not, of course, just happen as nice things to do. They evolved from fierce competition to serve a demanding public. It was a grounding in the tough consumerism of North America which shaped my business philosophy, placing marketing and good customer practice in pole position for the race towards success. I had never come across a more discerning set of consumers than those you find in the malls, main streets, and in my case, the car rental counter of America.

Through constant and practical application of this customer service philo-sophy, Marshall rose through the ranks to become a Hertz Senior Executive. Later, in 1982 he returned to Europe to become the deputy Chief Executive of Sears, the British retailer. In 1985 he was appointed by Lord King as Chief Executive of British Airways, then a rather "moribund, over-manned and de-motivated state-owned airline corporation". Formed in 1972 after the merger between two public and unprofitable carriers — British Overseas Airways Corporation (BOAC) and British European Airways (BEA) — the new com-pany had from the start a rather complicated integration experience, with powerful unions contesting every serious attempt to restructure the organiza-tion. During the mid 1980s, under a radically new framework of labor rela-tions, Marshall undertook a vast turnaround of British Airways' operations, cutting down 20,000 employees, divesting non-core operations, and drama-tically focusing all employees' efforts on a commitment to customer service. In effect, one of his first actions, was to create a marketing department and institute regular customer service courses for every employee, regardless of whether he/she had direct client contact or not. As a result, Marshall was able to model a profitable company by releasing a relentless customer service culture upon its employees. The way he did that was based on relatively simple managerial principles executed with great skill and determination:

> The "customer first" concept sounds pretty obvious, doesn't it? And these days (...) it might seem naive to go on about it. But how few British companies thought that way, back in the '50s and '60s? And how many operate to that first, golden rule of marketing today? (...) When asked, I have often explained that the task of turning British Airways round, was something like an archaeological dig. Once the dust and debris of ages had been carefully brushed away, we uncovered the jewels. The brightest of them was the people of British Airways. They were, by and large, highly professional, well-skilled and knew instinctively that they were capable of being the best in their industry. What they lacked were the right tools, the right motivation and the right leadership. In short, they wanted an environment in which their skills and experience could be let loose to respond to their customers, rather than remain constrained and frustrated.

In carrying out this corporate transformation, Marshall's *execution orientation* was proverbial amongst British Airways staff. During his tenure as CEO, he is remembered as constantly going down to "talk to the troops" at dawn in Heathrow airport, bringing together and encouraging employees, following every development with a steely attention to detail. In later years, Marshall coined the term market-oriented company, to synthesize his vision of an externally focused company, dynamically committed to serve and satisfy customers in an entrepreneurial and innovative way. Marshall observes that a key characteristic of a market-oriented company is thus ingrained in a distinct execution-orientation, as well as in the management's personal involvement and commitment to customer service, as opposed to ritualistic marketing practices:

> ... in other words, there is no point in buying the most expensive pair of trainers if you are not an active sports person.

In the case of Pharmacia & Upjohn, a good deal of Jan Ekberg's skills in turning around cross-border acquisitions seem to have been sharpened in Sweden's domestic pharmaceutical industry. When he took over KabiVitrum in 1985, it was a Stockholm-based pharmaceutical company fully owned by Procordia (then a Swedish state-owned holding company) facing substantial losses, with a very small turnover largely concentrated in the Nordic area, and only about 200 researchers. A highly unlikely basis to build a leading global concern. Nevertheless, in five years Ekberg made a remarkable turnaround of the company, to the point that, in 1990, it took over Pharmacia, another Swedish pharmaceutical company based in Uppsala with Volvo as its major shareholder. Through a complex deal in which Volvo received Procordia shares as payment, KabiVitrum became Kabi-Pharmacia, and both companies started a most forceful integration process. Ekberg recalls:

The merger was very violent and the people in Uppsala [Pharmacia] felt raped by the people in Stockholm [KabiVitrum], because Pharmacia was the "beautiful", "successful" and "star" company here in Sweden, whereas Kabi was the "state-owned", "grey" and smaller company. Initially, Pharmacia and Astra were the star pharmaceutical companies in Sweden. But then in 1990 this small company, Kabi, took over Pharmacia, which was more or less interpreted as a disaster for the target company's employees. We started this merger in 1990, and by 1991 we could say that we had successfully implemented it. But it was a very, very difficult process, and we made all the mistakes you could imagine.

In 1992, the battle scars from the Pharmacia merger still recent, Ekberg went on to build Kabi-Pharmacia from a Nordic leader into a major European player, by acquiring Farmitalia-Carlo Erba in Italy (FICE), a company which also was the product of a domestic merger. As described in detail in Chapter 8, it is curiously pointed out that, although prior to this acquisition, the national cultural differences between Sweden and Italy were perceived as being a significant issue, the lessons learned in the Kabi-Pharmacia merger made this cross-border effort comparatively easier to lead. In November 1995, Pharmacia, having already achieved a leading European stature, announced that it had reached a merger agreement with US-based Upjohn, creating one of the world's largest pharmaceutical companies at that time, renamed Pharmacia & Upjohn. However, integrating Pharmacia and Upjohn posed new and substantially different challenges than those faced during Pharmacia's previous acquisition deals. In particular, Ekberg remarks that the *execution skills* learned through Pharmacia's acquisition of FICE, in certain cases were quite different from those required in the implementation of Pharmacia and Upjohn's "merger of equals":

[When implementing the merger between Pharmacia and Upjohn] we more or less copied the process we had carried out in Italy [after we acquired FICE]. The problem was: In Italy it was a takeover treated as a merger, where I could make the final decisions. But when implementing the Pharmacia & Upjohn merger, we had to reach the final decisions together all the time.

As a result, two years after the announcement of the Pharmacia & Upjohn merger, it was becoming increasingly apparent that the new company was experiencing the pains of executing a major global integration effort. Pharmacia & Upjohn's sales and earning declined continuously during most of 1997, while a newly appointed President and CEO was replacing a three regional "pharmaceutical product centers" (in Italy, Sweden and the U.S.), with a centralized global structure covering all prescription pharmaceutical operations. As will be further discussed in Chapter 8, both Pharmacia's past successes and difficulties highlight the importance of direct experience and learning-by-doing, to foster a company's *execution skills* in global M&A activity.

In Japan, leaders such as Koji Kobayashi, a former President and a Chairman Emeritus of NEC until his death in December 1996, came to epitomize the particular combination of *execution orientation* and practical, detailed and down-to-earth, knowledge of their business, which allowed them to rebuild their country's industry after World War II. Kobayashi was President of NEC for 25 years, between 1964 and 1985. Under his tenure, NEC grew forty-fold to become the world's largest telecommunication company, drastically diversifying its revenues from an almost exclusive domestic public sector orientation to cover the Japanese private industry, and initiating its first determined expansion effort overseas. An engineer by profession, Kobayashi was the first NEC President to have grown through the ranks of the company, through 35 years of an uninterrupted career encompassing research, sales, marketing and staff functions. As such, he had first-hand experience of the drawbacks implicit in NEC's monolithic organization and basic research prior to the mid 1960s, which at the time were common to other major industries in Japan. Thus, as President, Kobayashi radically reorganized the previously conservative NEC structure into a far more decentralized divisional system, with localized marketing responsibilities. He also restructured NEC's research division along more decentralized lines, introducing a technology research approach closely linked to consumers needs. Kobayashi simultaneously replaced the traditional statistical defects controls in manufacturing, with "zero defect" methods which he learned from US-based Hughes Aircraft Company during a visit to that country in 1964. Throughout these major reforms, Kobayashi's hands-on, communicative and direct management style, constituted a profound departure from other Japanese corporate leaders, whom at the time often privileged a rather distant and detached managerial approach. In this sense, Kobayashi describes the curious mix of responses he initially found amongst NEC's plant workers — rather unused to personal contacts and direct communications with a company President:

> I recall one incident that took place during these conversations at the Sagamihara plant, and which gave me a strong sense that many NEC employees felt an unarticulated mixture of high hopes, uneasiness, and curiosity about their new president. A long-serving group leader said, "I am in total sympathy with your ideas and intentions, and we are all delighted to hear them; but if you listen directly to the views of everyone from the top executives down to the lowest new recruit, how can you conduct the business of a large-scale corporate organization and still maintain order within the company?"[12]

In all the major strategic areas chosen to underpin NEC's radical corporate transformation during his tenure as President, Kobayashi achieved such successful results, that, following NEC's lead, divisional marketing, consumer based technology research and zero defects production lines were comprehensively embraced by many other corporations in Japan since the mid 1960s, often leading to astonishing product development and productivity performances. As a result, these industrial traits have come to be increasingly associated with the "Japanese way" of manufacturing, often with archetypal and culturally rooted connotations. Nevertheless, the experience of leaders such as Kobayashi suggests that sound strategic vision, *execution orientation* and the *practical ability* to carry out a complex corporate transformation and an ambitious international expansion program such as NEC's may have played at least an equally important role in shaping these widely adopted organizational and manufacturing methods in Japan.[13]

Execution-Oriented Leaders Pragmatically Building on a Company's Historic and Cultural Endowments

Even if a particular corporate leader often shapes a company's vision and functioning structure to varying degrees, a number of studies have highlighted that these can be as much influenced by its specific corporate history and previous leaders.[14] In the context of cross-border M&As, the ability of *execution-oriented* leaders seem to be one of swiftly recognizing the historic strengths of a company, and pragmatically build upon them in order to skillfully stretch the organization's capacity for change. In military terms, this would be comparable to a general's ability to appraise his troops fighting skills and morale and, based on such examination, ready his army and march quickly to anticipate an enemy, providing carefully thought targets that push soldiers to the limits of what they can achieve. Although a relatively simple notion, this is, again, an area where a critical gap between theoretical concepts and the practical *execution skills* to carry them out can often be observed. In effect, a target company's resilient corporate culture, its historic complacency, or conservatism, compounded with national cultural issues, are frequently cited as major detrimental factors by international acquirers that fail to carry out integration efforts overseas. As a result, these factors are often viewed not as practical opportunities to build upon, but rather as insurmountable barriers preventing corporate leaders and key managers from taking appropriate actions, or outright paralyzing them.

Contrary to these notions, we have found numerous cross-border M&A instances illustrating the *execution-oriented* leaders' ability to build upon an acquired or a merging company's historic endowments, without compromising the need to simultaneously execute profound corporate changes. The resulting renewed organization is often, paradoxically, deeply embedded in the company's historical strengths, taking advantage of its *gnosis* of the local informational contexts, and insertion within the national cultural and institutional fabrics of the countries it operates in. These characteristics are difficult to copy by competitors who have to build up such a critical local *gnosis* and experience from scratch, or whom are less able to integrate and build upon their existing base of acquired companies.

During the radical transformation which followed the merger between ASEA and Brown Boveri in 1987, Eberhard von Koerber, then the company's European Regional Director, used to remark that "the important thing is to judge how much you can rock the boat without sinking it". Indeed, as the leader of ABB's restructuring efforts in Germany right after the merger was announced, von Koerber himself tested the very limits of the new company's capability to change. Being the largest of the merging companies' operations, the sweeping restructuring of ABB's German subsidiary put the very credibility of the merger at stake, but was nevertheless carried out within a rather consensual, conservative national cultural environment, and in spite of a half-century history of independent operations, the opposition of all-powerful unions and local institutions, and a strong corporate culture extremely hostile to the changes that had been initially proposed. Similarly to von Koerber's exploits in Germany, the ability of ABB's leaders to build upon the merging companies' historic strengths, were demonstrated by the overall organizational design implemented — a complex and exceedingly demanding multi-domestic structure which nevertheless proved to be within the practical reach of the company's employees.

As mentioned, ABB was formed by the merger of some of Europe's oldest and most respected companies, historically part of the industrial establishment *élite* in countries such as Sweden, Switzerland, Germany, and to a certain extent also in Italy and France. In this context, observers have often highlighted Barnevik's role in radically shaking the merging companies old values and structures, and almost single-handedly replacing them with totally new corporate values and organizational designs. However, upon more attentive examination, it appears that Barnevik was as much intent on conserving and building upon many of the merging companies' historic characteristics as in instilling new values, structures and mechanisms. Thus, throughout this process, a central aspect in the creation of ABB's multido-mestic organization appears to have relied on its leaders' *practical ability* to transform historical structural endowments and constraints into sources of competitive advantages internationally.

Going back into ASEA's history helps illustrate this point. Founded in Sweden at the close of the 19th century, ASEA was, well into the 1970s, a fine example of a highly conservative international company, with a strong corporate culture and a number of long-standing structural rigidities. Conspicuous examples of this included: Employment security (the company took pride that no personnel had been discharged since the 1930s), advancement policies (which tended to favor technical and engineering competence over functional business skills), and a rather patriarchal business style throughout. However, during the second part of the 1970s, a world-wide industrial recession dramatically affected ASEA's growth and capacity utilization levels. As a result, the company's profitability and financial strength declined alarmingly, and certain aspects of ASEA's company culture and people management, started to be publicly questioned amid the company's critical financial situation. Driven by financial complications and slow growth, by 1979 it was increasingly evident that ASEA was finding it difficult to compete successfully against its much larger international rivals, such as General Electric in the USA, Brown Boveri in Europe, and some of the major Japanese industrial conglomerates.

Percy Barnevik was initially singled out by Curt Nicolin, the company's previous Chief Executive, and appointed President and CEO of ASEA by Marcus Wallenberg shortly before his death in June 1980. Building on a strong support from ASEA's Board of Directors, Barnevik, a non-engineer in a traditionally engineering-dominated company, embarked in the most radical turnaround the company had experienced throughout its long history. The way he swiftly carried out fundamental changes in a most conservative company, historically revered as a major industrial flagship in Sweden, has since become a classic example of business turnaround surgery. Three critical stages can be recognized in this process. First, as mentioned, Barnevik reduced head office from 2,000 employees to 200, and replaced ASEA's current organization at that time with a matrix structure embedding geographic, operational, and technology-based responsibilities world-wide. Secondly, he extensively downsized ASEA's operations to regain cost efficiency. Lastly, Barnevik proceeded to expand ASEA's operations internationally through acquisitions, such as Strömberg in Finland (1986) and Elektrisk Bureau in Norway (1987).

This is the better known part of ASEA's history, often referred to as a prefatorial note in ABB's relatively recent corporate transformation. However, after closer examination, it is apparent that Barnevik was as determined in shaking ASEA's complacency and uprooting its conservative culture, as in building upon the company's considerable historical strengths and experience in conducting business internationally. The same approach was applied during the integration with Brown Boveri, following the 1987 merger agreement with ASEA. Nicolin observes:

> Mr. Barnevik invented the expression multidomestic. And he also suggested the meaning of the term, which we accepted. It essentially meant that a company in any given country should establish itself in the society where it lived, and that, whenever possible, we should have local executives to lead and manage it. If on occasions we couldn't find a suitable local person to head a company in a certain country, then we might appoint a foreigner. But then we wanted to have at least one or two local managers next to the top man, and of course we made sure that we knew and understood the laws and customs of any country we entered. When we [ASEA and Brown Boveri] joined together, these principles became much more important, but I haven't looked over the picture too much today. But if you do, you will find that in most cases we have local people

running the various companies. This principle was already there, before the merger [between ASEA and Brown Boveri], but we didn't have the name, the definition multidomestic, although we did have a clear idea of how to manage across borders, what type of management we should appoint overseas, etc.

Thus, in the case of ABB, a multidomestic solution represented a way of retaining the historically strong national cultures and insider characteristics of the merging companies. Based on their separate historical experiences, the local identities of these businesses provided considerable upside benefits which the new company was determined to maintain. Besides, going against the national sensitivities of ABB's constituting companies at the outset of the merger, could have proved both a prohibitively and unnecessary uphill battle, in view of their long historical tradition and the unprecedented attention which the merging companies received from all quarters in their countries of origin. Thus, by retaining the key local characteristics of the merging companies, ABB pragmatically turned apparent structural constraints into a pattern of organizational advantage which could be applied well beyond these initial integration efforts. Says Barnevik:

> There was no way you could make this a Swiss company, or a Swedish company or even a German or American company. We could pick English as a language and the US dollar as a currency for the whole business. But to reap the benefits we had to retain our local strengths and local identity in each market. For example, the strength we had in Finland, where we have a big market share: We don't want to give that up, and be seen as a foreigner. I want to be close to the present Prime Minister in Finland. I want to get funding for export. I want to get help to move into St. Petersburg.

The decision to build upon the particular historical characteristics and existing competitive strengths of the merging companies, also meant that the new ABB structure was de facto providing the opportunity to combine extensive local market knowledge, contact networks and business approaches in several countries, with the economic advantages of a global concern. The latter was achieved through the practical development of global co-ordination functions, a strenuous endeavor which could nevertheless leverage to an extent on ASEA's and Brown Boveri's extensive international business know-how, dating back to the turn of the 20th century. Thus, the resulting multidomestic organization was from the beginning deeply embedded in the merging companies' distinct historical experiences, making it difficult to be replicated by competitors possessing vastly different backgrounds. Barnevik remarks:

> We have been created from companies in all parts of the world. As a comparison, it would be like putting together a new competitor consisting of parts of Siemens in Germany, parts of Ansaldo in Italy, parts of GE in the United

States, parts of Alsthom in France, and a bit of Mitsubishi in Japan. That's what it would take and that's why it's so difficult to copy.

The 1984 acquisition of Italy-based Zanussi by Sweden's Electrolux is another example of an international acquirer building on a target's historical strengths, local networks and established market presence. As mentioned, these strategic aims led to Electrolux's determination to maintain Zanussi's employee base and product brands virtually intact across all of the company's core product areas (i.e. dish washers, washing machines and dryers), while the non-core areas in which the company had diversified, such as real estate, were quickly divested after the acquisition.

Following major cross-border M&A agreements, restructuring initiatives by corporate leaders easily get headlines, and often lead to swift transformations and a variety of performance outcomes. Indeed, in many of the cases we researched, *execution-oriented* leaders have not been shy on embarking in sweeping restructuring efforts when the need was perceived to be there, often involving themselves personally in these activities and directly confronting the associated emotional tolls. Nevertheless, far less noticed have been their concurrent *execution skills* to maintain and build pragmatically upon a company's historical strengths, often by adapting strategic and organizational designs to suit its corporate history and leverage on its traditional insertion into the local cultural and institutional environment. By creatively and skillfully balancing these apparently contradictory aims, corporate leaders in companies such as ABB, Electrolux-Zanussi, Daewoo and British Airways, have executed highly effective organizations, often turning initial constraints into practical advantages embedded in historical, cultural and organizational factors which are not easily replicated by competitors.

Small-Country Characteristics Foster People's Historic Openness Towards Global Co-operation

Throughout our research, there has been a recurrent theme underlying the development of a company's *execution skills* to manage effectively across national cultures and borders. These skills take many forms depending on a company's particular industry, strategic aims and organizational characteristics. However, what these skills seem to have in common is that they benefit greatly from a genuinely open attitude to work together with people from different national cultural backgrounds on an international level, across a company's key managerial and employee ranks. In this context, it is often the case that a specific country environment seems to play an important role in shaping their people's international openness and basic ability to interact with diverse national cultures. These people's qualities are generally considered to be highly valuable by companies seeking to routinely perform critical global co-ordination functions.

Take a country's environment and the special circumstances surrounding its industrial development. It can be argued that countries with relatively small domestic markets, which have nevertheless managed to develop a sizable and advanced industrial base very early on, had to rely from the initial stages on a significant international presence through exports and direct investments. This is indeed the case of Sweden, Switzerland and the Netherlands, which, presumably as a result of their relatively precocious industrial internationalization, have faced the need to develop open ways of working across borders from very early on compared with countries which based their initial industrial development relying heavily on comparatively large domestic markets. On the other hand, the industrial development of countries such as Korea has been recent compared to Sweden or the Netherlands. However, the size and limited purchasing power of Korea's domestic markets during the emerging stages of economic development have also made its companies particularly reliant on exports and international access to key technologies from the very beginning. In turn, these factors may have significantly influenced the ways in which companies in these countries have historically developed their peculiar approaches to managing internationally.

The prime effects of a country's initial domestic market conditions may become embedded in a company's specific ways of conducting operations overseas, even long after their home countries have achieved large-scale industrial internationalization. For example, they may play a role shaping their people's attitudes towards diverse, foreign cultures and individuals. Pharmacia & Upjohn's Ekberg observes:

> We can see many US pharmaceutical companies selling their products abroad, but they are not truly international companies. For example, some of us still remember when the big American multinationals entered Europe during the 1950s. Many of these companies failed because they treated Europe as if it was their own home market. They thought that the rest of the world was similar or exactly the same as the USA. However, Sweden is a small country which from the beginning had to accept and adjust to many different cultures to grow its industrial base.

Thus, a small country's early industrial internationalization in general appears to foster a more cosmopolitan, outward-looking cultural traits in people, which are seen as an important asset by organizations in need of routinely performing critical co-ordination functions across borders. By contrast, it is observed that in larger industrialized countries it is more difficult to find such cultural openness to work across borders or to willingly adapt to foreign cultures. In these countries, sizable internal markets have often made the local industries much more domestically focused historically, in certain cases fostering a tendency for ethnocentrism. These traits appear to be particularly relevant in the context of cross-border M&As, JVs and alliances, where implementation difficulties related to national cultural differences usually are compounded with the emotional issues and people sensitivities generally associated with these agreements. Says Barnevik:

> It is no coincidence that there are so many small-country people in international business. Because, the bigger country you have, the bigger the domestic market and the smaller the need to go out in the world to get new markets. And international openness is important to make an organization like this [ABB] work.

Likewise, openness to work co-operatively across borders, and interact with people showing markedly different national cultural values, can often be amongst the critical factors making an international alliance work in practice, along with other strategic and operational issues. This was the case of the highly visible international alliance in the computer industry between Italy's Olivetti and US-based AT&T. Elerino Piol, who led Olivetti through that effort in 1983, explains the reasons why the alliance was terminated after a few years:

> First of all, the alliance was conceived in the wrong strategic context (...) The second problem was to suppose that AT&T was going to be able to manage the computer business competitively. But at that time [1983], they just couldn't. They didn't have the right culture. (...) One thing was the company culture. The computer business is fast, dynamic, responsive, and AT&T was at the time a monopoly, had been a monopoly and had the culture of a monopoly, not used to competition. Another thing was the international openness of the Americans who had to work with Olivetti in this agreement, which was a cross-border alliance. I'll give you an example of this. I remember that when we were doing the due diligence of both companies, a team of eight American "evaluators" had to come to Italy, but arrived with a two week delay with respect to the agreed date. It turned out that this was because they had to get their passports. Can you believe this? These persons had never been out of the USA, this was their first trip abroad. And in addition, this alliance was the first real international experience for AT&T.

Thus, people's openness and disposition to work together with individuals from different countries and in diverse national cultural environments are consistently described as a critically valuable characteristic for companies which are required to establish complex global co-ordination functions, i.e. following a major international M&A, JV or alliance. In small countries, where an early industrial internationalization may have favored the development of such traits in people, this is perceived as an advantage by organizations which have to constantly devise specific ways and skills to manage across borders.

In other cases, a small country's particular historic circumstances can be turned into unexpected advantages by its business leaders, even if industrial internationalization takes place at a relatively recent stage. This appears to be the case of Korea, where the historical urge to develop its basic industry, after a civil war during the 1950s comprehensively ravaged the country, has been skillfully used as an opportunity to transform the lessons learned in dramatic episodes such as these, into concrete business advantages internationally. Kang observes:

> Korea's first five-year economic development plan began in 1962, when the annual GDP was only US$ 83 per capita. In addition, Korea had experienced the Japanese colonial rule from 1910 to 1945, and had suffered a three year war against communism from 1950 to 1953. But today [in 1996], the annual GDP has grown to over US$ 10,000 per capita. We are formally joining the OECD as a result of this development. We have experienced total poverty but have subsequently achieved a very significant economical progress. And we can share these experiences with other developing or emerging countries. We suffered greatly from the restrictions in the transfer of important technologies which had been imposed by certain developed countries. As a response, we did our best efforts to develop our own technology. And of course, we know that other developing countries will also catch up sooner or later, which is why we try to foster a partnership with them to develop their economies. Under the World Trade Organization system two trends are clear. One is that the world is becoming one market. But from a practical perspective, we find ourselves facing economical blocks, such as the European Union, NAFTA or Mercosur. It's a great obstacle we are facing. We either find a way to participate in these developments or our industry will not survive. This is why we are learning how to understand these countries' people, cultures, history, because we have to adapt in order to do business with them.

Korea's first-hand *gnosis* and dramatic experiences handling neighboring communist regimes and growing its industrial base with unprecedented speed from a rather underdeveloped starting point, can be turned into unique business assets in certain regions. Indeed, right after the fall of the Berlin Wall in 1989, and the subsequent fall of communist regimes all over Eastern and Central Europe and the former Soviet Union, Korean *chaebol* (a word denoting industrial conglomerates) such as Daewoo, preceded most Western European and US companies in pioneering the economic development and the restructuring of whole industries in those areas. Most remarkable for a country with virtually no strong historical or cultural ties in the region, the commercial links established by Daewoo and other *chaebol* in many cases made it possible for the Korean government to start formal diplomatic relations with many countries in Eastern Europe. As a result, in less than one decade after the fall of these formerly communist regimes, Daewoo's wave of major international JVs has made it one of the largest foreign investors in countries such as Romania and Poland, where it owns significant or majority stakes in JVs ranging from commercial vehicle production to shipbuilding. Indeed, this massive spree of investments in the region was seen by Korea's industrialists partly as a way to capitalize on a unique opportunity to compete in Western Europe's rich markets, from within the EU economic block.

Such developments, as Daewoo's Kang points out, are revealing examples of how Korea's troubled recent history, mixing early national tragedies and astonishing economic success, combined with its current commercial position *vis-à-vis* the emerging regional economic blocks, has provided its leading companies with both the urge and the opportunity to internationalize its operations in unique ways. Throughout these efforts, it is maintained that people's openness to understand, accept and adapt to different local and foreign cultures, has proved to be a valuable trait for the effective internationalization of Korea's industry, conducive to the effective management of resources across nationalities and overcoming the country's initial structural weaknesses. Says Kang:

> This [Korea] is a small country. Let's say united Korea would have a population of just over 60 million. This is why our human resources are very limited [in number]. And we need foreign technology to grow our industry abroad. Therefore, we have to be open to work with people from other nations, understand their cultures, adapt and accept each other.

Sometimes, evidence of the practical business implications associated with the traditional international openness of certain small industrialized countries can be detected in specific characteristics of seemingly little significance. For instance, when the handling of M&As, JVs and alliances takes place across countries with different languages, some of the resulting communication-related problems are often represented as major cultural obstacles to implementation. In this context, it is interesting to observe that in countries like Sweden and the Netherlands a very reduced population of native-language speakers has acted as a stimulus for people to learn foreign languages to conduct their regular activities, not only business-related. For instance, in Sweden significant parts of the domestic TV programming takes part in English, the original production language, including transmissions destined for under-age audiences. In the few cases where tailoring to the local audiences take place, this mostly involves subtitles in the native tongue, which preserves the original spoken language form. Contrary to this, in Germany, France, Japan, or Italy, TV productions originating from English (or non-native) speaking countries are almost invariably dubbed for the "benefit" of domestic audiences. In another small country like Switzerland, the three major languages spoken in the country (Italian, French and "Swiss-German") are also native to very large national communities outside its national borders, but the reduced size of the population drives many people to learn and speak fluently these languages in order to carry out regular activities.

Partly as a result of these characteristics, it has been widely observed that, in these small countries, an astonishingly large amount of individuals are able to communicate fluently in a foreign language, relative to, say, sizable industrialized economies such as Japan, France or Germany.[15] In the latter societies, the emphasis on the national language which can be found, has been de facto accentuated in certain cases, responding to a perceived need to preserve a country's national culture, or (perhaps as a conspicuous side-effect) to protect specific industries seen as embedding such national cultural patrimony. Thus, during the mid 1990s, the French government was visibly attempting to enforce legislation requiring "minimum contents" of native language transmissions upon the radio and TV networks operating in the country, a move widely interpreted as targeting English speaking productions mostly originated in the USA. Other countries' experiences illustrate how practically difficult it is to open an unaccustomed population to wide foreign language proficiency, even when the benefits to do so have been broadly recognized at every level. For example, in Japan it has been often highlighted that, albeit increasing numbers of English language students, the prevalence of teaching methods emphasizing reflective and memorizing routines, and the relatively reduced opportunity to regularly speak or listen to this foreign language, in many cases leads to people not being able to fluently speak or understand spoken English, even after years of training.[16]

Can these factors be related to the relative expediency with which companies strongly linked to, or based in countries such as Sweden, Switzerland, the Netherlands and even Korea (e.g. Phillips, ABB, Pharmacia and Daewoo) have been able at different times to adopt internal official languages which were foreign to a large part of their employees? It is tempting to argue against this, as such a decision ought to be entirely based on the grounds of business convenience and efficiency. However, in countries such as Germany and Japan, whose native languages are not so widely spoken internationally as, say, English, national cultural sensitivities combined with practical difficulties, may significantly complicate a major company's decision to internally adopt a non-native language, even across a company's limited and selected managerial levels. In Japan, for example, industry leaders such as Yotaro Kobayashi, Chairman and CEO of Fuji-Xerox, the US-Japanese joint venture in the office equipment industry, stress the sheer management courage required to officially establish a non-Japanese language for internal communications within a major Japanese multinational, in spite of executives' perception of the significant practical benefits that could stem from such a decision. The latter is supported by the fact that a number of Japanese companies, such as NEC, have created highly successful internal language schools to support their executives' business activities abroad. In Germany, analogous language problems seem to have raised some issues in the past at Deutsche Bank's top management levels. This emblematic German company determinedly started a large scale internationalization effort during the mid 1980s, leading to a massive and unprecedented level of international investments in the financial industry, including its £950 million acquisition of Morgan Grenfell in 1989, a prestigious British merchant bank.[17] Following this acquisition, Morgan Grenfell's John Craven became the first non-German member of the bank's Board of Directors before retiring in 1996. His ability to understand German was at the time seen as a distinct advantage in Deutsche Bank's Board. By contrast, the lack of German language proficiency in other Deutsche Bank's executives was viewed then as a major professional disadvantage. Arguably, in the highly international investment banking sector, Deutsche Bank's initial insistence on maintaining German as the "official" language at the highest management ranks was limiting its access to a global pool of top executive talent. Recognizing this, some of the bank's executives remark that today, English is informally becoming the *de facto* second language at the top management levels. This is seen as facilitating communication within the increasingly cross-border network of Deutsche Bank's operations, and contributing to the bank's internationalization efforts by helping attract top executives from different nationalities and cultural backgrounds. Indeed, after Deutsche Bank announced a new Group management structure in July 1996, about one-third of the thirty-six members of the Group Executive Committee were of non-German nationality. When all the members of this Group Executive Committee meet — roughly every three months — the sessions are conducted in English.

"The Art Is Not in the Concept": *Execution Skills* to Successfully Manage Cross-Cultural M&As, JVs and Alliances

The empirical evidence concerning the performance of cross-border M&As, JVs and alliances so far presented suggests that, when handled effectively, a company can actually turn national cultural distance or initial deep-rooted cultural resistances into lasting practical advantages. Through *execution oriented* managerial approaches, a company's leaders and key managers can crystallize the potential upside associated with functioning global co-ordination mechanisms across national borders and local cultures. Superior *execution* of such mechanisms is holistically based on both technical knowledge and *gnosis*, a significant part of which is not easily codifiable but lives in a company's practical experience, processes, methods, subjective group skills and organizational repertoires. Building on cross-border M&As, JVs and alliances, a company may implement *execution* mechanisms leading to global economies of scale, scope and other similar advantages, in a way that makes them more difficult to copy by competitors. Thus conceived, managerial *execution* becomes an area of primary strategic importance to the performance of global M&As, JVs and alliances.

A company's peculiar *execution skills* can be traced back to the continuous *execution orientation* of a company's leaders and key managers, their business knowledge and subjective experiences, the way in which strategic and organizational responses have been adapted in order to build upon an acquired, merging or partner company's historical strengths and local insertion, and, particularly during the initial internationalization stages, perhaps even to a country's historical openness to conducting business overseas, as well as the associated cosmopolitan orientation of its people.

Nevertheless "the art is not in the concept", as previously indicated by one senior executive: In order to illustrate how *execution skills* can generate sustainable practical advantages to a company in the context of international M&As, JVs and alliances, it is necessary to examine the way in which some of the associated *execution* mechanisms actually operate in practice, across national borders and local cultures. We therefore dedicate the following chapters to characterizing the way in which leading multinational companies approach *execution*, throughout the assessment, negotiation and implementation phases of overseas M&As, JVs and alliances.

Notes and References

[1] Hedlund, G. and J. Ridderstråle. "International development projects", *International Studies of Management and Organization*, 25 (1-2), 1995, pp. 158-184; Hedlund, G. "The hypermodern MNC — a heterarchy? *Human Resource Management*, 25 (1), Spring 1986, pp. 9-25; Bartlett, C. A. and S. Ghoshal. *Managing Across Borders: The Transnational Solution*, Harvard Business School Press, Cambridge, MA, 1989; Doz, Y. L. *Strategic Management in Multinational Companies*, Pergamon Press, Oxford, 1986; White, R. E. and T. A. Poynter. "Organizing for a world-wide advantage", in C. A. Bartlett, Y. Doz and G. Hedlund (eds), *Managing the Global Firm*, Routledge, London, 1990, pp. 95-116.

[2] Handy, C. "Balancing corporate power: a new federalist paper", in *Managerial Excellence. McKinsey Award Winners from the Harvard Business Review (1980-1994)*, Harvard Business School Press, Boston, 1996.

[3] Morosini, P., S. Shane and H. Singh. "National cultural distance and cross-border acquisition performance", *Journal of International Business Studies*, in press.

[4] *Pharmacia AB Annual Report* 1994, pp. 9-10; Pharmacia & Upjohn, Inc., *Annual Report*, 1995, p. 29 (italics have been introduced by the author).

[5] Morosini, P. and H. Singh. "Post-cross-border acquisitions: implementing 'national culture compatible' strategies to improve performance", *European Management Journal*, 12(4), December 1994, pp. 390-400.

[6] Bleeke, J. and D. Ernst. "The way to win in cross-border alliances", *Harvard Business Review*, November, 1991, pp. 127-135; Lorange, P. "Human resource management in multinational cooperative ventures", *Human Resource Management*, 25(1), Spring 1986, pp. 133-148.

[7] See for example: Hofstede, G., B. Neuijen, D. Daval Ohayv and G. Sanders. "Measuring organizational cultures: a qualitative and quantitative study across twenty cases", *Administrative Science Quarterly*, 35, 1990, pp. 286-316.

[8] See, for example: Datta, D. K. "Organizational fit and acquisition performance: effects of post-acquisition integration", *Strategic Management Journal*, 12, 1991, pp. 281-297; Deal, T. and A. Kennedy. *Corporate Cultures*, Addison-Wesley, Reading,

MA, 1982; Pettigrew, A. "On studying organizational cultures", *Administrative Science Quarterly*, 24, 1979, pp. 570-581.

[9] Peters, T. and R. Waterman. *In Search of Excellence: Lessons from America's Best-run Companies*, Harper & Row, New York, 1982.

[10] For example, see: Lorange, P. "Roles of the CEO in strategic planning and control processes", in a seminar on "The Role of General Management in Strategy Formulation and Evaluation", co-sponsored by ESSEC, EIASM and IAE, Cergy, France, 28-30 April 1980.

[11] Kets de Vries, F. R. and R. de Vitry d'Avaucourt. "Percy Barnevik: the corporate transformation wizard. An interview", INSEAD, Fontainebleau, 1994 (italics have been introduced by the author).

[12] Kobayashi, K. *The Rise of NEC. How the World's Greatest C&C Company is Managed*, Blackwell Publishers, Cambridge, MA, 1991, p. 3.

[13] A number of comparative studies between US and Japan manufacturing performance, have also pointed out that superior performance levels on the part of the Japanese, are not to be uniquely associated with "cultural advantages" or "national culture traits", but are rather the result of systematic implementation of sound, basic management practices. See, for example: Gavin, D. A. "Quality on the line", in *Managerial Excellence. McKinsey Award Winners from the Harvard Business Review (1980-1994)*, Harvard Business School Press, Boston, 1996.

[14] See: Pettigrew, A. *Op. cit.*, 1979.

[15] See: "Euro-tongues wag in English", article appeared in the October 25th, 1997 issue of *The Economist* page 48. See also: Takubo, K. "Cross-cultural problems in overseas business communication", NEC Culture Center, Ltd., Tokyo. From a Conference in Cross Cultural Aspects of Human Resource Management, Singapore, March 24-25, 1983; also see an article by the same author: "Learning English by Teaching English", published in the newspaper *The Daily Yomiuri*, on March 15 1990.

[16] Takubo, K. *Op. cit.*, 1983.

[17] For more details on Deutsche Bank's internationalization, see Chapters 2 and 9.

Part III
Turning National Cultural Differences into Lasting Practical Advantages

CHAPTER 7

Assessing M&As, JVs and Alliances across National Cultures

The same consequences which have uniformly attended long discussions and councils of war will follow at all times. They will terminate in the adoption of the worst course, which in war is always the most timid, or, if you will, the most prudent. The only true wisdom in a general is determined courage.

Napoleon Bonaparte

Although both top executives and consultants often regard it as a soft issue, a growing hard empirical evidence increasingly lends support to the notion that cultural differences can make or break an M&A, JV or alliance. The available statistical and anecdotal evidence covers a broad spectrum of culture as characterized in Part I, from national to corporate aspects of it.[1] In addition, our empirical findings concerning cross-border acquisitions suggest that a direct link between national cultural distance and post-acquisition performance appears to exist, significantly explained by the acquirer's *execution ability* to handle the target's national cultural traits during the implementation stages. In particular, we found that some companies' particular approaches to assessing international M&As, JVs and alliances can increase the chances of building genuine trust and co-operative working relations with a potential target or partner, taking advantage of the diversity of skills and national cultural differences which may exist. The latter can have an enduring and positive impact during the subsequent negotiation and implementation phases.

Complementarity, Openness and Similarity in Business Values to Build Trust Across National Cultural Differences

A number of value creation acquisition theorists have classified these transactions into related or unrelated categories, based on their strategic potential for transferring functional kills (i.e. in R&D, manufacturing, marketing or distribution) between the acquirer and the target. Related acquisitions can be further subdivided into related-complementary and related-supplementary transactions, depending on the degree of strategic fit or existing overlaps between the merging companies functional and market-based activities.[2] However, as mentioned in Chapter 1, many empirical studies have overwhelmingly reported a high failure rate of acquisitions, across a broad range of performance measures, industry sectors, geographic areas, and time periods. The existing evidence includes rather mixed results for related acquisitions, some studies actually maintaining that unrelated transactions have performed better than related ones.[3] Although this dismal track record has been generally associated with poor managerial control, strategic shortcomings or cultural and organizational difficulties arising during the post-acquisition integration period, one empirical study has pointed out an interesting distinction, suggesting that acquisitions allowing access to new but related markets, will create the most value for shareholders. Analogous evidence suggests that strategic cross-border alliances focusing on filling functional gaps and potential complementarities between the partners' core and related activities, generally achieved significantly higher performance than those where more functional overlaps existed.[4] From a similar perspective, senior executives interviewed in our research have consistently highlighted the importance of business *complementarity* to significantly increase the chances of success in carrying out major M&As, JVs or alliances across borders. In some cases, such awareness has been strenuously built as a result of serious integration problems experienced with related-supplementary acquisitions. Former Olivetti senior executive Elserino Piol observes:

> I see in a better light international agreements based on complementarity, call it acquisitions, strategic alliances or joint ventures. The situations that worked out in the worst ways for us [in Olivetti] were our acquisitions of very similar companies, based on economies of scale or on the expectation of gaining market share. These are difficult propositions because, the higher the similarity between the acquirer and the target, the greater the cultural difficulties, conflicts and integration problems. Based on the opposite reasoning, in the past we acquired companies which were doing the same things we were doing. For example, back in the early '80s Olivetti acquired Triumph Adler, the German leader of type-writing machines, and an old, traditional company. It is one thing to choose a partner who complements your own strong points. But try to convince the German leader of type-writing machines that the buyer of his company is better at producing type-writing machines! And it was the same when we acquired Hermes, the Swiss producer of type-writing machines.

In the case of the 1987 merger between ASEA and Brown Boveri, a very strong complementarity between these companies' areas of excellence underpinned both the purpose and rationale of the deal, which was from the beginning conceived as a 50/50 "merger of equals". Curt Nicolin, former CEO and Chairman of ASEA, and a primary architect of this company's merger with Brown Boveri, remarks that ensuring that a strong complementarity existed between both companies was one key aspect of his evaluation:

> Of course, they [Brown Boveri] were one of our good competitors, so I knew them reasonably well. But the fact that we had very complementary abilities was also one good thing which was part of my evaluation. We had very good reasons to admire certain parts of Brown Boveri's operations, and they also had good reasons to admire certain things that we [ASEA] made. But everything wasn't gold, neither with them nor with us. But it's more important that you have some very good things that another company can admire, rather than being average in everything. And that was true for both companies but in different areas: Our best areas were never one of the best areas of Brown Boveri and vice versa. As a result, complementarity was very great, like an alliance.

The electrical engineering industry is a multi-product type of business, where the complementarity lies in the approach to the customer. An electrical company requiring a new power generator, typically chooses between several technologies, such as: Nuclear, gas turbine or steam turbine, which the provider needs to offer. Moreover, building power stations or transportation plants requires a myriad of sophisticated components, ranging from energy transformers to control, transmission and distribution equipment, a set of differentiated products which have to be provided and assembled by the building company. This is distinctly different from industries such as automotive, electrodomestics, or pharmaceuticals where production is often organized around well-defined manufacturing lines, each of which is made up of virtually identical products that can be mass produced. By contrast, multi-product industries such as electrical engineering are very seldom organized based on line production systems. Although small electrical pieces can be manufactured utilizing mass production and associated logistic methods, the larger power, transmission or distribution components which form the core of the electrical engineering industry, typically are highly customized and command hundreds or even billions US dollars a piece. In this context, ASEA's and Brown Boveri's activities offered a very broad potential complementarity *vis-à-vis* the customer, from a technological, functional, product and geographic perspectives. Says Nicolin:

> There were many areas of complementarity between ASEA and Brown Boveri. For instance, at ASEA we had already come rather far on the development of robots. And today ABB, built on that start from ASEA, is the world's largest manufacturer of robots. And in many other areas, this merger was also very valuable in the sense that it was complementary. If you look at our companies' skills, for instance, they were among the very top in the world for large gas turbines, whereas we were outstanding in other areas, such as power transmission, transformers and high voltage DC. There was also very good geographic complementarity. If you take Brown Boveri as an example, they were well

175

introduced to certain markets where we had very little business, and we had a good presence in certain countries where they had very little activity. So, we addressed the market complementarity in many countries, not just in terms of market share, but especially the people, who have the network and know the market.

One crucial characteristic of global M&As which are broadly designed based on related-complementarity, is the overriding need for mutual co-operation that is established from the outset, as opposed to the more substitutive dynamics which might be associated with transactions largely based on strictly supplementary or overlapping resources between the merging companies. As a result, it has been mentioned that major international M&As based on related-complementarity are constantly referred to by senior executives as mergers of equals or alliance type of agreements. Beyond the rhetorical connotations that may occasionally accompany these expressions in a business context, in the case of international complementary M&As, JVs or alliances, they often tend to stress the need for effective working co-operation between the partners to realize in practice the potential value of combining resources across borders. Indeed, a strong strategic complementarity has led Ekberg to describe Pharmacia's 1992 purchase of Italy's Farmitalia-Carlo Erba (FICE) as an acquisition treated as an alliance. In this case, FICE's world-class research capabilities in areas such as oncology, and extensive presence in the European markets, constituted a nice complementary fit for Pharmacia, which at the time operated mostly in the Scandinavian arena, with no recognized area of research leadership at the European level.

Openness to work co-operatively across national cultural differences

However, in this kind of related-complementary mergers or acquisitions, the very need to establish an alliance type of environment, fostering effective co-operation between international partners, often implies a careful evaluation of the existing national cultural differences prior to the deal. As already mentioned, a vast empirical and anecdotal literature concerning the performance of M&As, JVs and alliances, has identified the implementation phase following the conclusion of the deal, as a period where most complications arise between the companies, ranging from national to corporate cultural difficulties and personnel or organizational complexities. As a result, a large part of performance disappointments in M&A, JV or alliance activity can be traced back to integration problems taking place after the deal, even in cases where these transactions appear to have been conceived on sound strategic grounds.[5] In the case of M&As, JVs or alliances based on related-complementarity, one way to assess the impact of national cultural differences on building effective collaborative relations, is to examine previous experiences and similar situations. Pharmacia's Lars Lindegren observes that this assessment suggested that, in spite of the relatively large national cultural distance between Sweden and Italy, people from both countries were generally open to establish co-operative working relationships:

> In 1992, when we were looking to acquire FICE, we realized that there were very big cultural differences between Sweden and Italy. So we asked ourselves: What is the track record of Swedish companies in Italy? We looked at major Swedish multinationals who had acquired Italian companies, such as SKF and Electrolux, and realized that Swedish business in Italy had been in almost all cases a success story. I believe there is a reason for this: Italians do not see Swedes as a threat. In Italy, people are open and prepared to work with us because they consider Swedes to be honest and transparent people who can be trusted. And at the higher levels of FICE and Pharmacia, there was of course no problem if you were Italian or Swedish or whatever, because as international companies we were already used to work across different nationalities.

One of the main cases studied by Pharmacia, the 1984 acquisition of Italian Zanussi by Sweden-based Electrolux, is interesting because during the pre-merger evaluation not only functional and geographic complementarity seem to have been considered as key factors, but also the complementary skills historically embedded in the highly distant national cultures of Italy and Sweden.[6] Moreover, from the perspective of building collaborative working relations after the acquisition, the acquirer's openness to build on the local resources and work co-operatively across national cultural differences, were once more seen as a determinant factor for success. Gianmario Rossignolo, who advised Electrolux in the Zanussi acquisition and subsequently led the integration of the new company as its first CEO, explains:

> It is important that two national cultures are complementary and not supplementary. The cultural differences that exist between Sweden and Italy are complementary, because we Italians have a tendency towards more hierarchical and bureaucratic organizations, while the Swedes — because of their nature, their history and their particular needs — have a lesser tendency towards this type of rigid organizations. And this is an advantage when you try to combine both cultures. We also set out with two countries that are geographically distant but had traditionally moved across complementary areas of business influence which did not overlap. For example, the Scandinavians had a strong presence in the UK, before we Italians had any. But we had a stronger and more successful presence in Germany. Another fundamental reason is that people's skills are very complementary. What is the advantage of the Scandinavians to the Italians? It has been that Sweden, being a small country with a rather limited domestic market, since the end of the first world war has always been prone to move through acquisitions made in different geographic areas. This has forced them to become very internationally open from very early on, for example adopting international accounting systems. Instead, Italy's international presence in business has been more recent, and our baroque, Mediterranean accounting with many standards, renders us hardly understandable to work abroad. On the other hand, Italians are much more creative, more aggressive,

more flexible than the Swedes. But the Swedes, being a nation of few people, has very good managers but not in great numbers, which ensures that whatever country they go they do not destroy resources, but try to build, to accept, to integrate. And it is a fact that, instead of imposing everything Swedish, they try to always adapt to a country's own traditions and ways of doing things.

In the airline industry, it has been mentioned that a relatively broad availability of internationally open people, who are used to day-by-day working co-operatively across diverse national cultures, is considered to be a distinct advantage in the sector, in many cases facilitating the implementation of co-operation agreements and business alliances amongst international carriers such as British Airways. In the case of ASEA, an analysis of the merger candidate's country of origin *vis-à-vis* Sweden was an important part of the selection criteria. However, similar to Pharmacia or Electrolux-Zanussi, this examination focused more on a country's international business experience and historic track record overseas, rather than on generic national cultural differences or distance considerations *per se*. The implications of these specific country characteristics on the people's international openness and their traditional disposition to work cooperatively across diverse national cultures were seen as important factors to make the purpose of a merger of equals function from the beginning. Observes Nicolin:

> I don't know if Swedish companies have been, as a whole, successful acquirers abroad, but of course being as small as Sweden is, we have had a lot of experience in that comparatively. But the fact that we were small and had a fairly advanced industry has also made us work a lot in the international markets, and has created big exports. So we were trained in meeting customers abroad and sometimes cooperate with somebody on a specific deal. And that of course helped in a situation like this [the merger between ASEA and Brown Boveri]. And the same goes for Switzerland I would say. This was important because my criteria when evaluating merger candidates was <u>not</u> to favor big companies from large countries because they tend to impose their own national cultures, and they feel that they know best. That's not a good attitude for cooperation.

Similarity of business values to build trust across national cultural differences

Along with people's openness to work across national cultural differences, assessing similarities in business approaches and company values has been consistently stressed as a critical aspect to make related-complementary M&As, JVs and alliances work internationally. Common approaches and ethical standards greatly facilitate building genuine trust between the partners' or merging companies' top management, paving the way to establishing mutually collaborative relations across other managerial levels and bridging any national cultural differences which may exist. Trust has been singled out as a key factor in people management and performance across a wide variety of business areas, including manufacturing methods, co-operative links between customers and suppliers, as well as target or partner selection in acquisitions, JVs and alliances.[7] Supporting this, Colin Marshall observes that British Airways' careful assessment of its potential partners' business approaches has been a key aspect in successfully establishing the company's global network of alliances:

> I stress that it is very important to choose a partner who shares your business culture, your approach to selecting, training, leading and communicating to people, and who also has analogous practices and approach to international co-ordination of operations. In our case, a paramount business value is of course a dedicated and authentic customer service approach. Building on these basic similarities in business cultures, national cultural differences are not an obstacle, but I would even say that, if and when our potential partners are as open and tolerant to work across borders as I believe we are in this company, it is actually quite the contrary.

In the case of ASEA's evaluation of Brown Boveri as a potential merger candidate, Nicolin remarks that, along with business complementarity, it was crucially important to ensure that ethical standards were both similar and coherent to each other, and that there was a good fit between the top management of both companies:

> Strong complementarity between the two companies was an important part of my evaluation [of the merger candidates]. But equally important was my evaluation of the ethical standards and personalities. Let me say that I have spent my life with ASEA and became Managing Director in 1961. And I maintained, and that was the policy I established in ASEA, that the most important asset that we have is the quality of our name. That means that I wouldn't like to ever see us at a court. We should resolve disagreements with customers or others outside a court. And particularly when it comes to customers we should not seek the last [Swedish] krona of the deal in question. We shall rather make a sacrifice but make them feel happy, so that they can come back in the future. And the same thing between individuals in our organization: Very high ethical standards. If we had anybody, a boss or whomever, that didn't follow the ethical code, they have nothing to do with our company. Now let me finish by saying: It was also my understanding that the ethical standards in Brown Boveri were good and coherent with ours.

In the case of Fuji-Xerox, similarity of business values between the partners has also played an important role in transforming it from a relatively small company into a multibillion US$ concern and a Japanese leader in office equipment and technology. Formed in 1962 as a 50/50 joint venture between US-based Xerox Corporation and Japan's Fuji Photo Film, Fuji-Xerox was one of the first business partnerships of its kind between the two countries, but has ever since outlived successfully most other similar US-Japanese JVs or alliances.[8] Based on an essential complementarity between its shareholders' strategic aims, this joint venture allowed Fuji Photo Film to introduce in Japan what at the time was considered to be a highly innovative xerography technology, whereas Xerox Corporation could establish a foot-hold in the fast-growing Japanese market of the 1960s. Yotaro Kobayashi, Chairman and CEO of Fuji-Xerox observes that at the time it was both a matter of pride and a practical necessity for Fuji Photo Film to bring into Japan this new xerographic technology as the would-be successor of the silver halide, conventional photography. In this context, a basic similarity of business approaches to developing advanced technologies, helped building an unusual degree of trust between the American and the Japanese partners, which was crucial to make the joint venture work in spite of the strong national cultural differences that existed. Says Kobayashi:

> There has to be, particularly in the case of a 50/50 joint venture, a very, very strong trust between the two partners' management. It's both natural and fair to insist with a non-Japanese partner to be present at all levels, to have someone living in Japan, and to demand at least something like 50 percent equity ownership. But in the case of Fuji-Xerox, we developed an extreme degree of trust between the partners, Fuji Photo Film and Xerox. And I don't think this is typical. And because of this unusual situation, we could have these first ten years, where we just didn't have any non-Japanese people. And this was all done with the perfect understanding on the part of the Xerox people, who realized that it was necessary to establish, a very strong Japanese identity for the new company. But the degree to which how local you can run an international joint venture depends on how strong trust you can actually have between the shareholders, and also on the kind of people you really have. I think we are fortunate that Fuji Photo Film, under this premise, felt totally responsible, that unless they brought in good people to run the joint venture, they would eventually be co-responsible for the lack of performance. It represented a very strong sense of commitment on the part of Fuji Photo Film's top management at that time: This is a joint venture, we are responsible for the operations, and if we are really serious, we have to send in the best people we can have. And I think Xerox strongly related to Fuji Photo Film's total commitment and seriousness to develop a key technology, because it was also part of their business approach.

Building upon this basic similarity in business approaches, Fuji Photo Film's determination to "walk the talk" and demonstrate its commitment to make its partnership with Xerox Corporation work, was determinant to practically foster mutual trust. One key way to do this was reflected by the type of resources it was ready to allocate to its joint venture agreement with Xerox, particularly in terms of people. Kobayashi observes:

> I was not among the first group who came from Fuji Photo Film. I came in the second year of operation. But I was watching the selection of those people who had been sent into this almost unknown joint venture, and the selection was being made from the main line of Fuji Photo Film. I was watching them: Why do they go into that small company? They were among the candidates to

become the top leaders of Fuji Photo Film. So, that signaled the type of commitment that Fuji Photo Film put into this joint venture [with Xerox].

Thus, similarity of business approaches, ethical standards and corporate values is an important factor to foster trust between two international partners' or merging companies' top management. This appears to be a particularly relevant requirement to enter a 50/50 merger, alliance or joint venture agreement, of the kind of ABB, Pharmacia & Upjohn, or Fuji-Xerox. Conversely, in culturally distant or unfamiliar countries where the potential partners do not share similar business values, or where it is difficult to assess one of the partners beliefs and approach to conduct business, it is recommended to avoid 50/50 arrangements, and instead look for a controlling stake. This is the case of countries such as China, where it is often difficult for a foreign multinational to identify common business values or approaches, partly due to the country's unique historic and political developments. As a result, any existing national cultural differences may be reinforced and magnified, taking longer time for the partners to build genuine mutual trust. However, Kobayashi observes that in the case of international JVs, strong trust between the partners is an essential pre-condition to grant the business autonomy implied in a 50/50 agreement:

> We also do business in China through Xerox in Hong Kong. It's a straight trade: We export products. We also ship components and products to Xerox own manufacturing venture in Shanghai. Now, are we willing to form a joint venture with the Chinese? Probably the general answer is yes. I think Taiwan Fuji Xerox is a joint venture between Fuji Xerox Asia Pacific [48 percent], local investors [48 percent], and other investors [4 percent]. But of course Taiwan and mainland China are very, very different and we don't really know what the answer might be. The Shanghai joint venture is between Xerox and the Chinese, where I think Xerox is the majority [partner]. But a 50/50 joint venture does require a really strong trust and relationship between the partners. But also a very strong sense of trust that the partners' parents and the shareholders have toward the joint venture. Unless you are willing to allow almost a maximum degree of autonomy to the joint venture, a 50/50 arrangement is very difficult to manage.

Accordingly, the advice of Western industrialists such as Curt Nicolin, regarding multinational companies' investments in what can be considered culturally unfamiliar countries from a certain perspective, is to proceed cautiously. In particular, in countries such as China, it is recommended from the beginning to single out and rely on key "local" individuals who can be trusted to build business within the Chinese institutional environment and according to their cultural traditions, but maintaining a majority position as long as the country's culture and ways of conducting business are not well understood:

There were a few things that I concluded after a trip to China some years ago [in 1991]. Number one, the time had come when Swedish companies should invest in China. And number two: Don't ever buy 100 percent of any company in China, because you don't understand the Chinese. You must have somebody who is involved in the business, whom you can trust and who can tell you what you can do and not do in China, and he must be part owner. But you [the non-Chinese acquirer] must never buy 49 percent. Then you are lost. You must buy between 51 and 75 percent, something like that, because here we really talk about different cultures. And I could imagine that there are many more Chinese people who understand the Americans or the Europeans than there are Swedes who understand the Chinese.

Proactive Approaches to Assessing Cross-Border M&As, JVs and Alliances

Upon closer examination, it is also apparent that when assessing national cultural traits, business values and the like, the way in which a potential acquirer or partner carries out its pre-deal evaluation can be almost as important as the factors under examination. From this perspective, a proactive approach to gaining first-hand working experiences with a potential international partner or target company seems to provide rather insightful indications of the degree of fit between the companies' values, managerial styles and personalities, and their actual ability to establish mutually co-operative relations across national cultural differences. Through a proactive approach to assessing these opportunities, a potential partner, joint venturer or acquirer, attains direct *gnosis* of these practical issues prior to concluding a major international deal, in many cases qualitatively complementing the associated strategic analyses and value estimates. This type of approach has been widely favored by British Airways, establishing marketing, training or sales agreements with other international airlines which in many cases are the prelude for wider, more comprehensive JV, alliance or acquisition arrangements. In the case of ASEA, already in 1970 the company attempted to establish a JV with Brown Boveri to build nuclear power stations, and entered a limited series of license agreements in other areas. Deutsche Bank established long-standing top management relationships and took a small equity participation in the UK-based investment bank Morgan Grenfell several years before acquiring it in 1989. Japanese NEC relies on the local commercial networks of the group's parent, Mitsubishi, whose international trading and banking activities are in many cases old-dated and well established, even within the so-called "emerging" economies. In the case of prospective cross-border acquisitions, JVs and alliances, this existing group network allows the company to gather reliable information and gain introduction to a country's cultural, social and institutional peculiarities. Atsushi Fukushima, Vice President of Corporate Planning at NEC Logistics, explains:

> Many Japanese companies don't utilize consulting firms when they want to do business abroad, as might be the case of some American or European companies. When we [at NEC] do business overseas, in Latin America for example, we initially rely on some Japanese Banks as well as trading companies so called Shosha, which in most cases have long business histories in these countries, and are well aware of the strong local players there. For example, in the case of Argentina we were helped by the Bank of Tokyo (now called Tokyo Mitsubishi Bank after their integration with Mitsubishi). We visited them many times over there, and then we hosted them in Tokyo. We also have about ten Japanese trading companies there which have been doing business in Argentina for a long time, and are well aware of the structures of interest over there and what interests are strong in what fields, and what company is looking for a new business in this field or that. After this initial assessment, we select the two or three most attractive candidates for us to associate with. Then we try to approach them, telling them of our intentions, and finding out whether they are interested in establishing some collaboration with us or not. Another way is to approach the government, because NEC's main job is in the field of public communications, such as telephone companies, which in many cases are still in government hands. When these governments introduce new technologies they normally organize tenders, often in connection with the existing local companies, with whom we may be interested in collaborating through joint ventures. So we check all these possibilities and, whenever possible, reach a decision to collaborate with the most suitable partners for us.

Another interesting variant of this proactive approach to assessing international M&A, JV and alliance opportunities, has been evidenced by Korean companies such as Daewoo. Alarmed by the emergence of regional trading blocs in Europe, North and South America (none of which Korea appears to naturally fall in), the Korean *chaebol* moved aggressively into the former communist regimes of Europe and the ex-Soviet republics following the fall of the Berlin Wall in 1989. These countries were seen as providing business opportunities in their own right, but also as a strategic bridge into the rich markets of the European Union. To address the unprecedented challenges of operating in culturally unfamiliar countries, which in most cases lacked any significant exposure to capitalism and market economy principles since the end of World War II (or even during most of the 20th century in the case of Russia), Daewoo organized an intensive series of pioneering visits to these countries, starting several years before the fall of the Berlin Wall. This allowed the company to gain a direct exposure to their history, society and culture, and develop a wide local network of contacts inside these countries. As mentioned, these early business contacts often preceded and facilitated the start of official diplomatic relations between Korea and former communist European countries, which in many cases had been considerably strained since the Korean civil war period during the 1950s. Says Kang:

> Before 1988, we [South Koreans] could not visit the former communist regimes of Central and Eastern Europe. But we had offices in Western Europe, in Frankfurt and in the former Eastern Berlin. We started to establish ourselves in Eastern Europe from that base. Our earliest contacts were probably started in 1988, in Hungary. From our Budapest office, a few Daewoo executives regularly visited other Eastern European countries. They studied the history and the culture of these countries, to understand the people and each other, and in the process we established valuable contacts. We haven't had enough time, because the normalization of diplomatic relations between Korea and the Eastern European countries took place just a few years after 1988. However, during that period we thought that if opportunities would raise before us in those countries, we could participate in the privatization programs to turn-around some of their industries.

Secrecy

As already hinted, a proactive attitude towards relying on internal resources to develop both knowledge and *gnosis* of diverse national cultures and other companies' business values is also reflected in the reluctance that some companies show to overly rely on external management consultants or outside experts during the evaluation phase of international M&As, JVs or alliances. Indeed, Nicolin maintains that keeping absolute *secrecy* during the evaluation stages of the merger between ASEA and Brown Boveri was a key factor in carrying it out in a relatively smooth fashion, with the added advantage that not involving any external advisors ensured that the potential deal was kept under control at all times. Since 1992, a similar approach was taken by Pharmacia during the pre-merger evaluation phases of both FICE and Upjohn, sharply contrasting with their extensive utilization of management consultants during the troubled acquisition of Pharmacia by KabiVitrum in 1990. As will be described in the following chapter, such a circumspect approach to assessing major cross-border M&As seems to continue well into the negotiation phases. This might at first seem excessive, as the planning of a cross-cultural — or indeed any kind of M&A, JV or alliance — is usually portrayed as a heavily analytical phase, dominated by strategic thinking and duly supported by management consultants, investment bankers and other *ad hoc* external professionals. However, in 1986, a US-based study by Jemison and Sitkin argued that the mismanagement of M&As could sometimes be traced back to the pre-acquisition appraisal process. This was due to a number of impediments, such as: excessive influence of outside advisors, over-reliance on analytical "activity segmentation", the complexity and financial attractiveness of the deal, the lack of experience at the board of directors, and the parent's financial, organizational and technical weaknesses. As a result, a mishandled pre-acquisition process tended to primarily focus on strategic fit issues, at the expense of organizational fit or post-acquisition integration issues. In the case of IJVs, it has been suggested that external advisors such as lawyers and accountants might be involved in codifying the basic agreements between the partners but should not determine them, as their involvement often leads to confrontational situations outside a commercial context.[9]

Self-assessment of execution skills prior to an international M&A, JV or alliance

Another key aspect characterizing a proactive, hands-on approach to evaluating global M&As, JVs and alliances, is constituted by a company's ability and thoroughness in assessing its *own execution* skills, international experience and overall implementation capabilities prior to the deal. In this area, the specialized literature has overwhelmingly focused on developing techniques to assess the potential value of combining two companies complementary or supplementary functional resources and market presence. However, this literature devotes comparably little attention to examining whether or how a rigorous self-assessment should be conducted with regards to a company's *execution skills* to handle complex post-acquisition cultural or organizational issues, or how this type of assessment may influence the value estimates which can actually be realized from a deal.[10] Nevertheless, the consistently poor performance record of M&As, JVs and alliances suggests that under-estimating integration and implementation difficulties following the conclusion of the deal, as well as over-estimating a company's practical ability to handle these effectively, might sometimes become closely related pitfalls in the real world. By contrast, in sciences other than management, such as the military theory, the evaluation of a strategic target is always made dependent on a careful assessment of an army's readiness and practical capabilities to conquer it. The latter is not only a mechanical result of the type and amount of weaponry and soldiers that are available at a given time, but it involves soundly appraising in advance an army's fighting skills and morale, its battle experience and *esprit de corps*, as well as the individual qualities of the Generalship, the Officers and Heads of Staff to competently carry out a plan of action. A strict adherence to these principles has been in evidence in every great military campaign since ancient history.[11]

Similarly, in order to achieve strategic objectives involving major M&As, JVs and alliances across borders, certain companies seem to pay a great deal of attention to conducting a self-assessment of their past experiences, as well as carefully selecting and developing implementation leaders who demonstrate the specific practical abilities required for the job.

In the case of Electrolux-Zanussi, Gianmario Rossignolo's previous experience with the acquisition of Italy's RIVE by Sweden's SKF was a primary factor in Electrolux's decision to implement an unusually decentralized integration model in Italian Zanussi, taking advantage of both the local skills of the people, and the international strength of the acquired company's electro-domestic brands. Says Rossignolo:

> What I call the "Swedish model" of decentralization is a winner compared to other models which at the end of the day impose their own cultures and global brands. Think global and act local: Many companies say that they espouse these principles, but lose out in implementation. We have not invented it, but forms part of our culture. In Italy, I don't call myself Electrolux. I call myself Electrolux-Zanussi. We have made a portfolio of brands with all the products of Electrolux, but Zanussi is also present across Europe: in Spain, in France, in Germany. But you have to have people who are capable of implementing this design. This is what makes the difference. And in my case, for example, before Electrolux-Zanussi, I had the experience of implementing these kinds of models working across the Swedish and the Italian cultures, when [Swedish] SKF bought RIVE, a producer of automotive bearings. We located the manufacturing where we could find the best skills, and it is a fact that here in Italy you find the best competence within the SKF group for automotive bearings. If SKF had given this responsibility to Gothenburg, for example, or to Schweiburg in Germany, it would have been a big mistake. And today, the leadership of this activity, the manufacturing and R&D capabilities, are Italian. This successful experience convinced me and Electrolux that we could build a similar model with Zanussi.

In Fuji-Xerox, the extensive international, and specifically "Anglo-Saxon" experiences of Japanese leaders such as Yotaro Kobayashi, have played an important role in nurturing the unusual level of trust with the American parent, which has been singled out as a key factor to make this 50/50 joint venture endure since the early 1960s. Indeed, Kobayashi's early living experiences in the UK and wide exposure to the US educational and business spheres have been highly unusual for a Japanese executive of his generation. This has been highlighted in the Japanese and Western business media, which likes to point out that Kobayashi's fluency in English, cosmopolitan attitude and American style approach to management are sharply in contrast with the traditional Japanese executive style, having gained him a following amongst young Japanese managers.

In the case of the 1987 merger between ASEA and Brown Boveri, Nicolin observes that a crucial aspect during the early negotiation stages, was to ensure that Brown Boveri would agree that Percy Barnevik, then ASEA's CEO, should be the Chief Executive of the merged Group. As mentioned, Nicolin had already in 1980 singled out Barnevik as the right man to lead the unprecedented restructuring and subsequent global expansion which the company was about to carry out. In the case of ABB, in spite of the underlying complementarity between the merging companies' businesses, an analogous phase of consolidation was expected to take place in some of their key markets after the conclusion of the deal, followed by a period of aggressive global expansion. However, it was not only these individual skills and experiences that were assessed at the outset of the ABB merger, but also other approaches that ASEA's top executives had previously experienced when managing other complex international mergers. For example, Nicolin observes that establishing a rotating Chairmanship at the Board level, was an important mechanism to foster co-operation between ASEA's and Brown Boveri's Board executives, across the national cultural differences that existed:

> When deciding what type of management and what kind of organization we [ASEA and Brown Boveri] should have after the merger, we had no difficulties to agree. But when we entered this merger, Mr. Wallenberg and I had of course experienced a similar situation at SAS [Scandinavian Airline Systems]. There you had three nations joining together to form one company, and in each of these three countries you had to consider the public, the government, the private investors, and the national airlines. There were six shareholders in SAS and we had one Chairman from each of the three countries involved. Every year one was elected as the leading Chairman, and the next year it was the turn of another country Chairman, and so on. After some years the same person could serve again as a leading Chairman. Of course, there are different qualities of people, different habits, etc. in the Nordic countries, although we understand each others' languages. But we also found that we could solve our disagreements on various matters. And at the time of the ABB merger, I had already been in SAS for fifteen years, and for ten years I had been one of the Chairmen. And that made me confident that we could form an organization with Brown Boveri where we also had two Chairmen. So, we agreed to try two co-Chairmen in ABB: One was the Executive Chairman for one year, and the next year it was the turn of the other one. That approach worked well.

Moreover, a pre-merger assessment of the level of *execution skills* that was required to integrate ASEA and Brown Boveri, was partly the result of a clear vision of the type of organization that was desired, as well as the practical difficulties inherent in implementing it. In this case, the vision of a multi-domestic structure was coherent with ASEA's and Brown Boveri's managerial experiences overseas, giving these companies a first-hand insight into both the upside and associated risks involved in implementing this kind of design. Thus, all the major strategic objectives, as well as the practical managerial challenges involved in creating a matrix-based global co-ordination structure, while simultaneously fostering flexibility through widely autonomous local operations and a small central headquarters, were already identified and assessed *before* the merger, and continue to represent ABB's organizational vision to this day. Nicolin remarks:

> We [ASEA] and Brown Boveri were similar in that we had a long experience managing across different countries, establishing ourselves in these countries' societies, and selecting top leaders from these countries to run the local operations. We were aware that it is very difficult to co-ordinate this kind of organization and still keep it flexible. However, I think that any large company must have a matrix organization. If there is something that we have made wrong

with ABB, is that we could possibly do with a matrix that is less complicated. We have three dimensions in our matrix and you get fairly big groups to make decisions, ordinary operating decisions. My ambition is to see if we couldn't simplify the matrix in the future. I am not saying that it doesn't work, but there is a little tendency to become a bureaucracy, which we, of course, in private business don't like. That was a great ambition and one of the necessary things before the merger: To have a small head office.

The highly diverse approaches to assessing international M&As, JVs and alliances that we have described in this chapter, have in common a strong emphasis on looking for broad business complementarity at the basis of a potential deal. Building on this underlying complementarity, a proactive appraisal is carried out of the degree to which a company can practically build mutually trustful and collaborative relations with a potential partner, in spite of the national cultural differences which may exist. This type of approach has been favored by companies such as: ABB, British Airways, Daewoo, Electrolux-Zanussi, NEC and Fuji-Xerox, which have consistently pursued collaborative M&A, JV or alliance agreements internationally, assiduously assessing their potential partners' degree of similarity in business values and openness to work co-operatively across national cultural differences prior to the deal. Moreover, an important factor for success at this stage is a company's ability to appraise its "own troops", specific capabilities and overall experience to handle the implementation complexities related to international M&As, JVs or alliances. The latter often combine national and corporate cultural issues, personnel integration difficulties and organizational complications, significantly affecting the value that can be actually realized from these types of deals during the implementation phases. Based on these assessments, in the following chapter we describe how these companies move to actually build trust and develop co-operative relationships during the negotiation of international M&As, JVs or alliances.

Notes and References

[1] See Chapters 1 and 3.

[2] See, for example: Salter, M. S. and W. A. Weinhold. *Diversification through Acquisitions: Strategies for Creating Economic Value*, Free Press, New York, 1979; Singh, H. and C. Montgomery. "Corporate acquisition strategies and economic performance", *Strategic Management Journal*, 8, 1987, pp. 377-386.

[3] Chatterjee, S. "Type of synergy and economic value: the impact of acquisitions on merging and rival firms", *Strategic Management Journal*, 7, 1986, pp. 119-139.

[4] For a performance analyses of acquisitions in new, but "related" markets, see: Shelton, L. "Strategic business fits and corporate acquisition: empirical evidence", *Strategic Management Journal*, May-June 1988, pp. 279-288. For an empirical performance study on cross-border alliances highlighting the value of "strategic complementarity", see: Bleeke, J. and D. Ernst. "The way to win in cross-border alliances", *Harvard Business Review*, November, 1991, pp. 127-135.

[5] Morosini, P. and H. Singh. "Post-cross-border acquisitions: implementing 'national culture compatible' strategies to improve performance", *European Management Journal*, 12(4), December 1994, pp. 390-400; Haspeslagh, P. C. and D. B. Jemison. *Managing Acquisitions: Creating Value through Corporate Renewal*, Free Press, New York, 1991; Lane, H. W. and P. Beamish. "Cross-cultural cooperative behavior in joint ventures in LDCs", *Management International Review*, Special Issue, 1990, pp. 87-102; Buono, A., J. Bowditch and J. Lewis. "When cultures collide: the anatomy of a merger", *Human Relations*, 38, 1985, pp. 477-500.

[6] Based on the numerical measure developed in our research, Sweden and Italy were the most "culturally distant" countries in the empirical sample utilized (see Figure 3.1).

[7] Sampson, A. *Company Man. The Rise and Fall of Corporate Life*, Harper Collins, 1995; Chan Kim and Mauborgne, R. "A procedural justice model of strategic decision making, *Organisation Science*, 1995; Blodgett, L. "Partner contributions as predictors of equity share in international joint ventures", *Journal of International Business Studies*, 22 (1), 1991, pp. 63-78; Geringer, J. M. "Strategic determinants of partner selection criteria in international joint ventures", *Journal of International Business Studies*, 22 (1), 1991, pp. 41-62; Parkhe, A. " 'Messy' research, methodological predispositions, and theory development in international joint ventures", *Academy of Management Review*, 18(2), 1993, pp. 227-268; Nahavandi, A. and A. Malekzadeh. "Acculturation in mergers and acquisition", *Academy of Management Review*, 13(1), 1988, pp. 79-90; Kumar, N. "The power of trust in manufacturer-retailer relationships", *Harvard Business Review*, November-December 1996, pp. 92-106.

[8] From a strictly legal stand-point, Fuji-Xerox Co., Ltd. (Japan), was formed in 1962 as a "50/50" joint venture between UK-based Rank Xerox Limited and Japan's Fuji Photo Film. However, the actual development and cross-cultural management of this joint venture have historically centered around the relationship between US-based Xerox Corporation (a majority shareholder of Britain's Rank Xerox Limited, established in 1956) and Japan's Fuji Photo Film. The US-Japanese relationship behind Fuji-Xerox was bound to be further enhanced after June 1997, when it was apparent that Britain's Rank Organization was taking steps to progressively sell its minority stake in Rank Xerox Limited.

[9] See: Jemison, D. B. and S. B. Sitkin. "Corporate acquisitions: a process perspective", *Academy of Management Review*, 11(1), 1986, pp. 145-163. For an empirical examination of the role of lawyers and accountants in IJV design, see: Lane, H. W. and P. Beamish. "Cross-cultural cooperative behavior in joint ventures in LDCs", *Management International Review*, Special Issue, 1990, pp. 87-102.

[10] For example, functional and strategic approaches to appraising M&As are well described in Porter, M. E. *Competitive Strategy*, Free Press, New York, 1980, p. 352; Copeland, T., T. Koller and J. Murrin. *Valuation. Measuring and Managing the Value of Companies*, John Wiley, New York, 1990.

[11] See: Dupuy, Colonel R. E. and Colonel T. N. Dupuy. *The Encyclopedia of Military History*, New York and London, 1970, revised edns New York and London, 1976, 1986; Laffin, J. *A Dictionary of Battles*, London, 1986.

CHAPTER 8

Negotiating M&As, JVs and Alliances across National Cultures

> In forming the plan of a campaign, it is requisite to foresee everything the enemy may do, and to be prepared with the necessary means to counteract it. Plans of campaign may be modified *ad infinitum* according to circumstances, the genius of the general, the character of the troops, and the features of the country.
>
> Napoleon Bonaparte

Although during the assessment of a cross-border M&A, JV or alliance, related-complementary cultural openness and similarity of business values are seen as fostering genuine trust and a collaborative attitude in spite of national cultural differences, the degree to which these are actually generated is made clear during the negotiation stages, when the potential partners proceed to establish direct contacts and relationships. Here, specific *execution* mechanisms built around circumspection, ownership arrangements, the establishment of a common managerial steering structure, and the sheer determination to generate mutual trust above strictly financial aspects, can lead to the creation of a collaborative and multicultural organization following an international M&A, JV or alliance deal, contrasting the notion that national cultural differences must necessarily have a detrimental impact in these situations.

Building Genuine Trust Across National Cultural Differences

It has been mentioned that a proactive approach to assessing international (related-complementary) M&As, JVs and alliances is often useful to establish whether similarities in business values and the personalities of the key top executives involved offer enough grounds for nurturing co-operative relationships across national cultural differences. However, when looking at the speed with which some major and complex cross-border M&A, JV and alliance deals have been negotiated and successfully concluded in the past, it is apparent that, beyond a proactive assessment approach, certain companies have *de facto* established a long period of quasi negotiation activities, where a particular deal, or series of deals, are tenaciously pursued. The 1987 merger between ASEA and Brown Boveri is a case in point to illustrate this. Although at the time it was the largest ever industrial merger since Royal Dutch and Shell joined their operations at the turn of the 20th century, the complex deal leading to the creation of ABB was reportedly concluded within a few weeks time. However, Nicolin suggests that this merger had actually been in the making for nearly twenty years. Here, it was not just a strategic business complementarity which led to the company's strong conviction to pursue merging with Brown Boveri, as other international candidates were examined which could have adequately fitted the bill from a purely functional or geographic perspective. Rather, it was the combination of the companies' relative size, and particularly the cultural characteristics of Brown Boveri's relatively small country of origin and similarity of corporate values, which deeply convinced ASEA that it could eventually establish trustful and co-operative relations with Brown Boveri following a merger, and as a result create value through the effective combination of the merging companies' complementary resources. Says Nicolin:

> In the late 1960s I was the Managing Director of ASEA, and Marcus Wallenberg was the Chairman. He then said to me: "I have the feeling that ASEA is too small to fight all these giants around the world in the long term, and I think it would be beneficial if we started to talk collaboration with some of our competitors. Would you give that some thought and make a suggestion on what you think should be the right company to approach?" I did that, and then I came back to him and said: "Number one I don't think that we shall look for a cooperation with a 'giant' because then we would disappear in the cooperation. I don't think that we could choose a very large company from a big country (this is an American company I was referring to), because then again we will be lost. Because large companies coming from big countries want to impose their own national cultures, and they feel that they know best. And that's not a good attitude for cooperation. And further, I think we should try to find a company where management of people have something similar to our values. It may not be identical, but at least similar." He agreed with me on that, but I also said that with these criteria, I had chosen Brown Boveri. And he was then a good friend of the Chairman of Brown Boveri, so it was easy to arrange a visit to Sweden for him and some of his colleagues. And then we discussed various forms of collaborations.

Although ASEA had experienced significant growth during the 1950s and 1960s, establishing itself as one of the ten largest electrical engineering companies in the world, with around 40,000 employees (three-quarters of them based in Sweden), and recognized world-class technologies in its field, throughout the 1970s Brown Boveri was on average four times larger than ASEA in revenue size. Although this still put Brown Boveri closer to ASEA compared to other, American-based competitors such as General Electric, it was perhaps as a result of this major difference in size that, when Nicolin first approached Brown Boveri, the time was not ripe to pursue a major collaboration scheme between the two companies, of the kind that Marcus Wallenberg had envisioned. Moreover, at the time there was no apparent urgency on Brown Boveri's side to embark in any major partnership with a third party. Nevertheless, Nicolin did not come back empty handed from this series of initial contacts, being able to start a limited series of co-operation agreements between ASEA and Brown Boveri:

> At the time, around 1970, they felt that we were rather unimportant. They didn't say it of course but it was there. We only achieved two things: first, we bought a license for very large steam turbines, and secondly, we made an agreement on certain areas where we had completely different technologies. In addition, it was agreed that we would open up our doors to each other in a number of specific fields, in order to see whether the combination of our different experiences could generate something better. But we did not generate a wider concept of co-operation.

During most of the 1970s, ASEA had to face a global recessionary market stagnation which had a highly detrimental impact on the aggregated demand for electrical energy. As a result, the company experienced very serious financial difficulties, but a compelling need to restructure its operations was at the time inhibited by a markedly conservative corporate culture and Sweden's powerful union organizations. However, in 1980 Percy Barnevik was appointed President and CEO of ASEA, and immediately embarked in one of the most comprehensive restructuring programs which had been carried out in the European industrial arena. Under his stewardship, ASEA swiftly closed dozens of inefficient plants around the world, significantly increasing the efficiency levels in the best production sites, drastically reducing the number of employees at headquarters, and aggressively expanding internationally through acquisitions and alliances. As a result of Barnevik's determined corporate shake-up, by 1987 ASEA had grown to match Brown Boveri in size and had actually surpassed it in profitability. The company which only seven years before had found itself in a precarious financial position, had vigorously expanded to the point that pursuing Marcus Wallenberg's early vision of global collaboration with a major competitor appeared within reach. It was at this stage, seventeen years after their first collaboration discussion had taken place, that a perseverant Nicolin re-opened a period of courtship with Brown Boveri:

> During the early part of 1987, a friend of mine told me that he knew the Chairman of Brown Boveri, and had got the impression that he would want to meet me. So I called him up to say that I would visit Germany shortly, and in that occasion it would be easy for me to come over for a meeting. But that didn't suit him. So three weeks later, I called him again, and said: "I am now coming

to Germany, couldn't you find time for a meeting?" No no, no. He couldn't. After that I visited Switzerland, but he couldn't meet me on that occasion either. And then after some time I called him again and said: "Now I will be in Germany. Can you see me on Sunday?" "Hmmm, excellent", he said. "Can you come then and then?" But two days later I got a call from his secretary, saying that unfortunately, he had to make a trip around the country. I said: "Which country?" "Germany", she answered. "Well, I am in Germany. Which city?" "So and so", she said. "But that is fine. I'm also in that city. At what hotel does he stay?" "So and so". "Hotel so and so? But I will also stay at that hotel!" And then: "Could you ask him whether we could have breakfast together?" Which we had, Monday morning, and then we made an agreement to meet with our respective general managers to discuss various areas of cooperation.

Thus, it was in 1987, after several years of comprehensive restructuring, that a renewed ASEA could resume merger negotiations with a major competitor from a position of financial strength. Although it had in the mean time examined acquisition opportunities to acquire major businesses from former Germany-based AEG and General Electric, when it came to form a truly global concern, it continued to tenaciously pursue a collaborative arrangement with Brown Boveri, which several years before had been already identified as the right company to merge with. Says Nicolin:

> But when he [Brown Boveri's Chairman] came home, he started to discuss whether it wouldn't be feasible to be legal competitors in certain fields and very close partners in other areas. Wouldn't that be a fine collaboration? We then concluded that maybe it wasn't. And then Brown Boveri had a different attitude to collaboration than before, because they had lost money for ten years, and we were making decent money at the time. So I went to Mr. [Peter] Wallenberg, who was then on our Board of Directors, and said to him that I had the feeling that Brown Boveri could consider not only a collaboration but that we join in a merger. So he immediately said: "If that is so, so much the better."

After it was sensed that the opportunity to negotiate a global collaboration agreement with Brown Boveri was finally within reach, ASEA's Nicolin quickly moved to establish closer personal bonds and relationships between the top management levels of both companies. These initial contacts were kept within a fairly reduced circle of persons, with the first face-to-face discussions being dominated by the need to ensure that, in spite of national cultural differences, a broad commonality of strategic objectives, business values and ethical standards effectively existed between the two companies. Nicolin recalls:

> When we met over lunch [Brown Boveri's Chairman and myself], I only tried to get him to speak all the time, and I asked questions. At the end of the lunch, I said: "Now I must check that I have not misunderstood you. I get the impression that you could consider a merger." Later on that day, we had a discussion

with our general managers, and decided that we should have a further meeting with our top representatives, the owners of our companies. On the first of July [1987], if I don't remember wrongly, Mr. Wallenberg and Mr. Schmidheiny [Brown Boveri's main shareholder at the time] came along, and we discussed this and came to "that would be a good idea." And we also discussed our company values and things like that.

Similarly, in the case of British Airways it is highlighted that the company carefully identifies potential international partners a long time prior to entering any serious negotiations, and moves to discuss business opportunities with another company only after genuine relationships of trust have been established at the top executive levels. Consistent application of this principle ensures that common customer service standards and working co-operation can actually be fostered across national cultural differences, throughout the company's international network of alliances covering Europe, Asia, Australia and the USA. For example, the airline had actively started to look for a potential alliance partner in the US market since the mid 1980s, soon after it was privatized. During early 1991, as the Gulf War erupted, leading to a dramatic decrease in the levels of passenger capacity utilization, British Airways moved to closely assess and monitor opportunities of combining operations with some of the leading US carriers at the time. However, it only started serious negotiations with USAir, after it had established friendly relationships at the top management levels, developing a direct "feeling" for the strong similarities that existed between the two companies' business and service philosophies. Marshall explains:

[In February 1992] our respective airlines, in the form of Roger Maynard and Frank Salizzoni, USAir's Executive Vice President, Finance, met by chance in the New York offices of Price Waterhouse, the accountancy firm called into advise financially troubled TWA. We had been invited to consider the possibility of acquiring TWA's international operation; USAir was looking at their domestic network. (. . .) As the talk of the TWA routes and how different ones might fit into either network, it slowly dawned on them that there could be far more compatibility between the USAir and British Airways than was on offer to each of us from TWA (. . .) It was beginning to look promising on paper, but an alliance would work only if our philosophies matched when it came to customer service and operational style (. . .) The only way to find out was to arrange a private meeting between Seth [Schofield, former USAir's CEO] and myself. This took place over dinner at the City Club in Washington one evening in the Spring of 1992. No one else was present, just the two of us. You will have to ask Seth what his first impressions were, but in him I found a soul-mate. Like me, Seth began his career in customer service — he as customer services agent for Allegheny Airlines at Washington National Airport, me as cadet purser on the ships of the old Orient Line. His views on the way an airline should be managed, ran parallel with our own British Airways way of thinking which places quality, value for money and customer service at the top of our list of priorities. He was putting this into practice with USAir and it became obvious that both our people and our customers would find comfortable "fits" with USAir and *vice versa*.

A first-hand acquaintance of the personality fit at the top managerial levels, as well as the strong commonality that existed between both companies' business approaches, ensured that the basic complementarity between British Airways' European links, and USAir access to the American domestic market, could be effectively exploited through a co-operative alliance agreement between the airlines. This took place in July 1992, with the work on the partnership starting immediately after, covering the establishment of common marketing and sales points, broad share-code flight programs between US and UK destinations, extensive joint customer service training, and sharing of international airport terminal facilities in the two countries. Overall, the partnership between British Airways and USAir lasted for about four years. In December 1996, it was abruptly severed shortly after it had been announced in June that British Airways and American Airlines had concluded their long-expected alliance agreement, the largest ever attempted in the international airline industry. However, it should also be noted that British Airways' relationship with USAir had become increasingly strained since January 1996, when Seth Schofield was replaced by Stephen Wolf as the latter company's CEO.

Deutsche Bank's acquisition of Morgan Grenfell, the prestigious British merchant bank, can be traced back to 1983, when a good personal relationship developed between F. Wildhelm Christians, at the time one of the two spokesmen at the Deutsche Bank Board, and Christopher Reeves, then Head of Morgan Grenfell. As a result, Deutche Bank acquired a 5 percent equity position in Morgan Grenfell during the early 1980s. Following this investment, a good relationship was nurtured between the two companies' Board members for a number of years, leading to Deutsche Bank's closer familiarization with Morgan Grenfell's "Anglo-Saxon" investment banking approaches, and the latter's first-hand exposure to the more conservative German commercial banking style. In October 1987, following the stock market crash, Morgan Grenfell had to face a substantial loss of around £50 million on its securities position. Following this event, Deutsche Bank's executives point out that Morgan Grenfell signaled a disposition to offer their securities business for sale. However, no conclusive results were reached at that time. It was only in early 1989, after Morgan Grenfell had dealt with their securities losses, that Deutsche Bank started to look at it as a serious prospective acquisition. During most of 1989, from February to early November, a dedicated team at Deutsche Bank's Group Strategy Department thoroughly carried out an internal acquisition analysis of Morgan Grenfell. Following their favorable conclusions, Deutsche Bank's top executives started direct negotiations with those of Morgan Grenfell during early November 1989. After just two-and-a-half weeks, a deal was concluded and announced publicly.

In the case of NEC, one key aspect of the company's policy when expanding abroad, is to start acquisition or alliance negotiations only in those countries where "our presence is welcomed". This has been a guiding principle throughout the company's global expansion efforts, ever since it was introduced during the 1960s by Koji Kobayashi, its legendary former CEO who first started in earnest the internationalization of NEC. This policy doubtless reflects a careful assessment of the deep-rooted cultural resistances and stereotypes that can be found in certain countries, and which even during the 1980s and 1990s have concretely affected many Japanese multinationals' expansion efforts overseas. Building on these experiences, NEC actively maintains a network of commercial contacts in the countries where it seeks to establish a presence, moving to negotiate alliances or acquisitions only after an appropriate level of personal relationships have been developed with a wide base of local businessmen and institutions. In the case of Daewoo's massive expansion within the former communist regimes of Central and Eastern Europe, as well as the ex-Soviet Republics, it has been said that the company's acquisitive spree was preceded by an intensive period of visits to these countries, to gain direct insights into their culture and history and build an institutional network of contacts. These took place over several years before the fall of the Berlin Wall in 1989, involving many of the company's top executives and officials, including Kim Woo-Choong, founder and Chairman of the group, who had an extensive and direct role in developing personal, long-standing relationships inside these countries' business and political spheres.

In Eastern Europe or within the former Soviet Union, Daewoo's emphasis on studying every country's history and culture prior to carrying out major expansion efforts can be partly interpreted in the light of the need to understand the psychology of people that are culturally distant from the perspective of Korean or "Asian" values. Moreover, countries such as the Czech Republic or Hungary, which had a strong industrial tradition prior to World War II, lent them to be treated strictly on a case-by-case basis, avoiding any generic "emerging economy" or "Eastern European" labels to be reflected in undifferentiated approaches to management in these countries. A reciprocal tendency can be noted in some Western European or US executives who need to conduct complex business negotiations in countries such as China or Japan. Nicolin observes:

> I think it is very important that you try to understand culture before you start to negotiate. I organized a trip to China several years ago to ensure that I understood the psychology of the Chinese, and I have studied the economic development of Japan since the middle of the nineteenth century, because I needed to understand the Japanese psychology. I think it is never negative to have a good general knowledge in these cases.

When establishing IJVs across culturally distant or so-called emerging economies, NEC's executives have also found that knowledge of a country's religious backgrounds can help understand the degree to which working compromises can be practically reached with the local partners, based on a shared cultural perception of common sense. Says Fukushima:

> When we negotiate joint ventures across various countries all over the world, one important problem for us is to identify at what point, or on what condition, we can compromise with our local partners. That depends upon the national cultures in the countries we work in. And for me, religious background, faith and traditions are very influential in this respect. If you do business in the Latin American countries, their values are based upon Christian cultures. But China was said to be traditional according to the teachings of Confucius as well as Buddhism, like other Asian and Near Eastern countries. We have to look deeply into these traditions. In Latin America, for example, our conception of common sense coincides with theirs. But in China, Near Eastern or African countries, we don't know what common sense is. In Latin America we can have an OK from headquarters regarding the agreements we reach: "We have thought that we have come to this point, and now, we should have a compromise." But in China, for example, today we agree on this point, but tomorrow they ask for more, because they have other companies offering better conditions than us, so our Chinese partner comes back and says: "We have a better offer from your competitors, would you like to accept this? If you don't, you can go home."

However, what all these diverse approaches to negotiation have in common, is that establishing long-standing personal relationships across national cultural differences, ensuring that there exists a fundamental similarity of business values, and seeking to understand a country's diverse historic, religious and cultural traditions, are ultimately seen as ways to develop genuine trust between two potential merging companies or international partners. When this level of mutual reliance on each other does not reach the appropriate managerial echelons, or comes across without the required intensity, specific steps are taken to foster trust as early as possible during the negotiation stages. Failure to do so may lead to detrimental performance during the subsequent implementation phase, or compromise the speed of the negotiations. Here, national cultural differences can play a significant role, as establishing genuine trust often means fairly different things according to the specific context in which business negotiations are carried out. The 50/50 merger between Sweden's Pharmacia and US-based Upjohn offers a good illustration of this. During the initial contacts between both companies, it was agreed that a consensual approach to decision-making should be taken whenever possible. However, Ekberg remarks that, already during the merger negotiation stages, it was made clear that having to constantly reach agreements between the two companies at every step was going to be a rather time-consuming process, aggravated by the considerable differences that were experienced between some of the US cultural traditions and those of Sweden:

> One crucial difficulty during the negotiations was of course coping with all the US legislation and traditions, which are totally different from the Swedish ones. We have a more open society, they have a more legal society. And to get all this together was very, very difficult. The US is a lawyer's paradise: They want to have everything on paper. In Sweden we can discuss and shake hands, and that's enough. But they [Upjohn's executives] wanted to have everything on paper, so we said: "You don't need that because we can trust."

In addition to the legal structure of the merger, and the considerable time demands required by the US "legalistic" traditions, Upjohn's insistence on reaching mutual agreements at every step of the merger negotiations may have also been related to its corporate background and ownership traditions, which were very different from Pharmacia's. Indeed, prior to their merger agreement, Upjohn had less international M&A experience than Pharmacia, being relatively centralized and concentrated in the US market. Founded in 1887 by W.E. Upjohn, the company was still tightly and conservatively run by the founder's family by the time of the 1995 merger agreement with Pharmacia, owning 20 percent of Upjohn's shares. However, one year earlier, in a move widely perceived as signaling the company's decision to enter the pharmaceutical global ranks, John L. Zabriskie was hired from rival Merck Sharp & Dohme, to become only the second non-family CEO of Upjohn. He immediately embarked on a comprehensive restructuring and cost-cutting turnaround which led to a 25 percent increase in earnings by the end of that year. More significantly, he managed to convince Upjohn's Board of directors and other key family members, to loosen their grip on the company and find an international partner in order to become one of the world's top pharmaceutical companies. This led to the initially complex and time-consuming merger negotiation process between Pharmacia and Upjohn.

"Merging before the merger" builds managerial trust to keep up negotiation speed

However, Pharmacia knew from its successful experience integrating Italy's Farmitalia-Carlo Erba (FICE) in 1993, that only by creating mutual trust across every key managerial levels in both companies would the merged organization manage to integrate at the required speed. Therefore, in order to break out of the sort of vicious circle that had been created during the negotiations with Upjohn, Pharmacia's leaders simply proposed to "merge before the merge". In other words, both companies decided to start drafting their post-merger integration plan together, already during the negotiation phase and prior to the official shareholders approval of the merger. This agreement effectively turned a potential weakness into an advantage, by allowing both companies to produce a joint merger plan at the appropriate speed, in spite of all the cultural sensitivities and burdensome legal procedures that had to be carried out. Says Ekberg:

When we were in the negotiation phase, we could see that it was going to be very costly to make a deal. Then we held up the negotiations, because, based on our previous experiences with FICE and Pharmacia, we realized that we had to make our business plan together, as well as the steering structure and the management philosophy of the merger. So we created management teams together, and they started to work with these business plans for the next three, four, five years after the merger. At the beginning, they [Upjohn] couldn't see the advantage of doing that, because: "Isn't it better that we make a deal, announce it, and after that start working through all these issues?" Whereas our experience was that the first day when you announce this kind of deal, it must be ready, because the organizations become paralyzed, and a number of questions come up. You must have answers to all these questions.

However, to jointly produce a formal post-merger integration plan during the negotiation stages was not the only benefit from this initiative. More importantly, many senior managers from both companies who were expected to lead the implementation of the merger, had the real opportunity very early on of working together, getting to know each other, openly discussing their views and obtaining a first-hand experience of the profound cultural diversities that existed. Ekberg explains:

The advantage was not only that we produced the pre-merger integration plan, but we also got to know each other. People from our side got to know their people. It was about ten or eight people from both sides [Pharmacia and Upjohn], who got acquainted, started to like each other and appreciate their different experiences and views. This was very important because the post-merger steering structure was not easy to design: They [at Upjohn] were a very centralized and functionally organized company, whereas we were a decentralized, profit center organized company. We had to find a mix between these two approaches in the new company.

The process of merging before the merger was initiated two months before the deal went public in August the 20th, 1995, and was carried out until early November 1995. By that time, Pharmacia had finally succeeded in securing the vote of 90 percent of the shares of its 440,000 private shareholders, a strenuous effort which was required as a result of the company's privatization in 1994. Once Pharmacia's and Upjohn's shareholders approval was granted, a more detailed planning phase ensued to address every aspect of the merger integration.

Although Pharmacia and Upjohn managed to timely negotiate a merger agreement, the initial post-merger management structure maintained a high level of decentralization. The new organization consisted of three pharmaceutical product centers (PPCs) in the US, Sweden and Italy, rather facilitating the preservation of the corporate cultural identities of the main groups involved in the merger. This approach had been adopted in Pharmacia's 1992 acquisition of FICE, but proved not to be as effective in this "merger of equals". Maintaining three separate regional PPCs did not promote the creation of a single corporate culture in Pharmacia & Upjohn, which added to the difficulty of co-ordinating across borders such critical areas as R&D and manufacturing/supply operations. In mid-1997, after the appointment of Fred Hassan as the new CEO (following the resignation of John Zabriskie), Pharmacia & Upjohn adopted yet a different organizational structure which centralized global R&D and manufacturing/supply operations, and consolidated the management of pharmaceutical R&D.

Structuring a Cross-Cultural Deal in Secrecy

One of the striking features of the 1987 merger negotiations between ASEA and Brown Boveri was the great lengths taken by both companies' top management to ensure that mutual trust and the conviction of joining together as one company were there. These, rather than overly analytical, strategic or financial aspects, seem to have been the dominating themes throughout the pre-merger negotiation stages, since both companies were already convinced of its strategic merits. An important factor behind this type of approach might have been the particular ownership structure of the merging companies, where decision-making had traditionally been concentrated on a few dominating shareholders compared with the wider ownership base of many US- or UK-based multinationals. Supporting these impressions, it should be noted that the merger negotiations were kept in extreme secrecy, without the participation of any external consultants or advisors, and that the final decision to merge was taken by a small group of six individuals from both companies, based on an extremely thin legal document. Following the merger agreement, all the related documentation was locked away in a Swiss bank with the intention of it being released 25 years later. This strong emphasis on privacy and confidentiality can be partly explained by the fact that ASEA and Brown Boveri were amongst the *élite* industrial jewels in their countries of origin, responsible for building a large part of Sweden's, Switzerland's and Germany's electrical and industrial infrastructure throughout the companies' long histories. Thus, knowing of their pre-merger negotiations in advance could have had unpredictable effects on these countries' business spheres and public opinion. In addition, Nicolin argues that secrecy was fundamental to build a shared conviction on the agreements and decisions to be reached by ASEA's and Brown Boveri's top management, continuously fostering an environment of mutual trust and understanding of their national cultural differences, and without allowing for any external interference. It is in fact suggested that not strictly adhering to this principle constitutes a major pitfall during the negotiation phase of M&As and alliances:

> The number one mistake is that they [the merging companies or partners] don't keep quiet. It gets known. Sometimes it gets known to journalists before certain Board members know about it. And when the press talks about a merger

between two companies, you don't know what they can invent. That's not good. And I have always made a point that important things should be explained when you know the whole story, not when you have half of it. Keep quiet until it's ready, and you will avoid misunderstandings.

In the case of Pharmacia and Upjohn, secrecy was key to smoothly reach a 50/50 capitalization of both companies through the stock markets, allowing them to enter a merger of equals quite literally from a contractual stand-point. In this merger agreement, there were no financial or other type of assets changing hands between both companies. Rather, Pharmacia and Upjohn simply put their complementary assets on the table to combine and optimize them on a global scale. However, Ekberg explains that ensuring that each party could own exactly 50 percent of the combined company, was a most critical pre-condition during the negotiations:

> The merger was legally concluded in August [1995], but during the whole evaluation and negotiation process it remained a top secret. It was particularly important to keep it secret during the negotiations, because of the stock market situation: We were not allowed to merge unless it was a 50/50 capitalization. But they [Upjohn] had a much higher market capitalization as they were valued in the US. It was about 60/40 [stock capitalization for Upjohn/ Pharmacia respectively]. Then in May 1995 we started to negotiate whether it was going to be possible to really make a merger of equals. We presented our ideas to our respective Boards of Directors. And then their market capitalization started to go down while ours increased a bit. I don't know if there were some rumors in the financial markets, but I don't think so. But as a result, when we started to make our negotiations, we were at a 55/45 capitalization level, or something like that. Then we said: "OK, now it must be possible to equalize our market capitalization to reach a 50/50 level."

Based on the poor performance record of international M&As, JVs and alliances to date, it is difficult to take these guidelines of secrecy lightly. Indeed, it has been previously described how international acquirers or part-ners can be concretely affected whenever the negotiation of a deal becomes part of the public domain. Although in some cases this leads to no major detrimental consequences for the parties involved, widespread speculation at the outset of M&A or alliance negotiations often translates in financial spec-ulation. Even more pointedly, when these negotiations cannot be kept secret due to legal or procedural requirements, public speculation can occasionally spin out of control, escalating into seemingly chauvinistic, or even nearly xenophobic reactions which can considerably modify the outcomes expected from a deal. Such situations have been variously experienced by companies such as British Airways, Sony or Daewoo, throughout their international M&A, JV and alliance activities.[1]

Thus, apart from genuinely building trust at the top management levels, it is perhaps to prevent these kinds of events from happening that ASEA and Brown Boveri went to such great lengths to ensure secrecy and circumspection during their merger negotiations. After all, the radical and widespread tribal resistance found by ABB in countries such as Germany and Switzerland at the very start of the merger implementation, could have easily affected its very existence had the merger negotiations been made public at some stage. In particular, the companies ensured a total absence of external consultants or advisors throughout the entire negotiation phase, which may have even affected the value estimates of the deal, as well as the degree to which the stock markets — without a full disclosure of the merger agreement — could fairly reflect the actual value of ABB, the combined company. From this perspective, what makes this approach to negotiations quite unique is that even pricing and other related considerations seem to have deliberately taken a relatively secondary place *vis-à-vis* ensuring that the conviction to merge really existed on the part of both companies' top decision-makers, and that all the key appointments and "difficult" decisions could be smoothly sorted out from the outset, within an environment of privacy and mutual trust. Says Nicolin:

> [In July 1987] before we went into our meeting to discuss the merger with Brown Boveri, the three of us, Mr. [Peter] Wallenberg, Mr. [Percy] Barnevik and myself, had discussions on how we should go about it. And someone said that, having come this far, we should employ an American company that was a good consultant. But I said: "No, I don't think we should. What we need to know is whether we want to make a merger with Brown Boveri or with some other company. That is the important thing. Whether we pay ten percent more or less is a secondary notion. The important thing is that we really join the right company." And we seemed to agree on that. And the fact is that Brown Boveri is quoted on the stock exchange and so is ASEA, but I am sure that if we go to our own hearts, we both think that we are valued too little on the stock exchange. But if we ask a consultant to come in, they would move around within the two groups and we will be head news in all the economic papers around the world long before we had made any agreement, and that could cause us a lot of damage. So we shall keep quiet. And we shall have everybody to sign a silence agreement. So we agreed that we would not ask for a consultant, but we would try to have an agreement between the three plus three gentlemen that met. And we succeeded on that. And then Brown Boveri agreed that Mr. Barnevik should become the Chief Executive of the group, which was exactly what I had intended to propose.

Hence, Nicolin's nearly obsessive determination to ensure that ASEA and Brown Boveri could really be able to work co-operatively after their merger agreement, and as a result effectively combine the companies' complementary resources across borders, led to their emphasizing secrecy, trust and managerial aspects over strictly financial ones during the negotiation stages. This type of approach arguably lies oddly *vis-à-vis* widely proposed negotiation strategies based on bidding the right price, and ensuring that a fair stock valuation is reached in the context of a merger or acquisition. Indeed, these views often cite a tendency to paying excessive equity premiums, or engaging in overpriced acquisition or merger transactions, as fundamental pitfalls leading to their poor overall performance record.[2] The premium level paid for a firm often reflects a bid's hostility which raises the price for the target's equity. An empirical study examined the performance of takeovers by leveraged buyout companies during the 1985-1995 decade, based on the bidders' ability to earn back the cost of capital employed in these transactions. However, it found "no consistent link between the size of the premium paid for a firm (even if it is a bid's hostility that raised the price) and a merger's long-term ability to create value",[3] estimated on its capacity to earn returns above the cost of capital employed. Along with these views, ASEA's friendly approach to negotiations with Brown Boveri suggests that post-merger performance can be seen not only in relation to the relative prices paid at the outset, but also primarily as a function of the merging companies' ability to practically realize the merger's expected benefits *after* the conclusion of the deal. Thus, Nicolin remarks that not being able to handle the implementation complexities of a merger, often leads to additional costs or unforeseen investments over the bid price initially paid:

> To acquire a company sometimes sounds very attractive. But to really be capable of integrating the two organizations, to reduce manufacturing places, to decide where you produce one thing or another thing, and all that: That costs a lot of money! So the investment is not what you pay for the company you acquire, but what it takes to follow it up and to streamline it.

As a result of their consistently conducting their negotiations in secrecy, ASEA's and Brown Boveri's 1987 announcement that they had decided upon merging their operations to form a new company, took the entire business world by surprise, although at the time it constituted one of the largest industrial mergers ever attempted. Nicolin remembers:

> We had agreed that we would both announce to the press what we had agreed upon when we had our next Board meetings. Brown Boveri had their Board meeting in Switzerland, and we had ours here [in Sweden]. I think it was two o'clock in the afternoon when we simultaneously announced the merger to the public, but none of the journalists had the faintest idea of this agreement, which, after all, created one of the world's largest businesses! Mr. [Peter] Wallenberg, Mr. [Percy] Barnevik and myself were convinced that this had to be kept secret until we were ready. And as I said, I didn't want to use any consultants because they may have leaked it to the public.

In Pharmacia's 1992 purchase of Italian FICE, the acquirer decided not to involve any external consultants, experts or advisors during the negotiation stages. Instead, the choice was to develop and rely on internal project leaders from the outset, who could subsequently take over the integration process. This leveraged on the troubled experiences which Kabi Vitrum had to face following its 1990 acquisition of Pharmacia, when it extensively employed outside management consultants to provide support throughout the assessment, negotiation and implementation phases. Says Ekberg:

> In 1990, when we made the merger between Pharmacia, Procordia [Kabi Vitrum's owner] and Volvo [Pharmacia's main shareholder], we relied on outside management consultants. But suddenly the consultants took over the whole process, and when they left after the merger, all their knowledge went out of the company. We said: "Let's develop internal people from FICE to carry out the integration process. That's the best education these middle managers can get! And it was fascinating how they could develop their own management capabilities in this process."

Secrecy was undoubtedly useful for companies such as ABB and Pharmacia & Upjohn during their merger negotiation and deal-structuring phases. Nevertheless, such a hermetic degree of circumspection might be difficult to replicate for companies working within different regulatory environments, or possessing diverse ownership structures. However, even when the negotiation of an M&A has to be made public at the very early stages due to normative requirements, some mechanisms, such as ABB's drafting and committing upon a gentlemen's agreement at the outset of negotiations, can still be helpful in minimizing misunderstandings and cultural conflicts between the parties involved. The 1989 acquisition of Britain's Morgan Grenfell by Deutsche Bank offers a good example of this, although these companies went much further than signing a succinct silence agreement. Cultural differences were early on identified as a significant factor during the negotiations between Deutsche Bank and Morgan Grenfell. Here, it was not just strong national cultural differences which played a prominent role, according to Deutsche Bank's executives, but these were *anchored* and magnified by the corporate cultural diversities that existed. At the time of its acquisition by Deutsche Bank, Morgan Grenfell was, after all, Britain's oldest merchant bank, having been around for longer than a century and being actually 30 years older than its acquirer.[4] Throughout its long history, Morgan Grenfell had become a well-established banking institution in the City of London, with a distinct corporate style and values. On the other hand, Deutsche Bank is an emblematic and highly conservative German institution, which at the time of the Morgan Grenfell acquisition had developed few inroads into the global investment banking business.

During the negotiation stages, potential cultural conflicts and misunderstandings were avoided and dealt with by utilizing two mechanisms. First, Deutsche Bank made it clear and explicit to Morgan Grenfell that it was determined to entirely preserve its British character and corporate culture by adopting a hands-off management policy after the acquisition. Secondly, both institutions wrote and agreed upon a 25-page "memorandum of intent" clarifying every potentially conflicting point which could be identified at that stage. As the acquisition negotiations could not be carried out in secrecy, given that under the UK legal framework a third-party advisor and a tender offer were mandatory, this memorandum was instrumental to conclude an agreement in a very short time period. The contents of this document intended to work out in advance any potential conflicts between Deutsche Bank and Morgan Grenfell, by having these institutions explicitly agree upon the adoption of a simple rule. In those businesses where a significant overlap between Deutsche Bank's and Morgan Grenfell's operations existed, the strongest player would in principle manage the combined operations. In the cases where such an overlap did not exist, minimal or no changes would be implemented as a result of the acquisition. However, these guiding principles were carefully applied on a case-by-case basis along the existing lines of business of Deutsche Bank and Morgan Grenfell. Thus, all of the M&A operations in investment banking, for example, became the responsibility of Morgan Grenfell, which had the Head of investment banking in Germany reporting to it in the UK. In other areas, such as institutional asset management, Morgan Grenfell was also left with a considerably discretionary role, taking over world-wide responsibility (except for Germany and the rest of Continental Europe, largely due to the differing local fiscal and regulatory frameworks), and directly reporting to a Board Member in Frankfurt. In certain markets such as Japan, where the local regulations in specific areas stipulated that only one operating license could be granted to each financial institution, Morgan Grenfell took over the group's combined operations as it had a stronger and more developed business in Japan at the time when it was acquired by Deutsche Bank.

Ownership Arrangements Leading to a Multicultural Steering Structure

When building an international merger of equals or a co-operative JV agreement, establishing a fair ownership structure constitutes one crucial test to make the new company work co-operatively in practice. This aspect can have a particularly direct effect at the Board levels, where a sound and willfully accepted ownership arrangement often paves the way to the building of a multicultural steering structure based on the combined talents of the senior executives available. By contrast, ownership arrangements not fully reflecting the combined companies' expectations often end up arousing national cultural sensitivities, or seeking at all costs a balanced national representativity within the new company's Board, which is not always in direct correlation with the balance of skills required following a merger of equals or a co-operative JV agreement. In turn, being able to put together a truly collaborative and multicultural steering structure right after this type of deal has been concluded usually sends a positive signal to the rest of the new organization, making it start on the right foot.

ABB constitutes a good example to illustrate these notions. Although, as mentioned, all the documentation concerning the 1987 merger agreement between ASEA and Brown Boveri was kept secret, Nicolin describes the main lines of how it was structured. Building on the strong strategic complementarity and the similarity in size between both companies, Nicolin maintains that reaching a truly 50/50 ownership structure was crucial to ensure that it could work in practice as a merger of equals, with both companies fully committed to build mutual trust and work co-operatively after the conclusion of the deal. Therefore, at least from an ownership stand point, the merger agreement between ASEA and Brown Boveri seems to have deliberately avoided to create the dividing line between winners and losers which is usually associated with these types of deals. In order to be able to reach this position, ASEA, as the most profitable company at the time, willingly modified its asset structure to ensure that it went into the merger in equal terms *vis-à-vis* Brown Boveri. Nicolin explains:

> First of all, we very early on concluded that ASEA represented a higher value in millions of Swedish Crowns or Swiss Francs than Brown Boveri did at the time, essentially because we had a higher profitability. On the other hand we couldn't suggest that ASEA should own 55 percent, and Brown Boveri's shareholders should own 45 percent of the new company. This had to be a sort of joint venture, a 50/50 deal. That was absolutely necessary, otherwise we didn't believe in its working. Therefore we agreed that ASEA should take out certain corporations that didn't belong to the core business of heavy electrical industry. There was for instance an electric power company in Sweden, and a company that produced certain war materials. There were a total of four or five companies that we brought out of ASEA's group. And on their side, Brown Boveri promised to put in more share capital before the merger to compensate for the remaining difference. In this way, we came to the same capitalization level and made a 50/50 agreement.

This 50/50 ownership structure both reflected and reinforced the strong mutual trust that had been skillfully built between the top management of ASEA and Brown Boveri. Moreover, the extreme determination demonstrated by these companies to reach a truly balanced ownership at the base of the merger deal, undoubtedly facilitated forming a post-merger steering structure which could bridge nationalities to work as a co-operative group. Here, additional mechanisms, such as a rotating Chairmanship, brought in as a result of some of ASEA's leaders' previous multicultural Board experiences,[5] further facilitated the constitution of a collaborative Board of Directors in ABB, working effectively as a team regardless of national cultural differences. Nicolin explains that, building on this co-operative attitude and mutual trust at the top, the merger had a real chance of succeeding during the implementation phase:

When it comes to decision-making, we have never been in a stalemate. You could think that one said: No!, and the other: No! no!, and then: No! no! no!... At times we had fairly long discussions perhaps, but then we have united, either on a compromise or on one point. So, I wouldn't say that our disagreements were so essential that I even remember them. I only remember that we had discussions. But both of us were convinced that we had to agree in the end.

Also as a result of this mutual trust and the team spirit that was created between the merging companies, ABB's Board appointments could be primarily based on competence rather than nationality, leading to a steering structure which truly represented the mixed talents and multicultural skills that were required to combine both companies' complementary resources in practice. Nicolin explains:

If you look at the top management of ABB, [in 1987] we happened to have more Swedes than Swiss people. And we had a couple of discussions regarding whether that was right, and whether we shouldn't have an equal number [of Swiss executives] reporting directly to Mr. [Percy] Barnevik. But we didn't really make any change on that argument. Because, again, the main objective was to make a success out of the whole thing. That's why you must appoint the individuals that are best suited for one job or another. We benefited from having other nationalities, different connections, different outlooks and different experiences, which we brought to the table when we had an important matter before us. But we did not have difficulties dealing with these differences.

By contrast, following the merger agreement between Pharmacia and Upjohn in November 1995, both companies initially decided upon forming a Board of Directors which included exactly the same number of Swedish and American executives, seeking to balance nationalities across every other aspect of the top management structure. For example, the corporate governance requirements introduced after the merger between Pharmacia and Upjohn stipulated that, if the company's CEO was of US nationality, the Chairman of the Board had to be European (and vice versa). These kinds of arrangements may have sought to attenuate the widely different Swedish and U.S. cultural traditions and practical approaches to building trust at the top management levels — relatively informal in the case of Sweden, more "legalistic" in the case of the US. Says Ekberg:

The overall concept was to make a merger of equals, so we decided that, at the beginning, the new Board and the top management should be composed of exactly the same number of individuals from both companies. At the same time, it was also very important to find the right person for each job regardless of nationality, but we expected to get that among the sixteen executives that initially constituted our top management. Of course we tended to have more Pharmacia people leading the market companies in Europe, and more Upjohn people in the US in those positions. But adding them all together it was a nice balance.

However, since the second half of 1996 Pharmacia & Upjohn issued three consecutive profit warnings, while sales and earnings continued to decline throughout 1997. By the end of that year, a newly appointed CEO replaced Pharmacia & Upjohn's initial post-merger steering structure — which had increased to 19 members — with a five-person executive group. Rather than obtaining a balance of nationalities *per se*, the new steering structure which was put in place gave clear priority to execution aspects, seeking to simplify Pharmacia & Upjohn's top management structure and streamline decision-making.

A 50/50 ownership arrangement combined with a strong degree of trust between the merging companies' top management levels, usually facilitate building steering structures based on what is right for the company regardless of nationality, in a collaborative joint-venture fashion. An extreme example of this is provided by Fuji-Xerox, the 50/50 joint venture between Japan's Fuji Photo Film and US-based Xerox Corporation. Although IJVs involving Japanese and Western partners have been relatively short-lived and markedly characterized by national cultural difficulties (with Japan-US combinations being particularly complex to manage from a cultural stand-point[6]), Fuji-Xerox has enjoyed a comparatively long corporate life since it was formed in 1962. However, Kobayashi observes that the original objective of Fuji-Xerox' shareholders did not contemplate establishing a 50/50 ownership arrangement, in spite of their pursuing inherently complementary business objectives. As a result, national cultural differences became an important issue during the negotiations between the Japanese and American parties, only after they were required to form a collaborative joint venture:

> At the time of the negotiation and the pre-negotiation phases, cultural aspects were almost totally out of consideration. The reason is very simple, because at Fuji Photo Film the Japanese were fundamentally interested in bringing in this technology called xerography, which in their minds was to be the new photographic technology. So initially, in the pre-negotiation phase, Fuji Photo Film was totally interested in bringing in this particular technology [to Japan] on a licensing basis, where culture plays no role. And Xerox wanted to get access to the Asian and Japanese markets for their technology, but were interested in coming into Japan as a 100 percent owned subsidiary, or at least on a majority basis. However, Xerox and Rank Xerox were told by the [Japanese] government that 50/50 was the best deal that they could expect. So the whole joint venture itself was a compromise. But before they had to compromise, neither Fuji Photo Film nor Xerox had wanted to establish a joint venture. After the parties [Fuji Photo Film and Xerox] agreed that this was the second choice for both of them, a 50/50 joint venture was the vehicle they had to create. Then of course, the national cultural aspects did become a very big, very important issue.

However, the strong level of trust that had been developed during the negotiations between Xerox and Fuji Photo Film, was instrumental to creating a working steering structure strictly reflecting the business requirements for the new joint venture. Although it had been conceived as a 50/50 ownership arrangement, the US-based shareholder Xerox quickly recognized that, in order to act as a real insider within the Japanese informational context, Fuji-Xerox needed to develop a strong local identity from the outset, being able to function and be recognized as a thoroughly Japanese player. As a result, it trusted the Japanese party to develop the new joint-venture's steering structure in complete autonomy, allowing Fuji-Xerox to develop a distinct Japanese character and corporate values in a largely independent way *vis-à-vis* its shareholders. Says Kobayashi:

> The national cultural issues [between US-based Xerox and Japan's Fuji Photo Film] were resolved by saying that, although this was a joint venture, it was going to be a Japanese company. An international Japanese company, run by a Japanese CEO, with all the operational decisions made by the Japanese Board Members. But a number of strategic policy issues were certainly left for the joint venture partners to decide at the Board level. In this way, the national cultural issues were resolved by saying that, operationally, the joint venture was going to be a Japanese company, therefore it will have Japanese staff and Japanese people. As a result, during the first ten years the joint venture took a very extreme form of manning the whole company totally by the Japanese from top to bottom. But all this was done in complete agreement with Xerox, which had an extreme degree of trust in Fuji Photo Film to give it complete operational autonomy in Japan, to the extent that [at Fuji-Xerox] we didn't even have a resident member of the Board from Xerox or Rank Xerox, until today [in 1996].

From a broader perspective, British Airways' approach to fostering collaborative working relationships within its global network of alliances, is to signal its commitment by engaging in minority equity participation with their alliance partners. Thus, although the partners' national identity and business approaches are normally maintained in accordance to the local demands and cultural traditions, British Airways creates a financial linkage as a basic undertaking to co-ordinate key resources or transfer specific service-related know-how to their international counterparts. As a result, the company's approach to building global alliances has led to a series of financial participations, in many cases representing substantial equity investments in the company's partners.[7] Says Marshall:

> If we find a partner sharing our basic business values and who we can trust, the other important factor in our approach is, of course, that we usually go beyond a marketing alliance with our partners. Rather, we demonstrate our commitment by investing money in their equity, by buying a participation in their company. In this way, you create a bonding, it is more difficult for either of us to walk away at the first difficulty. You are motivated to make it work.

Along with equity investments, some companies negotiate termination clauses when building an international network of alliances, in order to minimize national cultural conflicts between the partners during the implementation phase. Although this may seem paradoxical, Olivetti's Piol explains that an "exit clause" adequately reflecting the relative strategic importance that an alliance has for the parties involved, fosters a hands-on attitude to resolve internal rivalries and work co-operatively to combine an alliance's complementary resources across national cultural differences:

> You have to examine carefully the complementarities between you and your potential partner. But then, a fundamental thing to make the alliance work is the termination clause. Many people forget about this. It sounds contradictory, but a clear termination clause strengthens an international alliance, not vice versa. This is because, if you know the exit price, the probability of staying together with your partner increases significantly. And this persuades you to avoid national cultural conflicts or rivalries between the partners: If I realize that it is my partner who has the competence in certain area, then it is my partner who takes charge, independently of nationality. Moreover, what I am really talking about is a structural fact, that it is very unusual that an alliance is equally important for both partners. So, an exit clause is not some kind of blackmailing your partner because you know that he's got a lot more at stake in its alliance with you. It can be rather a factor of strength, not blackmail, to demonstrate to the other partner that there will be a serious effort to make the alliance work. Therefore, you establish the exit clause to balance things out. If one of the partners has to work harder because the alliance is structurally more important for him, then it is the other partner who has to pay more in the case of termination.

Overall, a skillfully executed negotiation of a related complementary M&A, JV or alliance internationally, usually is preceded by a period of building long-standing personal relationships at the top management levels of the companies involved, within a friendly atmosphere of privacy and circumspection whenever possible. At the basis of a collaborative relationship across borders, the ownership structure of a complementary deal needs to reflect fairly the type of co-operation which will be required from the joining companies, ranging from majority acquisitions or a 50/50 alliance type of merger, to broader agreements taking place within the logic of establishing a global network of alliances with different partners across diverse geographic or functional areas. When handled effectively, these factors often lead to implanting a steering structure based on a strong degree of mutual trust between the joining companies, in spite of the national cultural differences that may exist. As a result, top management appointments often reflect the companies' diversity of talents and expertise *vis-à-vis* the implementation of a new structure after the deal, leveraging on a "multicultural" base of practical skills and experiences, and the determination to work co-operatively to combine resources across borders. However, during these implementation stages, a whole new set of *execution* mechanisms come into play to ensure that international M&As, JVs and alliances can actually work in practice. We will explore some of these mechanisms in the next chapter.

Notes and References

[1] See Chapter 2.

[2] The detrimental consequences of engaging in "overpriced" M&A transactions have been widely highlighted in the specialized literature. See: *Mergers & Acquisitions: The Dealmaker's Journal*, Philadelphia, MRL Publishing Company, since 1965.

[3] This quotation can be found in *The Economist*, 4 January 1997, p. 61. It is based on a study by management consultancy McKinsey, cited in the article "Why too many mergers miss the mark".

[4] Deutsche Bank was founded in 1870.

[5] See Chapter 7.

[6] Reich, R. B. and E. D. Mankin. "Joint ventures with Japan give away our future", *Harvard Business Review*, March-April 1986, pp. 78-86; McKinsey & Company, Inc. *Japan Business: Obstacles and Opportunities, A Binational Perspective for US Decision-makers*, prepared by McKinsey & Company, Inc. for the US-Japan Trade Study Group (under the editorial direction of K. Ohmae), Wiley, New York, 1983; Peterson, R. B. and H. F. Schwind. "A comparative study of personnel problems in Japanese-American joint ventures", *Academy of Management Review*, 3, 1978, pp. 796-804.

[7] For example, in August 1995 British Airways held a 49 percent equity participation in Germany's Deutsche BA and France's TAT European Airlines, as well as a 25 percent equity investment in Australia's Qantas Airways and America's USAir Group (Source: *British Airways Fact Book*, 1995).

CHAPTER 9

Combining M&As, JVs and Alliances' Resources across National Cultures

> To know the country thoroughly; to be able to conduct a *reconnaissance* with skill; to superintend the transmission of orders promptly; to lay down the most complicated movements intelligibly, but in a few words and with simplicity: These are the leading qualifications which should distinguish an officer selected for the Head of the Staff.
>
> Napoleon Bonaparte

When it was announced in 1980 that ASEA would engage in a major restructuring of its world-wide operations, many international observers heralded it as an overdue effort with little chance of success. At that time, the Swedish electrical engineering group was a highly respected but conservative company, suffering from overmanned and unprofitable operations which made it a rather unlikely prospect for global market dominance, relative to its much larger rivals in the USA, Europe and Japan. During the same time period, British Airways was a loss-making state-owned carrier, with a demotivated work-force and an uncertain future *vis-à-vis* British Caledonian, another government-owned commercial airline in the UK. Also during the early 1980s, few in Western Europe or the USA (and certainly fewer within the still communist nations of Central and Eastern Europe) had heard of the Korean *chaebol* such as Daewoo, and those few tended to describe them as emerging industrial conglomerates prospering on low-cost industrial production outsourced by more established multinationals.

However, only sixteen years later, ABB, a widely admired and innovative multidomestic organization, formed after the 1987 merger between ASEA and Brown Boveri, was being regarded as one of the world's leading electrical engineering companies, posting record profit and revenue figures as a result of dramatic productivity and efficiency increases, as well as from an international expansion effort including major acquisitions and alliances in the USA,

Western Europe, Asia, and pioneering large-scale investments into the former European communist bloc, where it was acquiring at a rate averaging more than one company per month. Also by 1996, a privatized British Airways was consistently ranking as the world's most profitable airline and the leading international air carrier, having built an extensive network of acquisitions and alliances in France, Germany, Asia, Australia and the USA, where it and American Airlines had just concluded the largest international alliance ever attempted in the industry. During the same years, largely driven by the *chaebol*'s extensive acquisitions and greenfield operations in sectors ranging from semiconductors and automotive plants, to consumer electronics and shipbuilding, Korea had become one of the leading investors in the UK, surpassing even Japan as Asia's largest investor within the former European communist countries, with companies such as Daewoo, Samsung and Kia being poised to become household names in Russia and the former Soviet republics. In particular, Daewoo was seen as one of the most aggressive Korean players in Western Europe, through major acquisitions of microchip and consumer electronics companies in Britain, having become a dominant foreign investor in nations such as Poland, Romania and Uzbekhistan at a time when most of its Western European neighbors were still reluctant to consider developing major operations in these countries.

How have companies such as ABB, British Airways or Daewoo developed a major global presence in their industries starting from such inauspicious beginnings? How do they manage to swiftly integrate M&As, JVs and alliances across a wide variety of local cultural contexts and market environments, consistently succeeding where most companies fail? Time and again, these companies have faced stiff and deep-rooted resistances after concluding cross-border M&A, JV or alliance deals, such as ABB during its 1988 post-merger restructuring efforts in Germany and Switzerland, or British Airways during its 1996 acquisition of Air Liberté in France, or Daewoo following its acquisition of France's Thomson Multimedia during the same year. However, these organizations have consistently risen to these challenges by demonstrating the ability to flexibly manage major organizational, cultural and market complexities, and as a result consistently reaping the benefits of M&As, JVs and alliances internationally.

How do they do that? Speed. Communication. Practice. Developing people. Basic principles such as these are at the roots of every company's success in implementing M&As, JVs and alliances world-wide, and as a result have become commonplace notions in almost any management text-book on the subject. However, what makes a company consistently successful in this area is hardly conveyed in a generic recipe. Rather, the difference between making or breaking an M&A, JV or alliance in practice often lies in a company's ability to match unforeseeable series of events with sound responses that take into account all the unique internal and contextual circumstances that are relevant. Following a cross-border M&A, JV or alliance, complex phenomena such as national cultural symbols and manifestations can take innumerable forms and exert strong influence over a company's crucial co-ordination functions and overall performance. Here, the *execution* responses of a company need to be as vivid, holistic and flexible as the phenomena they address, allowing it to timely attain the upside benefits of an international M&A, JV or alliance. The skills required to consistently do this reflect both a company's technical and organizational knowledge, as well as its international business experience and *gnosis* of the multiple cultural and informational contexts that need to be concomitantly managed, particularly during the implementation phases. Such *execution skills* and capabilities are both difficult to develop and to imitate by competitors, and thus can be seen as providing formidable practical advantages to an organization, allowing it to successfully integrate and combine with other companies' resources across borders, based on a functioning global co-ordination structure.

Post-M&A Organizational *Design* and the "5 Percent" of Management

Cross-border M&As, JVs and alliances that are carried out from a value-creation perspective (such as related-complementary transactions), often require a significant combination of the merging or partner companies' specialized resources following the conclusion of the deal in order to attain the associated benefits — i.e. in terms of economies of scale, scope and market power.[1] In turn, this strategic need to combine resources invariably implies a degree of co-ordination across the companies' key structural dimensions. One of these critical dimensions concerns the level of global control *vis-à-vis* the degree of local autonomy that needs to be applied to effectively co-ordinate the merging or partner companies' specialized resources. On the one hand, standardization and centralized control over specific local operations can create opportunities to generating scale economies and other related benefits on a global scale. On the other, functional autonomy at the local level can lead to greater structural flexibility and responsiveness *vis-à-vis* the domestic market conditions and distinct cultural manifestations of every country. The resulting strategic dilemma significantly influences the organizational choices and the associated complexity of the co-ordination mechanisms that are often implemented after a major cross-border M&A, JV or alliance. However, from a wide perspective, this dilemma can be considered a fundamental issue underlying a company's co-ordination functions *vis-à-vis* its global constellation of resources. Arguably, companies that are skilled in practically co-ordinating critical resources on a global scale, will find it to be an advantage throughout the implementation of M&As, JVs and alliances across borders.

In the case of ABB, a strong strategic complementarity between ASEA's and Brown Boveri's global resources, and the objective of fostering organizational flexibility and entrepreneurship at the local level, led to the design of a post-merger multidomestic structure. This design was conceived as a network of heavily co-ordinated national companies, which are in turn divided into 5,000 relatively small profit centers. By intensively co-ordinating resources across national borders, each of the company's profit centers can continuously benefit from global economies of scale, scope and business knowledge, without eroding their "local" flexibility and advantages. These dual benefits constitute the upside of this matrix-based "multidomestic" structure. Barnevik explains:

> If you compare three transformer plants in Italy—one of ABB's, a family-owned transformer plant, and one from our larger Italian competitors, and say each has US$ 30 million a year in orders. All Italian, all living in Italy. But ours has better technology, and export markets allocated where they have already existing distribution channels. They can buy porcelain 10 percent cheaper out of Eastern Europe. So they have a lower cost base because they belong to a family. But as Italians running an Italian company, they look identical to the other Italians. That's a big advantage.

One side of ABB's organizational matrix divides the company into four business segments: Power generation, power transmission and distribution, industrial and building systems, and financial services. A fifth business segment, transportation, was transferred to a 50/50 joint venture with Daimler-Benz AG in January 1996. The business segments constitute a functional and technology-driven dimension of the matrix, each segment being led by an Executive Committee member who reports on its performance results as a separate entity. In turn, each business segment is made up of a number of business areas (BAs), each of which is responsible for the world-wide optimization of the manufacturing of a multi-product sector (e.g. nuclear power plants) or the delivery of a service (e.g. project and trade finance) across the organization. In 1996, there were a total of 37 BAs, each of which was regarded as a global business and led by a global manager with overall strategic and operational responsibility for worldwide optimization and co-ordination of resources. A corporate R&D function, along with the business segments, involves the company's research centers based in several European countries, supporting its technology development and special corporate programs.

Another side of ABB's structural matrix encompasses a geography-driven dimension, dividing the company's operations into three regions: Europe, The Americas and Asia Pacific. Each region is led by an Executive Committee member, and is further subdivided into that region's individual countries with a local Head presiding over each country's legal entities and profit centers. Thus, quite remarkably, a global network of 5,000 local profit centers employing over 200,000 people and generating US$ 35 billion in sales in 1996, was led by an Executive Committee of only 8 individuals, overseeing

55 BA global managers, and 44 regional and country managers.[2] By continuously co-ordinating the technology, geographic and operational dimensions of its organizational matrix, ABB's global managers can optimize production, quality standards, research funds, as well as the transfer of internal resources and business knowledge across the local profit centers, while maintaining their strong national identities and cultural traits.

British Airways' organizational structure is similarly based on the principles of decentralization, allowing for a common service approach to be tailored to the local cultural idiosyncrasies across its global route network of 169 scheduled destinations in eighty countries.[3] Says Marshall:

> We define ourselves as an international airline with a British accent. By that I mean that we are aware of our origins as a British airline, a UK national air carrier which was given renewed international growth impetus upon privatization. However, we try to operate in every country as a local carrier with an unparalleled international network. So, we are an American company and have been so for the past two decades, we fly to 23 American cities and have built a terminal at NY JFK airport. We are American orientated as all airlines are. But in Italy, we are an Italian company, tailoring to every Italian customer's needs, as much as any other Italian company. And the same goes for India, and so on.

Based on these principles, British Airways' operating structure is composed of an Executive Team of ten individuals reporting to the Group Managing Director. Each of the Executive Team members has responsibility for a specific functional area, such as customer service, passenger business, corporate resources or investments and joint ventures. Co-ordination of global operations is carried out at several levels, with particular attention devoted to developing and maintaining common service standards, as well as ensuring the best possible asset utilization of the company's air fleet world-wide. Regarding the former, the company has developed highly structured training and customer service programs that are continuously carried out internationally, adapting common service standards flexibly to account for the local cultural demands in every country. Regarding the global optimization of fleet and related resources, key management levels are the Regional Directors, responsible for co-ordinating the allocation of these business assets from the perspective of a single region. There are four regional organizations in British Airways: America, Europe, Asia-Pacific, and UK plus Africa, all of which report to the Director of Passenger Business. From an operational perspective, the company's growing network of international alliances, JVs or acquisitions are co-ordinated at the regional level by the corresponding directors of each relevant geographic area. Service standards, approaches and know-how are also intensely shared with British Airways' global partners, based on the company's existing training and customer service structures.

Daewoo's organizational design also reflects the importance that the company gives to being local across its various international operations, in particular concerning its series of acquisitions within the former communist regimes of Central and Eastern Europe, as well as in the ex-Soviet republics. Kang remarks:

> We believe that the so-called globalization requires localization in the first place. This means understanding the local people in every country, their culture and history. We approach them in this way in order to understand each other. We invite our international employees to our own factories in Korea, for three to six months in order to train and re-educate them. Then they go back to their home countries, such as Romania or Poland, where they apply what they learned to increase productivity, efficiency and improve their people management skills. We do not deploy Korean expatriates permanently in those countries, given that our managerial human resources [within Korea] are very limited in number.

Accordingly, Daewoo's organizational structure intends to confer a great degree of autonomy to its local businesses. To achieve this, the company has been divided into six areas: Trading, motor vehicles, heavy industry and shipbuilding, electronics and communications, construction and hotels, and finance and service. In turn, each area consists of several companies concentrating on major products or services, ranging from steel and metal products, chemical products, machinery and automobiles, to electronic goods, textile, aerospace and defense products. There are a number of Executive Directors reporting to the President of each area of business, responsible for co-ordinating specific geographic areas with the Heads of the local operations. In February 1995, Daewoo announced a radical re-organization to foster greater independent managerial responsibility and specialization for the companies in the group. A new company Chairmanship system replaced the former group-level Management Committee and the Planning and Coordination Office, which had served as the group's top decision-making bodies. As a result of this re-organization, in 1997 Daewoo Group consisted of 31 member companies, ten of which were listed in the stock market.

Sony has also resorted to the organizational principles of attempting to build a strong local presence while benefiting from global advantages of scale, scope and business knowledge across operating, technological and R&D areas. These principles have influenced both the company's approach to people development, and the organizational structure that has been put in place. Tsunao Hashimoto, Vice Chairman of Sony Corporation, observes:

> Through experiences and training programs (. . .), Sony managers are nurtured to think globally, and act locally; keeping global management philosophies and policies in mind, and networking with their global colleagues, while taking the initiative to help further Sony's goals at their local operations. (. . .) My final point is that corporations need to practice good corporate citizenship in the countries where they operate. Being a good corporate citizen shows that the company is committed to playing a positive role in the community, and

increases the attractiveness of the company to prospective employees. Understanding Sony's global philosophy and strategy, and working within the community to become a good corporate citizen is what we at Sony refer to as "Global Localization".[4]

To structurally foster its principle of "Global Localization", in 1996 Sony reorganized its operations into ten companies, along business and product lines, with an executive organization providing global co-ordination and corporate cohesion. Sony's US$ 5 billion acquisition of US-based Columbia studios and Records Group in 1989, were organized into separate companies: Sony Music Entertainment Inc. (SME), and Sony Picture Entertainment (SPE). This reorganization underscored the company's willingness to manage on a more decentralized basis, with a greater degree of autonomy being conferred to its different businesses and local operations.

Overall, the key organizational principles applied by these companies are far from new or unprecedented. An essential concept underlying the multi-domestic organizational design, to "think global and act local", has been pioneered by a number of multinational companies prior to ABB, ranging from financial institutions to consumer goods and industrial concerns. Moreover, structural designs of the kind implemented by companies in such diverse industries, as represented by British Airways, Daewoo or Sony, explicitly pursue similar principles of decentralization in different ways, looking to combine the seemingly contradictory aims of being local with respect to a country's cultural context and domestic market conditions, while simultaneously enjoying the advantages of a global base of knowledge, skills and resources. However, many companies attempting to implement these types of designs have often returned to more centralized country or regionally based organizations after experimenting the practical difficulties of co-ordinating effectively across highly diverse global and local informational contexts.[5] In particular, when a company's global expansion significantly involves M&As, JVs or alliances, the attempt to introduce effective co-ordination structures across borders while simultaneously allowing for a certain degree of local autonomy, can be further complicated by mutually reinforcing national and corporate cultural resistances, as well as other related organizational difficulties usually arising during the implementation phase. In our research, this has in fact raised the attention to the *execution skills* required to flexibly handle these issues at both the global and the local levels.[6]

A similar observation can be made from the point of view of the formal approaches to post-acquisition integration or implementation that have been developed so far. A large part of the literature concerning post-merger and acquisition implementation phenomena has tended to take a process view, highlighting theoretical principles of general applicability.[7] Thus, crucial actions, such as "moving fast" to implement a post-acquisition structural design early on are identified as beneficial to performance, but comparatively little attention is devoted to the practical skills required for a company to systematically achieve this speed of *execution*. As a result, many companies that plan their integration efforts well ahead, and move early to implement them, often find complex barriers to *execution*, ranging from organizational, to cultural and personnel related difficulties. Supporting this, a number of studies have shown that, although formal models, general principles and recipes for "successful" post-acquisition integration have been around in the management literature for a relatively long time (some of the basic principles having been identified many centuries ago within the military and the political spheres[8]), most M&As and alliances fail to generate the expected results largely due to the already mentioned cultural and organizational difficulties arising during the implementation phase.[9]

The above arguments suggest that knowledge of post-acquisition integration models and approaches, as well as the general organizational principles underlying decentralized designs and global co-ordination functions, can be regarded as a necessary but not sufficient condition leading to a consistently successful implementation of international M&As, JVs and alliances. Indeed, strategic thinking, organizational design and general implementation principles have been curiously referred to as constituting the 5 percent of management effort by a senior executive in our research. In the context of cross-border M&As, JVs and alliances, this further highlights the importance of the *execution skills* required to translate even basic implementation and organizational principles into actual gains. These skills often depend on the internal availability of people with a holistic cognition and direct experience of how to handle the highly diverse and variable (global and local) informational contexts during the implementation phase of these agreements, as well as the specific *execution* mechanisms and methods that have been developed within the organization.

Making a Post-M&A *Design* Work in Practice is the "Remaining 95 Percent"

During the implementation of a cross-border M&A, JV or alliance, a company's particular *execution orientation* and specific mechanisms utilized illustrate the degree to which it is able to derive concrete advantages based on widely cited organizational and integration principles. Many of these specific *execution* mechanisms neatly reflect a company's history and previous experience, both in managing operations and resources internationally, and in carrying out M&As, JVs and alliances across borders, properly handling the national cultural and other related complexities that usually arise in these situations. The ability to advantageously apply these mechanisms in practice, often reside on the unique ways in which a company combines them together

within its multiple informational contexts, pulling all of its human and organizational resources with great skill and determination to support *execution*.

The importance of developing people with cross-cultural skills

Following a cross-border M&A, JV or alliance, the strategic need to integrate
and co-ordinate resources from the merging or partner companies, often
requires that people from vastly different national cultural values and backgrounds must work co-operatively and effectively within teams or group-task
forces that are critical to performance. The international human resource
management literature has examined the role and concerns of the expatriate
manager from the perspective of multinational corporations. The topics studied include the recruitment, selection, compensation and training of managers and executives who are expected to function and perform abroad.
However, it has been observed that this literature has often examined the
selection and adaptation of international executives outside the business context and the specific behavioral issues inherent in implementing cross-border
M&As, JVs and alliances.[10]

From a practical perspective, companies seem to invest significantly in
expatriating personnel but with highly mixed results. Statistics published in
1996 estimated that more than 2.2 million Americans were residing and
working abroad, while international assignments in American companies
operating overseas had increased by about 25 percent since 1990.[11]
However, 5 to 15 percent of US managers in international assignments
were reported to be unsuccessful in business. In addition, it was estimated
that one-third of the total of US managers carrying out international assignments became "brownouts" — that is people who stayed abroad but were
consistently under-performing in business. This can constitute a significant
financial drain, as in 1996 an American company spent an average of US$
300,000 "to send someone overseas and then turn around and bring them
back".[12] Indeed, some observers have argued that the rapid growth of management consultancies in the USA during the 1990s might be linked with
their providing consultants with international experience to American multinationals that wish to implement ambitious strategies of global expansion,
but are unable or unwilling to develop internationally experienced executives
internally, facing all the related costs of continuously expatriating and re-
absorbing staff. Thus, especially in the USA, it has been highlighted that the
globalization of markets and business strategies, often implying the development of a world-wide network of acquisitions and alliances, is not always
accompanied by a corresponding increase in the internationalization of
staff.[13] In our research, an apparent illustration of these issues in the context
of an international merger has been provided by Sweden's Pharmacia. After
it was acquired by KabiVitrum in 1990, it extensively relied on the support of

management consultants during the implementation stages. However, it realized that by overly relying on external assistance, it had largely failed to internally develop professionals capable of leading the new company's operations internationally. Thus, during its subsequent acquisition of Italy's Farmitalia-Carlo Erba (FICE) in 1992, Pharmacia decided to entirely rely on developing internal champions to lead throughout the implementation stages.

In short, companies expanding globally through a series of mechanisms including M&As, JVs and alliances, seem to crucially rely on managers with cross-cultural co-ordination skills. Although many of these companies are investing significantly in these kinds of managerial resources, few seem to be consistently successful at developing people capable of carrying out complex co-ordination functions across diverse national cultural environments. Here, it is not theoretical approaches, but the practical and contextual aspects of developing these international managers that are usually missing. As a result many international M&A, JV and alliance failures have been traced back to the lack of intercultural or cross-cultural managerial co-ordination skills.[14]

Developing "global managers" in ABB

During ABB's post-merger integration phase, the company needed from the outset to develop people with the skills to carry out critical global co-ordination functions across national borders and local cultures. However, Barnevik explains that developing this type of people can be a very difficult task in almost any company environment:

> When you build this type of [multidomestic] structure, you have to understand and realize that people aren't global. They are very local. They like the family, their friends and their relatives. If you ask an Italian to build a team, he chooses other Italians, because he knows them. And you cannot force him to choose a non-Italian to make up a team. Or a German comes up and says: "I have a proposal for three people for my team. They happen to be all German but they're the best, you know. And, Mr. Barnevik, you have agreed that we have to pick the best." So these are the situations you face when trying to make the multidomestic idea work.

Throughout the post-merger integration of ASEA and Brown Boveri, an early emphasis on *execution* and multidomestic organizational flexibility dramatically concentrated the management's energy and attention into developing people with the skills to work effectively across "local" cultures. Some empirical studies have in fact suggested that people's skills are generally the key to attain organizational flexibility, whereas excessive reliance on knowledge systems and automated routines inevitably lead to relatively rigid structures. However, the existing models of post-acquisition integration have overwhelmingly stressed the role of formal process routinization, knowledge codification, and knowledge management mechanisms. Although in these approaches cultural fit and compatibility are sometimes included as important factors, they are often ill-defined and lacking in practical applicability, partly because cultural symbols tend to be inherently difficult to formalize or codify, requiring subjective cognition, direct experience and *gnosis*.[15]

In the context of a complex international merger such as ABB, the company had to develop rather sophisticated processes and information management systems capable of supporting a highly decentralized organization across multiple service levels, coping with both the increasing speed of technological change and the associated number of change initiatives. However, Barnevik remarks that it was also important that the individual and collective skills of global managers could lead to applying global co-ordination functions and processes in a flexible way, constantly reflecting and adapting to the different national cultures and the local informational contexts.

As previously mentioned, ABB's critical co-ordination functions constitute the specific responsibility of a limited number of global managers, possessing a mix of functional knowledge and cross-cultural *gnosis*. Indeed, one of Barnevik's first and most pressing tasks to get ABB's multidomestic structure in place, was to *identify* individuals capable of becoming global managers, and move fast to implement the flexible and effective global co-ordination functions that were required. However, given that the entire pre-merger negotiation phase was carried out very rapidly and in the utmost secrecy, there had been little opportunity to pause and work out in detail the new company's key managerial appointments at the operational levels. In order to do this quickly, Barnevik spent the three months following the public announcement of the merger, working fourteen hours a day non-stop, to personally interview around 500 people from both organizations, approximately half of whom were Brown Boveri employees. Later on, he has referred to this experience as the most straining in ABB's integration process, but one where his own personal involvement, together with other company senior executives, was crucial to success. Indeed, the first assignments for global manager roles were extremely delicate, as the newly formed company was under unprecedented attention in the countries where major changes were expected, and as a result could not afford to make too many mistakes at the outset. Moreover, it was rather difficult to find standard profiles or fixed formats to identify global managers in the new company, as successful individuals from diverse countries often tend to look very different from one another. However, Barnevik decided against picking ASEA's people, or indeed Swedish nationals for all the key posts — although he knew them well. Instead, he also relied on many of Brown Boveri's employees, whose performance he was less certain about, and whose values were not necessarily the same as ASEA's at the outset of the merger. The risks involved in this operation were tempered by the senior executives' personal involvement in the selection process, seeking for factual achievements in the candidates backgrounds, that were in accordance with the extremely demanding global management roles. According to Barnevik, these were:

> ... people who had demonstrated the ability to lead others, with humility and respect for other cultures. Extremely patient and open minded to understand, appreciate and work within the diversity of traditions and ways of doing things in different countries. Individuals who are "givers" more than "receivers", in the sense that they continuously develop people and make them available to the rest of the company, rather than constantly demanding people from other parts of the organization. At the same time, tough-skinned individuals with outstanding technical and commercial knowledge, working experience in several countries, good language ability, and the stamina to become "superstars" in their field.

Besides outstanding functional and managerial capabilities, it was therefore important that the candidates singled out to perform global co-ordination functions had a well-rounded insight of the countries in which they were to operate. A few years after the initial merger between ASEA and Brown Boveri, the company acquired extensively on a global scale, including companies within Eastern European countries, the former Soviet republics and the "emerging" economies of the Far East, at the time regarded as rather difficult locations from a cultural standpoint. The global managers that were selected by ABB to co-ordinate resources in these countries had to demonstrate a genuine interest and knowledge of their language, history and cultural manifestations, as these managerial roles required spending a significant amount of time on the road, constantly interacting with the relevant local people, and developing the *gnosis* to build internal networks and act as real insiders in these locations. Thus, it was also important that the candidates' spouses or close relatives could share his/her genuine interest in these countries. Barnevik explains:

> When you expand into China, you don't want a manager coming there without knowing anything about the country. Both the manager and the spouse really have to have an interest. They can't be just narrow-minded industrial or technical people. You need people who know and have an interest in the Chinese language, history and culture, because his or her job is to create a network. You can't create a Chinese network if you don't have that interest, especially with the language, which is quite difficult to learn. I wouldn't dream of having a manager running the Ukraine business, who didn't speak the local language. It wouldn't be possible. You have to have that anchorage, to really be accepted.

Another important characteristic sought after in a global manager was his/her human qualities to sensibly carry out people issues during the post-merger integration period. Particularly regarding highly delicate decisions involving job redundancies and dismissals across the company's international locations,

Barnevik's direct experience in handling these issues helped defining the selection criteria that was required:

> I also think it is important to go out of your way to deal with the people issues in these situations, the families, the financial side of it. But to do that without compromising what you have to do in the end can be difficult. (...) If I have someone who has to do this type of work, and he is a pretty ruthless, unemotional character, I think he is not suitable for the job. You asked me what is difficult. This is something that will really grind you down. Fortunately, it is not a thing that you do everyday. I have the advantage now, when I deal with other people who have to do it, that I know how it feels. I have done it personally, physically, with my own hands.[16]

The next step was to effectively mobilize and develop the global managers that were selected, to work co-operatively and co-ordinate the company's critical resources across local borders. In order to do this, Barnevik organized a three-day working seminar in Cannes which took place from 1 to 3 January 1988, with the attendance of the 250 global managers that had been initially identified. There, he explained ABB's new organizational structure, the roles expected from the global managers within the multidomestic organization, and the world-wide guidelines of behavior. The latter was made explicit in a brief document especially produced for that occasion, internally referred to as "ABB's Policy Bible", or "ABB's Book of Values". Altogether, the date, the venue and the attendance seem to have provided the right frame for ABB to launch its new vision, organizational structure and one-company values, with ABB's Policy Bible explicitly representing its new practical principles of behavior.

However, regular meetings such as this or written policy documents often are not enough to create effective cross-cultural teams in practice, even in the case of people with previous international experience and language abilities. Deep-rooted habits, resistances, or simply communication and other practical difficulties involved in working in different environments usually make it initially burdensome for people from diverse national cultures and backgrounds to work together in teams. However, a global manager is required to routinely travel abroad to co-ordinate with the local companies and profit centers, continuously devising business solutions that are adapted to and respect the local cultures, traditions and institutional environments. To develop enough people with such cross-cultural skills constitutes a major challenge for any organization. In spite of these difficulties, the credibility of the ABB merger was from the outset highly dependent on developing global managers with the *execution skills* to co-ordinate effectively across borders and local cultures. This was the key to make a multidomestic organization work in practice, and to actually deliver the benefits of the merger in terms of lower costs, economies of scale and scope, and business knowledge. Therefore, Barnevik involved himself personally to ensure that the selected global managers actually took the first steps to work together in teams, and learned to overcome their initial national cultural resistances early on in the merger integration process. This was achieved by ensuring that people from different nationalities were picked to be part of critical teams and task forces, even at the risk of interfering with selection decisions and criteria from time to time:

> How do you make a German [for example] choose people from other nation-alities to work in teams? Well, I do it by saying: "Take your time. Travel to the United States, travel to Italy, Scandinavia, and other countries, and then look at 15 candidates or so. Talk to them, check their references inside the Group, and then come back with a maximum 1 German. Two are from among these other people." Because it's not the case, of course, that only 3 Germans can do the job. He just happens to know 3 Germans.

Once a cross-cultural team was formed in this way, the organization had to be ready to cope with the short-term misunderstandings, efficiency losses and the resulting additional costs that were often incurred as the global managers learned how to work together across language and national cultural barriers. By willingly facing these initial difficulties, ABB signaled its determination and commitment to making cross-cultural teams work in practice. More importantly, the individual team members were given actual opportunities to learn and *experience in practice* the concrete benefits that can be generated through this cross-cultural co-operation. Says Barnevik:

> The first time we went to build a power plant in Saudi Arabia with ABB SACE Sadelmi from Italy, together with America's Combustion Engineering, we had quite a few misunderstandings. Now, after the first plant, there came the second plant. Now they knew each other. They started to become friends, they started to know each other, trust each other. And then, of course, they started to see the benefits, that in Saudi Arabia you can use Italian financing or American poli-tical support, and combine your strengths.

However, not every mechanism to encourage global co-operation across national cultures involves the possibility of interfering with a global man-ager's selection criteria, or generating short-term inefficiencies. Persuasion and involvement are other ways to continuously foster this kind of cross-border collaboration amongst global managers. In this sense, ABB has notor-iously pioneered practices such as "cloning", "adopting" and international "centers of excellence", which (as described in detail in the remainder of this section) effectively mobilize large parts of the organization to provide learn-ing opportunities on a global scale, foster continuous operational support to specific areas such as "emerging" markets, and generate the *gnosis* to over-come initial national cultural resistances to global co-operation. This is sys-tematically achieved through explicit delegation mechanisms and incentive systems. The latter are not exclusively monetary. For example, following the first global managers meeting in Cannes, Barnevik institutionalized the event, regularly utilizing it to provide positive feedback and motivation to specific internal initiatives with the potential to serve as models of global co-operation to the rest of the organization. Observes Barnevik:

> In November 1995 we had 400 managers in Montreux for one week. And I spent a lot of time discussing leveraging our global strengths. I had certain people come up presenting case studies illustrating how they were able to overcome national obstacles, marrying companies together in cooperation. How ABB SACE in Italy was building the business in Texas. They had said: "Let's get together and look at the customers in America, and at manufacturing in Bergamo, let's do something together, as though Bergamo were situated in Texas, and then we share the total profit". And their sales of standard products went from US$ 2 million to US$ 20 million with that approach. Because they came together.

Developing "project champions" at Pharmacia-FICE

As mentioned, in the case of Pharmacia's 1992 acquisition of Italy-based FICE, developing a few local project leaders with the ability to work across the highly distant national cultures of Sweden and Italy was the key factor to championing a significant organizational transformation within the target company. By coaching, promoting and empowering these project leaders into functional responsibilities within the new organization, the integration process was completed in two years, in many cases exceeding the cost, productivity and R&D improvements that had been initially targeted. Ekberg remarks that a crucial part of Pharmacia-FICE merger integration was to identify and develop a few project leaders capable of working across the highly diverse Swedish and Italian cultures and traditions:

> In the merger between Pharmacia and FICE we singled out the best people in FICE and trained them to lead the integration projects. We appraised many people in the process of appointing the new management. After being appointed, these new managers developed their ability to work together across their different national and corporate cultures, because we asked them to work face to face with a few Swedish expatriates who actively participated in the design of our implementation plan. And I would say that in this way they started to build the combined culture of the two companies, because they got to know each other, sorting out their national cultural differences from very early on. This has been very important for us to be able to reap the benefits of the merger.

International "missions" for Korean co-ordinators at Daewoo

In the case of Daewoo, the company greatly relies on a reduced number of internal co-ordinators, mostly of Korean nationality, to effectively turnaround acquisitions in overseas locations, from Britain to Eastern European countries, Russia and Vietnam. These co-ordinators help to quickly transfer key organizational and technological know-how not only to target companies and JVs but also across Daewoo's numerous greenfield and start-up investments overseas, as well as to carry out operating functions involving the Group's headquarters and international network of resources. Kang explains:

> For example, when we started up a 100 percent owned VCR production company in Northern Ireland in 1988, Daewoo Electronics dispatched twelve managers, engineers and technicians. However, after eight years less than five Korean expatriate managers remain there. They are: the Managing Director of the company, the Finance Director, and another manager. This Division factory in Northern Ireland is a subsidiary of Daewoo Electronics in Seoul, and therefore some co-ordination is needed with headquarters in Seoul, which is largely under the responsibility of our Korean expatriate managers. But otherwise, the factory is managed by "locals", and is a purely Northern Irish company. We completely localized critical components like decks and drums in Northern Ireland, and invite Korean medium-sized manufacturers and other producers to see our Irish factory and order these critical components from there. In this way, we have been exporting Irish production to countries such as Germany.

To co-ordinate and communicate effectively with the local people can be an extremely difficult task, particularly in nations that are significantly distant from Korean culture. In this area, Kang curiously observes that his country's unique historical experience in economic development and long-standing familiarity with neighboring communist regimes has shaped the Korean people's openness, experience and predisposition to relate to environments such as the former communist countries of Central and Eastern Europe, the ex-Soviet republics, and the "emerging" economies of Asia and Latin America:

> We have to understand the people first. How they think, what is it they like to do, etc. The human content is crucial for an organization, and we do not manage it like an army: "I'm the Managing Director, so I instruct you to do just what I want you to do." We don't like to work in that way, we prefer to use persuasion. This is partly due to historical reasons, because in Korea, we have experienced growth, and from being a very poor country we have become a developed nation in less than one generation. We have experienced isolation, privacy, a three year war against communism. This gives us an insight to work with the so called emerging economies, or within the ex-communist dictatorships. We know that they are going to develop, just as we did, and so we are open to share our experiences with them.

From a wide perspective, it would be difficult to underestimate the role that this sort of collective *gnosis* has played in the *chaebols'* aggressive and pioneering entry into the former communist regimes of Eastern Europe and the Soviet Union, at a time when most Western companies had an exceedingly risky perception of these markets. However, the company leverages on this existing base, providing a highly structured program of long-term *missions* to overseas locations for their young and bright Korean managers. These *missions* seek to provide an in-depth academic, working and living experiences to these future international co-ordinators, both in Western locations, but particularly across emerging economies as far apart as Russia, Vietnam or Romania. There, these managers get direct exposure and learn the country's language, culture and history, and have the opportunity to extensively develop a local network of contacts. Says Kang:

> Our people in Korea already have an insight on how to work in transitional economies and uncertain environments, and we continue to build on this base. For example, we identify our best managers, and help them gain experiences in other countries. We send many people to MBA courses in the United States, but also to other countries from which we have lots of things to learn, such as Singapore. We are also sending about ten students every year to famous universities in China. First they are given the opportunity to learn the Chinese language over there, and then they take special assignments to learn about Chinese culture, history and visit industries they are going to work with upon coming back to Korea. We also send a few persons every year to Brazil, Colombia, Argentina, and other Latin American countries. We have sent three people to Vietnam to study the country's language and culture at the local university there, and we send many managers to Russia, Poland, Romania, France, Germany, etc. in these kinds of extended training. Overall, these people spend on average one year in a given country, including the summer vacation.

Kang himself is a good example of how these programs of international *missions* constitute an important school for the development of Daewoo's leadership. As a young company manager, he spent three and a half years in Ecuador, before being transferred to Europe on a long-term *mission*, to work in Britain and Germany. In all these cases, an important part of his training was learning the language and the history of these countries. This, according to Kang and other Daewoo senior executives, is a prerequisite to really understanding the culture and the mentality of a foreign country, particularly those that are relatively distant from a Korean perspective. However, in some cases, young candidates for international *missions* feel reluctant to spend several years in certain emerging countries or culturally distant locations, requiring persuasion and leading by example. Says Kang:

> Our company invests a lot educating its young staff. And the interesting thing is that most of our Executive Directors and Management have had expatriate and overseas training experiences in developing countries rather than developed economies. But today many people that are appointed to developing countries are not necessarily happy, although at the end most of them say: "This is my turn", and willingly go abroad. Afterwards, when there is an opportunity for

them to become business co-ordinators in these countries, they know the places well because they have lived and worked in Poland or Vietnam.

Senior executives at NEC also highlight the practical difficulties involved in implementing similar long-term international assignment programs for their Japanese staff. Language, environmental and internal organizational barriers constitute powerful practical deterrents to continuously build cross-cultural *gnosis* among key company personnel. Iwane Takahara, Counselor Member of the Board at NEC Logistics, explains:

> When we go abroad to set up joint ventures, or to acquire companies, we send some Japanese staff to manage the local personnel. But of course, the first handicap or barrier we as Japanese face abroad is the language. Secondly, Japanese people on assignments outside Japan are supposed to stay abroad at least two or three years, but in reality I'm afraid that 99 percent of these people come back to Tokyo as soon as they can. They feel safe here [in Japan], and they don't want to face any trouble abroad. Another reason is that Japanese people don't want to be far away from their Tokyo headquarters for too long, because they see it as important to be close by, for career promotions and things like that. [Japanese] production or general managers going abroad for a long time, often face problems when people at headquarters tend to "forget" them. Tokyo headquarters, philosophically and "politically", is a hundred years away, and people become afraid for their future if they stay abroad for too long. But, at least in my experience, managers should stay abroad not two years, but ten years. One decade is necessary. If you go somewhere for one or two years, you are still quite "innocent" and a stranger. But after that, you start to become familiar with the customers and management ideas of a different country.

Implanting post-merger co-ordination functions that work across local cultures

Following a cross-border M&A, JV or alliance, the ability to develop people with cross-cultural skills has to be complemented with the capability to translate complex global co-ordination designs into specific roles and commonly accepted practices, methods and organizational procedures, in order to obtain the expected benefits from these agreements. One way to realize these in practice is based on promoting internal competition to optimize key resources. This type of approach is favored by British Airways in areas such as fleet asset allocation, in order to co-ordinate multiple demands on an essentially undifferentiated resource base, according to specific business optimization criteria. These demands are placed by the company's regional divisions, but also include British Airways' international acquisitions, alliance and JV partners. Marshall observes that the availability of people with great cross-cultural familiarity in the international airline business, combined with the rather indistinguishable nature of fleet resources across borders, leads to a strictly competitive allocation process on a global scale, not likely to be affected by national cultural or other related complexities in a significant way:

> We carry out the co-ordination of our global operations, in order to gain the advantages consistent with our large international network. In this area, key management levels are our Regional Directors, who are responsible for co-ordinating our business from the perspective of a single region. Each of them continuously compete for the company's limited resources, which allows us to ensure the best possible utilization of any given asset all year round. They all report to the Director of Passenger Business, who will examine the merits of every request with the Executive Committee. For example, the Regional Director for the Americas will co-ordinate our business across the Atlantic region, North and South. He will fight for resources, a Boeing 767, 747 or an Airbus 400, a level of cabin crew, etc. His or her team will produce a business case, and the Executive Committee, including Bob Ayling [British Airways' CEO], will decide on it based on how good his case and arguments are compared to the other Regional Directors. Decisions are based solely on business merits, no country favoritism or bias attached to them. Through this process, we also manage to co-ordinate our operations with our partners worldwide.

Other aspects, such as regulatory issues—what can or cannot be done in the different countries within this heavily regulated industry, are raised by the Regional Director and addressed by the company's Government Affairs department.

However, in multi-product industries, or industrial conglomerates such as the Korean *chaebol*, there typically exists a myriad of production, distribution and logistic dimensions along with geographic and technological areas, which need to be continuously harmonized. As a result, it is difficult to establish strictly competitive co-ordination mechanisms, as in many cases functional, geographic or operating units may at the same time present overlapping as well as complementary areas, based on the great diversity of products, services and technologies within the company's international locations. In this type of organizational contexts, a company's global co-ordination mechanisms ought to simultaneously foster internal competition and international co-operation across the companies structural dimensions. These mechanisms are both complex and potentially paradoxical, but become critical to integrate international acquisitions effectively within a company's web of global resources. Referring to Daewoo's global co-ordination mechanisms, Kang observes:

> For example, in the electronics plant we started up in North Ireland in 1988, we had a few Korean managers. Their function was to co-ordinate the Irish company's operations with headquarters in Seoul, and then engage in outsourcing parts and components competitively. If they could find better parts from Singapore, they bought from Singapore. We are not forced to bring our own parts and components to our overseas factories. As a result, sometimes our

overseas factories compete against each other, but when it is needed they co-operate and trade between them.

One of the most sophisticated examples of global co-ordination mechanisms in a multi-product industry is provided by ABB. Following the 1987 merger between ASEA and Brown Boveri, the company's multidomestic matrix organization pursues the seemingly contradictory goals of fostering global co-operation amongst a world-wide network of 5,000 highly competitive profit centers. This emphasis on cross-cultural co-operation intended to avoid functional duplications after the merger, ensuring a high degree of local flexibility and entrepreneurship, while handling the deep-rooted cultural resistances, misunderstandings or even open infighting which could arise between the multidomestic dimensions. Accordingly, the activities of the global and the local units had to be organized around precise rules in order to smoothly function side-by-side, avoiding overlaps and inefficiencies, and making it possible to combine the merging companies' complementary resources. Says Barnevik:

> The responsibilities of the global Business Areas involve standardization, common engineering, global supply, to support market building in some areas. It takes huge effort to orchestrate the build up of the emerging markets for example. They have a very big, clear role, these BAs. At the same time, the countries have a big role too. It's the other side of the matrix: Lead and accomplish the change process, reinforce customer rules. Working together with the BAs, the emerging economies' country managers have a lot of work to do.

Along the BAs and the country organizations, key managerial roles were made explicit and specifically different from one another:

> An Italian who happens to be placed in Zurich, and has a global responsibility for General Contracting in the world has to be not only Italian but also very American, and German, and Austrian, and Asian and what have you, because he has activities in 30 countries. He has a global responsibility. But an Italian in Italy doesn't have to be global. He has to understand the Italian workers, the unions, the customers, the prices, and then he has to cooperate within the Group. But he doesn't have to understand the Americans and the Swedes, and the Japanese, because they take care of themselves in their countries. And the Italian customer wants to talk to somebody representing ABB. So you have to have an Italian family, a strong leadership in Italy. The role of the Italian manager is extremely important as a networker, a leader in Italy, and as a line manager for these fifty companies you have in Italy. At the same time, each of them operates under that global Business Area structure. So these roles are complementary and well understood.

However, the crucial issue remained: How does ABB actually ensure that its global and local roles work co-operatively to combine the merging companies' resources across the highly diverse local cultures? Here, a number of basic organizational building blocks facilitate ways of co-ordinating effectively across the diverse nationalities that form part of ABB's multidomestic network. Amongst these: a common official language (English), a common reporting system and currency, and a common set of company values and guiding principles contained in the company's Book of Values. As mentioned, a recurrent principle in this Book of Values refers to global collaboration amongst ABB's managers, spelling out in detail what the company expects from each individual, and how certain rules of behavior ought to be observed when dealing with other managers and company personnel, particularly when this involves people from different countries and national cultures. In this sense, a large part of ABB's Book of Values can be interpreted as a manual of conduct, a practical guide of action for individuals with the mission of integrating a major cross-border merger by leading people, managing resources, generating consensus and influencing decisions across differing national cultural and regulatory environments. Thus, simply aspirational phrases are found along with more specific personnel policies stressing broad competence and performance as the only selection and promotion criteria, intensive cross-border rotation and exchange programs for key managerial levels, as well as direct and down-to-earth advice on the potential difficulties of working in a multicultural environment. Based on these written principles, ABB's senior executives strive to build cross-cultural co-operation through persuasion and motivation, leading by example and continuously showing the positive side of developing international personal networks within the company. Barnevik observes:

> Regular global managers meetings, international assignments, trainees, sharing best practices externally and internally, recognition for behavior that helps the Group, all that has to do with communications and building relations.

However, besides this positive encouragement towards cross-cultural co-operation, ABB's Book of Values also very clearly states the causes for dismissal of those who do not comply with the company's high standards of competence, integrity, internal co-operation and loyalty towards the company. Abundant anecdotal evidence suggests that the company's leaders are as determined in positively encouraging cross-cultural co-operation amongst their global managers and other key personnel, as in summarily removing those who fail to show competence in the role, or to work co-operatively within the Group. Barnevik remarks:

> In this organization you get kicked out if you aren't good. Because if you don't contribute, if you're looked upon as being disloyal to the Group, or as promoting a certain country at the expense of the overall Group performance, you won't be effective. You can't work.

Another key way of ensuring that global co-operation takes place in reality, is to apply standardization rules pragmatically and flexibly, taking into consideration the particularities of every business area and location. In this way, the global managers attention is overwhelmingly focused in those areas where co-ordination is really needed, while the remaining functions remain strictly local. For example, two key areas of global co-ordination are production and marketing. By specifying the manufacturing responsibilities and the marketing and sales territory of every local organization, ABB was generally able to avoid major duplications and to quickly attain significant economies of scale and scope in most functional areas a few years after the merger.

Nevertheless, in the real world it is often difficult to harmonize the apparently contradictory principles of bottom line orientation and global co-operation among profit centers. Many large multinational companies have found this combination insurmountable, not only due to cultural and language barriers, but also to conflicts of interest regarding internal pricing, operational or technology decisions, often reflecting internal political struggles within a company's local and global roles. For ABB, this situation was further complicated by the strong national identities of the merging companies, with long-established and highly independent country subsidiaries in the case of Brown Boveri. The new multidomestic organization established extremely demanding work-loads for the global managers and country Heads, so that political conflicts or empire building tendencies were inhibited. As mentioned, this was combined with the senior executives' personal example and continuous direct involvement, instilling the value of global co-operation, no-nonsense application of the company's explicit code of behavior, the constant encouragement of cross-cultural co-operation and the development of international networks within the company. These are considered more gratifying to the individual and beneficial for the Group in the long term, than a single-minded pursuit of financial results.

Apart from international assignments, rotation programs, cross-cultural team building and regular communication events such as the global manager meetings, ABB has utilized a series of mechanisms to effectively foster co-operation amongst profit centers in their newly acquired companies. For example, in the USA, the company had to create a collaborative attitude across a myriad of different companies, including the former subsidiaries of ASEA and Brown Boveri, as well as the subsequent acquisitions of Combustion Engineering and Westinghouse in 1988, immediately following the ABB merger. In this context, establishing a common headquarters early on was a useful step to foster mutual acquaintance, trust, and internal networks among this initially heterogeneous set of companies.

Another mechanism extensively utilized by ABB to build its new structure after the merger, involves cultural education for the company's global managers. This often takes the form of open seminars where managers from different nationalities have the opportunity to discuss and learn from each others' cultural perspectives. Such understanding is critical to effectively carry out co-ordination functions involving people from different nationalities, cultural backgrounds and traditions. Thus, cultural education based on open seminars and discussions are important to reinforce and complement the cross-cultural *gnosis* attained through first-hand international exposure.

Once ABB's global roles and co-ordination mechanisms had been implanted, the organization could move boldly to absorb further resources from international acquisitions, JVs and alliances. These took place unabatedly through the following eight years to build a global network of local profit centers in both the industrialized countries and the so called "emerging" economies. In particular, pioneering acquisitions in culturally distant, or at least unfamiliar environments, such as the former communist countries in Central and Eastern Europe, Russia and the former Soviet republics, took place at a rate exceeding one company per month between 1988 and 1995, requiring an average of two years to restore them to profitable levels. As explained in the rest of this chapter, the specific *execution* mechanisms developed by ABB in these cases, allowed the company to quickly and successfully integrate acquisitions within environments where not only significant national cultural differences were expected, but also a lack of exposure to even the most basic principles of market-oriented economies.

Overall, global co-ordination is an *execution* area where a company's international management experience can make a crucial difference. ASEA and Brown Boveri's century old international experiences may have played an important role in their implanting a multidomestic design effectively across the merging companies' well established national subsidiaries and local cultures. By contrast, companies without this type of international exposure have had to develop their organizational know-how and *gnosis* of global co-ordination in a relatively short time period. This often implies a strenuous effort on the part of the organization, requiring a major amount of managerial patience, will and determination. Few areas can illustrate these aspects as clearly as the international banking industry. A growing number of international banks such as ING and Citibank have pursued specific global advantages based on their ability to offer through their world-wide networks an extensive range of banking products and services appealing to multinational clients. This strategy is seen as instrumental to achieve a critical mass of business and long-term contractual relationships, thus generating specific global economies of scale and scope. However, in these areas, Deutsche Bank's executives conceded in 1996 that there was still "room for improvement", as their efforts to acquire and expand internationally had been recent relative to other long-established global banks.[17] Since 1995, efforts to achieve a greater integration of their products and services towards the customer, particularly those related to cross-border acquisitions such as DMG,[18] "look good on paper but are not so easy to get in practice". Curiously, these executives note that Deutsche Bank seems to have made more progress in co-ordinating between its

North and South American operations and its Asian businesses, than in establishing cross-border co-operation mechanisms amongst its European subsidiaries. It is observed that this is partly due to the fact that Deutsche Bank's European operations generally present a much stronger local character, and it is therefore more difficult for them to foster co-operation across borders. By comparison, their non-European operations tended to be born with the Deutsche Bank imprint: "Our Italian operations started in 1917 as non Deutsche Bank units, whereas the feeling with our recent Asian operations, for example, is that they always belonged to us".

After Deutsche Bank started an aggressive international expansion effort during the 1980s, the company's pursuit of global advantages through operational co-ordination tended to rely on their employees' personal experiences and informal networks. Well into the mid 1990s, there was no official "Deutsche Bank book of values" to be followed by all employees internationally. People got to know each other through the group's increasingly available exchange and expatriate programs across borders. Here, language barriers have become a significant issue. Although Deutsche Bank's top and middle managers tend to use English internationally (since there is not an apparent readiness to extensively learn and use German), language problems do exist, particularly at the lower levels in the organization. These often translate into operational difficulties, so that Deutsche Bank has had to implement other solutions. For example, a "liaison officer" figure has been introduced mostly in the bank's German offices: An employee who interacts with a foreign country, learns the local language (if he/she doesn't already speak it) and develops a network of contacts. He/she subsequently returns to Germany to work as a liaison, or trouble-shooter *vis-à-vis* that foreign country across specific business areas.

Commendable as they are, Deutsche Bank's executives conceded in 1996 that their efforts to consistently reap global advantages across national cultures were still at an early stage. Indeed, it is pointed out that "the average banking business is very local" across Deutsche Bank's international network, and "cannot be transferred cross-borders". Thus, being able to keep large parts of its international operations as local as possible is rather seen as an advantage: "Credit operations are quite different in Singapore than in Argentina". In this context, it is restated that Deutsche Bank does not normally attempt to change the "average local character" of its international businesses. It is indicated that this partly stems from the fact that many of Deutsche Bank's clients abroad are mid-size German or local corporations, which tend to rely heavily on excellent personal relationships, a good local presence and the effectiveness of "the man on the spot". As an example, it is pointed out that Deutsche Bank has just created an extensive finance program for Mannesman in Asia, a 200-strong company which is a world leader in a highly specialized tool machinery market niche. "Goldman Sachs would not care to provide such service to a company of this size", remark Deutsche

Bank executives, whereas they see these types of institutions at the very core of their client base.

However, Deutsche Bank's executives recognize that in the long term a more formal global structure may be put in place. The current absence of a global matrix to facilitate tighter co-ordination of its international businesses will be "eventually fixed" over time, as in 1996 Deutsche Bank appeared to be in no hurry to carry out more drastic organizational changes. A major element cited to explain this gradual approach concerns the relatively favorable market conditions experienced in 1995 and 1996, which have provided Deutsche Bank with some breathing space to gradually absorb its international acquisition and expansion initiatives. Another element which could be added to explain Deutsche Bank's gradual approach to building a global organizational structure, is related to the bank's ownership structure. Surprisingly as it may seem for an institution of its size and influence, Deutsche Bank's executives confirm that "nobody knows in detail the ownership structure of the bank". In 1995, about one third of Deutsche Bank's shareholders identities could be openly traced back, as they were mostly employees or owners of shares held in custody within the bank. However, the remaining shareholders, representing two thirds of the bank's stock capitalization, were unknown to the public at large. Nevertheless, they appear to have traditionally favored a long-term outlook for Deutsche Bank's operations compared to, say, US or UK-based banking shareholders. The latter, normally less inclined to anonymity, usually constitute the major stimulus for organizational changes of the kind Deutsche Bank was rather gradually approaching during the mid 1990s.

Co-ordination mechanisms are also key to manage a global network of alliances and JVs

As mentioned, similar to cross-border M&As, international JVs and alliances have been shown to present a high failure rate, not only due to market issues, but as a result of day-to-day conflicts between people from different national cultures, who are required to function co-operatively within a corporate setting.[19] Against this background, during the late 1980s Olivetti was recognized as a pioneer and an aggressive player in the field of international alliances and JVs, engaging in major agreements across Europe, the US and Japan, covering a wide range of office equipment technologies, computer hardware and software. In 1997, a strategic alliance with Germany-based Mannessmann was central to Olivetti's rapid recovery from a chronically troubled financial situation, and its transformation into a strong European telecommunications player. Prior to this, a series of overseas partnerships around Omnitel — a telephone operator co-owned by Olivetti — had turned the company into Italy's first privately-owned telecommunications provider.

Former Olivetti executive Elserino Piol has provided a succinct description of the company's experience in making international JVs and alliances work despite of the national cultural differences which may exist between the partners or shareholders. This approach is based on a strictly hands-off policy on the part of the shareholders or partners, both from the day-to-day operational activities and from a cultural perspective; a clear and skill-based allocation of the partners' main areas of responsibility from the outset; and the need to ensure that the new company operates in complete consonance with the business requirements of the "local" informational contexts:

> Regarding national cultural differences, there are three ingredients for success in a strategic international alliance or joint venture. First of all, it has to be clear from the beginning "who" gives "what" contribution to the alliance. And whoever gives the contribution should take charge of it. Secondly, the loyalty of the people who belong to the joint venture has to be first with the joint venture, and next to the shareholders. In other words, there has to be a clear separation between the management and the shareholders. The management cannot divide its loyalty with the shareholders, otherwise the shareholders will interfere, and conflict between the partners will be inevitable. When one creates a joint venture, everybody has to be clear on the fact that a new thing is being created. This new thing is not to be managed day-to-day by the partners, who are the owners of the joint venture. A third consideration is that there should not be a "prevailing culture" in the joint venture. In other words, none of the partners should pretend to make its own culture prevail over the other partner's culture in the context of a joint venture. The prevailing culture should in any case be on line with the market in which the joint venture operates. The key to ensure that this happens is to choose, in one way or another, the best people for every job independently of which company or country it comes from. This is why, even if there has been pre-alliance agreements regarding who should do what after the deal, such agreements should not always be taken literally.

In the case of Fuji-Xerox, it has been already described how a broad adherence to these principles of hands-off shareholders attitude, and the development of the new company as a totally Japanese concern, led to it becoming an established player in Japan's highly competitive markets for office equipment technology. Moreover, in spite of the conflicting relationship that has often characterized similar US-Japanese JVs, Fuji-Xerox has grown successfully since the early 1960s sharing a 50/50 ownership structure with US-based Xerox. Here, an unusual degree of mutual trust between Fuji-Xerox' shareholders has been at the basis of their being able to eventually sort out their occasional misunderstandings and national cultural differences which, as CEO Yotaro Kobayashi elegantly points out, "are not unlike some of the misunderstandings between the Japanese and the American governments". However, this model of trust-based 50/50 ownership functioned well enough for Fuji-Xerox to be willing to adopt it as the pivotal mechanism of the company's expansion efforts overseas. Kobayashi explains:

Fuji-Xerox was setting a good example of an effective joint venture, and so we said: Why not repeat the same thing overseas? And this is why we never insisted on the majority when expanding into other markets through joint venture agreements. We told our international partners: "50/50 [ownership] is OK with us". In some cases we were successful, but in others we had to follow the local regulations. In the case of the Philippines, for example, our business was defined as consumer business, a sector where the maximum foreign capital participation which was allowed was 40 percent or 30 percent initially, so we just couldn't go into the 50 percent level. But elsewhere, we applied the same principle as with Fuji-Xerox: 50/50 ownership, local management and all that.

Through Fuji Xerox Asia Pacific Pte. Ltd. — a 100 percent owned concern established in Singapore in 1991 to coordinate regional policy — the company has expanded in the fast growing Asia-Pacific markets using a mixture of fully owned subsidiaries and joint ventures with local investors. Apart from Philippine Fuji Xerox, in 1996 these arrangements included: Korea Xerox (50/50); Thai Fuji Xerox (49 percent owned by Fuji Xerox Asia Pacific), and Taiwan Fuji Xerox (48 percent owned by Fuji Xerox Asia Pacific).

However, making an international arrangement work on an individual basis, and co-ordinating resources within a global network of JVs or alliances, can be two very different things. An international JV or alliance can indeed be built as a local player in order to keep it close to the requirements of the markets in which it operates, while at the same time minimizing potential day-to-day difficulties related to national cultural differences. However, when a cross-border JV's operations become large enough to cover other countries and geographic locations, this makes it increasingly ripe for the kind of global co-ordination mechanisms that have been previously described. Moreover, when an international JV or alliance operates within a global business logic with regards to its shareholders' operations, or *vis-à-vis* other similar international partnerships, the need to internally develop people with the ability to co-ordinate resources and work co-operatively across national cultural differences becomes increasingly paramount. Fuji-Xerox experiences attempting to develop crucial technologies in co-operation with its American shareholder, Xerox, aptly illustrate these notions. Observes Kobayashi:

In the so-called reprographic technology, the color is becoming more important. And at one time initially, we were behind Cannon in this area although we had been the first one to come into the market with color products. Xerox and Fuji Xerox had developed their own color products separately, but we decided to put our efforts together to fight Cannon. As a result, we sent about 30 engineers to Rochester, Webster NY, to start a joint development with Xerox. But unfortunately it didn't work. I think that what didn't work was probably culture, more specifically, the working relationships with the vendors. In Japan it is not unusual for vendors to work with our manufacturer on a normal 24-hour basis, and they are willing to work extra time. But there is a more "business as usual" type of attitude in the United States. And that results in missed deadlines, delayed products and schedules, and added cost. We just couldn't live with these differences, and so the decision was made to bring these people back to Japan to continue developing our own products. But we left a few key engineers, because Xerox wanted to continue developing this product. We continued our own effort, and today the color products that are marketed world-wide are all Fuji Xerox products. But we are not saying that this is the best arrangement, because we know Xerox has a tremendous capability in color. So we are back to square one, where we said: "Let's develop our color strategy into the next century, and let's divide our capabilities so that together we can actually come up with a strong color portfolio". But it is easier said than done. In between, there's an uncomfortable feeling and sense of competition, and no Japanese and no American engineers want to be on the losing side.

In the international airline industry, British Airways' web of cross-border alliances and JVs are effectively managed as a global network. According to Sir Colin Marshall, this implies establishing effective global co-ordination mechanisms amongst the partners. In certain cases, such as fleet allocation, these mechanisms can often be applied smoothly across national cultural differences, on a strictly competitive basis. In other areas, such as the international co-ordination of marketing and sales resources and skills, or the transfer of critical customer service know-how, implanting global co-ordination mechanisms requires the availability of people who can work effectively and co-operatively across national cultural differences. Based on these people's abilities, global co-ordination mechanisms can be applied flexibly and on a case-by-case basis, taking advantage of the complementary resources, unique skills and know-how of the various partners involved:

> An important consideration when implementing global alliances, is that we carefully identify the areas of co-operation and work on them. The rest is better managed independently by our partners or ourselves. For example, in the case of USAir, we did not go into common branding. However, we did lend our customer service know-how and expertise, helping them create their "Business Select Service" in Pittsburgh. Our routes were highly complementary, so we worked at integrating and combining only those areas where an overlap or a "link" between our networks had to be addressed. To sum it up, the underlying objective of any alliance is to integrate networks and resources, so you have to generate a commitment to develop people who are capable of making this co-ordination happen in spite of any cultural differences which may exist to an extent.

Fuji-Xerox seemingly illustrates how a company's growing internationalization increasingly establishes different demands on the skills that are required from its people at key managerial levels. This evolution seemingly follows the dynamics illustrated in Chapter 5 (see Figure 5.2). During the initial, primordial mist stages of international expansion in the innovative xerographic technology of the early 1960s, technical know-how was the dominant factor for market success. Hence, an international licensing agreement or a fully owned subsidiary were initially identified as the vehicles to commercialize this know-how in Japan. Accordingly, national cultural and related issues became crucial aspects between the shareholders, only after it was required from Fuji Photo Film and Xerox to build a 50/50 JV within Japan. However, Fuji-Xerox could effectively handle these issues at the operational level by insisting on being structured and managed entirely as a local Japanese company. Nevertheless, as it grew consistently during the next few decades, Fuji-Xerox internationalized its operations on an increasingly global scale. At the same time, many of the initial technological developments in office equipment became increasingly proceduralized and transferable, whereas Fuji-Xerox's non-Japanese operations took a progressively more important role, both as potential markets as well as sources of technological innovations and know-how. During these stages, it has become crucial for the company to develop more formalized global co-ordination mechanisms to take effective advantage of Fuji-Xerox's international strengths. As a result, similar to previous cases, the company has experienced the growing need to develop key people with both the *gnosis* and the technical ability to work co-operatively across national cultural differences and misunderstandings. Here, one of the initial steps relates to developing the language skills to communicate effectively across borders within Fuji-Xerox international operations. Kobayashi candidly highlights these and other significant practical difficulties, as well as the time-frame required to increasingly implement global co-ordination mechanisms within Fuji-Xerox, which could be applicable to other companies in similar situations:

> At Fuji-Xerox we probably are at the fairly early stages of internationalization. We still have to blend the capabilities from our non-Japanese operations. We know that there is a lot of talent out there, but we have not even decided certain things. For example, ABB says that their official language is English. Do we have the courage to say: Our official language is English? I don't think so. Yet Japanese is not a universal language. We are encouraging our people to learn local languages, we have programs to send people to learn Chinese, and Thai, and other languages. In ten years time we will probably have developed enough key people to allow us to really blend our international talents, but we are still far away from that. We know that a lot of new developments, in software for instance, are coming from countries like Indonesia, Thailand, Korea, Taiwan and Australia, but we have not really began to effectively blend our multicultural talents into the so called Fuji-Xerox value system. This is absolutely important and we are in the process of doing it.

Continuous rotation of people across borders is key to achieve speed of execution

To move fast after an acquisition. To carry out critical tasks during the "first 100 days". To have a thoroughly planned and well thought-of plan of action to quickly implement changes and integrate the merging companies operations smoothly. Principles such as these have been commonly mentioned in the management literature, emphasizing the central value of speed in successfully carrying out M&As, JVs and alliances. And yet, abundant anecdotal evidence illustrate how often acquirers and company partners find it difficult to keep the momentum after the deal has been concluded, being slowed down or nearly paralyzed by unforeseeable events, cultural and personnel related issues, or organizational complexities. When these operations are carried out across borders, vague references to national cultural differences, as well as language and institutional barriers, are usually added to the list of difficulties that are cited to account for a poor performance or outright failure. Thus, in many cases, international M&As, JVs and alliances that are well conceived from a strategic standpoint, and thoroughly planned for, nevertheless fail to live up to performance expectations during the implementation phase.

However, parallel to these situations, some companies have consistently demonstrated the ability to rapidly turnaround acquisitions as well as build JVs and alliances across borders, even within former communist societies and emerging economies characterized by difficult cultural and social local contexts *vis-à-vis* industrialized market economies. Indeed, these rather extreme cases are particularly useful to illustrate the effectiveness of *execution* mechanisms that are largely centered around the principle of rotating people across national borders and diverse cultural environments. As a result of extensive international exposure, a company's key executives or managers can develop the skills to continuously and effectively tailor business requirements to the local cultures and informational contexts. The associated flexibility to carry out complex assignments across borders, can be crucial in achieving speed of *execution* in the implementation phase of international M&As, JVs or alliances. Simple as it may seem to be, this basic principle is often very difficult to implement in practice, with relatively few companies being able to advantageously apply it in specific business situations. Thus, in the context of our research on cross-border M&As, JVs and alliances, international employee rotation, along with other related implementation practices, has continuously emerged as a key principle through a variety of *execution* mechanisms.

Cloning

In 1994, five years after the Berlin Wall came down, most Western companies still regarded the former Central and Eastern European communist countries, as well as Russia and the ex-Soviet republics, amongst the riskiest markets in the world and systematically refrained from entering them. However, at about the same time, ABB had already acquired and turned around over thirty companies in the region, employing around 20,000 people. This included 7,000 employees in eight factories in Poland, another 7,000 across five manufacturing companies in the Czech republic, mainly in the eastern city of Brno, and over 2,000 people in nine companies across Russia. These acquisitions continued at a feverish pace during the subsequent two years, with total business in the region jumping from only US$ 200 million in 1990 to US$ 1.7 billion in 1995, including over US$ 200 million in exports to countries outside the region. Thus, in less than one decade, ABB had built a network of manufacturing profit centers across this whole region, with production lines ranging from electrical turbines, electrical transmission equipment and power generation components, to railway design and equipment, and emission control devices.

This remarkable turnaround was largely achieved by relying on local people and the existing employees of the newly acquired companies, whom in most cases had only a rudimentary knowledge of basic market economy principles. In countries such as Poland and Ukraine, drinking in the job was a serious and endemic problem, whereas even the most basic Western manufacturing methods in areas such as quality and productivity control were virtually unknown. Besides these internal problems, during the initial years following the fall of the Iron Curtain in Europe, many of the former communist countries were still largely dominated by the highly bureaucratic and non transparent ways of doing business which conspicuously characterized the old regime. Within these rather specific informational contexts, ABB initially relied on people who were very familiar with the local cultural and institutional environment, taking advantage of their personal networks of contacts. However, at the same time, it faced the challenge of quickly developing local leaders capable of turning around and bring the acquired companies up to Western standards within a reasonable time period. This was systematically achieved by resorting to execution mechanisms somewhat resembling a process of organizational *cloning*. Barnevik explains:

> Management candidates in Ukraine were too state-oriented, and job assignments were often not based on ability but political reasons. So we looked for younger Ukrainians in the Group, maybe someone who was working in Germany or Italy <u>before</u>. So one or two years before concluding the deal, we had 10-15 candidates working in the Western world, younger Champions who could be catalysts inside the Ukraine organization. And then some of these become senior managers.

Thus, people who have been brought up in Eastern European countries, Russia or other "emerging" economies, possessing a first-hand *gnosis* of the local cultural and institutional environments, were "acquired" by ABB several years before the fall of the Berlin Wall. These professionals were then typically deployed in one of ABB's leading plants in countries such as Germany, Sweden or the USA, living and working abroad until they became fully familiar with the company's methods and ways of working. After a number of years, they were transferred back to newly acquired companies in their countries of origin to "clone" or replicate these ways of working in accordance to the local informational context. ABB has found that this apparently simple execution mechanism can represent an enormous advantage in terms of speed of *execution* and effectiveness to turn around acquisitions, bridging across significant national cultural differences and the highly diverse local manufacturing practices and ways of doing business:

> When we wanted to get into Ukraine, we didn't understand the country well. So, we took a group of Ukrainian and Russian people we already had working with us in Kazakhstan and in Poland, managers and engineers who were Ukrainian or had lived in Ukraine. They know the Slavic mentality, they all came out from communist dictatorships, top-down allocation economies, without market prices, that type of thing. They understand it. Then you build on the base you have in Central Europe. We already did the work five years ago, a turnaround of the Czech and the Polish businesses, and you have 15,000 people there now. That gives you quite a pool of talent, people who can help build the business further East.

Some researchers highlighting potential information gaps between the acquirer and the target in relation to linguistic, institutional, cultural and political factors, have stressed the value of a gradual approach to cross-border acquisitions, initially focusing on environments that are relatively close from the perspective of the acquiring company.[20] Organizational risk considerations, and the need to internally develop learning mechanisms and "knowledge" of culturally distant environments, appear to give theoretical support to these types of approaches. However, ABB's pioneering acquisition experiences in the former communist countries of Eastern Europe and the ex-Soviet Union, illustrate an interesting practical departure from these approaches. The company *de facto* reduced the potential risks involved in entering these culturally unfamiliar markets by relying on an extensive network of acquisitions, mixing a few relatively large ones in Poland, Russia and the Czech republic, with a myriad of smaller targets across the whole region. In addition, by moving to acquire early on while its competitors were still shunning the region as overly "risky", ABB was able to pick the best prospects in every market it had targeted, often negotiating terms and conditions which benefited from both the lack of alternative bidders and these countries' compelling need to attract foreign investment, following the financial collapse of the Soviet Union during the early 1990s. Moreover, in these countries ABB ensured that it acquired a controlling or majority stake in the target companies, an essential condition to carry out the required changes as swiftly as possible. However, perhaps more importantly was the fact that the company's approach to appraising acquisition opportunities in the region was fundamentally proactive and *execution oriented*. Thus, after it had singled out the region's business potential during the late 1980s, it quickly moved to "acquire" and develop people with the holistic *execution skills* to work cooperatively within both ABB's organizational structure and the different national cultural contexts involved. The associated execution mechanisms which were developed early on, such as *cloning*, suggest that strategic opportunities to enter culturally distant countries through acquisitions might not be necessarily constrained by a gradual approach. An organization can bridge potential communication gaps and other complexities related to national cultural differences, based on its practical ability to identify in advance concrete market opportunities in culturally distant or unfamiliar locations, and move quickly to develop key individuals with both the functional knowledge and cross-cultural *gnosis* to champion major company transformations in those locations. Says Barnevik:

> Right now we have 3,000 people in Russia, and we may be 10,000 to 15,000 people in 10 years time. So we have a number of Russians in America and Europe that we train. Some of them we move from one Russian company to another. We spent tens and tens of millions of [US] dollars on that training. And the Italians, and Swedish, and Swiss, and Germans, etc. set aside money in their budgets to receive all these people.

Another crucial advantage of organizational *cloning* (and more generally a consequence of developing local people and domestic manufacturing capabilities from early on) is that an acquired company can be comprehensively transformed in a short time period while keeping intact its national character and inside networks in the countries it operates in. In the complex national cultural and institutional environments of Eastern Europe, Russia and the ex-Soviet republics, ABB has repeatedly found that the ability to crystallize in practice this basic multidomestic organizational principle can lead to concrete benefits. A typical example of this was provided in March 1996, when the company won a US$ 100 million contract from Omskenergo, an electric utility in Omsk, to refurbish its power station jointly with Russian power engineering companies. Under the contract, it was agreed that new technology 55 MW gas turbines will replace a less-efficient and polluting oil-fired plant. The turbines were to be produced in ABB Nevsky, a joint venture based in Saint Petersburg, and the generators were to be made by Sila, another company based in Saint Petersburg and participated by ABB. In winning this contract, it was crucial that ABB was perceived as a thoroughly local player, managed by Russians, relying on local manufacturing and technological capabilities, and loyally contributing to the domestic economy. Similar to this example, throughout the region ABB continuously leverages on its local companies' national character, strong cultural identity, inside networks and domestic manufacturing capabilities, to generate tangible business advantages *vis-à-vis* less flexible international competitors.

Adopting

Another execution mechanism extensively utilized by ABB to quickly turn-around acquisitions in Eastern Europe, Russia, and other culturally distant countries, is *adopting*. As already hinted, it crucially complements *cloning* by ensuring that the few managerial champions with the mission to transform a newly acquired company, are not initially isolated or cut-off from the company's global network of resources, but are placed within an adequate context where they can really deliver the changes that are required. Particularly during the first years following an acquisition, the businesses typically required significant functional, technological and human support to be able to sustain major changes and overcome deep-rooted cultural resistances internally, before they were capable to run smoothly as members of ABB's global federation of companies. The initial but critical changes usually included dividing the acquired company into profit centers, implementing a Western accounting and reporting system, installing quality control and testing practices to raise standards to Western levels, as well as starting English language lessons for middle managers, in order to co-ordinate internally and communicate with headquarters. However, under ABB's strictly decentralized and delayered organization, this type of support had to be provided without adding any functional or supporting staff at headquarters. Barnevik's response was to promote a comprehensive program of internal *adoption* for these newly acquired companies:

> Senior managers in a well-developed market like Germany, Sweden or Finland adopt a country. That's their baby. They develop it, help it, support it, build export business, buy companies. Then five years from now, the adopted businesses can stand on their own feet. You have to nurture them along. These are things that broaden your horizons, beyond your country.

The *adopting* countries are carefully selected, not only based on existing functional or technical capabilities, but also taking into consideration deep-rooted cultural and historical affinities, as well as long-existing relationships between countries. Thus, following the fall of the Berlin Wall, ABB was able to skillfully exploit Austrian experience in dealing with Hungarians and Slovenians, traditional German and Finnish links with Russia, and the already mentioned historical relationships between the Scandinavian countries, Poland and the Baltic states. This mixture of comprehensive functional capabilities and existing *gnosis* of the *adopted* countries, effectively assisted the parenting companies in comprehensively turning around acquisitions in former communist countries and "emerging" economies, contributing to quickly bring them up to higher standards of performance.

Thus, *adoption* mechanisms foster cross-cultural co-operation through a two-way flow of both technical knowledge and organizational *gnosis* between the *adopted* and the parent companies. Since the additional responsibilities involved were seldom accompanied by an increase of the *adopting* company's resources, a new set of incentives was put in place in order to ensure that the critical support intended was effectively delivered:

> Let's say, for example, that an ABB company in Milan building generators takes responsibility for a company in Southern Poland, and helps them: Accounting, language, organization, supply, quality assurance, pricing, the whole thing. And then I say to them: "OK, you're measured in Lira on your profit in this generator plant but you're also 25 percent measured on how well your adoptee performs in Poland".

Besides monetary incentives, there are enormous stimuli, sense of achievement and motivation involved in pioneering whole new markets through *adoption*. Contributing to substantially improving the economic, technological and environmental standards of former communist societies and "emerging" economies, spearheading the integration of these countries into the wider global economic system, are perceived as bringing more than mere shareholders value and can develop a sense of pride and belonging amongst employees. In ABB, this type of motivation has been extensively promoted internally, with recognition being awarded and widely communicated to the rest of the organization through the company's global manager meetings and other mechanisms. In this way, other country organizations may become eager to participate in the company's rather challenging and visible *adoption* efforts.

There are additional and important side-effects from *adoption*. A parent company can obtain concrete benefits in the form of increased exports to its daughter company, or a lower cost of imports across certain products or services. Also, by internally promoting and rewarding *adoption* mechanisms, the organizational knowledge and cross-cultural *gnosis* developed during this process gets continuously magnified and outwardly projected. Thus, not only the *adopting* companies move on to develop similar locations after completing their initial parenting roles, but also the *adopted* companies that learned first-hand the benefits of organizational support and co-operation, can in turn become *adoptive* parents. This can turn *adoption* into a virtuous circle for continuous organizational learning and cognitive holism, leading to rather concrete results.

For example, in 1995, less than six years after they had been *adopted* by an Italian company following the fall of the Berlin Wall, ABB's operations in the Czech Republic were in turn parenting companies further East, within the former Soviet republics. At the end of that year, it was reported that ABB's revenues in the Czech Republic had nearly doubled to Kc 8 billion, from a total of Kc 4.1 billion in 1994. Profits had risen to Kc 495 million from Kc 317 million in 1994, while orders had increased 17 percent to Kc 10.2 billion. Exports in 1995 represented 24 percent of orders, a sharp increase from a year earlier, although the company was planning a further increase of 40 percent for 1996. ABB's Czech exports consisted mainly of turbines and power equipment to Germany, Poland and Slovakia, being the leading supplier to the domestic power industry. Although the company had invested Kc 1.6 billion in modernizing infrastructure, machinery and equipment, allowing it to double revenues per employee to Kc 1.2 million per worker, this was still 25 percent the ABB group average, leaving ample room for further productivity growth. Similar to the Czech Republic, continuous application of *adoption* mechanisms have allowed ABB to flexibly expand and turnaround acquisitions at a formidable speed in Eastern Europe, the former Soviet republics, and across emerging economies in Asia, Latin America, and the Middle East. This has been achieved without adding staff to ABB's 200 strong headquarters in Oerlikon, Switzerland.

Fixed consortium

In ABB, a "fixed consortium" provides another example of the concrete business benefits of global co-operation. This mechanism is extensively utilized not only to support on-going delivery of major orders and operational start-ups, but also in the development of international alliance projects, or to swiftly upgrading technological and production capabilities following an international acquisition. A fixed consortium is a cross-cultural team, formed with the explicit objective of carrying out a large and complex project, such as building manufacturing and distribution capabilities for electrical components and equipment, anywhere in the world. It typically includes employees representing all the operational, technological, functional and country network capabilities which are required to complete a project regardless of nationality. Thus, a fixed consortium constitutes a sort of virtual organization, able to rapidly assemble, concentrate and deploy the company's global resources, cognition and expertise in any given geographic location. By working both co-operatively and effectively across national cultures, the members of a fixed consortium can design and deliver innovative solutions, creating significant technological and cost advantages *vis-à-vis* competitors. Explains Barnevik:

> We combine our global managerial resources to form international teams which can effectively carry out large and complex projects. In one recent case, we formed a team with managers from Italy, Sweden, Switzerland and other countries, to build a major project in Italy. Their combined talents could simultaneously obtain EC funding from Brussels, compete against Ansaldo, convince the Italian Government to support our project, and involve Pirelli as a local partner. In addition, we were able to cut the total costs of the project by 25 percent by forming this fixed consortium.

As in the case of previous *execution* mechanisms, fixed consortia can be combined with *ad hoc* monetary incentives and recognition to continuously develop *execution skills* in cross-cultural team work and global co-ordination within an organization. For example, ABB has utilized fixed consortia to assist in the development of joint venture and alliance projects in emerging economies in South East Asia or North Africa, where engineers and technicians from places as far apart as Scandinavia, Italy and Saudi Arabia, worked together to set up a wide range of local assembly and manufacturing capabilities. After working closely with the local Thai or Moroccan employees, these have in turn become members of other fixed consortia, being deployed elsewhere to create a virtuous circle of technical learning and cross-cultural skills-building within the organization.

Cross-cultural rotations

Long-term international assignments and continuous rotation of key personnel across overseas locations constitute a key mechanism to effectively integrate cross-border acquisitions. Overseas rotations crucially complement the advantages of cross-cultural teams, allowing a company to integrate larger operations from highly diverse national cultures in a rather flexible way relative to single-nationality approaches.

In this area, companies such as ABB invest heavily in continuously creating opportunities for people to develop not only functional knowledge on a global scale, but also subjective insight or *gnosis* of managing effectively in culturally distant locations. Says Barnevik:

> I am not thinking so much of young people who spend six to 12 months abroad as part of their training and development, nor of the hundreds of people from newly acquired companies in former Comecon or Asian countries, who every year learn about modern company operations and get introduced to ABB's values and policies in western Europe and North America. What I have primarily in mind is young western Europeans being transferred to Asia or America, and North Americans being assigned to Europe, Asia or Latin America. When after some years they return home, they have got a deeper insight into different cultures, and may even have picked up another language. They will have learned that their own culture is not the measure for all things.[21]

After an international acquisition, rotation of specialists with this kind of long-term cross-cultural exposure can effectively transfer best practices avoiding internal resistances and other culture-related difficulties. This can considerably shorten the time required to turn around acquisitions, particularly those taking place in culturally distant or unfamiliar locations, such as the "emerging" economies of Eastern Europe, Asia and the ex-Soviet republics. However, it is often difficult to maintain a policy of long-term cross-cultural rotations in practice. For one thing, local managers usually feel reluctant to give up their young top performers who are the natural candidates for this kind of rotations. Also, the need to re-train or develop foreign personnel often takes time, patience and resources in the local companies, until the transferred professionals are able to perform effectively in their new and significantly diverse cultural and social working environments. Thus, internal documents such as ABB's Book of Values explicitly establish a number of organizational principles stressing the key value of these mechanisms to the company, highlighting the need to ensure that they take place on a continuous basis:

- We must strive to have managers who are "givers". They attract and develop talented people and thus provide internal candidates not only for themselves but also for other parts of ABB. We cannot afford "receivers", who always need to recruit from someone else or externally. We must promote a "giver" mentality among our managers so that we can maintain our policy of normally recruiting and promoting from within the group. (. . .)
- We must speed up the flow of managers across organizational and geographical borderlines. At higher levels horizontal moves should be used to create challenges and opportunities. Only in exceptional cases should transfers be stopped because that person is badly needed where he [she] is.[22]

Beyond this type of written principles, ABB has taken concrete steps to adhere to them. The combination of a *giver* attitude and the strict implementation of cross-cultural rotations, is firmly embedded in the company's corporate culture and reward systems. Regarding the former, the benefits of continuous international rotations are constantly communicated to key personnel and managerial levels, with the CEO and other senior executives personally involving themselves to ensure that these take place at the right pace throughout the organization. Moreover, every year a group of 500 to 600 global managers and other selected individuals across many geographic locations, are closely followed by ABB's CEO and the other members of the Executive Committee, all of whom spend a significant amount of their time reviewing their career path, professional development, international mobility and overall performance. Here, one key criteria for global manager promotions and monetary incentive decisions is based on the number of people made available by the manager to the group's international assignments and positions. Through these kinds of mechanisms, ABB makes sure that the organization continuously develops people with a significant reservoir of functional knowledge and cross-cultural *gnosis* to execute complex global co-ordination assignments, such as the effective integration of international acquisitions.

As in the case of global co-ordination mechanisms, a company's ability to carry out cross-cultural rotations in practice can significantly reflect its previous international management experience. Thus, companies with a lower degree of internationalization relative to well established multinationals, often resort to rotation programs overseas as a way to rapidly learn and improve on their ability to expand and manage on a global scale. After initiating an aggressive internationalization program during the mid 1980s, which included several major cross-border acquisitions, Deutsche Bank faced serious language and co-ordination problems *vis-à-vis* its growing overseas operations. As a result, the bank's executives interviewed indicated that the group has established specific practices in order to create a German-based network operating across its international subsidiaries and legal entities. Employees are regularly sent abroad in expatriate programs of at least three years — in Asia the program length being usually four years. "Our larger clients tend to be quite international", it is remarked, "and so, those who served them have to be very international too." Up until 1996, these programs have largely benefited German and Germany-based employees. Nevertheless, Deutsche Bank was increasingly extending its global expatriate network, both in numbers and scope, sending, say, Spanish employees to Argentina, or Portuguese professionals to Brazil. It was also encouraging an increasing number of its internationally based professionals to visit Deutsche Bank's operations in Germany, either in a one-year international staff exchange programs, or on a long-term basis. Thus, in 1996 it was remarked by some of the bank's executives interviewed that: "Nowadays you will hear three out of ten employees in our Frankfurt elevators speaking in a language other than German at any given time."

International centers of excellence

Throughout ABB's post-merger integration, as well as during the subsequent cross-border acquisitions that were carried out, the company faced the need to quickly raise the productivity and quality standards across its extensive network of manufacturing and assembly plants. Often, this involved comprehensive restructuring programs and the constant implementation of major change initiatives in the company's internal network of profit centers. For example, the continuous application of programs such as the "T-50" campaign, implemented since December 1992, effectively halved production times across the company's world-wide network of electrical and transportation plants. To carry out these complex transformation efforts, ABB often relies on the existing management and employees, even in relatively less developed and culturally difficult locations such as Eastern Europe, Russia or other "emerging" economies. In many cases, the need to change was initially met with stiff resistance by the plant managers and employees, sometimes due to fear of breaking with the *status quo*, the perceived level of uncertainty surrounding the benefits that were expected from these changes, or simply a disbelief that the major improvements that were often demanded could be achieved within a relatively short time. Often, carefully reasoned arguments illustrating the feasibility and resulting benefits of major change programs, were bluntly countered by the deep-rooted conservative tendencies of the local cultural environments where these transformations had to be applied. This initial cultural resistance to change following an international acquisition, was not only characteristic of "emerging" or former communist economies, but was also typically found across many Western and industrialized countries:

> Here you may see some cultural differences. Americans tend to be quite open to change, even repetitive change. Continental Europeans are more conservative, while the Scandinavians are somewhere in between. Some people come to me and say: "We have had all these changes, opening Eastern Europe, Asia, these acquisitions. We have doubled our profits. Never in our history have we been at this level of profitability. Can we now get some stability?" Some executives may even feel that I must be mentally ill because I always want more and more. (. . .) They think that I am never satisfied, never happy. Of course that is not true. I am trying to explain to people that the world is changing, that our competitors are not standing still. It is like being on an escalator that moves against you. If you stand still you glide backwards; you need to go faster than the escalator to move up.[23]

In this context, an effective *execution* mechanism utilized by ABB to break initial resistances to change early on, is based on the so-called "centers of excellence". These are manufacturing sites or assembly locations singled out based on its high performance or "best practice" standards relative to other ABB centers. Once a major change initiative is required somewhere, ABB invites the managers and other key personnel to visit a relevant center of excellence to see how best practices, ways of working and productivity standards are achieved and maintained. Often, the centers of excellence are carefully selected in locations and environments that are culturally similar to those where the change initiatives need to be carried out. For example, a number of Brown Boveri plant managers fearing the loss of their Swiss-German culture after the 1987 merger with ASEA, were invited to see some of the latter company's manufacturing plants in Sweden. There, they had the opportunity to observe methods and practices leading to doubling or tripling the levels of efficiency of similar Swiss and German plants. When they returned to Switzerland, they applied the lessons learned to quickly turn around their local loss-making profit centers. A year earlier ASEA had bought Strömberg, a Finnish loss-making company, and immediately invited several of its plant managers to visit similar high-performing ASEA sites in Sweden and Germany. Partly as a result of this direct exposure to new manufacturing methods and practices, these managers quickly embarked on a radical restructuring program. This led to the comprehensive transformation of Strömberg into ABB's most profitable operation five years later, generating 5 percent of the company's turnover but 20 per cent of its profits in 1993. About the same time, following their acquisition of Nevskij Zavod in

Russia, ABB's officials who had been initially refused the dramatic productivity improvements proposed, invited their Russian colleagues to visit similar plants in Poland. There, they discussed in Russian with Polish plant managers, becoming so impressed by the degree of autonomy and local control allowed by ABB, that they quickly agreed to carry out the internal changes required at Nevskij Zavod.

Another result of creating visible centers of excellence is that they foster cost and productivity competition amongst profit centers on a global basis. Manufacturing and assembly units strive to become centers of excellence and a source of know-how for the rest of the organization, while already existing centers continuously innovate and improve themselves to maintain their key role in transforming the organization. Overall, benchmarking of operational performance and internal transfer of best practices become an accepted routine across local borders.

Communications: The importance of mobilizing people around global values

The assertion that effective and continuous communication is at the very cornerstone of the integration success of M&As, has become rather common place in management. However, there are few areas where the crucial difference between generic theoretical notions and *superior execution skills* becomes more apparent, than in the practical ability to communicate effectively and mobilize an international audience following a major cross-cultural M&A or alliance. In this context, it is not easy to exaggerate the profound and almost obsessive attention that certain companies place in communicating articulately to build new company values and a commonly accepted mission during the implementation of an international merger or acquisition, or through the development of a global alliance or JV.

Effective top management communications: "walk the talk" and lead by example

Successful post-merger communications invariably start from the top of an organization. The way in which a senior executive approaches communications with the key managers and staff in the acquired company, constitute a crucial showcase of the degree to which he/she is determined to "walk the talk" from the outset of the post-merger phase. In the case of cross-border M&As, JVs and alliances, it is important that the new company's leaders are aware of the national cultural differences that exist, and how these can concretely affect a well thought of communications strategy. A good example of how to handle these issues was offered during the integration phase following the 1993 merger between Sweden's Pharmacia and Italy-based Farmitalia-Carlo Erba (FICE). Although it was crucial to communicate all the way to the bottom of the Italian organization, Pharmacia found that Italian executives usually stopped distributing critical information at the middle management levels. Says Lindegren:

> In Sweden we tend to work in groups and share information openly, without so many hierarchies. But Italians are very individualistic people: You realize that at any Italian bar every morning when you see Italians order coffee in a hundred different ways! They believe very much in control, a lot less in delegation. They believe that knowledge is power and do not share it. I learned this the hard way when I arrived at FICE and started distributing information to the management group. After a while I realized that this information was not reaching the places I had intended. This was worrying because soon after a merger deal is concluded everything becomes dependent on smooth communication. So I started to send key people around to check what information was reaching whom. Then I organized a meeting with our managers, and convinced them that sharing information was not going to reduce their power. But the best convincing argument was leading by example. I was the first one to constantly share information across all levels, and did that until the message started to get through. For example, last August [1995] I had six meetings with 100 people each. In addition, we have wall papers, journals, videos, worldwide interviews with the company's Top Executives, etc.

This type of no-nonsense and direct style of communications, with heavy involvement from the top executives of the merging organizations, was crucial to the success of the Pharmacia and FICE merger. Lindegren observes that a mixture of communication techniques at the end manage to get information through to the desired managerial levels, and across the national cultural differences which may exist:

> As top manager, you should be out there, talking to people, and constantly informing them. If you think that you don't have anything to communicate, you should still do it, because there are a lot of questions coming up. During the merger between Pharmacia and FICE, we held more or less weekly meetings where a lot of people participated, allowing them to ask questions, and obtain answers. If on occasions we can't answer, we say: "It's too early", or "we don't know". But we come back to answer these issues as soon as information is available. Personal meetings work across national cultures. A little bit different in some countries than in others, like Sweden or Italy, but if you continuously use all these ways to communicate: Written communication, videos, gatherings, etc. you will eventually reach your audience and they will see that you really want to inform and involve them.

Articulating communications and coaching programs to create global values

British Airways organized a highly structured communication framework to foster the company's crucial values of customer service and orientation across its world-wide network of acquisitions and alliances. It combines conventional communications mechanisms such as international gatherings and internal company media, as well as sophisticated technological aids, to continuously build a service and customer awareness amongst employees from different nationalities and cultural backgrounds. Says Marshall:

> We need to make sure that our company mission, goals and customer service approaches are shared amongst every one of our employees, not only those in direct contact with the customer, such as the cabin crew members, but also any employee, no matter where he/she is working, has to perform knowing that at the other end it is always the customer who will judge us based on how his or her tasks were carried out. This also applies to our international partners and franchises with whom we co-operate internationally across several routes. In order to make this happen, we have communication professionals in every company department, whom keep track of any relevant business development in relation to our common goals, objectives and company values. We use cc-mail, produce an internal newspaper, weekly magazines, and are even experimenting with an internal TV broadcast. We use any state-of-the-art means of communication when we think it can help us communicate and follow up on our common mission and goals. In addition, there are more formal, cascade type mechanisms of communication along the organizational levels, and regular "Business Exchanges" at Heathrow to discuss business issues and present financial results.

In parallel with these communication programs, British Airways has developed a continuous customer service training program based in the UK. Consistent with its communications strategy, this program is widely offered to the company's personnel, including those without direct customer contact, and is also required for British Airways' international alliance partners and acquired companies. In the cut-throat price competition which has characterized the international airline business throughout the 1980s and 1990s, British Airways continuous investments in such wide-ranging customer service training have been in drastic contrast with its competitors' radical price cutting initiatives during the same time period. Even during the Gulf War of 1992, when it was facing severe financial problems and a sharp drop in passenger capacity utilization, the company did not stop investing in its comprehensive employee customer service training programs. This determined approach to developing its employees and building a global customer service culture has lent credibility to British Airways communication programs, sustaining its legendary approach to building service excellence across its global network of alliances and acquired companies. More importantly, through its particular combination of continuous communications, employee training, branding, marketing, and customer service excellence, British Airways has developed a formidable competitive weapon embedded in its company culture, allowing it to steadily command a slight premium price for some of its higher-end services at a global scale. As a result, it has consistently been one of the world's most profitable international airlines during the mid 1980s and 1990s, a time period during which most other global carriers have lost billions of US dollars every year. Marshall observes that British Airways' particular customer service training approach, has been key to make the company values accepted and shared by employees from fairly diverse national cultural backgrounds:

> With regards to the training of our people worldwide, you have to understand that our company culture is first and foremost based on the customer. And we want everybody to live up to it, without taking away the national character and values of our people. These values have to hold across diverse cultures and country environments, and we work hard to make it happen. So, for example, since 1983 we have built a continuous customer motivation program. I stress the word continuous because, unlike some of our competitors, ours has been created as a permanent feature, one that each of our employees will go through regularly — on average every two years. Everybody comes to the UK for this program, including employees from our international partner companies. This gives them a first hand chance to get to know us, the kind of company they are joining or partnering with. Apart from this, there is a great variety of training programs focusing on customer service techniques, on the importance of winning and retaining customers. In fact, we go much further than anybody in the UK on this respect, being the only company which awards an actual diploma in customer service, a professional qualification after a one-year part-time program we run jointly with the Manchester University. I believe other companies such as Disney and McDonalds have organized similar programs in the US. Since we started ours, several thousand employees have gone through this type of training.

"Global manager meetings": building common company values across diverse national cultures

Following the merger between ASEA and Brown Boveri, former CEO Barnevik passionately involved himself in preparing, delivering and following up on a highly structured and continuous program of post-merger communications with the company's global managers and key staff around the world. Partly due to Barnevik's ceaseless globetrotting, communicating and delivering presentations during the integration phase of the merger, ABB earned the nickname of "the 10,000 slide company". These communications took a wide variety of forms, from day-to-day routine communications to regular Group Executive Committee meetings and continuous visits to ABB's local companies abroad.

However, communications reached a somewhat climatic level during the annual meetings organized by ABB with the attendance of the company's global managers. Each of these meetings was proposed as a natural continuation to the previous one, being utilized to foster and consolidate company values, practices and past achievements, as well as to focus the global managers energies on the new challenges and "themes" for the future. As mentioned, the first of these meetings took place — quite symbolically — on 1 January 1988, in Cannes, shortly after the announcement of the merger between ASEA and Brown Boveri. It was largely used to proclaim the five basic values of the new company: Meeting Customer Needs, Decentralization, Taking Action, Respecting an Ethic, and Co-operating. A year after, the global managers meeting was located in Geneva, and opened ABB's Customer Focus concept aimed at increasing quality levels reducing cycle times. During the 1993-1994 recessionary downturn, ABB underwent a painful restructuring phase globally. Then in 1995, Barnevik announced to his annual audience of global managers gathered in Montreux, that the consolidation phase had ended, and that a leaner ABB was ready to resume growth through international expansion in Asia, Latin America, and particularly across the former communist Eastern European countries, Russia and the ex-Soviet republics. Thus, by relentlessly pursuing this kind of communication plans, the company's global managers got to know each other, creating bondings across local cultures and nationalities and building direct relationships with the company's top management. Simultaneously, an *esprit de corps* was skillfully built under Barnevik's leadership, around a few, clearly understood values and practical guidelines of behavior, focusing on specific targets that changed from time to time.

ABB's global manager conferences were turned into a conspicuous educational tool to help harmonize in practice the culturally unnatural demands of global co-ordination mechanisms. At the very heart of this practical challenge, the company attempted to instill a common mentality of *global co-operation*, a group sense of unity and a single code of behavior across the company's key managerial ranks. In the case of this multidomestic company, strictly divided into a myriad of small and autonomous profit centers with a highly heterogeneous mix of national cultures and strong local identities, instilling a genuine attitude of co-operation was indeed crucial to really combine the complementary resources of ABB's global array of acquisitions, JVs and alliances. This value of global collaboration across national cultures and backgrounds, was also a fundamental pre-condition to implant functioning global and local roles, which in ABB's matrix structure are highly interactive and mutually dependent on each other.

As mentioned, ABB's Book of Values was an important initial step to building these corporate values across a culturally heterogeneous group of global managers. Although English is the company's official language, its Book of Values was translated into several languages, and extensively distributed within the company. To help turning these values into living behavior, Barnevik made this book a centerpiece of ABB's global managers meetings, constantly discussing, following up and enriching its contents with the group:

We first produced it in 1987. Then, in 1991 we had 200 work groups revise it, and we expanded into environment and some other areas, such as the value of corporate unity, business ethics, customer focus, employer focus, quality, environment, action orientation and values. We went out with 38,500 copies in English, 25,000 in seventeen other languages.

Within ABB, this Book of Values is widely proposed as an exacting guide of behavior and practical advice for the company's global managers and other key managerial levels. In order to achieve this goal from the beginning, it was not so much developed around generic organizational principles and aspirations, but mostly included specific day-to-day advice and practical guidelines of professional and personal behavior. For example, regarding the integration process between ASEA and Brown Boveri, it gave down-to-earth managerial guidance fostering a positive attitude and warning against the potential misunderstandings, demoralization and personal conflicts which typically arise following an international merger:[24]

Merger process — important considerations

The true merger process does not come automatically or naturally — it is unnatural and takes management determination.

- Combat "us" and "them" syndrome vigorously.
- Strive to mix talents and experiences from the partners.
- Listen and take time to understand other viewpoints.
- English as group language is foreign to 80-90 percent [of our employees] — watch out for miscommunication.
- Show respect and recognition — do not "rub in" past failures or poor performance. Look forward.
- Inform repeatedly — "over-inform". (...)

Specific guidelines of action leading to speed of *execution*, constitute another important aspect of ABB's Book of Values, particularly regarding the company's constant acquisition turnaround activities internationally, as well as the continuous programs for productivity and technological improvements that are implemented on a global basis:

Policies for change

- Identified necessary changes have to be implemented as fast as possible. We have to concentrate on those with the biggest profit improvement potential (80/20 rule).
- After the fact it is rarely regretted that the speed of change was too high, but very often that it was too low.
- The risk of negative consequences of changes is often exaggerated because natural forces tend to resist change, arguing against them and trying to delay them.

- Avoid the syndrome of more investigations, which often becomes a way of at least delaying, if not altogether avoiding, necessary changes.
- Get "negative" changes over with all at once and avoid prolonging the process by cutting it up in pieces.
- Most major changes must be started in the first year, because what is not started in the first year will be a lot more difficult to do later. A "honeymoon" of small changes for ABB would be detrimental to our development.(...)

Generic multidomestic organizational principles championed after ABB's original cross-border merger have also been translated into specific guidelines of action in its Book of Values, arguing persuasively for the observance of a collaborative and positive attitude when applying them:

Organizational policies

ABB's organization must allow us to abide by our principle of "think global, act local". Functions and responsibilities in our matrix organization must be clearly understood.

- A fundamental guiding principle is to organize the group in clear profit centers with individual accountability.
- The many profit centers reflect a far-reaching decentralization of responsibility and authority into, as much as possible "self-contained and manageable" units with overview.
- [The "30 percent rule"] Minimize overhead and allowed costs. Special staff reduction projects will be conducted to safeguard a dramatic outback of central functions, financed by allocations. The method is:
  1. elimination of function (30 percent)
  2. decentralize function into profit centers (30 percent)
  3. create service centers which invoice services at market rates (30 percent)
  4. remaining central staff (10 percent).
- The roles of the two dimensions of the ABB matrix are complementary. They are interlinked and interdependent, and good communication skills are required to promote a widespread exchange of views. Any arising conflict at the interface between regions and business areas/segments must be resolved constructively. Only if the matrix works smoothly can we reap the full benefits of being global (economies of scale, technological strength, etc.) and of being multidomestic (a high degree of decentralization and local roots in the countries in which we operate).

(...)

Regarding the development of people, ABB's Book of Values not only includes the aspirational phrases commonly found in similar corporate documents. As already mentioned, it also contains specific guidelines showing how employees must be continuously developed and rotated across borders, supported by specific mechanisms in the company's internal reward and promotion systems. Moreover, ABB's Book of Values contains practical recommendations on how to handle all aspects of a manager's performance, including specific criteria for evaluation and dismissal:

Personnel policies

Employee Focus at ABB means fairness, openness, and respect in all our relations with our employees.

- The only selection criteria for managers must be competence in a wide sense. Our success within the ABB group will in the end depend on our being able to recruit, keep and develop the best managers in our industry.
- We will not show consideration by keeping a non-performing manager in his present job longer than necessary.
- Normally the "grandfather" principle should be used in recruitment and dismissal (means that management two levels up is involved).

(...)

ABB's global manager conferences are largely devoted to transforming the principles contained in the company's Book of Values into living guidelines of behavior for the group. Fitting a multidomestic organization initially formed and built through major international M&As, ABB's written code of behavior is likened to the constitution of a global federation of national companies. Global managers are thus given a great degree of autonomy and delegation, but remain accountable to a shared code of behavior. Accordingly, throughout ABB's global conferences, Barnevik championed the specific non negotiable rules that had to be rigorously observed by the group:

> Our directives, instructions and basic principles establishing our organizational structure and how we operate, can be regarded as the Group's Constitution, and just as any country's Constitutional Chart, it's mandatory. If we establish a sales commission charge around the world of 5 percent, it's not a matter of negotiation. These are the rules, and if you have them you have them. And of course it took a long time for people to realize that our Constitution is the glue that ties us together.

The number of ABB's "constitutional" rules continuously increased throughout the company's post-merger integration period, with the Book of Values growing correspondingly in size and content from the original 22-page version. Parallel to this, the structural complexity of the company's matrix organization has tended to increase along with the group's functional and geographic expansion. As a result, global co-ordination demands could easily grow to the point of betraying the company's intended organizational flexibility, requiring fairly big groups to make even ordinary operating decisions. Here, it was crucial that ABB's global managers get a common understanding and buy into the company's "constitutional" rules, above any national or local company loyalties. To help meeting these challenges, ABB's global managers conferences continuously relied on examples and cases, illustrating how the company's numerous rules and principles are to be applied in specific contexts.

ABB's global managers conferences are also a showcase to illustrate and promote the application of *execution* mechanisms such as *adoption*. As mentioned, the global managers that acted as "parents" to integrate acquisitions in the Czech republic, got an opportunity to share their experiences with the group, obtaining high visibility and recognition within the organization. As a result, other companies were motivated to become adoptive parents in these countries, including the initially *adopted* organizations. Additional examples illustrate how *adoption*, after becoming routinely established in Eastern Europe and the former Soviet republics, has moved across continents to effectively integrate similar acquisition and alliance situations in "emerging" economies across Latin America and Asia. The examples explain key criteria to successfully select *adopting* companies. In the case of Poland, Russia, or the Czech Republic, the parenting organizations were established ABB operations from locations that were culturally close to the *adopted* companies, possessing the *gnosis* to bridge potential language and cultural barriers. These examples intend to both encourage and facilitate the continuous implementation and global expansion of this type of *execution* mechanisms.

Overall, ABB's global managers conferences serve multiple communication purposes, helping to instill a group sense of unity in a company built through major international mergers and acquisitions, develop internal leadership, create a co-operative atmosphere and common guidelines of behavior across national cultures, and continuously increase both knowledge and *gnosis* of global co-ordination practices. Accordingly, the company has continuously fostered these communication events to take place on a larger, global scale. Barnevik observes:

> Communicating to these global managers is the whole thing. And the reason for having these four hundred top people meet regularly, is to have the Group Executive Committee go through all the key issues, hammer them home, show cases, motivate them, lift them up, show them that we are the best, we take the lead, creating cultural success and belonging together. And now this is done in other areas. It's done in the Europe Region, it's done in Hong Kong/ Asia Region, they do it all over the place.

Effective post-merger communications are also a matter of managerial stamina

However, effective post-merger communications require continuous and strenuous effort on the part of the top leaders of an organization. Normally, these have to ensure that a company's key managerial levels buy into the new organization's values, vision and mission, so that a trickle down process is effectively generated and goes through the middle and lower managerial levels. This requires direct contact with the top leaders, through visits, speeches, personal meetings and continuous involvement, but herein lies the crucial test of any such communication effort. Particularly when a major M&A or alliance involves people from highly diverse national cultural values and traditions, it takes time to reach out the key managerial levels, let alone mobilize them around shared values and goals to convince others. This process is compared to an educational effort which takes time, patience and sheer managerial stamina to continuously "evangelize" to people around common beliefs and objectives, and periodically monitoring that these are effectively trickled down to the lower levels of the organization. Says Ekberg:

> We have to adapt to the local cultures, and we have to build that attitude globally across our companies. This you do by training, education, and by constantly rotating people across borders. But it takes time, although you will eventually reach down to the middle and lower management layers of the company. You have to become humble when confronted with this immense task. *After merging large organizations, it takes at least two years to reach about twenty-five percent of the company managers.* So you have to be on the road all the time, visiting people, encouraging, training and educating them.

Execution Skills to Take Advantage of Culturally Distant Traits

When discussing our empirical findings showing a positive relationship between national cultural distance and cross-border acquisition performance in Chapter 3, it was suggested that routines and repertoires embedded in the target's national culture which were significantly different from the acquirer's (or *vice versa*), had the potential to enhance the combined company's performance after the deal. Amongst others, we mentioned routines and repertoires related to innovation and inventiveness, degree of entrepreneurship and working practices. In addition, we also found that the ability to effectively improve cross-border post-acquisition performance was crucially dependent on the acquirer's implementation of *execution modes* that were compatible with the target's national cultural traits. From a wide perspective, *execution mechanisms* such as "cloning", "adoption", "cross-cultural rotations" or "international centers of excellence", can continuously foster an expanding cognitive flow across multiple organizational dimensions, leading to rapid absorption and internal transfer of methods, practices and routines that are key to performance, including those embedded in the local cultures and informational contexts. However, during our case research and senior executive interviews, we examined cross-border transactions where the acquirer and the target were specifically based on culturally distant countries, such as Swedish-Italian acquisitions.[25] In this context, we found additional illustration on how the application of particular *execution skills*, in certain cases contributed to unleash creativity or absorb working practices and capabilities rooted in a country's culture, significantly influencing performance as a result.

Pharmacia and FICE: implanting new ways of working to take advantage of Italian creativity

In the case of Pharmacia's acquisition of Italy-based FICE in 1992, the Swedish buyer found that many of the target's skills and working practices were significantly different from their own. Both the detrimental and potentially positive aspects of FICE's "cultural ways of doing things" were seen as partly reflecting some of Italy's specific national cultural traits versus Sweden's. Says Lindegren:

> The Italians had a big problem because they lacked an understanding of the conditions under which research works. Creativity and innovation cannot flourish in a place where control and hierarchy are more important than delegation. Research means to innovate, to invent and create new things, and that needs freedom, delegation, guidance and teamwork. So the Italian way of working — hierarchical, individualistic and not cross-functional — was counter-productive in this context. However — paradoxically — this does not mean that Italians are not creative. On the contrary, Italians are often more knowledgeable [than the Swedes]. They know more history, art, and literature, and creativity and innovation are higher in Italy than in Sweden. I believe that this has to do with the culture of the family which is so strong in Italy. Italians take school much more seriously than Swedes, and the family structure makes sure this happens. In Sweden, this is not looked upon as important.

Thus, it was perceived that FICE's operational problems were not related to the people's capabilities *per se,* as the company already had a very good pool of scientists prior to being acquired by Pharmacia. It was rather a problem in the way of working within FICE, which, particularly in its R&D areas, was not particularly congenial to innovation and creativity. As a result, Lindegren's first moves following the acquisition, aimed at implanting a completely new way of working within FICE, relying on a more decentralized organization based on cross-functional research teams. The latter clearly focused on closing three gaps which had been initially identified:

- A gap in the pipeline, in other words, no new drugs were coming up from the research side to replace the older ones.

- A time gap, as a result of the former one, which meant that, since research into new drugs had been partly neglected, there had to be some time before FICE was in a position to developed good, new drugs.
- A technology gap, FICE's researchers were active enough in more modern approaches, such as autoimmunity, hormonal treatments and photo dynamic therapy.

In fact, at the time when Pharmacia acquired FICE, the latter depended heavily on three old drugs which had been developed more than twenty years earlier. Thus, by promoting a new way of working, Pharmacia attempted to significantly cut the time-to-market of new products, and to effectively unleash the potential innovativeness and creativity of FICE's researchers. This was achieved by utilizing a rather simple expedient. Lindegren and other Swedish executives from Pharmacia singled out a few young and bright FICE professionals, and appointed them as team leaders of twenty projects which had the objective of closing the gaps that had been identified. These young leaders were given great autonomy and functional responsibility, and were promoted internally to champion the new cultural ways of working throughout the organization. By concentrating their efforts on these internal champions, Lindegren and his Swedish colleagues effectively turned them into catalysts for a radical organizational change which trickled down across all organizational levels. Says Lindegren:

> We identified the twenty best individuals in FICE and trained them to work and lead teams. We then gave them responsibility to lead actual teams. In this effort I was not alone. Doctor Borg was with me: We had worked together in Astra from 1976 to 1978. In Astra, where he was also a Top Executive, he and I had tried to understand how to improve time to market in research, and things like that. We also brought in personnel consultants to help train our twenty project leaders.

The delicate changes in FICE's "cultural ways of working" were carried out within two years in a remarkably smooth fashion, in spite of the significant differences that were perceived between the two companies' national and corporate cultures. However, when Lindegren and other executives at KabiVitrum had attempted to implement very similar changes following their acquisition of Pharmacia in 1990, a strongly violent reaction had ensued although both companies shared the same national cultural values. What had made the outcomes of these acquisition integration efforts so different? Here, Lindegren remarks that their strenuous experiences integrating Pharmacia had given him and his colleagues the specific knowledge, as well as the cultural sensitivity and tact to anticipate and handle similar situations within FICE's considerably diverse informational context:

> We did it all respecting the people, the local uses and ways of thinking. And then, we brought only a few of us Swedes, it was not the case of a lot of us "invading" the whole place and giving orders to the Italians. There was no takeover, no hordes of consultants "leading" the integration effort. As a result, the Italians didn't feel that we had come in to take their jobs or kick them out of their company. Besides, we made commitments and kept them. One way of measuring the success of the FICE integration is the fact that we have achieved higher cost savings than expected. During the first year, we targeted to save the equivalent of 7 percent of total costs, and achieved 16.7 percent. In the next year, we will be 20.7 percent and for the third year we look forward to achieve a 25 percent target. However, we achieved this by divesting away from non-core activities. We haven't cut one head in R&D, which is a commitment which I made with the FICE people when I came in. We did let go 850 people but not a single one of them was from R&D. The only exception to this was 60 research people from Pierrel, a company which Kabi Pharmacia owned and which we divested after the FICE acquisition. So, at the end of this three-year process we had a clearer product line to project based on a much stronger research efficiency. We empowered a lot of the bright, young people around here, releasing all those ideas which were previously unheard. As a result, the whole atmosphere changed, and we obtained faster results from our projects.

Appointing FICE's best individuals as cross-functional team leaders signaled Pharmacia's high appreciation and expectations on the acquired company's internal resources and capabilities from the very beginning. Also, by insisting in giving these champions specific responsibility and wide autonomy, Lindegren effectively started to rebuild FICE's long-term cross-functional organization based on these young leaders. They were effectively empowered, and from very early on had the opportunity to develop cross-functional and project management knowledge, as well as the experience and *gnosis* required to practically co-ordinate resources across Pharmacia's and FICE's organizations, bridging any national or corporate cultural issues which may arise. This focus on developing internal people from the outstart of FICE's post-merger integration process was a thorough success factor, in stark contrast with KabiVitrum's reliance on outside management consultants to integrate Pharmacia's operations three years before.

Thus, the merger between Pharmacia and FICE could well be described as FICE bringing in specific research and scientific talents, while Pharmacia provided a new "cultural way of doing things" which, particularly within the R&D areas, led to FICE being able to run projects much faster and much more efficiently than before. The key to this company transformation was the ability to identify, develop and empower a few champions to effectively lead teams and co-ordinate critical resources, constantly bridging the diversity of national and corporate cultures which was apparent after Pharmacia's acquisition of FICE. Young and talented project leaders that had previously been reluctant to speak up within a rather hierarchical organization, were encouraged to regularly share their ideas in *ad hoc* meetings that were organized to that effect, whereas Lindegren involved himself personally to ensure that critical information which was previously kept at higher organizational levels, was regularly shared with these champions. As a result, by instilling team-work practices and a more decentralized structure, an open and more transparent climate was fostered, in which the flow of ideas could be communicated across FICE's organizational levels.

Embracing "Anglo-Saxon" practices at Deutsche Bank

According to Deutsche Bank executives, their internationalization and expansion efforts started during the early 1980s, had already caused a strong impact in the organization after less than one decade. It was previously permeated by an exceedingly conservative German culture, embedded in the country's traditional post-war social and corporate policies. These generally emphasized relatively low wage differentials and the absence of aggressive, "Anglo-Saxon type" of productivity-based bonus or share options schemes of executive compensation. In turn, such policies tended to foster stability, relatively extensive social benefits, and the consensual management style which have arguably constituted the cultural norm in Germany's corporate world.[26] In this context, Deutsche Bank's recent acquisition and executive "hunting" activities abroad, particularly the 1989 acquisition of Morgan Grenfell, an old-established British merchant bank, by 1996 had already led to a widespread increase of salary levels and monetary bonuses internally. These are apparently becoming more in line with the "Anglo-Saxon" incentive practices of the institutions Deutsche Bank had acquired and heavily recruited from. In addition, during early 1996 it decided to introduce executive share options for top management, roughly at the same time when Daimler-Benz, based on an epochal and divided vote of its supervisory board, also introduced an executive share option scheme for its top management. At the same time, the incorporation of Morgan Grenfell's aggressive "Anglo-Saxon" approaches had led to a positive impact on Deutsche Bank's profitability, with its international investment banking activities reportedly constituting as much as one-third of the bank's profits in 1995.[27]

From a different perspective, Deutsche Bank's greater awareness of "Anglo-Saxon" style pension systems since its late 1980s international acquisition and expansion efforts, has helped it modify deeply held cultural conceptions at the very heart of Germany's welfare system. During early 1996, Deutsche Bank started campaigning for a US style corporate pension plan in Germany, allowing banks to make cash investments outside balance sheet, into professionally managed pension funds. Consistent with its preaching, Deutsche Bank started its own US$ 330 million equity pension fund in April 1996, and placed it under segregated management control of an asset management subsidiary. It was expected that the bank will further increase this initial amount of investment, in a move that could extensively influence other banks and corporations, which in Germany comprehensively hold around US$ 170 billion in cash in their balance sheets. Indeed, the future ability of Germany's current pension system to support its rapidly aging population based on non-equity investments which are seldom managed professionally, had been increasingly questioned by the country's financial and economic authorities. In this context, Deutsche Bank's campaign to reform Germany's pension system along the lines of a US style system, was viewed as revolutionary, due to the profound legal and fiscal overhaul it may imply in the country. It was also seen as an unprecedented attempt to promote more liquid stock markets by introducing an equity culture of investment, which Germany ostensibly lacks, relative to "Anglo-Saxon" countries. Indeed, an extensive preference for less volatile, fixed income forms of investment in countries such as Germany, Italy and France, has been linked in the past with these countries' highly uncertainty-avoidant national culture traits, *vis-à-vis* countries such as the USA or the UK, which tend to favor more volatile, equity forms of investment.[28]

Apart from incentive systems and pension fund reforms as a result of Deutsche Bank's recent internationalization efforts, the introduction of "new blood" such as Edson Mitchell's, the Head of global markets recruited from US investment bank Merrill Lynch, has led to new ideas and practices been implemented across its operations. In particular, an improved and more extensive risk management was already apparent in 1995, compared to the relatively unsophisticated risk management techniques traditionally associated with many German banks. Asset management operations were also considerably greater in size (having grown from £13.2 billion to £35 billion during the 1990-1995 period) and truly global in scope. In addition to the positive impact in profitability, growth opportunities have also multiplied as the bank has aggressively expanded abroad since the mid 1980s: "Our net volume growth during 1995 was equivalent to five times our total size in 1968", Deutsche Bank's executives note. However, well into the mid 1990s, the one area where Deutsche Bank had led a less spectacular expansion was global equities. This area, according to Deutsche Bank executives approached at that time, needed "another Mitchell" to be turned around into a global operation from where it was in 1996. Nevertheless, these executives acknowledged that global equities tends to be "a more difficult area to build than fixed income", because of its heavy reliance on world-class research. They argued that these research skills are "harder to create" in corporate banking environments such as the German's or the Italian's, which have historically and overwhelmingly favored the relatively stable fixed income markets over the more volatile equity markets.

Electrolux-Zanussi: Creating a new industrial relations framework to absorb Italian flexibility and "Mittle-European" organization

When Swedish Electrolux took over Zanussi in 1984, the latter company already was one of Italy's most respected industrial symbols, a well-established European pioneer and leader in the production of washing machines and other white goods. Moreover, at the time of the acquisition, Zanussi's production volumes were nearly twice as much as those of Electrolux, leading many observers to believe that the underlying logic of the transaction was to gain scale economies in manufacturing, as well as a significant distribution boost for the acquirer's own brands in the Southern and Central European markets where it had been traditionally absent. However, former Electrolux-Zanussi CEO and Chairman Rossignolo observes that this transaction had a much wider set of motivations. Paramount amongst these, was the acquirer's desire to absorb what it saw as highly complementary skills in the target company. These were seen as embedded in the national cultural characteristics of its employees, manifesting themselves through highly flexible and creative approaches towards product design and manufacturing routines and repertoires:

> One fundamental reason for Electrolux to acquire Zanussi is that people skills were sufficiently complementary. In marketing and product design the Italian people were more creative, more aggressive, much more flexible. The Swedes instead have difficulty in being flexible. This was also present across the labor relations area, although we have presented an image in the world of an Italy where you don't work, with high absenteeism and factories that are in the hands of the Unions, etc. etc. All of this was true in the past, but Italy has made a silent revolution during the past ten years, as a result of which labor relations have substantially improved. For example, labor flexibility, the adoption of new technologies, working on Saturdays or Sundays have been easier here [Italy] than in Sweden. This flexibility is part of the Italian culture, and you could see many concrete examples of this in Zanussi. For example, I had initially thought that they [in Sweden] had an advantage in the area of methods or systems of production. But in fact this is not true, because in the area of productive systems we had introduced automation from very early on, as a result of having larger production facilities and higher volumes, and also due to the difficult labor regulations we had in the past. To further enhance its flexibility, the Italian industry has made big efforts in areas such as just-in-time, information technology, things that allowed us to bring under control the production processes. When I made sure that Electrolux bought Zanussi, I thought that Electrolux would bring the state-of-the-art of manufacturing. Instead, I later realized that we taught them excellence in manufacturing.

Zanussi was founded after the First World War by a native of Pordenone, a small city in Italy's North Eastern region of Friuli. As a war prisoner in North America, he had the opportunity to see the incipient electrodomestics which were being introduced for the first time into American homes. Following the end of the war, young Zanussi returned to Italy and, remembering what he

267

had seen across the ocean, founded a small manufacturing company named after him to produce electrodomestics. Thus, since the beginning of the 20th century, Zanussi pioneered the development of the electrodomestic market, first in Italy, and afterwards in Europe, as the company grew rapidly in size. However, from the very early stages, Zanussi relied on its own design, technical innovations and quality of manufacturing, developing the skills which made it an internationally renowned brand and a European leader in electrodomestics.

Zanussi's skills have been particularly in evidence within the local informational context of Pordenone, where it has traditionally continued to conduct most of its R&D, manufacturing, marketing and product design activities. There, Zanussi's contextual skills and assets appear to owe as much to the specific history and culture of the Friuli region, as to the more generic Italian cultural traits. This rather distinctive regional character of many Italian communities has been studied by some authors, who have for example linked their cultural diversity to a markedly varied disposition towards political institutions and ways of government across the many regions of the peninsula.[29] Within Europe, such regional cultural diversity also characterizes other nations such as Germany, which shares with Italy a similar history of long-standing political fragmentation until relatively recent times. In these countries, a myriad of comparatively small but lasting republics, well-established kingdoms and enduring governments have contributed to mold distinct regional traits until the late 19th century, when these political organizations were superseded by the kind of larger national states championed since the 15th century by France, England, Spain or Portugal.

In the case of Friuli, its present regional borders were already drafted during the pre-Christian era, when the Fresians, a group of Germanic barbarian tribes from Central Europe, were first incorporated into the Roman Empire's domains. During the first centuries AD, and following the fall of the Roman Empire, civilized Friuli suffered more than any other Italian region the marauding invasions of the Goths, Huns and other barbarian tribes, situated as it was across the strategic Alpine paths connecting Central and Eastern Europe to the Italian peninsula. It was already during these dark centuries that a few surviving chronicles described the Friulians as an exceedingly industrious community, persistently repopulating and rebuilding their savaged cities regardless of the perils continuously brought about by the barbarian invasions. During the 14th and 15th centuries, Friuli fell under the direct influence of the Republic of Venice, the leading European maritime nation at the time, which saw this region and the adjacent Veneto and Venezia Giulia provinces as its natural "hinterland", constituting today's Italian Tri-Veneto region. Friuli's rich alpine forests and the industriousness of its inhabitants were particularly attractive to the Venetians, whose famous Arsenal was the world's largest shipbuilding site at the time, constantly requiring large amounts of manpower, wood and other raw materials. It was under the centuries-long Venetian domination that Friuli's strong regional cultural traits may have been amalgamated in its present form. For one thing, the Venetian government was an exceptionally stable and enduring organization, two characteristics which few would associate with contemporary Italian political structures. The Venetian Republic's constitution, written during the late 8th century, survived almost exactly one thousand years with minor modifications, as the pre-eminent law of the Republic's aristocratic form of government. Thus, after the Venetian government eventually fell at the hands of Napoleon Bonaparte in 1798, its constitution had lasted longer than any other similar political document in history. However, during their lasting stewardship of Friuli and the adjacent Italian regions, the Venetians had widely introduced their characteristic commercial methods and manufacturing organization, which were highly sophisticated by the standards of the time. These included the invention of the double-entry book-keeping system during the 15th century, and the widespread specialization of manufacturing tasks on a relatively large scale. The latter methods were conspicuously applied to shipbuilding activities in the Arsenal, leading to it being described as a medieval precursor of the modern assembly line, for its capacity to entirely produce a warship ready for battle in one day during periods of emergency.[30] After Venetian domination faded away at the eve of the 19th century, the region was absorbed into the Austro-Hungarian empire during most of the following 60 years, until the formation of the modern Italian state. Throughout these historic events, the traditional industriousness, flexibility, working organization and tight sense of community of Friuli's people have been distinctively shaped, and continue to typify the region's character to the present day. Rossignolo indicates that the strong cultural traits of Friuli's people have played a relevant role in Electrolux 1984 acquisition of Zanussi:

> I have always said to the Electrolux Board: "When you acquire Zanussi you aren't just acquiring a company in Italy. You are acquiring a company in a 'country' which is situated in the North-East of Italy, Friuli, a region very close to Austria. Their inhabitants have the flexibility and creativity that all Italians have, but also possess a 'Mittel-European' culture of discipline and organization. And you have invested there." I would have never advised them to acquire Zanussi, had it been based in Naples, because there it would never have been managed as a company. So, I say that the relationship that we have developed in Friuli with the public administration, with the local unions, with the people and with the local authorities, is an incredibly good relationship! And this is an asset that Electrolux-Zanussi has and which should not be destroyed! Because one reason for our success is this: If I ask in Friuli a sacrifice for Zanussi, there is no question that they will do it. And in this way, we constantly achieve productivity increases, or product design improvements, for example. In Friuli, people have Zanussi in their hearts. The person who founded this company 80 years ago was a worker, an artisan who built this kind of culture in his hometown [in Pordenone], and so you don't buy just machine tools here in this company, you buy the people's culture, which is an asset to be preserved.

In order to absorb Zanussi's regional cultural assets into Electrolux's global network, the company implemented a flexible structure of "distributed leadership". Within this highly decentralized organizational design, production responsibilities are localized following the geographical distribution of technological and manufacturing skills. For example, Electrolux "cold" lines (refrigerators and the like) remained under the responsibility of Sweden, whereas the "wet" lines (washing machines, dish washers and dryers) were placed under Electrolux-Zanussi's leadership in Pordenone. To co-ordinate production and distribution at a global scale, Electrolux has created Business Line manager roles, located where the product skills are, and Portfolio managers, who are responsible for all the brands that are distributed in a particular country. In turn, these managers are part of organizational business areas which operate at a regional level (i.e. Europe, North America, etc.) and meet regularly to co-ordinate production, distribution, marketing and brand management initiatives across borders. The business areas largely follow product and technological lines, such as: vacuum cleaners or washing machines. This organizational design allows for a great deal of local autonomy between the company's large country-based operations, such as Sweden, Italy or the USA. However, perhaps more importantly in the case of Electrolux-Zanussi, it also ensured that all the relevant regional cultural assets developed throughout the acquired company's history could remain largely intact, including its characteristic brand names, the local employees embedding the company's R&D, product design, marketing and manufacturing capabilities, and the well-developed local community networks and institutional relationships in Pordenone, where Electrolux-Zanussi is still today the largest single employer. Rossignolo explains:

> If I had "married" a German or a French company, they would have sent expatriate managers to Italy. This would have been a disaster because it would have destroyed the culture that Zanussi had here in Italy. Instead the Swedes, a nation of few people, has very good managers but not in great numbers. Therefore, instead of destroying our resources, we have integrated them. In fact, we have not made the mistake of accepting everything from Sweden, or just buy factories as a point of production. They [Electrolux] didn't wish to impose the Swedish culture or their brand names in Swedish, a type of acquisition that we have seen implemented by some of our competitors. The Swedes' approach was much more pragmatic. We asked: What is a brand name? It's an asset. Why destroy it? So, we integrated our various brand names. We sell Zanussi, Electrolux, we sell Zoppas, we sell Castor, etc. In different countries we try to bring forward our value in terms of marketing, products and people. This is our fundamental reason for success. The type of organization we initiated and which has been so useful for improving communication between people, is called "distributed leadership". It can be defined as a structural model where the leadership follows the technical and people skills geographically. We locate the leadership wherever those skills are: in Sweden, Italy, France, etc.

However, implanting a "distributed leadership" design was just one critical step to ensure that Zanussi's regional cultural assets could be maintained and developed within Electrolux global structure. At the time of the acquisition, another crucial aspect was to ensure that the company could keep its local employee base and associated skills in spite of the company's difficult financial constraints and the highly confrontational atmosphere which characterized Italian industrial relations during most of the 1980s. During those years, any company of Zanussi's size had well-established and powerful union representatives, whom operated in close co-ordination with the National Labor representatives' directives, issued from Rome. Due to Zanussi's emblematic reputation, its deteriorating financial situation in 1984 which threatened thousands of jobs, and the fact that it had been acquired by a foreign company, establishing a mutually trustful and co-operative relationship with the unions was a necessary but exceedingly difficult step. Here, Electrolux-Zanussi's model of distributed leadership proved to live up to the circumstances. First of all, it had established a local Country Manager with wide responsibility to oversee his/her country operations and interface with the internal government, labor and industrial institutions. Secondly, it allowed great autonomy to its local organizations to develop industrial relations frameworks which best suited the particular cultural characteristics of the countries it operated in. Rossignolo remarks that, in the case of Electrolux-Zanussi, this combination allowed him to develop an innovative and eclectic model of industrial relations which was tailored to Italy's particular context:

> The industrial relations model many companies use in Italy today is called the "Zanussi model", which I introduced in the local market. Some critics said that it was imposed by the Swedes, but they imposed nothing. In fact, Sweden's labor relations model is widely criticized in their own home country, being an inflexible system where the Unions block everything. If I had adopted the Swedish system in Italy, it would have been a big mistake. Instead I sold them the concept of a participative model in the "Italian way". The only concept I kept from the Swedish model, is that we play with the cards on the table and don't keep them hidden under the table. All information should be correct, transparent and fair. We start from the stand point of wishing to make a deal and we neither distort facts nor massage data. Because if we start with a game, we will both keep on hiding our cards, and in this way we will accomplish nothing. The resolution of problems should be made with a maximum amount of information. Both sides can then take responsibility, and agree upon what needs to be done.

Transparent negotiation style and broad employee participation in decision-making were not the only innovative aspects of the Electrolux-Zanussi's model of industrial relations. It also crucially included a wide array of profit-sharing and stock ownership programs for its employees, which at the time had been largely shunned by the large Italian corporations, represented by Cofindustria, the country's main industrial association. However, in the case of Electrolux-Zanussi, both transparency and employee participation were crucial requirements to foster an atmosphere of genuine co-operation with the Unions, allowing the company to retain its employees' regional cultural skills, taking advantage of the local informational networks that had been created, and generating badly needed productivity and product development improvements. Says Rossignolo:

> To some people in the Cofindustria, my labor relations model of participation with the workers was at first seen as heresy. But we pushed it because we wanted to keep this asset, our people. As a result, today we have a wonderful relationship with the people and the community. We have moved a huge step forward, with the unions being part of our family and involved in all issues, not just productivity improvements, but also remuneration. My workers participate in the results of the operations and share the dividends of the company. We look at the bottom line, the profitability of the company, and then we distribute the benefits, so they [the employees] become real partners to produce more. And this is why they accept to work during Saturdays and Sundays: They [the employees] become more capitalist than the owner. We have created a system which is both intelligent and generous. And the results speak by themselves. This is why Italy and Sweden constitute a good business combination: In substance we Italians have managed to uphold a certain type of culture, that we did not have, but with their encouragement, we adapted it to the Italian context and to the local culture.

These initiatives led to a quick turnaround of Zanussi. In 1984 the company had lost Lit 150 billion. However, in 1985 Rossignolo had managed to reduced the loss to Lit 36 billion, and a year after turned it into a profit of Lit 36 billion, the real turnaround of the company taking place only 14 or 15 months after Electrolux took over. In the meantime, Rossignolo had to negotiate with the unions in Rome for 72 hours, non-stop, to be able to reduce 5,000 people, and then another 4,848 — "not more, not less" — who mostly worked in the non-core areas of the company, such as real estate and construction businesses. After refocusing on its core activities, Electrolux-Zanussi's head-count was reduced to 12,000. However, in these core areas — washing machines, dish washers and dryers — Rossignolo kept intact the employee base and managed to increase production by 50 percent a few years after the Electrolux acquisition. As a result, by 1996, the head-count had increased to around 16,000, with an ROA of 20 percent, and a profit of Lit 228 billion on total revenues of Lit 4,300 billion.

Making it Happen: "The Art is Not in the Concept"

Execution mechanisms of the kind described in this chapter, can be critical in quickly integrating M&As, JVs and alliances across national borders and local cultures. More generally, they may contribute to effectively co-ordinate an organization's global pool of resources, continuously generating economies of scale, scope and market power. However, in the end, the degree to which an organization is able to attain these benefits is not strictly dependent on any single set of *execution* mechanisms *per se*. Rather, a superior performance is also a function of the way in which multiple *execution* mechanisms are combined to continuously match a company's complex and changing informational contexts. This notion has been a recurrent one throughout this part of our research, being illustrated by the way in which ABB has successfully combined *cloning, adopting, cross-cultural rotations* or *global co-ordination functions* to quickly integrate major acquisitions in culturally difficult locations across Russia and Eastern Europe without adding staff to its 200 strong headquarters; or by British Airways' flexible and focused approach to develop highly consistent global service standards which are nevertheless tailored to the local cultures in which it operates; or by the strenuous international acquisition efforts of companies such as Pharmacia or Deutsche Bank, which doggedly developed their organizational knowledge and *gnosis* of integrating resources across national cultural difficulties. These cases provide numerous illustrations showing how a determined application of basic *execution orientation* principles, and learning-by-doing, can consistently develop the skills required to generate practical advantages through global M&As, JVs and alliances. For example, it has been pointed out that in culturally difficult countries such as China, the former communist regimes of Eastern Europe, Asia, and the ex-Soviet Union, controlling a majority stake in the target companies is crucial to rapidly carry out the major changes that are often required. However, Daewoo's experiences pioneering acquisitions and JVs in countries such as Vietnam, Poland or China, evidence the extent to which general implementation principles can meet significant barriers to *execution* in the real world. Says Kang:

> In those countries influenced by the so called socialism, or communism, majority shareholder doesn't mean anything. They don't know. They don't understand. For example in one joint venture we established in Vietnam, we had 75 percent of the company shares and the Vietnamese government the remaining 25 percent. But we could not make certain basic decisions in spite of the fact that we were the majority owners. Under a capitalist way of management, the majority owners should manage the company, but in our Vietnamese joint venture the minority was always complaining. They didn't understand capitalism completely. We were trying to implement market economy principles and the Anglo-American shareholder company system: The majority shareholder selects the management, who has the responsibility to run the company for a certain period of time and achieve results. But they don't understand that concept. In Poland we faced the same situation as well. So a lot of education is needed, but for how long?

Examples such as these give an insight into the practical importance of specific *execution* mechanisms in the real world of global management. When applied effectively, they become critical to handle the rather unpredictable

273

myriad of cultural and organizational difficulties that can arise during the implementation of international M&As, JVs and alliances. Moreover, they help putting into context how rather overdone terms such as: learning-by-doing, direct experience, or managerial determination, remain crucial to the successful integration of cross-border M&As, JVs and alliances. The international experiences of Pharmacia and Deutsche Bank, are interesting examples to illustrate these notions.

Pharmacia & Upjohn: Arduous but determined learning-by-doing

Pharmacia provides a singular example of a company that has sharpened key *execution skills* through direct merger and acquisition experience, leading it to grow dramatically within less than a decade, from its relatively small Swedish origins to the global pharmaceutical stage. It started in 1987, as Jan Ekberg was carrying out a dramatic turnaround of Stockholm-based KabiVitrum. At that time, he presented a long term strategy for the company's Board of Directors, delineating two fundamental alternatives to go forward. One was to sell the company after restructuring was completed and it had again returned to profitability. The other was to expand aggressively, not only based on organic growth but also through acquisitions, to become a leading company in Scandinavia, and subsequently turn it into a major European player. Procordia, the Swedish state holding company that controlled KabiVitrum, strongly endorsed the latter option, establishing specific investment limits and other policy guidelines. Thus, following this decision, KabiVitrum started to acquire a number of relatively small companies in Sweden, Germany, Spain and Italy. In 1989, it targeted Pharmacia, a leading European pharmaceutical company based in Uppsala (Central Sweden), which had Volvo as its major shareholder. However, the integration of Pharmacia turned out to be an exceedingly difficult ordeal. Lars Lindegren, then a senior executive at KabiVitrum, had a first-hand exposure to these difficulties:

> It became very, very touchy. Both companies' corporate cultures were quite different. On the one hand, KabiVitrum was not quoted in the stock market, was smaller than Pharmacia, and had a rather informal style. On the other, Pharmacia was the bigger company, quoted in the stock market and very proud of it, with an uptight style. In addition, there were a lot of mistakes during the post-acquisition integration of the two companies. First of all, we decided to keep the two CEOs on their places, which turned out to be quite a stupid thing to do at the end, because, after a while, the CEO of Pharmacia left amid quite a sour situation. And then, the Management Board had eight KabiVitrum Directors whereas Pharmacia only had two. All this contributed to create a distinct feeling in Uppsala that they were being raped by the people in Stockholm. It became a very violent merger, and although we tried to present it as a merger of equals, it was clear to everybody that Procordia always had the last word.

Pharmacia's size, long-standing international reputation, relatively success-ful operations and ownership structure, were in sharp contrast with the acquirer's comparatively provincial background, state-owned and strug-gling corporate history. Hence, many of the considerable tensions felt within the companies' top management after the KabiVitrum's acquisition of Pharmacia were indeed aggravated by the widely differing perceptions that each company's top management had on the other's outlook, corporate cul-ture and background, *vis-à-vis* their own. These difficulties at the senior levels naturally affected every other areas of the merging companies, creating mis-trust and an extremely negative and openly conflictive atmosphere between people from the two organizations. In addition, it was decided early on to bring in an outside management consultancy to facilitate and speed up the post-merger integration efforts at the operational levels. However, an exces-sive reliance on outside consultants at this stage, created a crucial issue for Kabi-Pharmacia in the medium-term, as suitable professionals with both the knowledge and *gnosis* to smoothly continue the integration process over time had not always been developed internally. As a result, middle managers with the co-ordination skills required to resume the amalgamation of Kabi's and Pharmacia's resources, had to be painstakingly developed well after the mer-ger integration had started.

Thus, from the time when it decided to expand aggressively in 1987, it took KabiVitrum five years before it could acquire and fully integrate Pharmacia's operations to create a new leading European pharmaceutical company, Kabi Pharmacia. In 1992 Ekberg was ready to make another presentation to the company's Board of Directors, where it was decided that the next step for Kabi-Pharmacia was to become a truly international company, not only active in Europe, but also in the USA and Japan. That was the underlying strategy leading to the 1993 acquisition of Italy's FICE, a company with strong R&D and commercial capabilities internationally.

Senior executives at Pharmacia unanimously concede that, even if the Italian national cultural environment is substantially different from Sweden's, FICE's integration was considerably easier than that of Pharmacia's. In effect, as previously mentioned, the valuable skills and les-sons learned during the arduous integration process of Pharmacia's, proved to be largely transferable across national borders and cultures. First of all, build-ing on these previous experiences, it was early on decided to appoint a single person to lead the FICE's integration efforts, to transfer only a reduced and necessary number of senior executives from Pharmacia, and to rely on inter-nal people as much as possible. As a result, Lindegren was chosen as President of FICE and moved to Italy with a few Pharmacia executives shortly after the acquisition deal had been concluded. In addition, it was decided not to involve any management consultancy during the integration of FICE.

Secondly, Lindegren found a relatively hierarchical company, not used to team-work and informality. Until 1990, FICE's R&D division reported directly to the company's owners, while Marketing and Sales answered directly to the CEO. In practice, this meant that research had little communication or co-ordination with the rest of the company. In this environment, the way of running research projects was to start them after specific guidelines by the owners, rather than putting them under a project leader. By the time Pharmacia took over, these combined factors had been adversely affecting FICE's innovation and creativity levels, with no new major drugs having come out of its R&D labs for over twenty years. In order to change this situation, Pharmacia implanted new ways of working within FICE. As mentioned, this was achieved by developing and empowering a reduced number of local team leaders, around critical projects that were identified to improve FICE's research and technology gaps. By subsequently giving significant functional responsibilities to these young leaders, Pharmacia effectively empowered them to champion FICE's new organization.

Throughout this process, it is not easy to exaggerate Pharmacia's accomplishments in smoothly integrating FICE's operations and profoundly changing its cultural attitudes and working practices. Italy and Sweden are quite far apart in terms of national culture traits, and their business related informational contexts are also correspondingly different in many aspects. Particularly in the pharmaceutical sector, Italian business practices have historically provided an uneasy mix of lack of transparency and political nepotism, as well as exceedingly bureaucratic processes involving the approval and launching of new drugs.[31] In addition, Pharmacia's acquisition of FICE in 1992, was the largest ever attempted in the Italian pharmaceutical sector, and one of the most significant industrial investments by a foreign company. As a result, in a country not used to large-scale lay-offs or radical industrial restructuring initiatives, there was a great amount of expectation and attention from both the business and the political circles in the country, following Pharmacia's integration initiatives in what was widely regarded as one of Italy's emblematic pharmaceutical companies.

Learning to move with speed through direct experience

Pharmacia's tactful and knowledgeable handling of FICE led to a relatively fast integration process, to the point that only one year after making this acquisition, Ekberg was yet again facing the Board of Directors, this time to propose turning the international Italian-Swedish company into a global pharmaceutical player. In terms of speed, this had been a sharp improvement over the five years it had taken the company to grow from a national to a European player through Kabi's 1987 acquisition of Pharmacia. Says Ekberg:

> What we have learned from FICE [the acquisition of Italy's Farmitalia-Carlo Erba], and what we also implemented now into the new merger [with US-based

Upjohn], is speed. Speed is the most important thing because as soon as you announce a merger, you create a lot of uncertainty and chaos in the organization. This is why we are really up to a very high speed in here when it comes to the planning and implementation of a merger. I think we are far better than other companies in our industry when it comes to keeping up speed of execution.

After a period of consultations and negotiations, in 1995 Pharmacia-FICE and US-based Upjohn decided to merge, creating one of the world's ten largest pharmaceutical companies at the time. Here, Pharmacia's successful experiences in integrating FICE, had to be tailored to the significantly different ownership and deal structure that had been agreed between the two companies. Indeed, both during the acquisitions of Pharmacia in 1990 and FICE in 1992, there had been an exchange of assets from the acquiring to the target companies. However, as previously described, Pharmacia's and Upjohn's particular merger structure did not involve an exchange of assets as such, but was rather based on a legal agreement to integrate two companies of remarkably similar size and market value, to form one. As a result, a "merger of equals" strictly reflected both the market value and the ownership structure of the contractual agreement which was implemented. In addition, Pharmacia and Upjohn initially sought to balance the diverse nationalities and the presence of both companies at the Board of Directors, by creating a relatively large steering structure which consisted of exactly the same number of individuals from each merging company.

Nevertheless, attempting to reach both companies' agreement across every aspect of the merger within a 16-person top management committee, was a rather cumbersome decision-making approach, which could potentially threaten the outcome of the whole integration process. As mentioned, this had been the bitter lesson of KabiVitrum's acquisition of Pharmacia, and the upside learned through the considerably more successful turnaround of FICE later on. These experiences had deeply implanted in Pharmacia the value of moving with speed, but with the concurrent ability to tailor and respond tactfully to the diverse local informational contexts and national cultural differences that existed. Thus, it was proposed and agreed with Upjohn, that both companies will proceed to "merge before the merger" during the negotiation stages, in order to develop the implementation plan before the deal had been officially approved by the shareholders.

As a result, all the crucial projects, people appointments and business objectives had been comprehensively thought of and jointly planned for prior to January 1996, the date in which the newly merged company could legally start carrying out decisions and making official appointments. Ekberg remarks:

> The key to successfully conclude the merger implementation plan with speed was the way in which we organized it. We first analyzed and planned, then we

took all the important decisions and started the implementation afterwards. However, the plan was that, even if the deal had not been accepted by the shareholders, we would have nevertheless started with the pre-merger work and the planning phase.

The arduous task of building global corporate values at Pharmacia & Upjohn

From January 1996 onwards, the merger integration process between Pharmacia and Upjohn remarkably followed the guidelines and structure which had been successfully experienced during the Pharmacia-FICE post-acquisition stages three years earlier. However, this approach proved not to be as effective within the considerably larger scope, global complexity and diverse ownership structure of the Pharmacia & Upjohn "merger of equals". The organization put in place at Pharmacia and Upjohn's inception in 1995, was designed to preserve the cultural identity of the main groups involved in the merger and to devolve decision making. Under this structure, three regional pharmaceutical product centers (PPCs) were created in the US, Sweden and Italy, with broad responsibility for discovery research, product development, strategic marketing, manufacturing, and support and admin-istration. In addition, the 16-person top management committee — which reflected the 50/50 balance of Pharmacia's and Upjohn's diverse nationalities that was sought after the merger — did not prove effective in blending the merging organizations global strengths into a unified corporate culture.

As a result, Pharmacia & Upjohn experienced continuous decline in sales and earnings during the second half of 1996 and throughout 1997. A new president and CEO was subsequently appointed, who proceeded to dismantle the three regional split of Pharmica & Upjohn's PPCs, and replaced it with a single global structure covering all of the company's prescription pharmaceu-tical activities. The company's top management committee was drastically reduced to a 5-person executive group, and the world-wide management of pharmaceutical R&D was consolidated. Throughout this arduous learning-by-doing, Pharmacia & Upjohn ostensibly shifted its priorities, from initially maintaining the corporate cultures while balancing the diverse nationalities of the merging groups, to a more centralized, streamlined and execution oriented steering and organizational structure. The new organization put in place after 1997 was designed to simplify the management and decision making of the combined group, increasing accountability, avoiding duplica-tions and fostering the creation of a single corporate culture under a centra-lized global structure.

Deutsche Bank's dogged determination to build a global banking presence

Executives at Deutsche Bank often regard their industry as a conglomerate of local businesses, rather than a global one, pointing out that their understanding of the banking business is significantly different than the "Anglo-Saxon" merchant or investment banks. Whereas the latter types of institutions often build global advantages based on a limited set of highly specialized banking products and services, Deutsche Bank intends to be the foremost European Universal Bank, serving "all kinds of clients with all kinds of products". This is a largely branch-based understanding of business, looking at the local aspects of commercial banking in every European country. However, driven by the financial de-regulation within the European Union, Deutsche Bank has considerably accelerated its expansion efforts throughout Europe since the mid 1980s, conspicuously seeking to achieve a leading market position in the larger European countries (i.e. Italy, France and Spain), comparable to their standing in Germany. In addition, Deutsche Bank's executives stress that "there is not a fixed approach" behind the development of such a European banking network, but rather a continuous but flexible set of initiatives.

The most recent phases of Deutsche Bank's internationalization efforts can be traced back to the mid 1980s, when Deutsche Bank established trading operations from scratch in New York (jointly with UBS), London, Singapore, Hong Kong and Tokyo. Along with Frankfurt's, these operations appeared sufficient in those days to give Deutsche Bank a global financial reach. However, it soon realized that this was not going to be the case when the thin business volumes achieved through this network slightly disappointed its expectations. Thus, while this initial expansion thrust led to the establishment of a series of Deutsche Bank's niche businesses internationally, the real strength of the Group clearly remained elsewhere: In Germany, and in Deutsche Marks.

However, during this time period a series of US leading merchant banks aggressively entered the German market. These new players introduced highly innovative financial techniques and could leverage on a vast pool of global resources. As a result, the likes of Goldman Sachs and J. P. Morgan were poised to grow rapidly in Germany, being able in some cases to establish several hundred strong offices from scratch after a few years. Deutsche Bank executives concede that, based on their existing organization at the time, they found it extremely difficult to compete internationally against these US-based competitors.

Therefore, the decision was taken to acquire a big outpost in the UK, and to pursue similar moves in Italy and Spain. Whereas the former responded to the strategic need of establishing a global investment banking presence, the acquisitions in Southern Europe were aimed at consolidating a leading regional position in Europe's retail and commercial banking businesses. Overall, these twin strategy intended to accelerate the "internationalization" process of Deutsche Bank, as an alternative to purely organic growth — i.e. gradually building on the 1,000 base of mostly German traders that the bank had established outside Germany since the mid 1980s. At the same time, it notoriously embarked in the most aggressive program of executive "hunting" which the banking industry has known for decades.

On both accounts, Deutsche Bank's investments have been staggering, demonstrating its commitment to its European strategy. When it announced the merger of its world-wide investment banking businesses under the name Deutsche Morgan Grenfell in July 1995, there were only two Germans in the sixteen-strong management committee, and one non-German but long-standing Deutsche Bank executive. The remaining management committee members included Edson Mitchell, recruited from Merrill Lynch, the US investment bank, Maurice Thompson and Michael Cohrs, hired from London-based S.G. Warburg, as well as British executives from the former Morgan Grenfell.[32] Apart from recruiting senior executives internationally, during those years Deutsche Bank also targeted middle managers across key banking businesses it intended to develop, hiring entire teams from competing banks. For example, in May 1995 it hired a complete team of option dealers from Citibank in New York in order to increase its profile in the derivatives market. Also, in April 1996 Deutsche Bank hired a team of three Wall Street executives who had been the key figures behind Morgan Stanley's high-tech banking group, a move which was described as "one of the biggest coups yet by a European bank trying to break into the investment banking business in the US."[33]

The figures involved in these expansion activities are impressive. In 1989, Deutsche Bank paid £950 million (around DM 2.7 billion) for Morgan Grenfell in what was widely regarded at the time as a rather "expensive" acquisition. In Italy, it invested around DM 1.5 billion in its acquisitions of BAI and Banca Popolare di Lecco, which gave it a high profile commercial banking presence throughout Italy, with 261 branches by the end of 1996. Hiring costs climbed to DM 400 million in 1995, a figure which included entry bonuses for 400 new professionals. Partly as a result of this, in 1994 it was forecast that Deutsche Bank's overall staff costs would double to DM 3.5 billion by 1999, raising doubts on the bank's ability to reach its publicly stated goal of a 15 percent after-tax ROE level before the end of the 20th century.

Two major factors have seemingly contributed to keep Deutsche Bank's expansion investments at sustainable levels during the first half of the 1990s. First, its move to partially embrace International Accounting Standards (IAS) in financial and book keeping reporting, unveiled large amounts of reserves which, under previous German accounting practices, had remained hidden. In March 1996, Deutsche Bank revealed that such hidden reserves amounted to DM 20 billion (US$ 13.4 billion).[34] According to the bank's executives, more hidden reserves could become available in due course as the bank continues to increasingly embrace IAS across the board. Secondly, as it turned out, Deutsche Bank's timing to expand internationally was quite fortunate. When it stepped up its executive "hunting" investments during the second half of 1995, the bond markets underwent a particularly favorable market cycle, benefiting Deutsche Bank as well as other financial institutions with traditionally strong positions in these markets. Nevertheless, it could be argued that the main test for Deutsche Bank's increased levels of investments and staff costs since the late 1980s, will remain its ability to sustain prolonged market downturns in the future.

However, Deutsche Bank's cross-border acquisition experience has met with mixed results. On the one hand, Deutsche Bank has successfully preserved the local character of its acquisitions by implementing hands-off approaches and granting them a high degree of functional independence. Deutsche Bank's acquisitions in Italy provide a good illustration of its post-acquisition management style. After it acquired Bank of America and Italy (BAI) in 1986, and Banca Popolare di Lecco in 1993, it gave them entire discretion on how to run their commercial banking business. The parent bank's intervention was limited to ensure a strict adherence to the group's accounting, credit, risk and other operational policies, which apply equally to every member of Deutsche Bank's Group across the globe. In these, as well as other international acquisitions, operations are largely left to be run in the hands of local managers once the Group's policies and standards are established.

On the other hand, the integration of Morgan Grenfell, the UK-based merchant bank, exemplifies some of the difficulties that Deutsche Bank has encountered when managing across significant national and corporate cultural differences. As long as it was kept as a highly independent merchant banking subsidiary, Morgan Grenfell was incorporated into Deutsche Bank's businesses in a relatively smooth fashion. However, after it created Deutsche Morgan Grenfell (DMG) in May 1995, in order to integrate Deutsche Bank's investment banking and asset management operations more closely with Morgan Grenfell's, major national and corporate cultural difficulties appeared to emerge, creating uneasiness as to how effectively these institutions could combine their strengths in the marketplace. From time to time, business difficulties or occasional control gaps at DMG have tended to make these cultural tensions resurface strongly and publicly. In spite of this, Deutsche Bank has managed to overcome these complications with a determined approach to make it to the top leagues of global investment banking within this century. For one thing, notwithstanding serious integration difficulties with DMG, it has so far refrained from centralizing its investment banking operations in Germany, ensuring that DMG's London-based management maintains its "Anglo-Saxon", aggressive investment banking approach, as well as a full access to the City's global financial resources and stature. Deutsche Bank's international expansion has also continued unabated by some of its problematic acquisition experiences overseas. Perhaps as a result of the latter, since the early 1990s it tended to vigorously emphasize on its executive hunting activities. These only appeared to slow down after a move to hire away dozens of highly ranked bankers from ING's Latin American operations drew widespread criticism from Deutsche Bank's competitors, complaining that the bank's aggressive tactics were raising salary levels to unacceptable limits in the industry. Deutsche Bank's determination to become a global banking player, capable of competing *tête-à-tête* against the leading American investment banks, was also severely tested in December 1996, when the influential Moody's banking rating agency downgraded its long-term obligations from the prestigious "triple A" to AA1, with an overall downgrading of the bank's rating to "B+" from a previous "A1". This was widely interpreted in the specialized media as one of the most visible costs of Deutsche Bank's resolute internationalization efforts, which had led it to invest massively into entering the profitable but relatively unstable businesses of investment banking and global equity markets. Nevertheless, as in previous occasions, Deutsche Bank's management took advantage of these difficult events to reaffirm its unwavering commitment to internationalization and global expansion.

Notes and References

[1] Salter, M. S. and W. A. Weinhold. *Diversification through Acquisitions: Strategies for Creating Economic Value*, Free Press, New York, 1979; Porter, M. E. *Competitive Strategy*, Free Press, New York, 1980. Alliances and joint ventures also imply the combination of the partner's resources, although in certain cases this is required to a more limited extent relative to mergers or acquisitions, usually responding to the partners "strategic" need of developing crucial technologies and business know-how, or gain entry into key markets. See: Contractor, F. and P. Lorange. *Cooperative Strategies in International Business*, D. C. Heath, Lexington, MA, 1987.

[2] Note: The source of all these figures is ABB's 1996 Annual Report.

[3] This information is dated July 1995 (from the British Airways Fact Book, 1995).

[4] Speech by Tsunao Hashimoto, Vice Chairman, Sony Corporation, at the Pacific Basin Economic Council, 29th International General Meeting, Sheraton Washington Hotel, Washington DC, Monday, 20 May 1996.

[5] Ghoshal, S. and C. Bartlett. "Changing the role of top management: beyond structure to processes", *Harvard Business Review*, January-February 1995, pp. 86-96.

[6] The "culturally unnatural" attempts to create global co-ordination functions after a major cross-border merger have been illustrated in Chapter 2.

[7] For a brief discussion on the applicability of formal post M&A integration models, see Chapter 3.

[8] There are many examples of this. Writing in the 16th century, Machiavelli stressed the crucial importance of acting with speed, for a Prince who aimed at consolidating power in a newly acquired state:

So it should be noted that when a man seizes power in a state, he should decide what cruelties are necessary, and carry them all out at once, so that he will not have to renew them every day. Once they are over, he can begin to secure the loyalty of his subjects and gain their affection by favors and benefactions. Anyone who follows the opposite policy, through timidity or bad advice, must always have his dagger in his hand; and he will never be able to rely on his citizens, because they, being subject to renewed and continual injuries, can have no confidence in him. Injuries should be inflicted all at once, so that their bitterness will last for a short time as possible and so cause less resentment; benefits should be dealt out a little at a time, so that their savour may linger for a long period. *The Prince*, J. M. Dent, London, pp. 46-47.

Also, in military science, speed of execution has been historically hailed as a key principle by all the great Captains and Generals of every nation. See: Chandler, D. G. *The Military Maxims of Napoleon*, Macmillan, New York, 1987.

[9] Marks, M. and P. Mirvis. "The stiff challenge in integrating cross-border mergers", *Mergers and Acquisitions*, January-February, 1993, pp. 37-41; Buono, A., J. Bowditch and J. Lewis. "When cultures collide: the anatomy of a merger", *Human Relations*, 38, 1985, pp. 477-500; Hayes, R. H. "The human side of acquisitions", *Management Review*, 68(11), 1979, pp. 41-46.

[10] See: Lane, H. W. and P. Beamish. "Cross-cultural cooperative behavior in joint ventures in LDCs", *Management International Review*, Special Issue, 1990, pp. 87-102; Lane, H. W. and J. J. Di Stefano. *International Management Behavior: From Policy to Practice*, Nelson Canada, Scarborough, Ontario, 1988.

[11] US Department of State Statistics, 1996; *USA Today, International Edition*, August 9, 1996.

[12] *Los Angeles Times*, Saturday, 13 January 1996, Home edition.

[13] During the 1990s, the growth rate of major international management consultancies was estimated to have been around 20 percent annually, which is supposed to have been at least double the growth rate of its major clients throughout the same time period. See: "Well fed and growing fast", *Financial Times*, 16 December 1996.

[14] Lane and Beamish. *Op. cit.,* 1990.

[15] See: Upton, D. M. "E il fattore umano la chiave della flessibilità", *Harvard Business Review*, Italian edition, May-June 1996, p. 46; Blake R. R. and J. S. Mouton. "How to achieve integration on the human side of the merger", *Organizational Dynamics*, 1985, pp. 41-56; Weber, Y., O. Shenkar and A. Raveh. "National and corporate cultural fit in mergers/acquisitions: an exploratory study", *Management Science*, 42(8), August 1996, pp. 1215-1227. For a discussion of the paradoxical aspects of deep-rooted symbols, see Chapter 4.

[16] Kets de Vries, F. R. and R. de Vitry d'Avaucourt. "Percy Barnevik: the corporate transformation wizard. An interview", INSEAD, Fontainebleau, 1994.

[17] This was not always the case. Looking at Deutsche Bank's history, one observes a curious discontinuity in the company's international presence. It had one of the world's premier international banking networks prior to the second world war, including major presence in Latin American, Asian and African countries. However, it lost most of it following Germany's war defeat in 1945.

[18] Deutsche Morgan Grenfell, a division established in May 1996 by merging investment banking and asset management operations of formerly separated Deutsche Bank and Morgan Grenfell entities.

[19] Lane and Beamish, *Op. cit.,* 1990.

[20] Johanson, J. and J. Vahlne. "The internationalization process of the firm: a model of knowledge development and increasing foreign market commitments", *Journal of*

International Business Studies, 8 (Spring-Summer), 1977, pp. 23-32; Johanson, J. and J. Vahlne. "The mechanism of internationalization", *International Marketing Review*, 7(4), 1990, pp. 11-24.

[21] *Financial Times*, Monday, January 17 1994.

[22] Excerpts from ABB's "Book of Values", quoted in Morcos, R. "Percy Barnevik and ABB", Case Study 05/94-4308, INSEAD, Fontainebleau, 1994, pp. 24-25.

[23] De Vries, F. R. and R. de Vitry d'Avaucourt. *Op. cit.*, 1994.

[24] All references to ABB's "Book of Values" are excerpts from the original, quoted in Morcos, R. *Op. cit.*, 1994, pp. 19-25.

[25] Based on the numerical measure developed in Part I, Sweden and Italy were the most "culturally distant" countries in our empirical sample (see Figure 3.1).

[26] Hampden-Turner, C. and A. Trompenaars. *The Seven Cultures of Capitalism*, Currency Doubleday, July 1993.

[27] During 1995, an official breakdown of Deutsche Bank's profits by area of business was not publicly available. Therefore, these estimates are only indicative, reflecting informal interviews carried out by the author. However, the following year Deutsche Bank announced that it would publish divisional results as part of its standard financial statements, starting with fiscal year 1996.

[28] Morosini, P. "Effects of national culture differences on post-cross-border acquisition performance in Italy", Doctoral Dissertation, Management Department, The Wharton School, University of Pennsylvania, 1994.

[29] See: Putnam, R. *Making Democracy Work: Civic Traditions in Modern Italy*, Princeton, 1993.

[30] It is possible that this astonishing manufacturing capability was developed by the Venetians long before the 16th century. The Arsenal was jealously covered with military secrecy by the Republic of Venice, but fortunately for modern historians, the visit of the twenty-three-year-old King Henri III of France in July 1574 was an exceptional occasion to unveil this most remarkable feat of medieval "assembly production". 16th century contemporary chroniclers report that the King was invited by Doge Alvise Mocenigo to see the Arsenal one morning, where he could observe workers assiduously starting to build a large warship. That afternoon, he was invited again to the same place, where he could see that the ship had been completed in every detail. Asking what was the secret of such diligence, the King received a minute explanation which could be described as the first objective lesson on the benefits of product standardization, functional specialization and production assembly lines. See: Norwich, Lord J. J. *A History of Venice,* London, Penguin Books, 1982, pp. 492-493.

[31] During the early 1990s, in one of the first major scandals unveiled by the "clean hands" anti-corruption campaign which swept Italy's political and business circles, a former Health Minister was prosecuted in relation to proscribed financing practices involving several major pharmaceutical companies and medical institutions in the country.

[32] In March 1997, DMG's management committee consisted of 13 members with the following nationalities: Eight British, four Americans and only one German.

[33] *Business Week*, 29 April 1996, p. 50. Also see: *Financial Times*, week-end 6/7 April 1996.

[34] Deutsche Bank's reserves of DM 20 billion revealed in March 1996 refer only to the listed securities among the bank's financial fixed assets. Due to International Accounting Standards (IAS) the bank applied market value to those securities instead of carrying out a valuation based on purchase costs (as it had been common practice prior to 1996).

CHAPTER 10

Concluding Remarks

By nature, men are nearly alike; by practice they get to be wide apart.

Confucius

Cross-border M&As, JVs and alliances, which have been increasingly used by multinational corporations during the last three decades of the twentieth century, usually fail to deliver the expected performance results to management and shareholders alike. While academicians, management consultants, and not a few executives have often single-handedly emphasized strategic and financial issues to improve on such a mixed track record, our empirical findings suggest that much of a firm's practical advantages in obtaining the expected gains from a deal depend on its *execution skills* to handle the multiform and pervasive national cultural aspects of overseas M&As, JVs and alliances.

However, few management fields have been so influenced by myths and preconceptions, which are the more difficult to eradicate as they often reflect factual realities to a partial extent (as most good myths do). Thus, in relation to cross-border M&As, JVs and alliances, national cultural aspects have been variously referred to as detrimental, mere managerial "hype" or even plainly irrelevant. Nevertheless, when these aspects are rigorously examined, a couple of notions emerge with singular consistency. First, national cultural distance is not necessarily detrimental to cross-border M&As, JVs and alliances, although it is linked to a myriad of managerial issues that are both determinant to performance, and extremely complex to handle practically. Second, a company possessing the *execution* capabilities to integrate and co-ordinate resources from M&As, JVs and alliances across national cultural differences, can build concrete advantages in a way that is difficult to replicate by competitors.

The latter has been the focus of particular attention in this book. We have examined how the cross-cultural *execution skills* and mechanisms widely utilized by a number of leading companies in their global M&A, JV and alliance activities, are holistically based on both knowledge and *gnosis*. This latter cognitive dimension is grounded on subjective and experience-based understanding of complex phenomena such as national culture symbols, that are both difficult to logically proceduralize and critical to business performance. As a result, a firm's *gnosis* of how to operate effectively across diverse informational and cultural contexts is often hard to develop, but it is correspondingly arduous for competitors to imitate. Thus conceived, we found that holistic *execution skills* are critical to mobilize and co-ordinate resources in practice across vastly different national cultural environments, leading to concrete performance benefits from overseas M&As, JVs and alliances. Conversely, the lack of such skills seems to be an outstanding reason behind these agreements persistently high failure rates, although they might have been soundly formulated from a strategic or a financial perspective.

These findings have potentially profound organizational implications for companies competing in the so-called global economy. Indeed, a large part of the available organizational design and strategic theories in this area have been influenced by a conceptual dichotomy between a firm's thinking and doer functions. This must constitute one of the most enduring management tenets, often regarding planning functions and roles *as opposed* to acting ones, or at best presenting the supposedly analytical and intuitive "approaches" to management, as if these were substitutive or exclusive to a significant extent.[1] Such a conceptual separation can be found conspicuously embedded in the formal techniques and strategic thinking trends that often underpin both a multinational company's structural paradigms, and their occasional re-organization efforts. As a result, the actual application of these frameworks in the real world has often been overly formal and one-sided, under-estimating the complexity of managing practically and adapting analytical tools to the diverse local cultural and informational contexts in which a global company operates. From this perspective, failure to manage international M&As, JVs and alliances could be considered a symptom of a company's deeper limitations to co-ordinate its global constellation of resources across borders — though not the only one. It has been noted that management initiatives similarly entailing intensive co-ordination skills internationally, such as global outsourcing, benchmarking, re-engineering or down-sizing programs, are often too uniformly and simplistically applied, leading to no significant long-term performance improvements. However, even when recognizing the shortcomings of such an over-reliance on reductionist management approaches, the proposed responses continue to be persistently one-sided — i.e. based on "critical thinking skills", "strategizing" and the like.[2]

By contrast, in our research we found that consistently successful cross-border acquirers, joint venturers and alliance partners, present a sharp *execution orientation* underlying their particular organizational structures. This has been crucially exemplified in the combination of strategic thinking *and* direct managerial involvement of senior executives across every implementation aspect of global M&As, JVs and alliances. In particular, this *execution orienta-*

tion extends to critical managerial levels of these organizations, responsible for co-ordinating specialized resources across national cultural differences. Thus, these companies' "global managers", "international co-ordinators", "project champions" and other similar roles, constitute a reduced number of people possessing a critical mix of technical knowledge and cross-cultural *gnosis* to carry out complex co-ordination functions following an international M&A, JV or alliance. In spite of the wide array of structural designs represented by the companies we studied, the ability to identify, attract and develop key managers capable of *executing* these types of functions was invariably crucial to organizationally support the implementation of these international agreements. In practice, nurturing these kinds of abilities often involved extensive and direct top executive attention to constantly coach and oversee these managers throughout their career paths. Moreover, at the structural level, the more successful international acquirers or company partners had developed practical co-ordination, control and communication mechanisms such as *cloning, adoption, international missions*, or *global manager meetings*. These *execution* mechanisms not only facilitate the creation, codification and distribution of knowledge, but also ensure that the flow of local *gnosis* speeds up the implementation of international M&As, JVs and alliances, without it being overly inhibited by bureaucratic or centralizing tendencies within the organization. Overall, these companies' *execution orientation*, global corporate values and co-ordination skills across borders, allow them to adapt and build effectively upon their targets' or partners' pre-existing strengths and deep understanding of the local informational contexts.

The practical and intuitive aspects of *execution orientation* could be easily over-emphasized as akin to "back to basics" or mainly "cultural" views of management. However, the cognitive holism underlying the *execution* mechanisms examined in this book, was found embedded and continuously reinforced by a company's leadership character, its corporate values, strategic aims, organizational practices and subjective skills developed over a long-time period. Thus, cultural, strategic and structural aspects were often inextricably linked in a company's particular set of *execution* mechanisms, with a degree of complexity that is difficult to codify and transfer outside a specific corporate context. Indeed, many of the companies we studied seemed to carefully reflect upon the importance of *execution* aspects from the very early stages of their international M&A, JV and alliance activities. In particular, the importance of a circumspect and proactive approach to evaluating these opportunities, thoroughly assessing a company's own *execution* and implementation skills, were stressed as crucial prior to the deal. These types of approaches generally prevented a company from taking an overly analytical perspective during the evaluation and negotiation of cross-border M&As, JVs and alliances, or underestimating the relevance of national cultural and other related issues to effectively realize the expected benefits from these deals. Moreover, the ability to implement practically these agreements was often directly related with a company's existing *execution* and organizational skills to managing resources across national cultural differences. As mentioned, in spite of the significantly diverse structures we examined, ranging from "multidomestic" to "global localization" or "distributed leadership" frameworks, it was not always the organizational design *per se*, but the underlying *execution* capabilities to resolve its inherent contradictions what ultimately determined its strategic and practical effectiveness. Paramount amongst these contradictions, a company's existent *execution* mechanisms to co-ordinate resources across fairly diverse global and local contexts, were found to be especially critical in the implementation of M&As, JVs and alliances across national cultures. Here, companies which had started globalizing their operations early on, generally acquired a valuable practical experience in handling co-ordination mechanisms across national contexts, whereas less internationally oriented companies often had to undergo exacting and long-term efforts to build such pragmatic skills when expanding abroad through M&As, JVs or alliances.

Although previous empirical models of national culture have overwhelmingly emphasized on its pervasive and resilient characteristics, our research has in addition highlighted the multiform, dynamic and unpredictable traits of national cultural symbols. When looked from the practical perspective of cross-border M&As, JVs and alliances, the managerial implications of these combined features of national culture can be far-reaching. For one thing, the cross-cultural *execution* mechanisms examined in this book can be regarded as a company's structured efforts to flexibly adapt organizational and technical knowledge to the local cultural environments — not the other way round. The knowledge thus disseminated can in itself be modified, enriched and fed back from the local context to the rest of the organization and *vice versa*. Therefore, from a national cultural viewpoint, *execution-oriented* organizations could be conceived as highly open *social* entities, continuously blending cultural *gnosis* and technological knowledge from various sources around the globe, in ways that are compatible with and leverage from diverse local informational contexts. By contrast, some authors have described certain aspects of modern organizational or technological knowledge as uniquely embedded in Western cultural values, with an overall conception of national culture that seemingly emphasizes its more resilient characteristics. These types of views tend to see the spreading of the so-called global economy not as the interactive adaptation of firms' knowledge in multiform ways *vis-à-vis* the local cultural perspectives, but as a belated and intrinsically confrontational attempt to enforce the convergence of a myriad of national cultural values into a single — i.e. Western — cultural paradigm.[3]

A key notion throughout this book has been to highlight the importance of holistic managerial roles within an organization, with both the knowledge and *gnosis* to carry out complex co-ordination functions across national cultures during the implementation phase of M&As, JVs and alliances. In our research, much of these managers valuable *execution skills* were found to be subjectively derived, but crucially facilitated by a company's organizational practices, as well as a country's particular cultural environment and government policies. However, in these areas we also found numerous barriers to *execution* at play during the implementation phase of international M&As, JVs and alliances. Regarding organizational barriers, our findings suggested that managers reluctant to enter culturally distant locations might be acting in their own interest rather than in the interest of shareholders. At a pragmatic level, overly centralized organizations might be inadvertently reinforcing this agency problem in a series of ways. On the one hand, excessively bureaucratic headquarters, red-tape and an abundance of centralized procedures makes a company less responsive to the local demands, and more insensitive to the *gnosis* and flexibility inherent in *execution* mechanisms of cultural adaptation. On the other, career promotion, salary schemes and other internal practices favoring centralized roles over more international or local ones, often have a detrimental effect on a company's ability to rotate key executives and generate cross-cultural *gnosis* inside the organization, inexorably attracting expatriate managers to headquarters after a short time period overseas. As a result, following an international M&A, JV or alliance, a company may find that it lacks enough managers capable of combining resources effectively across national cultural environments, although on a formal level it may have created multiple co-ordination mechanisms and standardized organizational procedures to that effect.

A country's specific policies can also inadvertently inhibit a company's ability to rotate key personnel across borders, or establish adequate flows of knowledge and *gnosis* at a global scale inside the organization. In our research, a number of senior executives directly associated these kinds of barriers to *execution* with a company's ability to develop good implementation skills *vis-à-vis* international M&As, JVs and alliances. For example, in certain countries such as Japan, the local school and university systems are both highly demanding and extremely difficult to homologize *vis-à-vis* other countries educational systems. These seemingly minor elements have an enormous discouraging effect on Japanese executives to live and work abroad with their families during extended time periods, fearful that upon returning to their home country, their children — and often themselves — will have to either spend longer years at school to "catch up" with the local educational demands, or face additional difficulties in entering the job market without a local university degree. Also, in countries such as Italy, Germany and France, emphasis on the local language across the media and cultural manifestations is much greater than in smaller nations such as Sweden or the Netherlands. However, continuous exposure to foreign languages and cultural manifestations from a very early age, has been associated with the latter countries' degree of openness to different national cultures, as well as its people's multilingual proficiency. In turn, these characteristics have been generally described as key assets for companies looking to co-ordinate a global constellation of resources across diverse national cultural environments.

Other government policies could also be subtly linked to a company's ability to develop the required cross-cultural *execution skills* in overseas M&As, JVs and alliances. For instance, government intervention to protect or support the local companies' business activities across culturally difficult foreign markets or *vis-à-vis* global competitors, may end up favoring those organizations with relatively little cross-cultural *execution skills*, or lacking the managerial determination to develop those over time. One highly visible example of this concerns some aspects of trade policy. Many major companies based in the USA, Japan, the European Union and other locations, have routinely invoked the intervention of their home countries' trade bodies to resolve important business issues, often stigmatizing other nations' "collusive protectionism" or "dumping" practices. The latter have supposedly opened these companies' "own" local markets to foreign competitors, whose domestic markets have nevertheless remained "unfairly" closed. However, the record of anti-dumping and similar trade policies across major economies does not necessarily inspire confidence in its impartiality. Here, a country's government is often both the judge and the jury concerning the application of its own laws and conceptions on competition. As a result, although in most cases these are grounded on appealing notions such as fair trade, liberalization or anti-protectionism, anti-dumping and related trade policies have in practice become a byword for virulent confrontation and jingoism between certain countries. It would be tempting to examine whether such vehement trade disputes could be generally drawing notice to those cases where a lack of *execution skills* to manage across culturally distant locations is greater, while examples of accomplished adaptation to culturally "difficult" markets are to be found elsewhere.

In short, in this book we have looked at how companies manage M&As, JVs and alliances across national cultural differences. This is an increasingly debated topic, but one which had previously received little empirical attention from management researchers and practitioners alike. Our findings suggest that both national cultural factors and execution aspects are quite important to consider when deciding about and implementing M&As, JVs and alliances overseas. In a global business milieu fostering greater interaction among culturally distant countries, these kinds of findings are expected to be of particular value to international companies managing across ever more uncertain environments.

Notes and References

[1] Hilmer, F. and L. Donaldson. *Management Redeemed: Debunking the Fads that Undermine our Corporations*, Free Press, 1996.

[2] Spitzer, Q. and R. Evans. *Heads You Win: How the Best Companies Think*, Simon & Schuster, 1997; Hamel, G. "Strategy as revolution", *Harvard Business Review*, July-August, 1994, pp. 69-82.

[3] Huntington, S. *The Clash of Civilizations and the Remaking of World Order*, Simon & Schuster, 1996.

Appendix

We present some results of the statistical regression analyses described in Chapter 3.

First, we show a summary of the results obtained concerning our hypothesis on the link between national cultural distance and cross-border post-acquisition performance. The detailed analyses can be found in: Morosini, P., S. Shane and H. Singh. "National cultural distance and cross-border acquisition performance", *Journal of International Business Studies*, in press (March 1998).

Next, we summarize some of the results on our hypothesis linking national culture — post-acquisition "execution modes" *interaction*, and cross-border post-acquisition performance. These findings are described in more detail in: Morosini, P. and H. Singh. "Post-cross-border acquisitions: implementing 'national culture compatible' strategies to improve performance", *European Management Journal*, 12(4), December 1994, pp. 390-400.

For additional details on the quantitative analyses carried out in this study, see: Morosini, P. "Effects of national culture differences on post-cross-border acquisition performance in Italy", Doctoral Dissertation, Management Department, The Wharton School, University of Pennsylvania, 1994.

National Cultural Distance and Cross-Border Post-Acquisition Performance

We specified a bivariate regression model in the following way:

Performance = f(CD, UA, RE, SI, IN, 87, 88, 89, 90, 91, TE, WA, BA, PH)

where:

Performance = percentage growth in sales for the two years following the acquisition.

CD = cultural distance score between Italy and the counterpart firm's country of origin.

UA = Hofstede's uncertainty avoidance score for the acquiring firm's country of origin.

RE = dummy variable for relatedness of the acquisition.

SI = dollar value of turnover of the acquiring firm.

IN = post-acquisition *execution mode* implemented by the acquirer.

87, 88, 89, 90, 91 = dummy variable for acquisitions which took place in 1987, 1988, 1989, 1990 and 1991, respectively.

TE, WA, BA, PH = Dummy variable for the textiles and clothing, waste management, banking and pharmaceutical industries, respectively.

TABLE A.1

Results of the ordinary least squares regression analyses

Variable	Coefficient	t-value
Cultural distance	0.13	2.04*
Uncertainty avoidance	0.01	2.23*
Post-acquisition execution mode	0.06	1.17
Relatedness	0.08	0.58
Size	−0.00	−3.14
1987	−0.30	−1.52
1988	0.08	0.37
1989	−0.1	−0.76
1990	−0.03	−0.14
1991	0.51	1.95
Banking	−0.37	−1.61
Waste management	−0.44	−1.46
Textiles/clothing	1.05	4.45*
Pharmaceuticals	−0.38	−1.69
Constant	−0.57	−1.85
Adjusted R^2	0.48	
Degrees of freedom	37.14	
F-value	4.35	
Number of observations	52	

*Significant at the $p < 0.05$ level or better in a two-tailed t-test.

Target's National Culture/Acquirer's "Execution Mode" *Interaction,* and Cross-Border Post-Acquisition Performance

We specified two different bivariate regression models to test this *interaction* for the target's "uncertainty avoidance" and "individualism-collectivism" national cultural dimensions, respectively. The specification and statistical results of these models are shown in Table A.2.

TABLE A.2

Target's national culture, post-acquisition execution modes and performance

	Model 1	Model 2
Dependent variable	Profitability1	Productivity1
Const	−1.63	−0.80
Target's uncertainty avoidance	0.02	
Target's individualism-collectivism		0.01
Target's uncertainty avoidance-PAE interaction	−0.27***	
Target's individualism-PAE interaction		−0.03***
Relatedness	−1.17	0.07
Size	1.53	0.11
PAS	1.40	−0.05
F	2.51***	1.64*
d.f.	49	51
R^2	0.22	0.15
N	50	52

*** Significant at $p < 0.05$
** Significant at $p < 0.10$
* Significant at $p < 0.20$
Profitability1, profitability growth comparison (1 year basis); Productivity1, net sales per employee growth comparison (1 year basis); Const, regression's constant coefficient; PAE, post-acquisition *execution mode* implemented by the acquirer (-1, 0, 1 scale); Size, size of acquired company; F, F-test; d.f., degrees of freedom; N, number of observations.

Selected Bibliography

M&As, JVs and Alliances

Barret, P. *The Human Implications of Mergers and Take-Overs*, Institute of Personnel Management, London, 1973.

Bartlett, C. A. and S. Ghoshal. *Managing Across Borders*, Boston, Harvard Business School Press, 1991.

Bleeke, J. and D. Ernst. "The way to win in cross-border alliances", *Harvard Business Review*, November-December 1991, pp. 127-135.

Buono, A. and J. Bowditch. *The Human Side of Mergers and Acquisitions*, San Francisco, Jossey Bass, 1989.

Chatterjee, S., M. Lubatkin, D. Schweiger and Y. Weber. "Cultural differences and shareholder value in related mergers: linking equity and human capital", *Strategic Management Journal*, 13, 1992, pp. 319-334.

Datta, D. "Organizational fit and acquisition performance: effects of post-acquisition integration", *Strategic Management Journal*, 12, 1991, pp. 281-297.

Haspeslagh, P. C. and D. B. Jemison. *Managing Acquisitions: Creating Value Through Corporate Renewal*, Free Press, New York, 1991.

Kogut, B. and H. Singh. "The effect of national culture on the choice of entry mode", *Journal of International Business Studies*, Fall, 1988, pp. 411-432.

Lane, H. W. and P. W. Beamish. "Cross-cultural co-operative behavior in joint ventures in LDCs", *Management International Review*, 30, Special Issue, 1990, pp. 87-102.

Lichtenberger, B. and G. Naulleau. "French-German joint ventures: cultural conflicts and synergies", *International Business Review*, 2(3), 1993, pp. 297-307.

Lubatkin, M. and H. O'Neill. "Merger strategies and capital market risk", *Academy of Management Journal*, 30(4), 1987, pp. 665-684.

Marks, M. "Merging human resources", *Mergers and Acquisitions*, 17(2), 1982, pp. 38-42.

Mirvis, P., H. Marks and M. Lee. *Managing the Merger: Making it Work*, Prentice Hall, 1992.

Morosini, P., S. Shane and H. Singh. "National cultural distance and cross-border acquisition performance. *Journal of International Business Studies*, in press (March 1998).

Parkhe, A. " 'Messy' research, methodological predispositions, and theory development in international joint ventures", *Academy of Management Review*, 18(2), 1993, pp. 227-268.

Porter, M. E. "From competitive advantage to competitive strategy", *Harvard Business Review*, 65(3), 1987, pp. 43-59.

Salter, M. S. and W. A. Weinhold. *Diversification Through Acquisitions: Strategies for Creating Economic Value*, Free Press, New York, 1979.

Seth, A. "Sources of value creation in acquisitions: an empirical investigation", *Strategic Management Journal*, 11, 1990, pp. 431-446.

Singh, H. and C. Montgomery. "Corporate acquisition strategies and economic performance", *Strategic Management Journal*, 8, 1987, pp. 377-386.

Weber, Y., O. Shenkar and A. Raveh. "National and corporate cultural fit in mergers/acquisitions: an exploratory study, *Management Science*, 42(8), 1996, pp. 1215-1227.

National Culture

Bellah, R. N. *Tokugawa Religion — The Cultural Roots of Modern Japan*, Free Press, New York, 1985.

Butterfield, H. *History and Human Relations*, Collins, London, 1951.

Carrol, R. *Cultural Misunderstandings*, University of Chicago Press, Chicago, IL, 1987.

Childs, M. *Sweden: The Middle Way*, Yale University Press, New Haven, CT, 1936.

Clark, G. *Understanding the Japanese*, Tokyo, Kinseido, 1983.

Gordon, C. in C. Randlesome (ed.), *Business Cultures of Europe*, Heinemann, Oxford, 1990.

Hall, E. T. *The Cultures of France and Germany*, Intercultural Press, New York, 1989.

Hampden-Turner, C. and A. Trompenaars. *The Seven Cultures of Capitalism*, Doubleday, New York, 1993.

Hofstede, G. *Culture's Consequences*, Sage, Beverly Hills, 1980.

Huizinga, J. *Homo Ludens: A Study of the Play Element in Culture*, Beacon, Boston, MA, 1970.

Maccoby, M. (ed.) *Sweden at the Edge*, University of Pennsylvania Press, Philadelphia, PA, 1991.

Michel, A. *Capitalism Contre Capitalism*, Edition de Seuil, Paris, 1991.

Schein, E. H. *Organization, Culture and Leadership*, Jossey-Bass, San Francisco, CA, 1985.

Suzuki, D. T. *Zen and Japanese Culture*, London and New York, 1959.

Complementary Perspectives

Anesaki, M. *The History of Japanese Religion*, London, 1930.

Berlin, Sir Isaiah (ed.) *The Age of Enlightenment: The 18th Century Philosophers*, Mentor Books/Houghton Mifflin, New York, 1956.

Boring, E. G. *A History of Experimental Psychology*, 2nd edn. Appleton-Century-Crofts, New York, 1950.

Cantwell Smith, W. *Islam in Modern History*, Princeton, 1957.

Card, C. R. "The archetypal view of Jung and Pauli", *Psychological Perspectives*, 24 & 25, C. G. Jung Institute, Los Angeles, CA, 1991.

Chandler, D. G. *Atlas of Military Strategy: The Art, Theory and Practice of War, 1618-1878*, Macmillan, London and New York, 1980.

Creel, H. G. *Confucius and the Chinese Way*, New York, 1960.

Davis, P. J. and R. Hersh. *The Mathematical Experience*, Houghton Mifflin, Boston, MA, 1981.

Drucker, P. F. *The Practice of Management*, Harper & Row, 1954.

Freud, S. *Three Essays on the Theory of Sexuality*, reprint of 4th edn of 1920, Basic Books/ Harper Collins, New York, 1962.

Hammer, M. and J. Champy. *Reengineering the Corporation: A Manifesto for Business Revolution*, Harper Business, New York, 1993.

Hofstadter, D. R. *Gödel, Escher, Bach: An Eternal Golden Braid*, Vintage Books, New York, 1989.

Jensen, H. *Sign, Symbol, and Script*, G. P. Putnam's, New York, 1969.

Jung, C. G. *The Collected Works of C. G. Jung*, Vol. 14: *Mysterium Coniunctionis*, Bollingen Series XX, G. Adler and R. F. Hull (eds), Princeton University Press, Princeton, 1963.

Jung, C. G. *Letters*, 2 Vols. Bollingen Series No. 95, G. Adler and A. Jaffe (eds), Princeton University Press, Princeton, 1975.

Kobayashi, K. *The Rise of NEC*, Blackwell Publishers, Cambridge, MA, 1991.

Kogut, B. and U. Zander. "Knowledge of the firm and the evolutionary theory of the multinational corporation", *Journal of International Business Studies*, fourth quarter 1993, pp. 625-645.

Kubose, G. *Zen Koans*, Regnery, Chicago, IL, 1973.

Löwith, K. *From Hegel to Nietzsche*, translated by D. E. Green, New York, 1964; London, 1965.

Maimonides, M. *The Guide for the Perplexed*, translated by M. Friedlander, London, 1928.

Machiavelli, N. *Il Principe*, 13th edn, Rizzoli, Milan, 1993.

Minsky, M. L. "Matter, mind and models", in M. L. Minsky (ed.), *Semantic Information Processing*, MIT Press, Cambridge, MA, 1968.

Mintzberg, H. *The Rise and Fall of Strategic Planning: Reconceiving Roles for Planning, Plans, Planners*, Free Press, New York, 1994.

Nagel, E. and J. R. Newman. "Gödel's proof", in J. R. Newman (ed.), *The World of Mathematics*, Simon and Schuster, New York, 1956.

Nietzsche, F. *The Birth of Tragedy and The Genealogy of Morals*, translated by F. Golffing, Doubleday, New York, 1956.

Pfeffer, J. *Competitive Advantage Through People*, Harvard Business School Press, Boston, MA, 1994.

Rose, S. *The Conscious Brain*, updated ed., Vintage Books, New York, 1976.

Robertson, R. *Jungian Archetypes*, Nicolas-Hays, York Beach, 1995.

Rózsa, P. *Recursive Functions*, Academic Press, New York, 1967.

Sloan, A. P. Jr. *My Years with General Motors*, Doubleday, 1963.

Smart, N. *The Religious Experience of Mankind*, Charles Scribner's Sons, New York, 1969.

Smith, D. H. *Chinese Religion*, London, 1968.

Smullyan, R. *Theory of Formal Systems*, Princeton University Press, Princeton, NJ, 1961.

Waley, A. *The Way and Its Power: A Study of the Tao tê Ching and Its Place in Chinese Thought*, London, 1934; New York, 1956.

Zimmer, H. *The Philosophies of India*, London, 1951; New York, 1964.

Author Index

Page numbers in **bold** type indicate where a reference is given in full.

299

Author Index

Subject Index

Subject Index

Subject Index